Joan M. Petersen

The Dialogues of Gregory the Great in their Late Antique Cultural Background

This study is a reassessment of the *Dialogues* of Gregory the Great (540 ?-604) in relation to their sixth-century literary and theological background and to modern hagiographical research; and a reconsideration of the influence of Eastern Christendom upon Gregory's spirituality and theology.

Chapters 1 to 3 examine the relationship between the sites of Gregory's miracles, the places of residence of his correspondents and informants, and the system of Roman roads. There is also a detailed study of the technique and language which he employs in introducing his own material and that of his informants, together with his attitude to the question of historical accuracy. Gregory is shown to have applied the methods of biblical typology not only to his homiletical and exegetical material, but also to the *Dialogues*. The study also considers the question of Gregory's relationship to the writers of the *Gesta martyrum*: it appears that, although these writers and Gregory were handling similar material, their aims and outlook were quite different, and that direct connections between Gregory and this group of writers cannot be proved.

The miracle-stories in the *Dialogues*, as seen in the context of those of other Western writers, and the doctrine of relics, as developed by both Gregory of Tours and Gregory the Great, afford examples of the interaction between Eastern and Western Christian teaching. No hard and fast distinction can be drawn, since there are many exceptions, but broadly speaking, in the West, the dead holy man heals the sick from his tomb, whereas in the East, the holy man performs miracles as a living agent. The miracles described in the *Dialogues* are generally performed by living holy men, which suggests that Gregory was not uninfluenced by Eastern Christian teaching.

The last two chapters of the book break new ground by conducting an enquiry into the Eastern Christian sources which may have influenced Gregory. In the past it has been commonly assumed that he knew no Greek and that consequently he could only have been influenced by Western writers, particularly Augustine. Although his knowledge of Greek – though not non-existent, as is often supposed – was not sufficient to enable him to read a patristic text in the original, Gregory was brought into contact with Eastern spirituality through the works of Latin writers who had been in contact with the Christian East and through Latin translations of Greek works. This study also offers some suggestions for solving the problem of how Gregory apparently obtained access to certain Greek writers, of which no Latin translations existed in his day.

This study reaches the conclusion that although the language barrier between Eastern and Western Christendom was becoming more rigid by the late sixth century, there was still in this period a corpus of ideas which were common to Christians in both the East and the West and which were indeed so much a part of the general Christian consciousness that they found expression in the writings of both Greek and Latin authors.

STUDIES AND TEXTS 69

THE *DIALOGUES* OF GREGORY THE GREAT IN THEIR LATE ANTIQUE CULTURAL BACKGROUND

by

JOAN M. PETERSEN

PONTIFICAL INSTITUTE OF MEDIAEVAL STUDIES

Acknowledgment

The author and publishers acknowledge with grateful thanks the award of grants from the Twenty-Seven Foundation and the Isobel Thornley Bequest Fund of the University of London, which have enabled this work to be published.

CANADIAN CATALOGUING IN PUBLICATION DATA

Petersen, Joan M. (Joan Margaret), 1914-
  The Dialogues of Gregory the Great in their late antique cultural background

(Studies and text, ISSN 0082-5328 ; 69)
Bibliography: p.
Includes index.
ISBN 0-88844-069-3

1. Gregory I, Pope, circa 540-604. Dialogi de vita.   I. Pontifical Institute of Mediaeval Studies.   II. Title.   III. Series: Studies and texts (Pontifical Institute of Mediaeval Studies) ; 69.

BR65.G542P47 1984   231.7´3   C84-098345-X

PRINTED BY UNIVERSA, WETTEREN, BELGIUM

Memoriae
parentum et fratris dilectissimorum
qui altera in ripa iam gaudent

Contents

Abbreviations IX

Acknowledgments XII

Note XIII

Introduction XV

1 Gregory's Raw Material and His Attitude Towards It 1

    A. Gregory's Sources of Information and their Relationship to
    the Contemporary Italian Background 1.   B. The Historical
    Aspect of the *Dialogue* 15.   C. Gregory's Use of the
    Dialogue Form 21.

2 The Typological Interpretation of the *Dialogues* 25

    A. Gregory's Biblical Formation 25.   B. The Use of Typo-
    logical Interpretation in the *Dialogues* 29.   C. Examples
    of Gregory's Use of Typological Interpretation 32
    D. Conclusion 54.

3 Gregory and the Stories of the Italian Martyrs 56

    A. Introduction 56.   B. The Nature of the *Gesta martyrum*
    and their Writers and Readers 59.   C. Gregory's Relation-
    ship to the Martyr-stories 66.   D. Literary Evidence for
    the Relationship between the *Gesta martyrum* and the
    Dialogues 73.   E. Conclusion 88.

4 The Miracle-Stories in the *Dialogues* Seen in the Context of Those
  of Other Western Christian Writers 90

    A. The Attitude of Augustine Towards Miracles 90.
    B. The Forms of the New Thaumaturgy 94.   C. The
    Origins of the Two-fold Tradition of Thaumaturgy 116.

5 Gregory of Tours and the Development of Relics 122

    A. Relics in Sixth-Century Gaul 122.   B. A Comparison of
    Gregory of Tours and Gregory the Great as Writers of Miracle-
    Stories 130.   C. Bodies and Relics: How Far Did the Burial
    Customs of East and West Influence the Cult of Relics? 141.

6 The Influence of the Spirituality of the Desert upon Gregory the
    Great   151

    A. Introduction 151.   B. Monasticism in the *Dia-
    logues* 153.   C. Some Theological and Psychological
    Concepts Common to Gregory and to the Eastern Christian
    Writers 160.   D. A Comparison Between Narratives and
    Character Sketches in the *Dialogues* and in Eastern Christian
    Writings 169.   E. Martin the Hermit and Symeon Stylites:
    was Gregory Acquainted With the *Historia Religiosa* of
    Theodoret? 181.

7 Epilogue   189

Bibliography   193

Index   217

MAPS

Map 1: Italy in the Late Sixth Century   XXII

Map 2: The Duchy of Rome in the Late Sixth Century   XXIII

Map 3: Ecclesiasitical Rome in the Late Sixth Century   XXIV

Abbreviations

AASS	*Acta Sanctorum*
AAST.M	*Atti della Accademia delle scienze di Torino*, 2, *Classe di scienze morali, storiche e filologiche*
AAWW.PH	*Abhandlungen der philosophischen-historischen Klasse der österreichischen Akademie der Wissenschaften*
ABenR	*American Benedictine Review*
ACW	Ancient Christian Writers
AnBoll	*Analecta Bollandiana*
Annales	*Annales: économies, sociétés, civilisations*
BÉFAR	Bibliothèque des Écoles françaises d'Athènes et de Rome
Ben.	*Benedictina*
BenM	*Benediktinische Monatschrift*
BGAM	Beiträge zur Geschichte des alten Mönchtums und des Benediktinerordens
BHG	*Bibliotheca Hagiographica Graeca*
BHL	*Bibliotheca Hagiographica Latina*
BISI	*Bolletino dell'istituto storico italiano per il medioevo*
BKV	Bibliothek der Kirchenväter
BMus	Bibliothèque du Muséon
Byz.	*Byzantion*
CCist	*Collectanea Cisterciensia*
CCSL	Corpus Christianorum Series Latina
CEtMéd	*Cahiers d'études médiévales*
CIL	*Corpus inscriptionum Latinarum*
CP	*Classical Philology*
CSEL	Corpus Scriptorum Ecclesiasticorum Latinorum
DA	*Deutsches Archiv für Erforschung des Mittelalters*
DACL	*Dictionnaire d'archéologie chrétienne et de liturgie*
DR	*Downside Review*
DSp	*Dictionnaire de spiritualité*
EuA	*Erbe und Auftrag*
FlorPatr	*Florilegium patristicum*
FSI	Fonti per la storia d'Italia
FThSt	*Freiburger theologische Studien*
GCS	Die griechischen christlichen Schriftsteller der ersten drei Jahrhunderte
HZ	*Historische Zeitschrift*

Iren.	*Irénikon*
Ist.	*Istina*
JEH	*Journal of Ecclesiastical History*
JRS	*Journal of Roman Studies*
JS	*Journal des savants*
JTS	*Journal of Theological Studies*
JWG	*Jahrbuch für Wirtschaftsgeschichte*
LCC	Library of Christian Classics
LCP	Latinitas Christianorum primaeva
Lib. pont. rav.	*Liber pontificalis ecclesiae Ravennatis*
LP	*Liber pontificalis*
Mansi	*Sacrorum conciliorum nova et amplissima collectio*, ed. G. D. Mansi
MD	*Maison-Dieu*
MÉFR	*Mélanges de l'école française de Rome*
MGH	Monumenta Germaniae Historica
AA	Auctores antiquissimi
Script.	*Scriptores*
SRL	Scriptores rerum Langobardicarum
SRM	Scriptores rerum Merovingicarum
MGMA	Monographien zur Geschichte des Mittelalters
MIÖG	*Mitteilungen des Instituts für österreichische Geschichtsforschung*
Nau	[Apophthegmata Patrum.] *Histoires des solitaires égyptiens* [anonymous collection]
OrChrA	Orientalia Christiana analecta
OrChrP	*Orientalia Christiana periodica*
PBA	*Proceedings of the British Academy*
PG	Patrologia Graeca, ed. Migne
PL	Patrologia Latina, ed. Migne
PW	Pauly-Wissowa-Kroll, *Realencyclopädie der classischen Altertumswissenschaft*
QSM	*Quaderni storici delle Marche*
RAM	*Revue d'ascétique et de mystique*
RBen	*Revue Bénédictine*
RÉA	*Revue des études anciennes*
RÉAug	*Revue des études augustiniennes*
RÉByz	*Revue des études byzantines*
Reg.	*Registrum epistolarum Gregorii Magni* MGH *Epp.* 1&2
Reg. Ben.	*Regula S. Benedicti*
RegBenSt	*Regulae Benedicti studia*
Reg. Magist.	*Regula magistri*
RÉL	*Revue d'études latines*
RH	*Revue historique*

RHE	*Revue d'histoire ecclésiastique*
RHP	*Revue de l'histoire de la philosophie*
RHPhR	*Revue d'histoire et de philosophie religieuses*
RHRel	*Recherches d'histoire religieuse*
RHSp	*Revue d'histoire de la spiritualité*
RIS	Rerum italicarum scriptores
RivAC	*Rivista di archeologia cristiana*
RLM	*Revue liturgique et monastique*
RMAL	*Revue du moyen-âge latin*
ROC	*Revue de l'Orient chrétien*
RQH	*Revue des questions historiques*
RSR	*Recherches de science religieuse*
RTAM	*Recherches de théologie ancienne et médiévale*
SBLTT	Society of Biblical Literature. Text and translation
SC	Sources chrétiennes
SCH(L)	*Studies in Church History (London)*
SE	*Sacris erudiri*
SeL	*Storia e Letteratura*
SHG	Subsidia hagiographica
SLH	Scriptores Latini Hiberniae
SMSR	*Studi e materiali di storia delle religioni*
SpicFri	Spicilegium Friburgense
SSAM	*Settimane di studio del centro italiano di studi sull'atto medioevo, Spoleto*
StAns	*Studia Anselmiana*
StMon	*Studia monastica*
StPatr	*Studia patristica*
TaS	*Texts and Studies*
ThH	Théologie historique
TU	Texte und Untersuchungen zur Geschichte der altchristlichen Literatur
VetChr	*Vetera Christianorum*
V.I.	Vetus Italica
VKHSM	Veröffentlichungen aus dem kirchenhistorischen Seminar, München
VSanti	Vite dei Santi
WSt	*Wiener Studien*
ZKTh	*Zeitschrift für Katholische Theologie*
ZSRG.K	*Zeitschrift der Savigny-Stiftung für Rechtsgeschichte. Kanonistische Abteilung*

Acknowledgments

This book is based upon the thesis which I presented for the degree of Ph.D. Lond. in 1981.

First of all, I should like to express my warmest thanks to those who have supervised my research, Professor Rosalind Hill and Dr Janet Nelson, for their wise and stimulating guidance. My thanks are likewise due to Dr Judith McClure, who has helped me on many occasions with her criticisms and suggestions and has kindly allowed me to read her own unpublished thesis; to Father Adalbert de Vogüé, OSB, monk of La-Pierre-qui-Vire, for the wise counsel and constructive criticism, which he has so generously given me from 1976 onwards; to the Rev. Professor Stuart Hall and to Professor Robert Markus for a number of valuable suggestions concerning the revision of the text for publication; to Dr Stanley King for drawing the preliminary sketch of the map on p. xxiii; to the Archbishop of Canterbury's Counsellors on Foreign Relations, for the grant which they awarded me in 1976 to enable me to visit La-Pierre-qui-Vire; and last but not least, to Mrs Barbara Baker, for her patient and devoted labour in typing my manuscript.

It would be impossible to list the many other scholars who have helped me with their criticisms, suggestions, and gifts of offprints, and the relatives and personal friends, who have given me so much encouragement. One who was both scholar and friend must be selected to represent them all, the late Miss Amy K. Clarke, my former teacher at Cheltenham Ladies' College, who followed the progress of my thesis with the keenest interest from its inception until her death in June 1980.

London 1982   J.M.P.

Note

With regard to place-names, I have been deliberately inconsistent, in order to avoid pedantry. Where there is a modern English form of the name or the modern Italian name is well-known, I have retained the forms in common use, e.g., Milan, Spoleto. In the case of places where the English and Latin forms are equally well-known, e.g., Nursia, Placentia, or of places of lesser fame, e.g., Fundi, Populonium, I have retained the Latin names.

All references to the text of the *Dialogues* are to A. de Vogüé's edition (3 vols., SC 251, 265-266 [Paris, 1978-1980]), unless otherwise stated.

Introduction

In post-medieval times the *Dialogues* of Gregory the Great have received little favourable notice. At best they have been regarded as a source for Italian social history in the sixth century, but for the most part, they have been seen as an excrescence upon the corpus of Gregory's works or as an aberration of an otherwise noble mind. From time to time doubts have even been expressed as to Gregory's authorship; the most recent sceptic is H. F. Clark, who at the international congress, *San Benedetto nel suo tempo*, held at three Italian centres in the autumn of 1980, read a stimulating but controversial communication on this subject. Until Clark's promised book appears, it is not possible to deal in detail with his arguments, which deserve to be taken seriously, but which have failed to convince me. Of those who accept Gregory's authorship of the *Dialogues*, the most famous hostile critic is Edward Gibbon, who referred to "the entire nonsense of the Dialogues," and added that the credulity of Gregory was always disposed to confirm the truths of religion by the evidence of ghosts, miracles, and resurrections.[1] In 1905 a rather more sympathetic critic, F. Homes Dudden, could express astonishment that "the clear-headed man, who managed the papal estates with such admirable skill," could have contributed to the writing of "these wild tales." [2]

Both Homes Dudden and U. Moricca, whose edition of the *Dialogues* was published in 1924, though they may differ in other respects, are at one in their mistrust of Gregory's critical powers.[3] Moricca is troubled because Gregory assigns equal worth to the testimonies of his informants, irrespective of their education or social position; Moricca thereby reveals a certain lack of critical sensitivity in himself. It is by no means obvious that the testimony of the well-born and educated is more reliable than that of the less fortunate. Much of Gregory's material must surely have been based upon oral tradition; here the truthfulness and accuracy of

---

[1] E. Gibbon, *The Decline and Fall of the Roman Empire*, ed. J. B. Bury (London 1911), 5: 103.

[2] F. Homes Dudden, *Gregory the Great: His Place in History and Thought* (London 1905), 1: 358.

[3] *Gregorii Magni Dialogi libri IV*, ed. U. Moricca (hereafter cited as "Moricca"), FSI 57 (Rome 1924), p. xxxII.

observation, which are often characteristic of country people, might be of more value than academic learning.

In addition to the charges of superstition and credulity, Gregory has also been accused of historical inaccuracy.[4]

These three charges seem to me to have been made against Gregory, because his critics have failed to realize what he was trying to do. They have not seen fully the scope of the *Dialogues* in relation to the culture of his age or compared them with the works of other writers with similar aims. The time seemed to me to be ripe for an investigation into the literary background of the *Dialogues* and for a reassessment of their purpose and value. Although my interpretation of culture is confined to literature and theology, I am well aware that there is scope for the treatment of the art and architecture of the sixth century. This is a field in which B. Ward-Perkins and C. Heitz are currently engaged.

It is my intention to show that the *Dialogues*, written in response to the request from Gregory's own circle (who were doubtless already familiar with the *exempla* cited in the *Homiliae in Evangelia*[5]) for an account of the miracles of Italian holy men, belong to that *genre* of late antique and early medieval hagiography, which was first subjected to criticism by Delehaye, Dufourcq, and Lanzoni in the earlier years of this century.[6] Their work has been followed more recently by that of three writers with a more radical approach: E. R. Curtius and E. Auerbach have scrutinized this material from a literary point of view, while F. Graus has examined it from the point of view of the anthropologist and sociologist. S. Boesch Gajano is currently engaged in a study of hagiography from a sociological standpoint; though I appreciate the value of her work, I do not always agree with her conclusions. W. F. Bolton has dealt ably with Gregory's attitude to history; I shall discuss this question further in chapters one and four. Here I shall confine myself to the comment that since it is now generally recognized that this literary *genre* cannot be regarded as history or biography, Gregory should not be censured for failing to achieve something which was never his intention. Like the other hagiographers, his aim was not to produce accurate history, but to tell inspiring stories to act as a substitute for the *passiones* of the martyrs in a nominally Christian society, where opportunities for martyrdom were virtually non-existent. It

---

[4] E.g., Homes Dudden, *Gregory the Great*, 1: 341.

[5] See J. McClure, "Gregory the Great: Exegesis and Audience," unpublished doctoral thesis (Oxford 1978).

[6] For details of the works of these and other authors to whom a general reference is made in this Introduction, see the Bibliography, pp. 193-215.

was immaterial to him, as it was to other writers in this class, that the same story was applied to more than one holy man; what was important was to attach to the subject of the hagiography an account of actions appropriate to a holy man as such.

The work of theologians in the field of biblical typology since 1945 helps to emphasize the non-historical nature of the *Dialogues*.[7] Once it is grasped that Gregory's use of typology is not confined to his biblical and homiletical works, the significance of his treatment of the miracle-stories becomes apparent, as I try to show in chapter two. This view of his exegetical methods counteracts the over-literal and over-ingenious interpretations of O. Rousseau and M. Mähler.

No reader of the *Dialogues* can fail to be impressed by Gregory's profoundly biblical outlook and extensive and detailed knowledge of the Bible. Jean Leclercq affords an insight into the methods by which this knowledge was acquired.[8] It was the daily *lectio divina* from the codex of the Bible assigned to him which, through the years of his life in the monastery of St Andrew, formed Gregory's mind and character and built up his spiritual life.

Scholars working on one or other aspect of Gregory's life and teaching have commonly assumed that, in spite of his six years' sojourn as *apocrisiarius* in Constantinople, he knew no Greek, and that consequently he was uninfluenced by Eastern Christian spirituality and theology. Many instances of this view could be cited; one of the most recent is to be found in an article by Claude Dagens, published in 1975:

> Un autre facteur risquait de rendre Grégoire encore plus étranger au monde oriental: son ignorance du grec. ... Dans le domaine culturel, l'Orient et l'Occident deviennent de plus en plus étrangers, l'un à l'autre; le Romain qu'était Grégoire ne pouvait pas ne pas se comporter en Romain, convaincu des mérites de la langue latine....[9]

The repetition of this opinion in his notable book, *Saint Grégoire le Grand: culture et expérience chrétiennes*, is to be regretted.[10]

---

[7] E.g., J. Daniélou, *Sacramentum futuri: études sur les origines de la typologie biblique* (Paris 1950); G. W. H. Lampe and K. J. Woollcombe, *Essays in Biblical Typology*, Studies in Biblical Theology 22 (London 1956); R. P. C. Hanson, *Allegory and Event* (London 1959).

[8] J. Leclercq, *L'amour des lettres et le désir de Dieu*, 2nd ed. (Paris 1963), pp. 19-24; see also A. Mundò, "'Bibliotheca': Bible et lecture de carême," *RBén* 60 (1950): 65-92.

[9] C. Dagens, "L'église universelle et le monde oriental chez saint Grégoire," *Ist.* 4 (1975): 457-475, at 464-473.

[10] Idem, *Saint Grégoire le Grand: structure et expérience chrétiennes* (Paris 1977), pp. 436-437.

Leclercq takes a different view. He points out that though (in his view) Gregory knew no Greek, a number of the Greek Fathers could be read in Latin translation, and that Gregory was undoubtedly influenced by some of them:

> Au sujet de sa dépendance à l'égard des Pères de l'église et du monachisme, l'état actuel des recherches n'autorise pas encore de résultats définitifs. ... Comparé à l'ensemble des Pères latins, Grégoire se distingue par une certaine saveur orientale, qui est actuellement bien difficile à définir et dont des études à venir préciseront sans doute les composantes.[11]

It is this last sentence which has formed the point of departure for my own research. In the first place, I am unable to accept completely the common assumption that Gregory knew no Greek at all. An inspection of the texts of Gregory in PL 75-77 has revealed the presence of a great many Greek words and phrases, some in Greek characters and others transliterated. I have tried to examine them by the same methods as the late H. I. Marrou applied to Augustine's Greek,[12] and have discussed this question more fully elsewhere.[13] The results of this investigation have been inconclusive; it may be that Gregory's own protests were *confessiones humilitatis* rather than admissions of ignorance, and that he had a slight knowledge of Greek, but it is unlikely that he was able to read the language to any great extent. The question of Greek influence upon Gregory through Latin translations is another matter, but here again it has not been possible to prove conclusively that Gregory had read any individual work, apart from the *de fuga* of Gregory of Nazianzus, the reference to which in the *Liber regulae pastoralis* is already well-known.[14]

What has emerged is confirmation of the belief that Gregory and other writers, both Eastern and Western, drew upon a common literary tradition. There might already be a linguistic division between Eastern and Western Christendom in Gregory's day, but there was as yet no theological or cultural division. The study of the common literary tradition and its influence upon Gregory's spirituality has involved the reading of a wide range of Greek patristic and apophthegmatic literature,

---

[11] J. Leclercq, in *Histoire de la spiritualité chrétienne*, ed. J. Leclercq et al. (Paris 1961), 2: 12-14.

[12] H. I. Marrou, *Saint Augustin et la fin de la culture antique* (Paris 1938), pp. 27-46.

[13] J. M. Petersen, "Did Gregory the Great Know Greek? A Reconsideration," unpublished paper.

[14] PL 77: 14; for the Greek, PG 35: 425; for general reference to Gregory of Nazianzus, see *Liber regulae pastoralis* 3, prol., PL 77: 49.

in the course of which a number of interesting correspondences and comparisons have been noted. The comparison of the *Dialogues* with the *Historia religiosa* of Theodoret has proved particularly interesting and fruitful. Though many of the resemblances are undoubtedly due to the fact that both Gregory and Theodoret were working within the same biblical and typological tradition, there is at least one, the correspondence between the descriptions of the earlier life of Symeon Stylites and that of Martin the hermit, which is too close to be accounted for in this manner.[15] I have suggested a solution.

There are undoubted resemblances between the *Dialogues* and the literature of the Desert, for example: Jerome's *Vitae* of Paul, Hilarion, and Malchus; the *Vita Antonii*; the *Historia monachorum in Aegypto*; the *Historia Lausiaca* of Palladius, the *Apophthegmata patrum*; the various *Vitae* of Eastern saints, including those of John the Almsgiver by Leontius, and of Euthymius, Sabas, and others, by Cyril of Scythopolis. Gregory was undoubtedly acquainted with the works of John Cassian,[16] but one cannot prove absolutely that he had first-hand knowledge of the other writings. If, however, we can accept that the translators of the Latin version of the subject collection of the *Apophthegmata patrum*, Pelagius and John, were identical with the popes of the same names – and an article by A. Mundò[17] shows convincing reasons for such acceptance – it seems inconceivable that Gregory did not know this translation at first hand. Indeed, apart from the probable identity of the translators, there seem to me to be other good reasons for assuming that he did, as I have attempted to show in chapter six.

In studying the literature of the Desert, I have been conscious of my debt to a number of workers in this field, notably A. J. Festugière, the late Derwas J. Chitty, the late Norman Baynes, the late André Wilmart, and Owen Chadwick, who has produced the only complete English translation (Helen Waddell translated only extracts) of the Latin version of Pelagius, with a useful commentary. More recently, C. M. Batlle, J. G. Freire, J. C. Guy, L. Régnault, and Sister Benedicta Ward have all made valuable contributions,[18] but a complete text of the Pelagius and John version, with a critical introduction and commentary and an adequate

---

[15] *Dialogue* 3.16, *Les Dialogues de Grégoire le Grand*, ed. A. de Vogüé, trans. P. Antin, 3 vols., sc 254, 260, 265 (Paris 1978-1980), 2: 326-337, at 334-335.

[16] See chapter six, n. 31.

[17] A. Mundò, "L'authenticité de la 'Regula S. Benedicti'," *StAns* 42 (1957): 105-158, at 129-136.

[18] See C. Philippart, "'Vitae patrum': trois travaux récents sur d'anciennes traductions latines," *AnBoll* 92 (1974): 353-365.

index, is badly needed. P. H. Rousseau's sensitive and sympathetic studies of asceticism in Late Antiquity have proved both illuminating and stimulating.

Once it is acknowledged that Gregory's raw material for the *Dialogues* largely consisted of a corpus of traditional stories common to both East and West, the claim that they are an important source for Italian social and economic history needs to be reconsidered, but it would be out of place to deal with this question in a work dealing with the literary background of the *Dialogues*.

No scholar working on this period can fail to be grateful to Peter Brown for the imaginative insight and penetration, which he brings to bear upon its problems, and for the stimulating quality of his writings, in particular for his important article on the rise and function of the holy man in Late Antiquity.[19] He has brilliantly revived the concept of *Romania*, that is, of the Mediterranean as a Roman lake, which was first propagated by the late Henri Pirenne in the 1930s.[20] My own intention is to show that this is as true in the cultural and theological sphere in the late sixth century as it is in the economic sphere, by taking a fresh look at certain widely accepted concepts and by juxtaposing with the *Dialogues* material emanating from the eastern Rome. Thus I hope to actualize the generalizations of both Leclercq and Brown, by defining more closely, so far as the *Dialogues* are concerned, that *saveur orientale* detected by Leclercq, and by attempting to explain the "Mediterranean-wide process of osmosis," [21] by which Brown believes that vital areas of culture were transmitted in the period of Late Antiquity. We have long been accustomed to view Gregory chronologically, as standing at the junction of Late Antiquity and the Middle Ages. We now need to see him geographically, so to speak, as the figure linking the old and new Rome.

There are necessarily some *lacunae* in my treatment of the subject but these are already being filled by the labours of other contemporary scholars. It is a remarkable fact that the bulk of the surviving literary sources for this period consists of theological material, including ecclesiastical history. What remains of secular literary material was, for long, despised on grounds of style and content, but Averil Cameron has done – and is doing – much to re-evaluate it and to reinstate it as an

---

[19] P. R. L. Brown, "The Rise and Function of the Holy Man in Late Antiquity," *JRS* 61 (1971): 80-101; see also his "Eastern and Western Christendom in Late Antiquity: a Parting of the Ways," *SCH(L)* 13 (1976): 1-24.

[20] H. Pirenne, *Mahomet et Charlemagne* (Brussels-Paris 1937), p. 9.

[21] Brown, "Eastern and Western Christendom," p. 6.

historical source.[22] My concentration on the literary raw material of the
Dialogues to the exclusion of their style and structure on the one hand,
and of Gregory's thought processes on the other, is due to the work of
Alessandro Brovarone and of Pierre Boglioni. Since Judith McClure's
unpublished thesis deals at length with Gregory as exegete, I have treated
this aspect of the matter only where the typological interpretation of the
miracle-stories and the question of Greek influences are concerned. She
has also dealt fully with the question of Gregory's audience. Recent work
by R. A. Markus on the episcopate in North Africa and in Ravenna has
been very helpful to me, as has his earlier writing on Augustine's mission
to England, which I have used in chapter six. The vexed question of
whether or not Gregory was a Benedictine has been settled once and for
all, in my opinion, by K. Hallinger, in the important article which he
wrote in reply to the somewhat ill-founded assertions of O. Porcel.[23] In
fairness, however, it must be admitted that Porcel has done a useful
service to scholarship by listing the correspondences between the *Regula
S. Benedicti* and Gregory's writings; and that Hallinger at times goes to
excessive lengths to prove his case. The two recent books by J. H.
Richards appeared when the preparation of this work was far advanced,
but in any case, their contribution to Gregorian studies is limited.[24]

To forestall potential critics, may I conclude by making clear what I am
not trying to do? It is not my intention to examine the wider question of
whether miracles can happen or to rationalize Gregory's miracle-stories,
unless very incidentally, by searching for some kind of scientific basis for
them. My efforts in the field of *Quellenforschung* will be directed chiefly
towards showing that there was in the Mediterranean area a common
fund of stories and teaching, upon which Eastern and Western Christian
writers alike could draw.

[22] A. M. Cameron, *Agathias* (Oxford 1970); ed., Corippus, *in laudem Iustini* (Oxford
1976); for her articles on the same theme, see Bibliography.
[23] For details of this controversy, see O. Porcel, *La doctrina monastica de San
Gregorio magno y la Regula monachorum* (Madrid 1950); reply by K. Hallinger, "Der
Papst Gregor der Grosse und der heilige Benedikt," St*Ans* 42 (1957): 231-319; rejoinder
by Porcel, "San Gregorio y el monacato: questiones controvertidas," (Scripta et
documenta 12) *Monastica* 1 (Montserrat 1960): 1-95. P. Verbraken in his review of
Porcel's article, *StMon* 2 (1960): 438-440, sums upt the arguments. P. Meyvaert, "Bede
and Gregory the Great," Jarrow Lecture 4 (1964) in *Benedict, Gregory, Bede, and Others*
(London 1977), pp. 1-26, at p. 26, 59n, rightly, in my opinion, contends that Hallinger's
thesis that Gregory hardly knew the *Reg. Ben.* and was little influenced by it, cannot
seriously be maintained. However, I accept as fundamentally correct, Hallinger's view
that Gregory could not have been a Benedictine in the modern sense of the term.
[24] See R. A. Markus, "Review: Consul of God, by J. H. Richards," *History* 65 (1980):
459-460.

MAP 1: ITALY IN THE LATE SIXTH CENTURY.

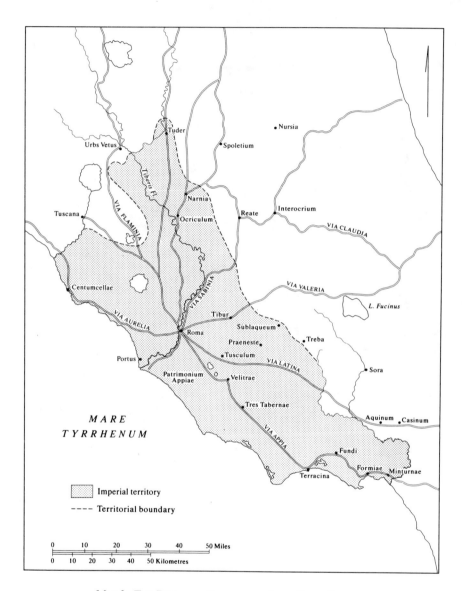

MAP 2: THE DUCHY OF ROME IN THE LATE SIXTH CENTURY
showing the convergence of the principal roads upon Rome.

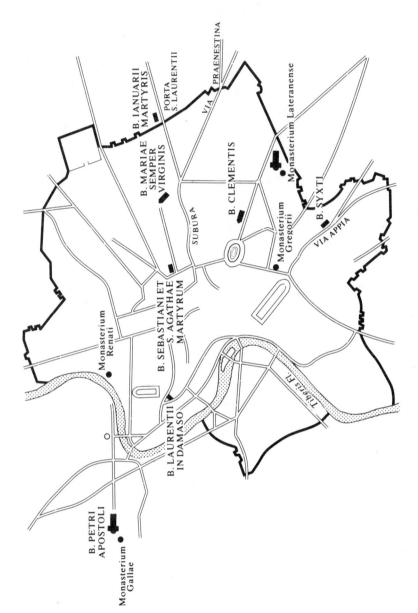

MAP 3: ECCLESIASTICAL ROME IN THE LATE SIXTH CENTURY
showing churches and monasteries mentioned in the *Dialogues*.

1

Gregory's Raw Material
and His Attitude Towards It

A. Gregory's Sources of Information and their Relationship to the Contemporary Italian Background

In previous studies of the *Dialogues*, the relationship between the political divisions of sixth-century Italy, the settings of the miracle-stories, and the location of Gregory's informants has not received detailed treatment; nor do the forms of language in which the informants are introduced appear to have aroused any interest. Yet an examination of these factors should be of some value in tracing the sources of the stories and in throwing some light on Gregory's own methods and motives in telling them.

This is not to say that these aspects of the *Dialogues* have been neglected. Homes Dudden and T. Hodgkin[1] have examined the evidence for the Lombard conquest of Italy; L. Duchesne,[2] in two articles written more than seventy years ago, and F. Lanzoni, in his slightly more recent work,[3] have supplied valuable interpretations of the state of the ecclesiastical organization of the Italian Church during this confused period (and both earlier and later, in the case of Lanzoni). Moricca has furnished us with an attempted chronology of the stories and with a classification of the localities in which the miracles described by Gregory are said to have occurred and also of the informants, according to status and occupation.[4] Most recent of all, A. de Vogüé has made a fruitful

---

[1] T. Hodgkin, *Italy and Her Invaders*, vol. 5 (Oxford 1875).

[2] L. Duchesne, "Le sedi episcopali nell'antico ducato di Roma," *Arch. Società Romana di storia patria* 15 (1892): 475-503 (= *Scripta minora* ... [Rome 1973]: 409-437); "Les évêchés d'Italie et l'invasion lombarde," *MEFR* 23 (1903): 83-116; 25 (1905): 365-399.

[3] F. Lanzoni, *Le diocesi d'Italia dalle origini al secolo VII (604)*, Studi e testi 35, 2 vols. in 1 (Faenza 1927).

[4] Moricca, Gregorius i, *Dialogi*, pp. xliii, 21-33.

examination of the relationship between the topography and the chronology of the *Dialogues*, of their audience, and of their literary antecedents.[5] What is lacking is a synthesis of our information, showing the inter-relation of the various strands and also taking into consideration such factors as the situation of the papal *patrimonia*, the proximity of the great trunk roads to the sites of the miracles or the homes of the informants, and the additional information which can be gleaned from Gregory's *Epistles*.

Let us first consider the political divisions of Italy at the beginning of Gregory's pontificate. The maps on pp. xxii-xxiii illustrate the situation as it was before the close of the sixth century, when Istria, Liguria, the Exarchate of Ravenna, the Pentapolis, a narrow strip of territory including Tadinum and Perugia, which linked this area to the Duchy of Rome, the Duchy of Naples, and areas of Calabria and Bruttium were all that remained in imperial hands in mainland Italy. The islands of Sardinia, Corsica, and Sicily were also in imperial hands; the last-named was of considerable economic importance as the granary of Rome.

Unfortunately no such clear map can be drawn to illustrate the situation of the papal patrimony, which, of course, must not be confused with the Duchy of Rome or with the later Papal States. Gregory's letters afford us considerable information as to how the papal estates were administered, and some idea of where they were situated, but in most instances, we do not know their exact geographical location nor their extent. For the present purpose we are considering only those estates which have some bearing on the subject-matter of the *Dialogues* and are therefore excluding those in Gaul and Dalmatia, but not those in Africa.

In Rome itself the papacy owned two valuable estates: the *Patrimonium Appiae*, which lay between the Via Appia and the sea, and the *Patrimonium Tusciae*, which lay on the right bank of the Tiber, perhaps in what is now the Vatican City, as well as property at Tibur. Not far away was the patrimony of Campania, which probably did not include Naples, but did include the off-shore islands. The patrimonies in Southern Italy receive mention in Gregory's letters, but not much is known about them; there is more information about Sicily, as befits its economic importance. Considerably less significant was the small patrimony in Liguria. As regards the *Patrimonium Samniticum*, the opinion of Homes Dudden is to be preferred to that of Duchesne. The latter may well be right in believing it to include the port of Ortona, but the fact that the inland area of the

---

[5] *Dialogue*, 1: 46-65.

Duchy of Beneventum, often called the Duchy of Samnium, was ravaged by the Lombards after Gregory's time (ca. 642) supports the view of Homes Dudden that this was part of the patrimony in Gregory's time.[6] However, Homes Dudden seems to be mistaken in believing that there were papal estates in the neighbourhood of Nursia:[7] in the first place, since Nursia was situated in the Lombard Duchy of Spoleto, Gregory would undoubtedly have lost them; secondly, the relevant letters deal with a purely ecclesiastical matter, namely, the scandal of priests in the district who were living with *mulieribus extraneis* (*Reg.* 13.38-39, 2: 401-402).

An analysis of the destinations of Gregory's letters shows that: there were apparently no papal estates outside imperial territory; and the only bishop – indeed, the only individual – in Italy outside imperial territory, with whom he corresponded, was the bishop of Spoleto.[8] There were other bishops from Lombard territory with whom he was in touch but these, as we shall see when we come to consider the whereabouts of Gregory's informants, were visitors or exiles in Rome.

It is not surprising that the area covered by Gregory's letters should be coterminous with the territory under imperial control; what is more surprising is the exception of the city of Spoleto and certain other places in that duchy, such as Nursia, where he also had correspondents. It is difficult to see the reason for this exception; one can only assume that this territory (as has been mentioned), between the Via Flaminia and the alternative route northwards via Todi and Perugia was a debatable ground, over which the imperial hold was uncertain. This view receives some support from *Reg.* 2.4, 1: 103, where Gregory is dealing with the situation in Narnia in 591: he writes of *Langobardorum sive Romanorum qui in eodem loco degunt.*

An examination of Moricca's list of the places where miracles occurred reveals that the majority of them were situated in territory which was under imperial control at the time when the *Dialogues* were written.[9] This territory, as has been mentioned, consisted principally of the Duchy of Rome, but also included places in the Exarchate of Ravenna, such as

---

[6] Homes Dudden, *Gregory the Great*, 1: 297; Duchesne, "Les évêchés d'Italie," pp. 83-116, at p. 97; see Paul the Deacon, *Historia Langobardorum* 4.44-46, ed. L. Bethmann and G. Waitz, MGH SRL (Hanover 1878), pp. 134-135.

[7] Homes Dudden, *Gregory the Great*, 1: 297; for a more recent account of the whereabouts and administration of the patrimonies, see J. H. Richards, *The Popes and the Papacy in the Early Middle Ages, 476-752* (London 1979), pp. 316-322.

[8] Duchesne, "Les évêchés d'Italie," pp. 83-116, at p. 111.

[9] Moricca, Gregorius I, *Dialogi*, pp. xliii, xlv.

Placentia and Ancona, and areas where portions of the papal patrimony were situated: Apulia, Sicily, and Africa. A few places are mentioned which we know to have been in Lombard hands at the time of Gregory's pontificate: Verona, Brescia, Lucca, Nursia, and Cample, possibly Narnia, and last but not least, Spoleto. Some of his informants were certainly exiles or visitors in Rome, or were travellers.

Once Gregory had decided to write an account of the miracles of the Italian Fathers, there were two important factors which would help him in the collection of information. In the first place, as we can see from the map on p. xxiii, the system of Roman roads was still in existence; we have no evidence as to their condition, but since Gregory was able to carry on such an extensive correspondence, it must have been possible for his messengers to use them. Secondly, there was an elaborately organized civil service, which administered the papal patrimonies, and which must have included runners and letter-carriers. The chief administrator of each patrimony was known as the *rector* and was usually a Roman *clericus*, appointed by Gregory. Under the *rectores* were officials known as *defensores*, who could be laymen, and who were assisted by clerks (in the modern sense of the word) called *notarii* or *cartularii*; these, like the *defensor*, could be clerici, but were often in minor orders and could be married. The lowest rank was that of the *actionarius*, who was a bailiff or lesser clerk and was usually a layman. It seems likely that people in all these ranks would be able to give Gregory the kind of assistance that he needed, since they would be in touch with farmers and country people (who would be steeped in local traditions), and would be in the habit of visiting Rome on official business connected with the estates. One of Gregory's principal informants was Julian the *Defensor*, who figures in the story of Equitius (1.4, 2: 38-55), and is cited as the source of the stories of Fortunatus, bishop of Todi (1.10, 2: 92-99) and of the prodigies announcing the death of Theodoric (4.31, 3: 104-107). Gregory's use of the expressions

> tam religiosorum virorum (3.1, 2: 266-267); religiosi viri Apuliae provinciae partibus cogniti (3.5, 2: 272-273); quidam religiosus et fidelissimus vir (4.10, 3: 44-45); quibusdam quoque religiosis viris (4.23, 3: 78-79); religiosi alii (4.35, 3: 116-117); and fideles ac religiosi viri multi (4.59, 3: 196-197)

is significant.

The term *religiosus* does not generally mean a monk, but a pious layman, though in 3.16 (2: 326-327), it is applied to Pope Pelagius II, who is classed with *aliis religiosissimis viris*. It may well be that some of the persons designated as *religiosi* could be members of the papal administrative service in the patrimonies, who had come to Rome on business and who had been received by Gregory himself. This seems particularly likely in the case of the *religiosi viri* from Apulia, which included the patrimonies of Hydruntum and Callipolis. Another of these individuals (4.10, 3: 44-45) told Gregory a story of travellers from Sicily (where there were papal estates), which island also figures in the story told by the *fideles ac religiosi viri* in 4.59 (3: 196-197). Gregory's informants also include a *senex clericus* (1.9, 2: 88-89) and *quidam clericus senex* (3.12, 2: 296-297), who could possibly be employees in the administration of the patrimonies.

These *religiosi viri* and *clerici senes* are categories in the much larger class of Gregory's anonymous informants. Anonymous expressions are sometimes used to designate individuals or definite groups, such as *coepiscopus meus* (1.5, 2: 58-59); *clericus senex*; and the *religiosi viri Apuliae provinciae partibus cogniti*; but more often they are vague in scope, such as *seniorum valde venerabilium* (1.prol., 2: 18-19); *nostri seniores* (3.25, 2: 364-365); *personarum gravium atque fidelium* (4.14, 3: 54-55); or simply *multi* (3.6, 2: 276-277); or *testes* (3.7, 2: 278-297; 26, 1: 366-367). We do not find the same contrast between the general and particular as in the *Moralia* and the *Homiliae*, to which Dagens draws attention,[10] perhaps because Gregory often has actual rather than theoretical examples in mind, even if he does not name them.

There is, however, some significance in the use of the anonymous to introduce a certain type of story, namely, one which is a *topos* or which has literary affiliations. Here Gregory seems to have taken over a traditional story or series of stories and thrown his material into a literary form having affinities with the work of some other writer. Important examples of such *topoi* are the story derived from the *senex clericus* (1.9, 2: 88-89, 90-91) of the infant Boniface giving his clothes to the poor,[11] and of the poisoned cup rendered harmless (3.5, 2: 274-275).[12] These are both themes which recur in late antique and early medieval literature.

Important examples of this kind of story, in which Gregory blends local information with literary material, are:

1. The two stories told by the *coepiscopus*: the first in which Constantius, the *mansionarius*, filled the lamps in the church with water,

---

[10] Dagens, "Structure et expérience," pp. 106-109.

[11] Cf. Cyprian of Toulon *et al.*, *Vita Caesarii episcopi Arelatensis* 1.3, ed. B. Krusch, MGH SRM 3 (Hanover 1896), p. 458; Venantius Fortunatus, *Vita S. Medardi* 2, ed. B. Krusch, MGH AA 4 (2) (Berlin 1885), p. 68; Gregory the Great, *Dialogue* 1.9, 2: 90-91.

[12] Cf. Sulpicius Severus, *Vita S. Martini*, *Vie de saint Martin*, ed. and trans. J. Fontaine, 3 vols., SC 133-135 (Paris 1967-1969), 1: 266-267.

which behaved as if it were oil (1.5, 2: 58-61), has affinities with a story told by Eusebius;[13] the second about Marcellinus, who turned back the flames from a burning house (1.6, 2: 262-265) resembles a story told by Sulpicius Severus and other writers.[14]

2. The group of stories (3.2-4, 2: 266-273) attributed to *religiosi viri* and set in Greece: these are apparently a blend of papal traditions and stories long current in the Mediterranean area, at least one of which was put into a literary form by Pliny the Younger and Lucian of Samosata.[15]

3. The story of the haunted temple of Apollo (3.7, 2: 278-285): *nec res est dubia, quam narro, quia paene tanti in ea testes sunt, quanti et eius loci habitatores existunt.* Presumably there were plentiful witnesses for the apparently scandalous story of bishop Andrew of Fundi and the nun, but the sequel has very close affinities with a story told by both Cassian and the apophthegmatic writers.[16]

4. The story derived from *senioribus nostris*, of bishop Paulinus of Nola (3.1, 2: 256-257) who is said to have gone to Africa as a captive slave in order to spare the only son of a widow. This is a remarkable elaboration of two very small pieces of historical information found respectively in Augustine's *De civitate Dei* and in the account of the death of Paulinus, by Uranius, of which more will be said in the next section.[17]

Gregory treats much of his material derived from named informants in the same manner. A favourite literary device of his is to attribute a story or stories to a named individual or group of individuals, and then to go on to describe *alia*, of which he has heard from other sources or has personally recollected.

---

[13] Eusebius, *Historia ecclesiastica* 6.9, ed. E. Schwartz, with the Latin trans. by Rufinus, ed. Th. Mommsen, GCS 9 (1) (Leipzig 1903), pp. 538-541. Gregory could, of course, have known this story from the Latin version.

[14] *Vita S. Martini* 14, 1: 282-283; cf. Gregory of Tours, *Liber vitae patrum* 6(6), ed. B. Krusch and W. Levison, MGH SRM 1(2) (Hanover 1885, anastatic repr. 1969), p. 234; Venantius Fortunatus, *Vita Remedii* 5, ed. B. Krusch, MGH AA 4(2) (Berlin 1885), pp. 65-66; Cassiodorus, *Historia tripartita* 12.10, ed. R. Hanslik, CSEL 71 (Vienna 1952), pp. 678-679.

[15] Pliny the Younger, *Epistulae* 7.27.4-11, ed. C. F. W. Mueller (Leipzig 1893), 1: 189-190; Lucian of Samosata, *Philopseudes* 30-31, in *Opera*, ed. M. D. Macleod, 3 vols (Oxford 1972-1980), 2: 194-195.

[16] Cassian, *Collationes* 8.16, *Conférences*, ed. E. Pichery, 3 vols., SC 42, 54, 64 (Paris, repr. 1966-1971), 2: 23; *Apophthegmata patrum, versio latina*, 5.5, PL 73: 885-886.

[17] Augustine, *De civitate Dei* 1.10, ed. B. Dombart and A. Kalb, 2 vols., CCSL 47-48 (Turnholt 1955), 1: 11-12; Uranius, *De obitu Paulini*, PL 53: 861-862; Gregory of Tours, *Liber in gloria confessorum* 108, MGH SRM 1(2), pp. 367-368.

Examples of this technique are:

1. Of Boniface: *huius multa miracula is qui adhuc superest Gaudentius presbyter narrat* (1.9, 2: 76-77), whereupon Gregory tells the story of the miraculous increase of wine and follows it with: *adhuc pauca aliqua, quae de Bonifati episcopi opere supersunt, quia eius memoriam fecimus, exequamur* (1.9, 2: 82-83). The three stories which follow are apparently recollections by Gregory.

2. Of Martin the hermit: *de quo multa ipse et beatae memoriae papa Pelagio decessore meo et aliis religiosissimis viribus narrantibus agnovi* (3.6, 2: 326-327). Here Gregory tells four stories; possibly he learned them from both these sources; at any rate, he does not say which are to be attributed to Pelagius II and which to the other informants. In this case there is a Greek source for much of Gregory's information, which will be treated in detail in chapter six.

3. The stories connected with Sanctulus: the first, the story of Florentius and Euthicius (3.15, 2: 314-319), is attributed to Sanctulus personally and appears to be derived solely from local tradition, but the other three (3.37, 2: 410-427) have been learned by Gregory *a vicinis suis sacerdotibus*. The first two of these are based on biblical types, while the third has a distinct affinity with the story of the recluse Hospitius told by Gregory of Tours.[18] It is interesting to compare Gregory's technique as narrator in two larger groups of stories: the life of Benedict, which occupies the whole of *Dialogue* 2, and the series of Spoleto stories (3.14-15, 2: 302-327; 21, 2: 352-357; 33, 2: 392-401). In the former he employs the technique (already described) of attributing the miracle-stories to a group of informants (the four disciples of Benedict in this case, *Dialogue* 2.prol., 2: 128-129), but does not assign any of them to a particular individual.[19]

The two exceptions, apart from Benedict's own account of his vision (2.35, 2: 238-241), are a story attributed to a disciple called Peregrinus (2.27, 2: 214-217), which is a *topos* relating to the miraculous arrival of money for the payment of debts,[20] and the reference by Aptonius (2.26, 2:

---

[18] *Liber historiarum* 6.6, ed. B. Krusch and W. Levison, MGH SRM 1(1) (n. ed., Hanover 1951), pp. 272-273.

[19] This technique is used by Greek writers, e.g., Lucian of Samosata, *Demonax* 67, 1: 57. Gregory probably borrowed it from Athanasius, e.g. *et ille enim vix potuerat tanta narrare, nam et ego suas a vobis modica illius rememorabo scribens vobis* (*Vita Antonii* 4, *Vita di Antonio*, ed. G. J. M. Bartelink, VSant. 1, Milan 1974, p. 6).

[20] For other miraculous appearances of money, cf. e.g., Gregory of Tours, *Liber in gloria martyrum* 43, MGH SRM 1(2), p. 67; *Vita Theodori Syceotae* 34, *Vie de saint Théodore de Sykéon*, ed. A.-J. Festugière, SHG 48 (Brussels 1970), pp. 30-31; Cyril of Scythopolis, *Vita S. Euthymii* 48 [Opera] *Kyrillos von Skythopolis*, ed. E. Schwartz, TU 49 (Leipzig 1939), pp. 69-70.

214-215) to the healing of his father's servant by Benedict. The vagueness of the attributions gives Gregory great scope for the superimposition of a literary form upon traditional material passed on by Benedict's disciples.

An interesting aspect of what may be termed "the Spoleto sequence" is that though the material is not always assigned to a definite informant, it appears to be principally traditional, without the superimposition from an external source: the two exceptions are the story of the consecrated virgin and the pig (3.21, 2: 352-355), which is derived from the Bible, and the story of the serpent in the servant's basket (3.14, 2: 310-311), which is identical with that of Exhilaratus (2.18, 2: 194-195). To give an example, in 3.14 (2: 302-315), we find a series of stories about Isaac the Syrian, which are attributed to the nun Gregoria, living in Rome, and to Eleutherius. Dufourcq and others have drawn attention to the close resemblance of these stories to certain stories, dealing with the same region, which are to be found in the *Gesta martyrum Romanorum*.[21] Since certain events described in these stories are undoubtedly *topoi*, Gregory probably decided to deal with them by the same technique as those stories more obviously capable of being linked with literary material.

We now approach those miracle stories which Gregory attributes to a single informant. Is there any difference in his method of handling them? In some cases, such as the stories to be found in 1.3-4 (2: 34-59; 10, 2: 92-111), where the informant is named, it seems that Gregory is giving a coherent form to a local tradition, but in others, particularly in *Dialogue* 4, there are literary overtones comparable to those in the stories for which Gregory employs the special techniques already described. It does not seem possible to discern any principle underlying his handling of stories attributed definitely to a single individual. We can only conclude that Gregory employs his special techniques for dealing with miracle-stories, for which there is an extensive written parallel in the Bible or the writings of other authors. In these cases, it is his practice to provide an anonymous informant or an imprecise attribution, and as the result of his intensely biblical formation and outlook and his general cultural background, to interpret his material in biblical terms or to impose upon it a literary form derived from other sources. We shall also see that he did not always refrain from these methods of interpretation in cases where the parallel was less obvious and where there was a named informant. The fact that it is not possible to schematize the whole of the material about his informants, with which Gregory supplies us, suggests that he was

---

[21] See chapter three *passim*.

working from genuine material supplied through personal enquiry and was not producing a series of names in order to give an appearance of verisimilitude to his work.

The connection between the papal estates, the road system, and the whereabouts of Gregory's correspondents is further confirmation of the genuineness of his efforts to collect material. The maps on pages XXII-XXIII represent an attempt to illustrate this connection. So far as one can see, the evidence brought to Gregory came orally through his informants, who travelled over the Roman road system, rather than by letters brought by messengers. Unfortunately the language which he employs to introduce his informants and their stories does not at once enable us to distinguish with certainty whether he received them in writing or through oral delivery, since the words *relatio* and *narrare* may be used both of speech and writing. However, it is possible for us to gain a little help from examining the tenses of the verbs employed. In Gregory's days the Latin language was in a fluid state; the imperfect was still employed to denote a frequentative action in the past, but it was being rapidly superseded by the use of verbs, such as *consuescere* or *solere*, followed by the infinitive, to denote habitual action. By looking at Gregory's mode of introducing informants, we can discover to some extent who were his habitual story-tellers and who were people paying him a single visit. It seems that the words *consuevit* and *solet* are applicable to persons still living (they both mean "he *is* wont") and *consueverat* or a verb in the imperfect to persons who are already dead at the time when Gregory is speaking.

Examples of the use of the imperfect tense are:

> Felix ... multa mihi ... admiranda narrabat (1.3, 2: 34-35); aiebat [Aptonius] (2.26, 2: 214-215); episcopus reperri qui se ... ora vidisse testabatur (3.31, 2: 392-393); ... miraculum narro, quod inquisitus mihi simpliciter et ipse [Eleutherius] fatebatur (3.33, 2: 394-395); [Redemptus] ... a me requisitus mihi ipse narrabat (3.38, 2: 428-429); quod vir venerabilis abbas Stephanus non longe ante hoc in hac urbe defunctus est, ... in eadem provincia Nursiae contegisse referebat (4.12, 3: 48-49); qui [Deusdedit] mihi narrabat (4.32, 3: 106-107).

The parallel usage, that is, of the pluperfect form with the imperfect meaning, *consueverat*, occurs in the following examples:

> quod eius discipulus, Peregrinus nomine, narrare consueverat (2.27, 2: 214-215); frater quidam ... ex multis quae nesciebam, me aedificare consueverat (3.18, 2: 344-345); Iulianus, qui ante fere annos septem defunctus est ... mecumque conloqui de animae utilitate consueverat (4.31, 3: 104-105).

Thus it seems that among people who were dead at the time of writing,
Gregory's frequent visitors had been Felix, called Curvus, the prior of
Fundi (easily reached from Rome); an older bishop, with whom he was
acquainted when serving as *apocrisiarius* at Constantinople, the holy man
Eleutherius, once abbot of St Mark's monastery at Spoleto, who died in
Gregory's own monastery in Rome (3.33, 2: 392-393); Redemptus, bishop
of Ferentis; the abbot Stephanus; a close friend named Deusdedit; an
unnamed brother in Gregory's own monastery; and Julian the *Defensor*.
Peregrinus, the disciple of Benedict, was evidently an habitual narrator,
but presumably belonged to an earlier age, since the word *mihi* is not used
in connection with him. Another regular visitor, now deceased, was
Sanctulus, the priest, *qui ad me ex Nursiae provincia annis singulis venire
consuevit*. Gregory has surely written this sentence, using *consuevit*,
before the arrival of the messenger bringing the news of the death of
Sanctulus (3.37, 2: 410-411).

Regular visitors who are apparently still alive, are:

> Laurentius religiosus vir, ... multa mihi de illo [Libertino] dicere consuevit
> (1.2, 2: 24-25); quidam etenim religiosi viri Apuliae provinciae partibus
> cogniti ... hoc ... testari solent (2.5, 2: 272-273); ... quod Probus omni-
> potentis Dei famulus, qui nunc in hac urbe praesto est ... mihi narrare
> consuevit (4.13, 3: 52-53); vir venerabilis Maximianus Siracusanus
> episcopus, qui diu in hac urbe monasterio praefuit, narrare consuevit (4.33,
> 3: 110-111); at contra Crisaurius, sicut Probus propinquus illius ... narrare
> consuevit (4.40, 3: 142-143).

Of these people, Laurentius and the men of Apulia were probably
members of the papal administrative service in the patrimonies; Maximianus was an old friend who, before becoming bishop of Syracuse had
been abbot of Gregory's monastery in Rome and with whom Gregory
was in constant touch by letter (*Reg.* 2.8, 1: 106-107; 24, 1: 121; 51, 1:
154-155; 3.12, 1: 171; 50, 1: 206-207; 53, 1: 210; 4.11, 12, 14, 1: 243-
247; 36, 1: 271-272; 42, 1: 78) and Probus, whom he appointed as abbot
of St Andrew's and St Lucia's (*Reg.* 11.15, 2: 275).

A careful examination of Gregory's other modes of introducing his
informants has not yielded any very significant results. It seems likely that
he used varying forms of words simply to avoid monotony and not to
denote any subtle shade of meaning. It would be tempting to see in his use
of the word *relatio* an indication that he was producing written evidence;
he uses this word in connection with Maximianus of Syracuse, to whom
he has written for information about Nonnosus (*Reg.* 3.50, 1: 206-207),
and from whom, since his correspondent was in Sicily, a written reply
might reasonably be expected. However, in 3.10 (2: 288-289) we find

perhibet, which is used only of the spoken word, in conjunction with *relatio*, which seems to dispose of this theory. There are three instances in which Gregory uses various forms of the verb *audire* (3.23, 2: 358-359; 4.42, 3: 150-151; 59, 3: 196-197) but he appears to do so only in order to emphasize that his evidence is based on hearsay and therefore is less reliable.

It is sometimes suggested that the letter to Maximianus is the one surviving example of a reply to a questionnaire sent by Gregory to the bishops of Italy in order to obtain material for the *Dialogues* but there are good reasons for a contrary conclusion. First of all, two examples of circular letters sent to a number of bishops by Gregory survive (*Reg.* 1.17, 1: 23; 9.45, 2: 72-73), which bear the names of all the intended recipients, whereas this letter does not. Secondly, the other bishops who were Gregory's informants were in or near Rome, whereas Maximianus was not. In 3.35 (2: 404-405) the reading Tifernae Tiberinae (the present Città di Castello) is to be preferred to Ferentinae,[22] in which case Floridus would be within reach of Rome. Indeed the wording *mihi ... narravit* suggests a single visit during which he could tell his story. Redemptus of Ferentis in Tuscany, not far from Viterbo, also told his story in person, *a me requisitus* (3.38, 2: 428-429). Felix of Portus, though he lived so near to Rome, was once among Gregory's correspondents (*Reg.* 9.98, 2: 107-108, dated 599), but the fact that no letter from him regarding the *Dialogues* survives seems to confirm the view that Gregory gathered information from him orally. Thirdly, the other episcopal informant, Venantius of Luna, was actually present in Rome: *adest quoque in praesenti venerabilis frater, Venantius Lunensis episcopus...* (4.55, 3: 180-181). It seems that Gregory wished to consult Maximianus, because he alone could give the required information about Nonnosus. Thus it was natural for Gregory to write to him on this specific point; indeed the letter gives the impression of a personal document, in no way resembling a circular.

Although the setting of the greater part of Gregory's miracle stories is the area of central and southern Italy under imperial control, the scene of some of them is laid elsewhere. Vogüé supplies an interesting analysis of the topography of the *Dialogues* in relation to their chronology in which he points out that it is not until *Dialogue* 3 that the geographical area is widened.[23] How did Gregory obtain his information about these more distant miracles?

---

[22] See *Dialogue* 3.35, 2: 405, ln.
[23] See *Dialogues* comm., 1: 62.

It will be convenient to begin with the northern part of Italy. The first story concerns a great flood of the river Adige, which seems to be contemporaneous with the great floods at Rome during the pontificate of Pelagius II (3.19, 2: 346-351). Gregory's informant is an official who was acquainted with Count Pronulfus, a witness of the disaster. This is an example of the remoteness of Gregory from some of his material, indeed what he describes is a *topos* in late antique and early medieval literature, namely, the preservation of a person, building, or object from becoming wet, when everything around is inundated by sea or river or soaked in a rainstorm.[24] The same informant, now *locum praefectorum servans*, in Rome (4.54, 3: 178-181) tells how in Brescia an evil-looking man called Valerianus was buried in the church, because the bishop wanted his money, and how the martyr Faustinus appeared to the sexton, telling him to remove the body, or he would be dead in thirty days – a fate which overtook him because he disregarded this advice. The story relating to Lucca (3.9, 2: 286-289) had been told to Gregory two days earlier by Venantius of Luna, who, as we have already seen, was in Rome at the time when Gregory was writing the *Dialogues*. Since his see remained in imperial hands, he was not an exile, like Albinus, bishop of Reate (1.4, 2: 46-47). While in Rome, Venantius was also able to obtain the corroboration of another river miracle, this time at Placentia, whereby the bishop Sabinus altered the course of the Po by means of a letter to the river (3.10, 2: 288-291).

Gregory's narrative relating to Populonium, the scene of two further miracles (3.11, 2: 292-297) is certainly confusing, but it seems that this city was in imperial hands at the time when *Dialogue* 3 was written. At the end of 3.4 (2: 272-273) Gregory indicates that he is now moving from past to present events: *sed oportet iam ut priora taceamus, ad ea quae diebus nostris sunt gesta veniendum est*. Among the *priora* are events which occurred *Gothorum tempore* (3.2, 2: 266-269) and *exigente causa Gothorum* (3.3, 2: 268-271). However, Gregory first holds up Cerbonius, bishop of Populonium, as one who gives proof of his sanctity *diebus nostris*, and then goes on to describe his courage and his miraculous experiences *Gothis supervenientibus* (3.11, 2: 292-297). Later in the same chapter Gregory tells us that since the Lombards were devastating Italy, Cerbonius retired to the island of Elba, where he died. After his burial, the clergy fled quickly to their ship, as he had instructed them, which was

---

[24] Cf. *Dialogues* 3.11-12, 2: 292-297; *Liber in gloria martyrum* 35, pp. 60-61; 43, pp. 67-68; Callinicos, *Vita Hypatii* 46, *Vie de saint Hypatios*, ed. W. J. M. Bartelink, sc 177 (Paris 1971), pp. 272-273.

fortunate as the cruel leader of the Lombards arrived almost immediately. It seems therefore that Cerbonius was bishop of Populonium ca. 546, when Totila captured Rome and when the miracle of deliverance from the bear is reported to have occurred. Cerbonius must have occupied the bishopric for a long period, since it was the arrival of the Lombards in Tuscany, between 571 and 574, which caused him to flee to Elba. Presumably it is the length of his episcopate which enabled Gregory to regard him as providing an example for men of his own time. Moricca is probably right in postulating a long vacancy after his death, since by 591, the diocese was in such a pitiable, leaderless state, that Gregory assigned its oversight to the bishop of Russellae (*Reg*. 1.15, 1: 16). Thus the Goths and Lombards seem to have come and gone.[25]

Of the other places mentioned, we have already seen that Narnia and Nursia are in areas of disputed control. The use of *qui hic de Narniensi civitate adsunt* as informants suggests the presence of a group of exiles from that city in Rome; in view of the statement in *Reg*. 2.4 (1: 103), to which we have already referred, that there was a mixed population of Lombards and Romans in the city, some of the inhabitants may have removed themselves to Rome for political or personal reasons.

The city of Nursia itself was in Lombard hands, whereas the country round it was imperial territory. The one story in the *Dialogues* which mentions the city (4.11, 3: 44-49, and which describes the building of the monastery of Cample, about six Roman miles from Nursia) is told by a *venerabilis vir*, who might conceivably be an exile. The existence of Nursian exiles in Rome is suggested by the reference in 1.4 (2: 44-45) to a man named Castor, son of Felix of the province of Nursia, *qui nunc nobiscum in Romana urbe demoratur*. On the other hand the references to the priest Sanctulus suggest that the local inhabitants had reached some kind of *modus vivendi* with the Lombards; Sanctulus, *ex Nursiae provincia*, used to visit Gregory annually (3.15, 2: 314-315; 37, 2: 410-427), and his death was announced to Gregory by a monk who had arrived three days earlier from the district (3.37, 2: 410-411) which implies that the journey from Nursia to Rome cannot have been unduly difficult or dangerous. We learn also from 3.37 that Sanctulus was regularly in touch with the Lombards (2: 412-413).

---

[25] See Duchesne, "Les évêchés d'Italie," pp. 90-91; Moricca, Gregorius I, *Dialogi*, p.165, ln; Lanzoni, *Le diocesi*, 1: 554-558. P. Conte, "Osservazioni sulla leggenda di S. Cerbonio, vescovo di Populonia," *Aevum* 52 (1978): 235-260, deals principally with the eighth-century *Vita Cerbonii*.

Lastly there is the question of Spoleto. We have already seen that Gregory corresponded with the bishop of Spoleto (*Reg.* 9.49, 2: 75-76; 59, 2: 82; 107, 2: 113-114; 166, 2: 164-165; 13.39, 2: 402), which suggests that messengers could safely carry letters to the Duchy and bring news of it. There were moreover sources of information nearer to hand; the consecrated virgin Gregoria, who lived near the church of St Mary Major in Rome and had known Isaac the Syrian (3.14, 2: 302-303); the holy man Eleutherius, who had been abbot of St Mark's monastery at Spoleto and who ended his days in Gregory's monastery in Rome (3.33, 2: 392-395); and Boniface, one of the monks of that monastery, who, until four years earlier, had lived *cum Langobardis* (3.29, 2: 376-377). It is almost certain that it was upon these people that Gregory relied for his information about Spoleto, since he virtually says so himself; though in the first series of stories (3.14, 2: 302-315) he employs his special technique by not assigning stories definitely to Gregoria or Eleutherius. Moreover he is dealing with the fairly recent past in the Duchy of Spoleto, rather than the immediate present.

So far our classification of Gregory's informants consists chiefly of employees in the papal administrative service, monks, and persons living in or near Rome, including several exiles. This group includes Gregory's episcopal informants, apart from Venantius, who was a temporary visitor, Maximianus of Syracuse, and his dead predecessor, Pelagius II.

There remains one other group to be mentioned: the travellers, among whom we may include Sanctulus. Many of the Italian informants are travellers in their own country by virtue of their occupation; the only one who appears to travel for the sake of it is the *senex pauper* (1.10, 2: 102-103), who might perhaps be some kind of wandering beggar or pilgrim. There are, however, other travellers who can bring Gregory news of more distant lands: *multorum, qui ab Hispaniarum partibus veniunt, relatione cognovimus* (3.31, 2: 384-385); and *Athanasius Isauriae presbyter*, making a long stay in Rome for a lawsuit, who describes the terrible event which he had witnessed at Iconium (4.40, 3: 144-147; *Reg.* 3.52, 1: 208-210; 6.62, 1: 437-438).

Finally we need to consider the distance of Gregory himself from his material. According to Homes Dudden,[26] there were only two cases in which he was personally involved: the first of these is that of Eleutherius, whom Gregory believed to have enabled him to fast on Easter Eve by the power of his prayers (3.33, 2: 396-399), the second is that of Amantius,

---

[26] Homes Dudden, *Gregory the Great*, 1: 342.

who came to Rome at Gregory's request, in order to demonstrate his healing powers, and actually cured a madman by the laying-on-of-hands (3.35, 2: 406-407). Gregory was not himself present, but he accepted the evidence of bishop Floridus and a servant. In point of fact there is a third example: the invisible pig, which departed from the church now known as Sant' Agata dei Goti, when it was consecrated for Catholic worship, after being in the hands of the Arians (3.30, 2: 380-381). *Populus, sacerdos, et custodes* are cited by Gregory as witnesses, but he was actually present himself, as we learn both from the *Liber pontificalis* and from his own use of the first person plural in this passage.[27] As further confirmation of the story about the pig, he mentions *quidam ex his, qui extra sacrarium stabant*. No doubt he was *intra sacrarium* and therefore missed the interesting phenomena in the body of the church.

We have already seen that in most of the stories the element of hearsay is very strong, and when we come to consider that in many of them Gregory unites local traditions with more sophisticated literary material, we may be tempted to regard him simply as a purveyor of stories based on inadequate testimony. We need to remember that: oral testimony is not necessarily unreliable, particularly among illiterate and semi-literate country people, who are accustomed to rely on their memories; and, it was not his object to produce a narrative history, based on unimpeachable sources.

B. The Historical Aspect of the *Dialogues*

There are three historical narratives in the *Dialogues* which are capable of being checked with external historical sources and a fourth, the Totila episodes in *Dialogue* 2, which does not occur in the works of any other writer, but which can be compared with other literary material.

The first of the group of three, to which Homes Dudden and Moricca devote much attention,[28] is the story of Paulinus of Nola (3.1, 2: 256-267), which Gregory believes to have been familiar to *senioribus nostris*, but which had hitherto escaped his memory. According to Gregory's narrative, the region of Campania was devastated, *dum saevientium Wandalorum tempore fuisset*, and Paulinus spent all the money that he could obtain from the diocese in ransoming poor captives. Finally he

---

[27] *Liber Pontificalis*, vols. 1-2, ed. L. Duchesne (repr. Paris 1957), vol. 3, corrections, etc., ed. C. Vogel (Paris 1957), 1: 311.

[28] Homes Dudden, *Gregory the Great*, 1: 304; Moricca, Gregorius i, *Dialogi*, pp. xxxvi-xxxviii.

made the heroic sacrifice of going to Africa himself as a captive, in order to allow the only son of a poor widow to return home. In Africa Paulinus worked as gardener to the son-in-law of the king of the Vandals, to whom he ultimately revealed that he was a bishop. The king allowed him to return home and promised him a present to take with him, whereupon Paulinus successfully petitioned for the liberation of all the captives from Nola.

Gregory also describes the death of Paulinus, referring to a written source: *de cuius etiam morte apud eius ecclesiam scriptum est....* He relates that while Paulinus was lying with a pain in his side, his cell was shaken by an earthquake and that all present were stricken with fear (3.1, 2: 264-265). The written source would appear to be either the *De obitu Paulini* of Uranius or the *Liber in gloria confessorum* of Gregory of Tours.[29] Unfortunately the greater part of this story is nothing but a work of the imagination. The difficulties of the narrative are well-known: in the first place, Paulinus, bishop of Nola, died in 431, but the Vandals, led by Genseric, did not arrive in Italy until 455;[30] secondly, the life of Paulinus is well-documented, but there is no evidence whatever for his having been in Africa as a prisoner. The nineteenth-century German scholar, A. Buse, suggested that Gregory had written Vandals instead of Goths and Africa instead of S. Italy, but this facile solution, which disregards much of the available evidence, was rightly rejected by P. Fabre (1949), though he suggested that there may have been a second bishop called Paulinus.[31] Moricca (1924) postulated the existence of a third bishop, who lived until 535 and was captured during the second incursion of the Vandals into Italy in the time of Thrasamund in 507 or 508. For this there appears to be no evidence at all.[32] Lanzoni (1927) postulated the existence of two bishops of Nola of the same name: (1) Pontius Meropius Anicius Paulinus, ca. 409-422; (2) a bishop, whom he designated Paulinus Junior and whom he believes to be the subject of *CIL* 10. 1. 1&2, 1340.[33]

---

[29] Uranius, *De obitu Paulini* 4-5, PL 53: 859-866, at 861-862; *Liber in gloria confessorum* 108, pp. 367-368. See A. de Vogüé, "Grégoire le Grand, lecteur de Grégoire de Tours?" *Anboll* 94 (1976): 225-233.

[30] Victor of Tunnuna, *Chronica, sub* A.D. 455, ed. Th. Mommsen, MGH AA 11 (Berlin 1894), p. 186; Procopius of Caesarea, *De bello Vandalico* 1.5, *De bellis libri I-VIII*, ed. J. Haury, rev. by G. Wirth, 2 vols (Leipzig 1962-1963), 1: 331-332; see also Cassiodorus, *Variarum libri XII*, 1.4.14, ed. A. J. Fridh, CCSL 96 (Turnholt 1973), p. 16, for the campaign of 439-440, but this occurred principally in Sicily, *pace Dial.* 3.1, 2: 442.

[31] *Paulin, Bischof von Nola, und seine Zeit*, 2 vols (Regensburg 1856), 2: 199-212; P. Fabre, *Saint Paulin de Nole et l'amitié chrétienne*, BEFAR 167 (Paris 1949), pp. 44-47.

[32] Moricca, Gregorius I, *Dialogi*, p. xxxvii.

[33] Lanzoni, *Le diocesi*, 1: 238.

However those who support ingenious theories about a succession of bishops called Paulinus disregard the two small pieces of information which are corroborated elsewhere and which leave us in no doubt that Gregory had the famous bishop of Nola in mind. The first is supplied by Augustine who tells us that *Paulinus noster Nolensis episcopus ex opulentissimo divite voluntate pauperrimus et copiose sanctus*[34] was taken prisoner by barbarians who laid waste southern Italy, including Nola itself, and that he escaped to tell his friends of his adventures. Presumably he was held prisoner only temporarily during a raid which occured in 410, probably a year after he became a bishop, when the Goths under Alaric ravaged Campania.[35] Augustine says nothing about his having been taken to Africa to work as a gardener there, and Augustine's contemporary, the historian Orosius, does not mention the episode at all. Possibly Gregory may have formed the idea of making Paulinus a gardener, because Paulinus uses a gardening metaphor about Paradise in the final paragraph of one of his letters, and displays affection for the *hortulus* of Felix in another, in which he tells Sulpicius Severus that he will honour him by receiving him *in gremio iam communis patroni domnaedii mei Felicis*.[36] Vogüé points out that there is a resemblance between this story and one told by Venantius Fortunatus in his *Vita S. Maurilii*, of an exiled bishop of Angers, who entered the service of a great man as gardener and was loved by all. Gregory may have known either the life by Venantius Fortunatus or the story from which Venantius Fortunatus derived his theme.[37] The other incident which can be checked with external sources is the death of Paulinus. Here Gregory follows the narrative of Uranius, with which we may compare the story told by Gregory of Tours in *Liber in gloria confessorum*. Both writers tell the story of the earthquake in the cell and stress the generosity of Paulinus in ransoming captives, but Uranius is concerned only with the death of Paulinus, and Gregory of Tours says nothing about his having been a captive in Africa, let alone of his having worked as a gardener there.

This is an example of the biographical and historical technique of Gregory the Great which we shall meet again. He was not an historian and the historical aspect of what he was writing was to him the least important aspect. What he has done here is to take pieces of information

[34] *De civitate Dei*, 1.10, 1: 11-12.

[35] Procopius, *De bello Vandalico* 1.5.1, *De bellis* 1: 331.

[36] Paulinus of Nola, *Epistulae* 11.14, *Opera*, ed. W. von Hartel, 2 vols, CSEL 29, 30 (Vienna 1894), 2: 72-73; 5.15-16, 2: 34-35; see also *Carmina* 16.284-289, 1: 81.

[37] *Dialogue* 3.1, 2: 442; Venantius Fortunatus, *Vita Maurilii* 16, ed. B. Krusch, MGH AA 4(2), p. 93.

from his own reading and to graft them on to a traditional story, which faintly echoes the story of Regulus, immortalized by Horace in *Odes* 3.5. In his anxiety to emphasize the sanctity of Paulinus, he attaches to him a story of noble deeds, such as a holy man like Paulinus might have performed, had he found himself a long-term prisoner in Africa. Much energy seems to have been wasted by scholars in discussing the lack of accuracy and the discrepancies in Gregory's narrative here. His object was to paint a picture of heroic sanctity, not to provide a biography of Paulinus. The identity of the invaders is therefore of little significance to him.

Again, in the second story (3.31, 2: 384-391), his intention is not to furnish an historical account of the death of Herminigild, but to glorify the latter's conversion from Arianism to Catholicism by Leander of Seville, the friend of his Constantinople days, whom he reports to be the source of his information. In point of fact there is less discrepancy between Gregory's account and the more strictly historical narrative of Gregory of Tours than might be expected. The latter's emphasis, however, is slightly different, because he was interested in the wife of Herminigild, the Austrasian princess Ingund, to whom he attributes Herminigild's conversion. The Arianism of the Spaniards is only of secondary interest to him.[38] It is possible that Gregory inserted the story for the benefit of Theodelinda, queen of the Lombards, to whom he sent a copy of the *Dialogues*,[39] because, though she herself was a Catholic, her second husband, Agilulf, was an Arian.

In the third story (3.22, 2: 390-393), Gregory tells how, in the time of Justinian, the Arian Vandals persecuted the Catholics in North Africa. They cut out the tongues of certain Catholic bishops, who nevertheless continued to be able to speak. In support of the story Gregory informs us that an older bishop, whom he had encountered in Constantinople, had actually seen these men when they were in exile there, and that one of them, who had misconducted himself, was deprived of his miraculous powers. It is easy to find objections to Gregory's narrative, if we view it

---

[38] *Libri historiarum* 5.38, pp. 243-245; 8.28, pp. 390-391. For a detailed discussion of these events, see E. A. Thompson, *The Goths in Spain* (Oxford 1969), pp. 64-73; J. N. Hillgarth, "Coins and Chronicles: Propaganda in Sixth-Century Spain and the Byzantine Background," *Historia* 15 (Wiesbaden 1966), pp. 483-508. For a discussion of Herminigild's martyrdom, see J. N. Garvin, ed., in Paul of Merida, *Vitas sanctorum patrum Emeretensium* (Washington 1946), pp. 485-491.

[39] Paul the Deacon, *Historia Langobardorum* 4.5, p. 117; see also Gregory the Great, *Reg.* 4.2, 1: 233-234; 4, 1: 236; 33, 1: 268-269; 37, 1: 272-273; 9.67, 2: 87-88; 14.12, 2: 431-432, where Gregory exhorts Theodelinda, who is reported to be wavering, not to stray from the Catholic faith.

as an historical source. The principal difficulty is that there was no persecution by Arians in Africa in Justinian's reign (527-565); in fact Procopius (d. ca. 562) states that after the defeat of Gelimer in 533, there was a general reconciliation.[40] He and three of his contemporaries, Victor of Vita (late fifth century), Victor of Tunnuna (fl. 555-565), and Marcellinus Comes (mid-sixth century), however, mention a fifth-century persecution in Africa, but do not agree as to its date. Victor of Vita and Marcellinus assign it to 484, Victor of Tunnuna to 479. All these writers differ from Gregory in making the persecution general, not of bishops alone. Procopius, Victor of Vita, and Marcellinus mention tongueless survivors in Constantinople; in fact Procopius and Marcellinus profess to have seen one of them. Procopius alone mentions that two of the victims lost the power of speaking without tongues as a punishment for sexual sin.[41] In a narrative slightly anterior to Gregory, the *Theophrastus* of Aeneas of Gaza, Libya is mentioned as the scene of the persecutions (Victor of Vita sets it in Mauretania), but no date is given. Aeneas reports that he could not have believed the miracle possible, had he not seen the victims (τοὺς ἱερέας) himself. Since Aeneas lived in the first part of the sixth century, this would bring the incident nearer to Justinian's reign, to which Gregory assigns it.[42] Here we are confronted with a difficulty, which occurs frequently in considering Gregory's possible sources. Was he able to read a Greek text, in spite of his protestations that he knew no Greek, or was this a story current in the Mediterranean area in his day? The latter seems to be the more likely answer since: the story appears with the same basic theme, but varying in detail, in the works of both Eastern and Western writers; and the martyr deprived of his tongue was a favourite subject at least from Prudentius (348-ca. 410) onwards.[43]

Why should Gregory have transferred the story to the reign of Justinian and how could his episcopal informant have seen these unfortunate men? There seem to be two solutions. The first is that some older bishop

[40] Procopius, *De bello Vandalico* 1.8, *De bellis* 1: 349-350.

[41] Victor of Vita, *Historia persecutionis Wandalica: libri III: Passio beatissimorum martyrum* 3.131, ed. C. Halm, MGH AA 3 (Berlin 1879), pp. 1-62, at pp. 47-48; Victor of Tunnuna, *sub* A.D. 479, pp. 92-93; Marcellinus Comes, *Chronica minora, sub* 484, ed. Th. Mommsen, MGH AA 11 (Berlin 1894), pp. 39-108, at p. 92. The evidence of Sigebert of Gembloux (11th century) relating to the exile of the bishops, is of little value, since he is almost certainly following Gregory the Great; see *Chronica*, ed. D. L. C. Bethmann, MGH *Script.* 6 (Hanover 1844, anastatic repr., Leipzig 1925), pp. 268-374, at p. 312; see also *De bello Vandalico* 1.8, *De bellis* 1: 345-346.

[42] Aeneas of Gaza, *Theophrastus*, PG 85: 1000-1001.

[43] E.g., Prudentius, *Peristefanon* 10, 959-960, *Carmina*, ed. M. P. Cunningham, CCSL 126 (Turnholt 1966), p. 363.

perhaps saw some tongueless men in Constantinople at an earlier era and
mentioned this to Gregory, with the comment that they resembled the
African martyrs; Gregory, with the passing of time, failed to report the
correct details. What seems more likely is that Gregory is drawing upon
his recollection of a work written in the reign of Justinian, which he read
during his time in Constantinople, and is assigning to that period events
of an earlier age which are described in it. It seems as though he is
combining his recollections of Victor of Vita, an *episcopus senior*, who
mentions a survivor, and Marcellinus Comes, who professes to have seen
some of the tongueless martyrs himself. Gregory was not writing history,
but following the conventions of hagiographical writing in his own day.
In reporting what he had read about what a holy man had said of other
holy men, he would not think it wrong to imply that he had heard it
himself. Since he was not writing history, it would not occur to him to
check his authorities, to see which chronicler reported that he had seen
the martyrs. What is important to Gregory here is not when, where, and
how the event happened, but what spiritual lesson is to be drawn from it.
What impresses him is the reward of retaining speech bestowed upon the
living martyrs and the punishment of deprivation of speech inflicted upon
the individuals among them, who fell from grace.

As Bolton points out,[44] for Gregory the historical form and chronology
of an event are its least important aspects; he looks at events *sub specie
aeternitatis*. His purpose is to lead his reader on from what is familiar to
understand the kind of fear of the unfamiliar which he ought to have
(4.32, 3: 106-109). He is suggesting that the lives of holy men are to be
interpreted as the Scriptures are, that is, *spiritualiter*.

Lastly, there is the story of Totila's visit to Monte Cassino and
Benedict's prophecies to him (2.15, 2: 182-185). P. A. Cusack has recently
shown that this story has literary connections elsewhere.[45] Its immediate
source appears to be the confrontation of Martin with the emperor
Maximus, as described by Sulpicius Severus, but this too has literary
antecedents. John of Lycopolis, an older contemporary of Martin, made a
prophecy to the emperor Theodosius, which is very similar to Martin's. It
is recorded in detail in the *Heraclidis paradisus* and in Rufinus's Latin
version of the *Historia monachorum*, and there are general references to it
in Cassian's *De institutis coenobiorum* and in the *De cura pro mortuis*

---

[44] W. F. Bolton, "The Supra-Historical Sense in the *Dialogues* of Gregory the Great,"
Aevum 33 (1959): 206-213, at p. 211.

[45] P. A. Cusack, "Some Literary Antecedents of the Totila Encounter in the Second
Dialogue of Pope Gregory I," *Studia patristica* 12 (Berlin 1975), pp. 87-90.

gerenda of Augustine, who discusses it more fully in *De civitate Dei* 5.[46] Gregory seems to have been acquainted with all these works.[47] It is therefore quite possible that the description of the visit of Totila to Benedict at Monte Cassino is without historical basis. It is not recorded elsewhere; moreover, it is in keeping with the practice of Late Antiquity to provide a set-piece for the display of those qualities, such as the gift of prophecy, which are regarded as the prerogative of the holy man.[48]

In general, we need to be careful not to judge Gregory by the standards of our own day, but to see him in the context of his period. In Chapter four we shall see that Jerome, who was a man of wider and deeper cultivation than Gregory, could yet write his three religious romances, and that Augustine, who at first tended to have a rationalistic approach to miracles, towards the end of his life could sympathetically describe in *De civitate Dei* 22.8 a series of healing and exorcisms, which anticipate those in the writings of Gregory of Tours. These are but two instances of a cultural change which came over educated Christians in Western Europe from the end of the fourth century onwards. Such an attitude became even more common in the fifth and sixth centuries. To expect Gregory to remain immune from it is comparable to expecting a scholar of our own day to be totally uninfluenced by contemporary ideas and inventions. Gregory and his *Weltanschauung* have to be accepted as they are.

C. Gregory's Use of the Dialogue Form

Before considering the reasons for Gregory's adoption of the dialogue for his account of the lives of the holy men of Italy, we need to examine the nature of the audience to which they were addressed. Since the general question of Gregory's audience has been dealt with recently by McClure,[49] only two points need emphasis here.

First, the *Dialogues* do not represent a lower level of culture than the other writings of Gregory. The idea that they are simple tales composed for the benefit of a popular audience, as opposed to an audience of learned

---

[46] *Vita S. Martini* 20, 1: 294-299; *Heraclidis paradisus* 22, PL 74: 301; *Historia monachorum* 1, PL 21: 391; Cassian, *De institutis coenobiorum* 4.23, *Institutions cénobitiques*, rev. text, ed. J.-C. Guy, SC 109 (Paris 1965), pp. 152-153; Augustine, *De cura pro mortuis gerenda* 17.21, ed. J. Zycha, CSEL 26 (Vienna 1891), pp. 655-656; *De civitate Dei* 5.36, 1: 161-163.

[47] See chapters four to six.

[48] E.g., Plutarch, *Solon* 27, *Vitae parallelae*, rev. ed. by C. Lindskog and K. Ziegler, vols 1-3 (Leipzig 1964), 1(1): 115-116.

[49] McClure, "Gregory the Great: Exegesis and Audience."

monks and clergy, is unacceptable. We are told by Gregory himself in
his letter to his friend Maximianus, bishop of Syracuse, that he had a
monastic and clerical audience in mind:

> fratres mei, qui mecum familiariter vivunt, omnimodo me compellunt
> aliqua de miraculis Patrum quae in Italia facta audivimus sub brevitate
> scribere (*Reg.* 3.50, 1: 206).

This passage suggests that Gregory was writing primarily for his own
familia or episcopal household rather than for the monks of St Andrew's
as such. According to the records of the Synod of Rome (595) he banished
all lay staff from his household and filled their places with monks and
clerics (*Reg.* 5.57, 1: 362-367; 11.15, 2: 275-276). His Roman associates
included Peter, his interlocutor in the *Dialogues*, John the *Defensor*, and
the *notarii*, Aemilianus and Paterius. Among the monks, he associated
closely with Maximianus, abbot of St Andrew's and afterwards bishop of
Syracuse; Augustine and Mellitus, who were subsequently sent as
missionaries to Britain; Marinianus, later archbishop of Ravenna; Probus;
and Claudius, to whose note-taking we owe our texts of Gregory's
commentaries on the Song of Songs and 1 Kings (= 1 Samuel).

We may picture the audience as being similar to that of the *Homiliae in
Ezechielem*. In Constantinople Gregory had addressed the *Moralia* to the
monks of his household. We may conjecture that when he became Pope,
the group was increased by the addition of the secular clerics who filled
the vacancies in his household caused by the departure of the laymen, and
the monks of St Andrew's, since the first book was dedicated to
Marinianus of St Andrew's and the second to his own brethren
(presumably the monks of his household as well as the secular clerics),
who had begged him to commit his discourses to writing. It seems as
though Gregory, once he became Pope, enlarged the kind of audience to
which he had become accustomed to address the *Moralia* in Constantinople. The use of the term *coram populo* (*Homiliae in Ezechielem* 1.1. *praef.*
3) surely implies that the discourses were given to an audience wider than
the household group.

Second, there is no evidence that the monks and secular clerics were
more highly educated than the secular congregations in Roman churches.
All of them would be influenced by the same cultural climate, which, as
we have already noted, had been changing since the end of the fourth
century. An indication of the cultural homogeneity of monastic, clerical,
and lay congregations is provided by the *exempla* used by Gregory in
the *Homiliae in evangelia* and the *Dialogues*: for instance, the choice of
Servulus, Redempta and Romula, Gregory's aunt Tarsilla, Probus, Theo-

phanius, and the prisoner, *pro quo sua coniux diebus certis sacrificum offerre consueverat* (4.59, 3: 196-197), suggests that these two works were intended for an audience with a similar background. Whether the *Homiliae in evangelia* were in fact delivered in the Roman churches to which they are assigned in Migne's *Patrology* is a disputed question, but internal evidence makes it clear that they were intended for a general congregation.

The two main reasons for Gregory's use of the dialogue form are practical and historical.

In terms of the practical, it allows the stories to be of varying length. Some are extremely brief, such as that of the nuns who gave the handkerchiefs to Benedict's monks (2.19, 2: 194-197), or of the man who had collected a large sum of money to support himself through the long life which he had been promised in a dream, and then suddenly died (4.51, 3: 176-177); on the other hand we find some lengthy narratives, such as the story of Romula and Redempta (4.16, 3: 62-69), or sequences of stories about individuals, for example, Isaac the Syrian (3.14, 2: 302-315), or Martin the hermit (3.16, 2: 326-337). If such material is presented as a straightforward narrative, the effect is disjointed and sometimes confusing, but if it is broken up by means of questions by an interlocutor, it at once becomes more lively and interesting. One has only to compare the *Dialogues* with the *Historia religiosa* of Theodoret to see what is meant.

In the historical realm, the dialogue was a familiar and popular literary form both in classical times and in late Antiquity. When a distinctive Christian literature began to develop, the dialogue form was found to be admirably suited to apologetics, because characters could be introduced to express the opposing points of view.[50] Some of the Christian writers adopted the Senecan form of dialogue, where there is no direct dramatic exchange, and the discussion is carried on like a conversation in a novel, with the interpolation of *inquit*. The earliest Christian dialogue in Latin, the *Octavius* of Minucius Felix (second or third century) is in the narrative style first employed by Plato and imitated by Cicero, who had translated much of Plato, as well as writing dialogues of his own. Here we generally find some attempt to provide a descriptive background, and to delineate individual characters, as in the opening speeches of Plato's *Republic*.

---

[50] For a discussion of the pre-Gregorian Christian dialogue, see B. R. Voss, *Der Dialog in der frühchristlichen Literatur* (Munich 1970).

Augustine in the Cassiciacum dialogues (386-387) [51] followed the Ciceronian model.

Gregory may well have been acquainted with Augustine's dialogues, but it seems more likely that he was influenced, on the one hand by the *Collationes* of Cassian, and on the other by the *Dialogues* of Sulpicius Severus. The latter were, in fact, a new development, since they are a blend of the narrative or Ciceronian form of dialogue with the Senecan form. They provide a physical setting, combined with an interlocutor of "feed", a device, by means of which tales of wonder can be brought before a general audience. Similarly Gregory sets his scene, a secret place (*not* named as a garden, as Homes Dudden and Moricca assume),[52] to which he withdraws with the faithful Peter, who urges him on to tell more and more tales of wonder, just as the audience persuaded Sulpicius Severus to do. The difference between the two sets of *Dialogues* is that Sulpicius Severus casts the interlocutor in the role of narrator.

Apart from the insistence of his brethren, Gregory may have had a didactic motive in writing the *Dialogues*. He may have believed that by means of stories of native heroes of the faith, he could provide suitable spiritual fare for his monks and restore the flagging spirits of Italian Christians in general, cast down as they may well have been by the Lombard invasions and the severe floods and outbreaks of plague during the 580s. Gregory's motives in writing the *Dialogues* will be discussed further in chapter three.

---

[51] *Soliloquia*, PL 32: 869-1904; *Contra academicos*; *De beata vita*; *De ordine*, ed. W. M. Green, CCSL 29 (Turnholt 1970).

[52] Homes Dudden, *Gregory the Great* 1: 324; Moricca, Gregorius I, *Dialogi*, p. lv.

2

The Typological Interpretation
of the *Dialogues*

A. Gregory's Biblical Formation

We have already seen that the basic raw material of the miracle-stories in the *Dialogues* was transmitted to Gregory orally by informants living in areas of Italy and elsewhere in the Western Mediterranean sphere of influence, which were still under imperial control, or in exile in Rome from areas under Lombard control. Gregory appears to have employed three principal methods of handling this material: (1) interpreting it in the light of biblical typology; (2) narrating stories linked with the martyrs and other holy men of Rome and Central Italy; (3) narrating stories found in the works of other writers both of East and West, which may well form part of the general Mediterranean cultural heritage.

No reader of Gregory's works can fail to be struck by his immense and detailed knowledge of the subject matter of the Bible and by the way in which it permeates his thought and writing.[1] He does not tell us directly how it was acquired, but we can form some idea of this from what we know of early medieval monastic practice. In the pre-printing era, when books were scarce, there were good reasons for cherishing what books there were and for becoming familiar with their contents, but the prime source of biblical knowledge among monastic readers was the *lectio divina*, which formed a regular part of their daily duties. Whether or not the monastery of St Andrew on the Caelian Hill followed the *Regula S. Benedicti* we may assume from a passage in one of Gregory's letters (*Reg.* 3.3, 1: 161) that the monks were expected to pass a certain portion

---

[1] R. Manselli, "Gregorio Magno e la Bibbia," *La Bibbia nell'alto medioevo, SSAM* 10 (1962, Spoleto 1963): 67-91.

of their day in reading.[2] In Late Antiquity and the early Middle Ages this entailed more physical activity than is usual today. The *lectio divina* was not only an optical movement, but also involved the lips, as they moved in pronouncing the words, and the ears, as they listened to them. It was not for nothing that the words were sometimes known as *voces paginarum*. This slow, careful reading caused the monk to think about the meaning of the Bible and helped him to remember accurately what he had read. It was indeed an activity, known as *legere et meditari*.[3] Gregory's vast knowledge of the Bible is surely the outcome of carrying out this practice daily over a period of many years.[4]

An examination of Gregory's methods of typological interpretation reveals something of his attitude to the miracle-stories in the *Dialogues*. In the early Church there was a corpus of types taken from the Old Testament and used to illuminate the gospel: typology may be defined as the interpretation of an event belonging to the present or the recent past as the fulfilment of a similar situation recorded or prophesied in Scripture.[5] Earlier patristic writers would have defined typology as the fulfilment of Old Testament types in Christ. A good example of such a definition is supplied by Hilary of Poitiers:

> Omne autem opus, quod sacris voluminibus continetur, adventum Domini nostri Iesu Christi, quo missus a patre ex virgine per Spiritum homo natus est, et dictis nuntiat et factis exprimit et confirmat exemplis. Namque hic per omne constituti huius saeculi tempus veris atque absolutis praefigurationibus in patriarchis ecclesiam aut generat aut abluit aut sanctificat aut eligit aut discernit aut redimit: somno Adae, Noe diluvio, benedictione Melchisedech, Abrahae iustificatione, ortu Ysahae, Iacob servitute.[6]

Gregory, however, would appear to have been influenced by the Alexandrian school of biblical exegesis, the members of which favoured a less historical and more allegorical style of interpretation, using the Scriptures as a "jumping-off point" for contemplation. It was thus a natural development for him, as indeed it was for earlier writers also, to look to the Scriptures to try to discover the origins of later ecclesiastical institutions and to see the holy men of post-biblical times not so much as

---

[2] For Gregory's encouragement of reading among the secular clergy, see *Reg*. 2.50, 1: 152; 52, 1: 155-156; 4.26, 1: 261.

[3] See introd., n. 12; Leclercq, "L'amour des lettres," pp. 19-20; B. Smalley, *The Study of the Bible in the Middle Ages* (Oxford 1941), pp. 13-23.

[4] For Gregory's view of the Bible, see *Homiliae in Hiezechielem* 1.10.3, ed. M. Adriaen, CCSL 142 (Turnholt 1971), p. 145.

[5] See R. P. C. Hanson, *Allegory and Event* (London 1959).

[6] *Tractatus mysteriorum* 1.1. Ed. by A. Feder, CSEL 65 (4), Vienna 1916, pp. 3-4.

directly fulfilled in Christ, as linked with figures in the Old Testament, who were themselves fulfilled in Christ. Origen saw monasticism as foreshadowed by the early Christian community in Jerusalem (Acts 2.42-47); Pachomius too found scriptural precedents for the monastic life. From this it was but a short step to the interpretation of the great ascetics of the Bible, Elijah, Elisha, and John the Baptist, as precursors and patrons of the founders of monasticism. The principal example of this form of interpretation is the *Vita Antonii* of Athanasius, in which an extraordinary similarity between the careers of Elijah and Antony may be observed.[7]

It is not surprising that Gregory, with his devotion to the monastic life, should have a predilection for the miracle-stories of the Elijah-Elisha cycle. It seems that he accepted the analogy of Elijah with Antony, the father of all the monks, and saw Benedict, the father of Western monasticism, as Elisha, the inheritor of Elijah's mantle. He may also have seen Benedict as a figure of eschatological significance. Daniélou has pointed out that the earliest typology of Noah is eschatological in character. Noah, the survivor of a physical world catastrophe, is a warning to the Christian of the cosmic catastrophe of the Day of Judgement.[8] Could it not be that Gregory saw Benedict as a Noah-figure, the type of the righteous man who survives? Benedict, like Noah, escapes from the wicked world, in his case represented by contemporary Roman society, to an "ark," that is, a monastery, Monte Cassino, perched on a mountain-top, and is accompanied by a "family" of righteous men who help him to preserve civilization. It is significant that he applies to Benedict the same title, *vir dei*, as is borne in the Scriptures by Moses, David, Elijah, and Elisha. B. Steidle points out that this is not an everyday name, but a special title for a miracle-worker.[9] Athanasius calls Antony ὁ τοῦ Θεοῦ ἄνθρωπος, which both Evagrius and the older translator render as

---

[7] For Elijah as the model of the first ascetics, see, e.g., Tertullian, *De monogamia* 8.10, ed. V. Bulhart, CSEL 76 (Vienna 1957), p. 60; Methodias of Olympos, *Symposium* 10.3, Συμπόσιον ἢ περὶ ἁγνείας, *Le banquet*, ed. H. A. Musurillo, SC 95 (Paris 1963), p. 292; Clement of Rome, *Epistola ad Corinthos*, *Épitre aux Corinthiens* 17.1, ed. A. Jaubert, SC 167 (Paris 1971), p. 128; Jerome, *Ep.* 58.5, *Epistulae*, ed. I. Hilberg, 3 vols, CSEL 54-56 (Vienna 1910-1918), 1: 533-534; Cassian, *De institutis coenobiorum* 1.1, pp. 36-37; *Collationes* 18.6, 3: 16-18; Palladius, *Heraclidis paradisus*, prooem., PL 74: 247; Basil, *Regulae fusius tractatae* 23, PG 31: 981; [Pachomius], *Vita S. Pachomii* [Greek 2] 4, ed. F. Halkin, SHG 19 (Brussels 1932), p. 87; [Latin] ed. H. van Cranenburgh, SHG 46 (Brussels 1949), p. 86; Athanasius, *Vita Antonii* 7, pp. 24-25.

[8] J. Daniélou, *Sacramentum futuri: études sur les origines de la typologie biblique* (Paris 1950), pp. 69-85.

[9] B. Steidle, "Homo Dei Antonius: zum Bild des 'Mann Gottes' im alten Mönchtum," *StAns* 38 (1956): 148-200, at pp. 149-152, 159-168.

homo Dei. Steidle, however, fails to observe that the expression "man of God" used in 1 and 2 Kings (3 and 4 Kings in the Vulgate) as an epithet for prophets, is sometimes rendered as *homo Dei* in the Vulgate and at others as *vir Dei*, apparently interchangeably. The latter is used no fewer than fifteen times of Elisha, whereas *homo Dei* is used only four times.[10] It is therefore only natural that Gregory, familiar as he was with the Bible, should use the epithet *vir Dei* of Benedict, whom he clearly regarded as the counterpart of Elisha.

There is a further, less obvious reason for Gregory's predilection for the Elijah-Elisha cycle. It may surely be regarded as a manifestation of his preference for a monastic life rather than a life of administration and action.[11] It is noticeable that all the miracles in the *Dialogues* which have affinities with this cycle are, with one possible exception,[12] performed by monks, whom Gregory saw as "sons of the prophets," reflecting something of the glory of Elisha and partaking of some of his powers.

Two articles by Benedictine authors, written in the post-war era, afford examples of the inadequacy of an interpretation of *Dialogue* 2 that looks for exact literary correspondences between texts and assumed sources.[13] We shall have occasion to refer frequently to these articles in what follows. The writer of the more recent article, M. Mähler, sees that it was Gregory's intention to create a portrait of Benedict as a charismatic figure, sharing in the spirit of biblical personages such as Moses, David, Elijah, Elisha, and the apostle Peter (2.8, 2: 164-167); he also notes the literary affinities with Athanasius and Sulpicius Severus, but in both cases he is troubled by certain discrepancies between Gregory and what he considers to be his model. His approach to typology is at the same time both too elaborate and too superficial. He offers no opinion as to Gregory's own attitude to his material, but he has grasped that the stories represent some

[10] *Homo Dei* is used three times of Elijah (2 [4] Kings 1.9, 11, 13) and four times of Elisha (2 [4] Kings 4.7, 22; 7.2, 8.2). *Vir Dei* is used twice of Elijah (1 [3] Kings 17.18, 24) and fifteen times of Elisha (2 [4] Kings 4.16, 25, 40, 42; 5.8, 14, 20; 6.10, 15; 7.17, 18, 19; 8.7, 8; 13.19). It is unlikely to be a coincidence that all those described as ὁ τοῦ Θεοῦ ἄνθρωπος, *homo Dei*, are reported to have brought a corpse to life.

[11] Expressed in e.g., *Dialogue* 1, praef., 2: 12; *Homiliae in Ezechielem* 1.3.9, p. 37; 11.5-6, p. 171.

[12] Severus, who raised a corpse (1.12, 2: 112-115) was a secular priest, but since this miracle-story is more akin to the returns from the dead described in *Dialogue* 4, it could be argued that it is not linked with the Elijah-Elisha cycle. It is significant that Severus is never called *Homo Dei* or *Vir Dei*, the epithets applied to other holy men who have raised corpses.

[13] M. Mähler, "Évocations bibliques et hagiographiques dans la vie de saint Benoît par saint Grégoire," *RBén* 83 (1973): 145-184; O. Rousseau, "Saint Benoît et le prophète Élisée," *RMAL* 144 (1956): 103-114.

kind of popular tradition, which Gregory's narrative attaches to the
historic traditions of Subiaco and its neighbourhood. He does not,
however, appear to have seen the article of our other Benedictine writer,
O. Rousseau, which appeared in 1956, and Rousseau, in turn, wrote too
early to have seen Steidle, since their articles appeared in the same year.

Rousseau is convinced that Gregory has selected 2(4) Kings 4-8 as the
framework of his life of Benedict; he lists the miracles of Elisha and
remarks that three of them have their replicas in Benedict's narrative. He
notes that in these three cases, the miraculous powers of Benedict surpass
those of Elisha, because whereas the latter had received a double portion
(*duplex spiritus*) of the spirit of Elijah (2[4] Kings 2.9), Benedict was filled
with *spiritu iustorum omnium* (2.8, 2: 166-167). Rousseau tries to show
the analogies between these three important miracles as performed by
Elisha and Benedict and to trace similar connections in the case of other
miracles, where the resemblance is less obvious.

Rousseau writes *in vacuo*, whereas Mähler pays some attention to the
literary background of *Dialogue* 2. Neither writer gives any indication
that he is aware of the work of scholars such as Auerbach and Lubac,[14]
which, elucidating the complicated theme of late antique and early
medieval typology, would have enabled him to set the figure of Benedict
in its context and have afforded clues as to the interpretation of the
Dialogues.

B. The Use of Typological Interpretation in the *Dialogues*

An examination of what Gregory himself has to say about typology and
of the details of those miracle-stories which appear to have biblical
affinities, will help to remove some of the difficulties raised by Rousseau
and Mähler and also by scholars of an earlier generation, and will afford
insight into Gregory's own cultural background and mental processes.

Let us first consider some examples of Gregory's use of typological
interpretation where a direct reference is made to stories in the Bible. Not
surprisingly he does not treat the Bible historically, but searches for
parallels of character and situation.

In his prefatory letter to the *Moralia*, addressed to his friend Leander,
bishop of Seville, Gregory states that he will expound the book of Job,

> per allegoriam sensus ... et per allegoriam quaedam typica investigatione
> perscrutamur (1.2).[15]

[14] For details, see Bibliography.
[15] For a useful comparison of the terms *figura*, *allegoria*, and τύπος, see E. Auerbach,
"Figura," *Archivum romanicum* 22 (1938): 436-489.

The *Moralia* abound in examples of the kind of typology which Gregory had learned from his study of the works of Augustine. One of the most striking is that of Job himself as the type of the Redeemer, his wife as the representative of the carnal life, and his friends as the expression of the *figura* of the heretics (*Moralia* praef. 6.14-16, 1: 19-21).

The same form of typological interpretation is found in the *Dialogues*. The earliest example is Gregory's reply to a question from Peter as to whether the miracle-worker Honoratus has been the disciple of a famous teacher, in which he cites Honoratus along with Moses and John the Baptist as types of the holy man who does not require a teacher because he has been taught by the Holy Spirit (1.1, 2: 22-23; Exod. 23.20). The resuscitation of a dead child by Libertinus on his way to Ravenna by means of the *caligula* of Honoratus affords Gregory the opportunity of comparing Libertinus to Elisha when he struck the Jordan with his mantle and of quoting him as a type of humility (1.2, 2: 30-31). In 1.4 (2: 54-55), where Gregory tells the story of the mistake made by Julian the *Defensor* in identifying Equitius and forming an opinion of his character, he instances David, when he passed a false judgement against the son of Jonathan, as a type of human fallibility (2 Sam. [2 Kings] 16.1-end). The conception of Elisha as the type of the holy monk Nonnosus is brought to Peter's attention (1.7, 2: 68-69), because he increased the supply of oil at his monastery through putting a flask containing a small drop upon the altar. In a discussion on predestination (1.8, 2: 74-75), Gregory expounds the story of Isaac and Rebecca, citing Isaac as the type of the man who prays effectively. A striking example of Gregory's typological mode of thought is to be found in his description of the quality of compunction (3.34, 2: 400-403). The two kinds of compunction are first compared to the rivers of water flowing from the eye of the penitent sinner (Lam. 3.48). Then he turns to the story of Achsah (Jos. 15.13-19), which he interprets in a typically Alexandrian manner; for intance, Achsah herself, riding upon an ass, exemplifies the soul which has gained the mastery over sensual desires; the dry ground, which Caleb has already granted her, represents the soul which has good desires but has not yet felt the need for tears; the land which was wet above and below, signifies the soul weeping from desire for heaven and dread of hell (3.84, 2: 402-403). Gregory reverts to the type of compunction in 4.61 (3: 202-205), where he presents Hannah, the mother of Samuel, as the type of the faithful Christian communicant.

Dialogue 2 is particularly rich in this kind of interpretation. In 2.2 (2: 138-139) there is a piece of Gregorian exegesis which recalls the *Moralia* and causes Peter to ask for a more detailed explanation. Gregory says that the *vasa*, the sacred vessels cared for by the Levites when, at the age of fifty, they have completed their twenty-five years of service in the Temple, typify the minds of those of the faithful who have gained self-mastery (Num. 7.44). There are four stories in *Dialogue* 2, which are strong in biblical overtones and which are regarded by Gregory as material for typological interpretation: 1. the sweating rock (2.5, 2: 152-155; 8, 2: 164-167; 3.16, 2: 328-329; cf. Num 20.2-13; Exod. 17.1-6); 2. the lost axe-head (2.6, 2: 154-157; cf. 2 [4] Kings 6.5-7); 3. Maurus walking on the water to rescue Placid (2.7, 2: 156-159; cf. Matt. 14.16-31); 4. the power of Benedict to discern spirits (2.13, 2: 176-179; cf. 2 [4] Kings 5.26). Gregory causes Peter to recognize the typological implications of all these stories and also of two others: Elijah is discerned in the obedience of the raven (2.8, 2: 162-163; cf. 1 [3] Kings 17.6); and David weeping for Saul (2 Sam. [2 Kings] 1.11) and for Absalom (2 Sam. [2 Kings] 18.33) is seen as foreshadowing Benedict mourning the death of his enemy, the wicked priest Florentius (2.8, 2: 164-165). In 3.18 (2: 344-347) Gregory causes Peter to make some further attempts at typological exegesis: he compares Gregory's story of the unsuccessful attempt of the Goths in Totila's reign to bake Benedict of Campania (not the saint) in an oven, with that of the Three Holy Children (Dan. 3). Gregory, however, points out that the details of the story are not the same, for Benedict was completely unharmed by the flames, whereas the bonds of the Three Holy Children were burned, though their clothing was undamaged.

The majority of Gregory's examples of the use of direct typology are taken from the Old Testament. Mention has already been made of the story of Maurus walking on the water, which Peter the Deacon compares with the story of the apostle Peter walking on the Sea of Galilee to meet Jesus (Matt. 14.29), but, as we shall see later, there may be a type for this story other than that found in the Gospel. There are, however, three stories in the *Dialogues* for which there is a direct New Testament type. In the first of them (3.17, 2: 336-345), Gregory attempts to link the story of the resuscitation of a corpse by the solitary of Monte Argentaro and the subdeacon Quadragesimus to that of Lazarus (John 11.1-45). Secondly, (3.21, 2: 352-355), he describes how a consecrated virgin of Spoleto drove an evil spirit from a villager into a pig, and expressly compares the incident with the story of the Gadarene swine (Matt. 8.28-9.1; Mark 5.1-20; Luke 8.26-39). The last story is that of Sanctulus of Nursia and the miraculous loaf (3.37, 2: 414-417), but Gregory is careful to explain that it is not precisely parallel to the feeding-miracle stories in the Gospels. The very fact that Gregory offers these brief explanations of the differences between his own stories and those of the Bible indicates that he is thinking typologically rather than trying to create precedents or to draw parallels. We shall also find a number of instances in which he employs typological interpretation in a more subtle manner, in cases where the biblical link is implicit rather than explicit as, for example, in the story of the raising of Marcellus from the dead in 1.10 (2: 106-111), or where there are small details which recall the Bible, such as the demon driven out by prayer and fasting (3.33, 2: 396-397; cf. Matt. 17.14-20).

There are two good reasons for the apparent discrepancies between Gregory's narratives and those of the Bible. In the first place, it was not his object to bring the Bible stories up to date by supplying them with a contemporary setting, where, however, the details corresponded exactly; his intention was rather to interpret stories transmitted to him, on the subject of contemporary or near-contemporary holy men in Italy (and elsewhere in the West) in the same spirit as stories of holy men in the Bible. Secondly, he was almost certainly relying on his recollections of the text of the Bible; in the days before printing, when human fallibility of the scribe did not ensure that every copy of a book could be completely accurate, the faculty of memory was regarded as being as reliable as the written word. The notion of verifying quotations or comparing one version of a quotation with another would be alien to him.[16] The story of Lazarus in John 11 is clearly the type of the story of the raising of Marcellus in 1.10 (2: 106-111), but here again he is relying on his memory of the gospel narrative (there are no quotations at all) to interpret the story offered to him by the *senex pauper*.

Once it is realized that Gregory's work as an exegete is not confined to his scriptural commentaries and homiletical writings, and that his typological interpretation is applied not only to biblical material but also to stories of the lives of holy men in Italy, the significance of his treatment of the miracle stories in the *Dialogues* becomes apparent, and the objections of some of his modern critics are less easily sustained.

C. Examples of Gregory's Use of Typological Interpretation

An examination of those of Gregory's miracle stories that are either capable of direct typological interpretation or possess, to a greater or lesser degree, distinct biblical overtones, will include not only the stories of

---

[16] The fact that Gregory's one attempt at a longer quotation from Kings (2 [4] Kings 4.27, *Dialogue* 2.21, 2: 200-201) consists of a mixture of the Vulgate and the V.I. (sentence structure from the V.I., but the two main verbs from the Vulgate) also suggests that he was quoting from memory.

miracles attributed to Benedict in *Dialogue* 2, but also material to be found in *Dialogues* 1 and 3. For the purpose of such an examination, it is useful to classify the relevant stories in categories which we will examine individually.

a. *Raising the Dead*

The experience of Lombard invasions and the natural disasters of the 580s may well have aroused interest in stories of resuscitation from the dead. In the absence of books, such stories, whatever their origin, may have been told so often that country people, such as the *senex pauper*, may have come to believe that the events described in them occurred locally, but too much importance should not be attached to this theory. Just as there had been in pre-Christian times a conception of the hero as a man who acted in a particular manner, so the Christian took over this conception and interpreted it in the light of Christian teaching. It had become customary by the end of the fourth century to attribute to a holy man miracles appropriate to his degree of sanctity. Consequently those who had achieved a high degree of holiness, such as Antony or Benedict, would tend to have attached to them stories of miracles comparable to those performed by the great prophetic figures of the Old Testament, by Jesus himself, and by the apostles. It is noticeable that in three out of five stories of raising the dead, told in *Dialogues* 1-3 (3.32, 2: 226-229; 3.17, 2: 336-339; 33, 2: 394-395), it is the disciples of the holy man who are responsible for informing Gregory. Such men would naturally be eager to heighten the prestige of their master by endowing him with the power to raise the dead. The biblical influence in the other two cases (1.2, 2: 24-31; 10, 2: 106-111) is so strong that we may assume that Gregory himself did much to shape the material supplied by *Laurentius, religiosus vir*, in the one case, and the *senex pauper* in the other. Indeed the words employed by Gregory in connection with the material supplied by Laurentius rather suggests this:

> multa mihi de illo dicere consuevit. Ex quibus ea quae recolo pauca narrabo.

The second *Dialogue* contains three examples of people apparently being raised from the dead. One of these (2.24, 2: 210-213), together with the story of the priest Severus (1.12, 2: 112-115), is better classified with the stories of returns from the dead (4.27, 3: 86-89; 32, 3: 106-107; 37, 3: 124-125), since all this material is similar in ethos. The issue of the story of the boy-monk apparently killed by a falling wall (2.11, 2: 172-175) is one of healing rather than resurrection, as Mähler rightly points out.[17] The third story (2.32, 2: 226-229) is the most interesting for our purposes, since it is treated by Gregory on similar lines to the stories of the widow's son at Sarepta (1 [3] Kings 17.17-24) and the Shunamite's child (2 [4] Kings 4.29-37); and it reproduces, with certain variants, the story told in 1.2 (2: 26-31), where Gregory makes an explicit comparison with Elijah and Elisha, quoting 2 (4) Kings 2.14. Two similar stories are told of Caesarius of Arles: in one of them Ravenna itself is the scene of the miracle (in *Dialogue* 1.2, 2: 28-29 it is the road to Ravenna) and the widow's son is a young adult (cf. the son of the widow of Nain, Luke 7.4-16); in the second, in which Caesarius is described as a second Elijah or Elisha (the reading is disputed), a young woman is raised from the dead through the prayers and tears of Caesarius at her bedside.[18]

The story of the resuscitation of the dead sons by Elijah and Elisha was a common type in both Greek and Latin hagiography. Other examples are the stories told by Sulpicius Severus of Martin resuscitating a dead catechumen and also a house-slave of Lupicinus, over whose bodies he stretched in prayer.[19] Gregory may well have known the *Vita S. Caesarii Arelatensis* by Cyprian and others, and the *Vita S. Martini*, but whether he did or not, it is clear that he and other writers were concentrating upon the same New Testament types.[20] It is important not to press the correspondence of details too far or to try to extract some obscure, non-biblical meaning, as Rousseau does, when he concludes that Gregory causes Benedict to surpass Elisha as a miracle worker, by reporting that he resuscitated two corpses, whereas Elijah and Elisha accomplished one each.[21]

Gregory's four narratives describing the raising of an adult corpse all share the type of the raising of Lazarus in John 11. Gregory's handling of the story of the raising of Marcellus by Fortunatus, bishop of Todi, affords a good example of his methods: there is no complete similarity of detail and there is correspondence of sentiment rather than language. The dead man, Marcellus, has two devoted sisters like Lazarus, and dies just before Easter. Gregory causes both sisters to approach Fortunatus, whereas it

---

[17] Mähler, "Évocations bibliques," p. 412.

[18] *Vita S. Caesarii arelatensis* 1.39, p. 472; 2.2, p. 484.

[19] *Vita S. Martini* 7-8, 1: 268-271.

[20] E.g., Paulinus of Milan, *Vita S. Ambrosii* 28, *Vita di Ambrogio*, ed. A. A. R. Bastiaensen, VSanti 3 (Milan 1975), pp. 127-241, at pp. 88-91; Theodoret, *Historia religiosa* 14.3, *Histoire des moines de Syrie*, ed. P. Canivet and A. Leroy-Molinghem, 2 vols, sc 234, 237 (Paris 1977-1979), 2: 12-13.

[21] O. Rousseau, "St. Benoît," p. 106.

was Martha alone who approached Jesus (11.29-32), while Mary sat at home (11.20). The sentiments of the Jews in verse 37 are repeated – and indeed amplified – by the sisters in Gregory's narrative. The story well exemplifies Gregory's inherently biblical outlook and his practice of relying upon his memory in creating a narrative based on a biblical type.

Two of his other stories of raising the dead have a single factor in common with this one: the tears of the miracle-worker himself. The weeping of Eleutherius (3.33, 2: 394-395): *illae lacrimae ex tam humili simplicique morte editae* recalls the simple grief of *et lacrimatus est Iesus* (John 11.35). The tears of Severus, on the other hand, are tears of penitence as much as tears of grief, because he arrived too late (1.12, 2: 114-115).

In these stories the typology is implicit but unexpressed. The last of the four stories, however, is regarded by Gregory himself as being linked to the story of Lazarus, though it has a certain latent affinity with that told in 2 (4) Kings 13.21, of a corpse flung into the sepulchre of Elijah which revived as soon as it touched his bones.

In 3.17, 2: 336-345 Gregory describes how the solitary of Monte Argentaro, clad as a monk, and his friend, the subdeacon Quadragesimus, resuscitated the dead husband of a poor woman by means of a combination of the application of dust from the altar of the church of St Peter (not the famous basilica) to the face of the corpse, by the solitary, and by the prayers of Quadragesimus. It is noticeable that the actual miracle-worker crept away and was seen no more by the witnesses of the miracle. This suggests, in the person of Quadragesimus, a devoted disciple who was anxious to build up the reputation of a holy man by attributing to him the power to perform the supreme act of the miracle worker, namely the raising of the dead.

Gregory's own attitude to physical miracles is epitomized in his attempt to link this story with that of the raising of Lazarus. Though it may be a *res mira*, the resuscitation of a body is of less consequence, *sub specie aeternitatis*, than the conversion of a soul. Consequently the raising of Lazarus is of less significance than the *conversio animae* of Paul (3.17, 2: 340-345).

b. *Restoring Lost Objects*

The single story in the *Dialogues* which deals with the finding of a lost object is contained in 2.6 (2: 154-157). Its type is the story of the recovery of the lost axe-head by Elisha in 2 (4) Kings 6.1-7. It is an interesting exercise to compare the two stories side-by-side, as an illustration of Gregory's typological method of interpretation; see table on p. 36. The

	2 (4) Kings 6.1-7	Dialogue 2.6, 2: 154-157
The scene	ad Iordanem	locus super ipsam laci ripam
The workers	filii prophetarum	... Gothus quidam pauper spiritu
The purpose	... ut tollant de silva materias singulas, ut aedificemus nobis ibi locum ad inhabitandum.	... ut de loco quodam vepres adscideret, quatenus illic fieri hortus deberet.
The loss	accidit autem ut cum unus materiam succedisset, caderet ferrum securis in aquam: exclamavitque ille, et ait: Heu heu heu, domine, mi, et hoc ipsum mutuo acceperam.	... ferrum de manubrio prosiliens in lacum cecidit, ubi scilicet tanta erat aquarum profunditas, ut spes requirendi ferramenti nulla iam esset. Itaque ferro perdito, tremebundus ad Maurum monachum cucurrit Gothus, damnum quod fecerat nuntiavit, et reatus sui egit paenitentiam. Quod Maurus quoque monachus mox Benedicto Dei famulo curavit indicare.
The miracle	Dixit autem homo Dei: Ubi cecidit? At ille monstravit ei locum. Praecedit ergo lignum, et misit illuc: natavitque ferrum, et ait: Tolle. Qui extendit manum, et tulit illud.	Vir igitur Domini Benedictus haec audiens accessit ad locum, tulit de manu Gothi manubrium et misit in lacum, et mox ferrum de profundo rediit atque in manubrium intravit. Qui statim ferramentum Gotho reddidit, dicens: Ecce, labora, et noli contristari.

basic story is the same, but there are numerous small differences. In the biblical narrative the sons of the prophets are accompanied by Elisha when they go down to the banks of the Jordan to cut timber for building themselves a larger house. Gregory, on the other hand, describes the Goth as already on the shores of the lake and cutting down thorn bushes to provide space for a garden. The son of the prophets who accidently drops the axe-head into the lake is chiefly distressed because the axe was borrowed, whereas the Goth is in fear and trembling on account of the prospect of punishment. He first runs to Maurus, who in turn goes to Benedict. Elisha, who is on the spot, cuts a piece of wood, which he hurls after the axe-head. Benedict, however, takes the axe-handle from the Goth and then throws it into the water. In the Elisha story, the axe-head floats to the surface, and he bids the sons of the prophets to pick it up. In Benedict's case, however, the axe-head comes up from the depths and fits itself on to the handle. Benedict retrieves it and gives it back to the Goth, telling him to go on with his work and not to distress himself further.

Our two Benedictine scholars have been unnecessarily troubled by this story.[22] Mähler does not concern himself so much with the details, but he claims to have discovered two far-fetched biblical parallels. Rousseau, with his conviction that the story should correspond as closely as possible to the narrative of 1 (4) Kings 6.1-7, is puzzled by Gregory's failure to mention that the axe was borrowed. He tries to fill this apparent lacuna by pointing out that Benedict had already performed a miracle connected with a borrowed object, namely the repair of the broken sieve of Effide (2.1, 2: 128-131).[23] However, a reference to the story of the axe-head in the *Moralia* suggests that Gregory was well aware that the axe in the biblical narrative was borrowed (*Moralia* 22.5, 2: 1098), which lends support to the view that he was not intending to reproduce the details of the biblical narrative here.

Rousseau sees that Gregory was not engaged in constructing an exact parallel to the biblical narrative, but has failed to grasp the basis of his method. He believes that Gregory is superimposing on the foundation of the Bible story *des faits plus ou moins semblables*.[24] He does not see that Gregory was interpreting typologically material which had been gathered locally with a view to dispelling the idea that no miracles had occurred in Italy.

[22] Mähler, "Évocations bibliques," p. 407; O. Rousseau, "St. Benoît," pp. 106-108.
[23] O. Rousseau, "St. Benoît," pp. 106-107.
[24] Ibid., p. 107.

The source of Gregory's information here was apparently the disciples of Benedict. Either they or Gregory or a combination of Gregory and the quartet of *discipuli*, consisting of Constantinus, Valentianus, Simplicius, and Honoratus, would be anxious to present Benedict as a miracle-worker comparable to Antony, father of Western monasticism, and possessing similar miraculous powers to the prophet Elisha. Indeed Benedict's powers exceeded those of Elisha in this instance, since he not only rescued the axe-head, but also caused the handle to fit itself into it.

c. *Increasing a Substance in Short Supply*

We have already seen that the resuscitation of a corpse was a *topos* of late antique hagiography.[25] A similar *topos* was a miracle achieving the increase of a substance in short supply, particularly oil or wine. Gregory handles this type of miracle in two distinct ways: the first may be described as a free interpretation of scripture: the biblical type is obviously 1 (3) Kings 17.16 and 2 (4) Kings 4.1-7, but Gregory's narrative in 2.28 (2: 216-219) bears a close resemblance to *Dialogue* 2 (3).3 of Sulpicius Severus, the authority for which is said to be a priest called Arpagius.[26] The setting of the stories is quite different. Sulpicius Severus tells a straightforward tale with the sole object of glorifying Martin as a miracle-worker. We are not told that oil was in short supply nor does there seem to be any reason why Martin should seek to increase quantity. The accidental fall of the flask, owing to the carelessness of the servant in leaving it by the window, and its miraculous preservation add nothing to the story other than to increase the prestige of Martin. Gregory, however, has a different motive. Like Sulpicius, he wishes to emphasize the gifts of his hero as a miracle-worker, but at the same time, he intends to stress his status as the abbot to whom monastic obedience is due. His object is akin to that of Cassian in the story of John of Lycopolis in *De institutis coenobiorum* 4, which may well have been known to him. In order to

[25] See in addition e.g., *De civitate Dei* 22.8, 2: 83; *Vita Ambrosii* 28, pp. 88-91; Cassian, *Collationes* 15.3, 2: 212; cf. *Historia monachorum in Aegypto* 9, PL 21: 423-424; 28, PL 21: 450-452; among Greek writers, Theodoret, *Historia religiosa* 21.14, 2: 90-93; Sozomen, *Historia ecclesiastica* 3.4, *Kirchengeschichte*, ed. G. C. Hansen, GCS 50 (Berlin 1960), p. 118.

[26] Sulpicius Severus, *Dialogue* 2(3).3, *Libri qui supersunt* [incl. *Dial.*], ed. C. Halm, CSEL 1 (Vienna 1866), pp. 200-201; cf. Cassian, *De institutis coenobiorum* 4.25, pp. 156-159, where John of Lycopolis is ordered to throw the only flask of oil out of the window; *Vita Caesarii arelatensis* 1.51, p. 477, where the flask breaks, but the oil does not spread; Eugippius, *Vita Severini* 28, *Das Leben des heiligen Severin*, ed. R. Noll (Berlin 1963), pp. 92-95.

achieve this object, he reverses the order of the story. Thus Benedict appears as the stern disciplinarian, who orders the flask containing the remaining drops of oil to be flung on to a rocky precipice (not a court-yard, as in *Dialogue* 2 (3).3 of Sulpicius Severus) rather than have the monastery defiled by a symbol of the disobedience of one of its inmates. We are also shown, in his desire to give Agapitus the sole remaining drops of oil, the practical application of the *Regula S. Benedicti* to treat a visitor as Christ himself. Then, as the result of this heroic gesture, Benedict is rewarded by the preservation of the flask, and after the monastery has been cleansed, as it were, by his *increpatio* of the *inobedientia* and *superbia* of the monk, his prayers bring about the increase of oil.

This story affords both an example of Gregory's literary skill in adapting material to illustrate a point and a commentary on his own conception of sanctity as contrasted with that of Sulpicius Severus. Both writers are evidently at work on the same traditional story, which seems to have been current in both East and West, and both see the ability to work miracles as a mark of the holy man, but whereas Sulpicius is interested principally in the outward event, Gregory is concerned with the inward spiritual excellence, of which the miracle is an outward manifestation. He accepts the idea that a man may be holy without being a miracle-worker:

> Vitae namque vera aestimatio in virtute est operum, non in ostensione signorum. Nam sunt plerique, qui etsi signa non faciunt, signa tamen facientibus dispares non sunt (1.12, 2: 116-117).

This can be taken as a form of the contrast between *intus* and *foris*, which is so well brought out by Dagens.[27]

Another example of a more free interpretation of a biblical type (2 [4] Kings 4.1-7; John 2.1-10) is the story of Sanctulus of Nursia (3.37, 2: 112-115), who brought about an increase of oil through flinging water on the olive press.

Gregory's stories of other Italian holy men who miraculously achieve an increase of a substance in short supply are treated from a more strictly biblical point of view. Nonnosus, whom Gregory asks Peter to compare to Elisha (1.7, 2: 68-69) achieves an increase of oil through pouring small drops into numerous vessels (cf. 2 [4] Kings 4. 1-7). Boniface (1.9, 2: 76-81) effected an increase of wine by similar methods and also performed a miracle on similar lines to that of Elijah in 1 (3) Kings 17.16, by giving a

[27] Dagens, "Structure et expérience," pp. 133-163.

small wooden vessel of wine to two Goths, which never ran dry on their journeys to and from Ravenna and during their visit there (1.9, 2: 88-89).

All these lesser miracle-workers had in common with Benedict himself the quality of humility, regarded by Gregory as essential in such people. Nonnosus was remarkable for his obedience to a difficult superior (1.7, 2: 66-67); Boniface was brought up in poverty, which teaches humility (1.9, 2: 92-93); Sanctulus was a man of singular sweetness of character (3.37, 2: 410-427). These men are all living examples of that inner life of holiness, the emphasis upon which differentiates Gregory from Sulpicius Severus and other writers of miracle-stories, as we shall see in chapters four and five.

Gregory's stories relating to the miraculous appearance of money to enable debts to be discharged are a form of "increase" miracle-story, but there is no need for a strained search after scriptural parallels, such as Rousseau pursues. He is troubled because the story in 2.28-29 (2: 216-219) does not correspond with 2 (4) Kings 4.1-7, and tries unsuccessfully to fill the gap by citing 2.27 (2: 214-217), where Benedict miraculously obtained the money to give to a poor man to discharge a debt. It is likely, however, that Gregory was not thinking primarily of the Bible here; this story and two others in 1.9 (2: 84-87) connected with Boniface and relating to the payment of debts, may have been inserted to enhance the latter's status as a holy man, who could achieve results similar to Benedict.

There are two other stories of famine in the *Dialogues*, for which biblical types can be traced. The first of them (2.21, 2: 198-199) relates to a period when there was a great famine in Campania, probably in 537-538. The monks were anxious, because they had eaten almost all their bread, and there was no wheat in store. Benedict gently upbraided them and prophesied that the next day there would be plenty. Just as he had prophesied, they discovered two hundred bushels of wheat in sacks in front of the gates of the monastery. Rousseau links this story with 2 (4) Kings 6.25-7.20, the account of the terrible famine in Samaria, when Elisha's prophecy that two measures of barley should be sold for a shekel and a measure of fine flour also for a shekel, came true. I cannot, however, share his opinion that there is a striking parallelism between the two stories.[28] He does not see that Gregory is here commenting in the spirit of the Bible on the kind of famine conditions that occurred in the sixth century. The second famine miracle is that of the loaf (3.37, 2: 414-415), which falls outside the terms of reference of Mähler and Rousseau.

---

[28] O. Rousseau, "St. Benoît," p. 110.

This story at once suggests latent New Testament precedents; nevertheless it has some affinities not only with the Elijah-Elisha cycle (except that in 1 (3) Kings 17.16, the barrel of meal, rather than a loaf, *non defecit*), but also with the story of the man from Baalshalishah, who brought *panes primitiarum* for the people to eat in time of famine (2 [4] Kings 4.42-44). Rousseau, who examines Gregory's story in connection with Benedict's prophecy in 2.21, is surely mistaken in believing that this story has no connection with famine.[29] Verse 38 of 2 [4] Kings 4 applies both to the story of the noxious pottage and to the story of the eating of the bread of the first-fruits. If the connection with the famine is removed, the story seems to lose its point. Here again, there is no need to attempt to draw strained scriptural parallels. It would be natural to Gregory to interpret on biblical lines the kind of events, such as famines, with which his audience were familiar, and it seems likely that this kind of interpretation would be met with a sympathetic response from an audience in sixth-century Italy, afflicted as the country was with so many disasters (e.g. *Dialogue* 3.38, 2: 430-431; *Homiliae in evangelia* 1.17, 16, PL 76: 1147; *Homiliae in Ezechielem* 1.9, 9: 149; 2.6, 22: 310-311; *Reg.* 3.29, 1: 187; 5.41, 1: 322).

d. *Changing One Substance into Another*

The type of the simple miracle story in the *Dialogues* which deals with the changing of one substance into another is the changing of water into wine at the marriage of Cana in Galilee, described in John 2.1-11. Gregory's story is that of the *mansionarius* Constantius at the church of St Stephen in Ancona, who, owing to lack of oil, filled the lamps with water and, as was customary, inserted a wick (*papyrus*); when lit, the lamps burned as if they had been filled with oil (1.5, 2: 58-61).[30] This story and the gospel narrative resemble each other, in that in neither case was there a prayer nor a command for the water to be turned into a different substance. This is one of that small number of Gregory's miracle stories, of which we have already seen examples, where there is an underlying biblical type, but where the immediate model is undoubtedly to be found

---

[29] Ibid., p. 109.

[30] For shortage of oil, see Augustine, *De ordine* 1.16, p. 92; *Regula magistri* 29, *La règle du maître*, ed. A. de Vogüé, 2 vols, sc 105, 106 (Paris 1964), 2: 160-163; for an earlier reduction in food supplies, see Procopius, *De bello Gothico* 1.15, *De bellis* 2: 78; the blocking-up of the aqueducts (ibid., 1.19, 2: 99) must have had a disastrous effect upon the water-supply and the production of flour, as the mills were driven by water-power. It is doubtful whether the temporary mills put up by Belisarius on rafts on the Tiber (ibid., pp. 99-100) could have lasted a further sixty years.

in the writings of some other author, though these too may be linked to the same biblical type.

In this case Gregory appears to have in mind a story contained in Rufinus's translation of Eusebius's *Historia ecclesiastica*.[31] The circumstances of this story are somewhat different: Gregory describes events which occured *quadam die*, whereas those described in Eusebius took place *in die sollemni vigiliarum paschae*, which makes the lack of oil appear even more serious. The protagonist in Eusebius's story is Narcissus, bishop of Jerusalem, who orders water to be brought. He prays and blesses it and then asks for it to be poured into the lamps. When they are lit, the water, as in Gregory's story, takes on the characteristics of oil: *natura aquae in olei pinguedinem versa*.[32] Thus the story differs from the gospel story in that a formal prayer and blessing were pronounced over the water. Gregory, on the other hand, causes the *mansionarius* to behave as Jesus did at the marriage, in that he displays an implicit faith in the power of God to change the nature of the liquid in the lamps. The use of the word *implevit* in Gregory's narrative suggests a reminiscence of the Vulgate, but otherwise there are no close verbal correspondences. Gregory uses the words *candela* and *lampas* for the lights, whereas Rufinus uses *luminar*. The opening words of the story, however, suggest that Rufinus may have had a stylistic influence on Gregory. They are reminiscent of the manner in which he introduces the stories of some of his more prolific miracle-workers.[33]

Both Eusebius and Gregory aim to stress the humility of the miracle-worker, but whereas Eusebius does so in the manner of an historian reporting a fact which is of significance in assessing the character of a bishop, Gregory writes of Constantius in such a way as to emphasize his personal holiness and his value as an example of a miracle-worker in Italy; his aim is put into the mouth of Peter:

> ut agnosco, vir iste magnus foris fuit in miraculis, sed maior intus in humilitate (1.5, 2: 62-63).

Gregory's informant about Constantius was a *coepiscopus*, who had lived for many years *in monachico habitu* in Ancona, and to the sanctity of whose life *quidam nostri* (presumably papal employees) could testify. In other words he was the kind of informant whose evidence, according to Moricca, should have been treated with greater respect than that of a

[31] See chapter one, n. 12.
[32] *Historia ecclesiastica* 6.9.3, p. 539.
[33] See pp. 6-7.

senex pauper or some peasant or workman. It is possible that such a man could have read Rufinus's translation of Eusebius, but on the whole it seems more likely that it was Gregory who took Rufinus for his model when giving the story literary shape. There is at least one other example of Gregory appearing to use Rufinus in this way in the *Dialogues*, as we shall see in chapter six.[34]

e. *Striking with Blindness*

There are two instances in *Dialogue* 2 of people being struck blind for beneficial purposes, owing to the intervention of Benedict. For one of these stories (2.10, 2: 172-173), Rousseau sees a biblical type, but the parallel is far from exact. In the Bible story, Elisha caused the Syrians to be stricken with blindness, so that he could lead them into Samaria; in Gregory's account, when the monks saw that their kitchen had been set on fire by an idol which they had dug up, Benedict, realizing that they saw flames which were invisible to him, caused them to sign their eyes with the cross, so that they were blind to the flames. The second story (2.4, 2: 150-153) is, to some extent, parallel with the first. In the case of an errant monk, Benedict's prayer enabled Maurus to see a little black devil on the monk's back, whereas Pompeianus remained blind to it. Rousseau does not mention this story, and Mähler does so only in order to show the relationship between *Dialogue* 2 and *Vita Antonii* 6, where the spiritual combat is concerned.[35] It is unfortunate that Mähler did not apparently know of Rousseau's article, since he would have been able to throw some light on the difficulty which Rousseau raises. *Il y a un point*, says Rousseau, *sur lequel nulle concordance – apparente du moins – n'existe entre le Livre des Rois et les Dialogues de saint Grégoire: c'est la présence et l'absence du diable*.[36] The explanation which he offers is that there are only four passages referring to the devil in the old Testament; that we have to wait for the coming of Christ to see him actively at work; and that the Fathers often see the enemies of the people of God as the type of the diabolic species. The difficulty about the absence, in this miracle story, of a biblical type of demonic possession disappears, once we realize that Gregory is not trying to categorize all the miracles in *Dialogue* 2 within the framework of 2 (4) Kings, ch. 4-8. The idea of the holy man being led by the devil to see flames where there were none is found elsewhere in

[34] See p. 174.
[35] Mähler, "Évocations bibliques," pp. 402-403.
[36] O. Rousseau, "St. Benoît," p. 112.

sixth-century literature. Gregory of Tours tells how Portianus, when the victim of diabolic attacks, saw his cell in flames though in reality all was well.[37] The presence of the *idolum* in Gregory the Great's story is not to be attributed to the difference between pre-Christian and Christian demonology. The *idolum* is parallel with the *niger puerulus* in 2.4. The latter is a phenomenon well known in Eastern Christian literature. Gregory may have known of him through the *Vita Antonii*, where μέλας παῖς is rendered as *niger puer* in the older version, or from Cassian.[38] Another possible source for Gregory's knowledge of this unpleasant little creature is the *Historia monachorum*.[39] All that Gregory was trying to do here was to show that through his human agents, God was able to strike men blind on appropriate occasions, just as had happened in biblical times.

A closer implicit parallel between Elisha and Gregory, which is not mentioned by our two Benedictine authors, because it occurs outside *Dialogue* 2, is provided by 2 (4) Kings 6.18-23 and Acts 6-12, and the two instances in *Dialogues* 1 and 3 of evil persons being struck blind: according to Gregory's informant Laurentius, abbot of the monastery of Fundi, the Franks, who had invaded Italy under Butilin, were struck blind when they charged into the chapel of Libertinus (1.2, 2: 26-27). The same fate overtook the Arian bishop who tried to gain possession of a church in Spoleto (3.29, 2: 376-379), according to the monk Boniface of Gregory's own monastery, who four years previously had been living among the Lombards. It is possible that Gregory knew the story told by Gregory of Tours of a heretic who was struck dead as a punishment for allowing a bishop to bribe him to sham blindness in order to demonstrate his, the bishop's, skill as a miracle-worker.[40] The first of Gregory the Great's series of stories (1.2, 2: 26-27) is the more exact parallel, since the inference is that Libertinus, through his personal sanctity, possessed similar miracle-working powers to Benedict and Elisha. In the story of the Arian bishop, it seems as though Gregory, like Gregory of Tours in the above-mentioned incident, wishes to present a picture of a man receiving punishment for his sins. From this story (and from two others in the same

[37] *Vita patrum* 5 (3), p. 229.

[38] *Vita Antonii* 6, pp. 18-19; Cassian, *Collationes* 1.21, 1: 105-106; 2.13, 1: 137; 9.6, 2: 45.

[39] *Historia monachorum* 7, PL 21: 411; cf. Cyril of Scythopolis, *Vita S. Euthymii* 50, *Kyrillos von Skythopolis*, ed. E. Schwartz, TU 49 (Leipzig 1939), p. 74. See B. Steidle, "Der kleine schwarze Knabe in der alten Mönchserzählung," *BenM* 34 (1958): 339-350.

[40] *Liber in gloria confessorum* 13, pp. 305-306; cf. Chunus, *Liber in gloria martyrum* 1.2, p. 137.

Dialogue, 3.30, 2: 380-393) we derive a picture of Gregory's hatred of Arianism and his desire to spread the truth. He is anxious not so much to explain what the doctrines of Arianism are as to stress the spiritual and indeed physical peril in which their devotees are placed.

f. *Rendering Poison Harmless*

As in the two latter stories of sudden blindness, there is only a tenuous and implicit connection between the Elijah-Elisha cycle – and indeed the Old Testament generally – and the stories in the *Dialogues*, of poison being rendered harmless. In two cases, the poison is neutralized by the sign of the cross: in 2.3 (2: 142-143) Benedict thus shatters the glass containing the poison destined for him by the dissident monks; in 3.5 (2: 272-275), the blind bishop Sabinus thus rendered harmless the wine poisoned by his scheming archdeacon. The three Old Testament types of this latter miracle relate to water or broth: the waters of Marah made sweet by Moses casting a tree into them (Exod. 15.25); the water purified through Elisha adding salt to it (2 [4] Kings 19-22), and the noxious pottage made harmless through his flinging meal into it (2 [4] Kings 4.38-41). In the third story (2.8, 2: 160-163), the poisoned bread offered to Benedict by Florentius, the treacherous priest, was carried away by the raven at Benedict's bidding. Rousseau is right when he points out that the fundamental difference between these two groups of stories is that in the Bible, the poison is placed in the pot through chance or ignorance, whereas in the *Dialogues* the motive is spite.[41] The story of the poisoned cup, whether or not inspired by the Scriptures, had long been in circulation. A similar incident, involving the sign of the cross, is described by Cyril of Scythopolis.[42]

g. *Prophecy and Discernment of Spirits*

Gregory clearly regards the gift of prophecy as one of the essential characteristics of the holy man. Not surprisingly Benedict is pre-eminent in this gift which can be regarded as two-fold: *ventura praedicere, prasentibus absentia nuntiare* (2.11, 2: 174-175). Neither Rousseau nor Mähler has completely understood this duality.

Rousseau, in his section vii, *Le don de prophétie d'Élisée*, takes as the biblical type of Benedict's prophecies 2 (4) Kings 6.8-23, which contains

---

[41] O. Rousseau, "St. Benoît," p. 108.
[42] Cyril of Scythopolis, *Vita S. Sabae* 48, *Kyrillos von Skythopolis*, p. 138.

only a prophecy of the second category, *praesentibus absentia nuntiare*, and then cites five examples of his revelations: the misdoings of the monks, who broke the Rule by eating outside the monastery, and of the brother of the monk Valentinian (2.12-13, 2: 174-181); the cunning of Totila (2.14, 2: 180-183); the identity of the monk who stole the napkins (2.19; 2: 194-197); the proud thoughts of one of his monks (2.20, 2: 196-199). He fails to mention another episode of the same type, where Benedict recognizes that some wine has been concealed (2.18, 2: 194-195).

The gift of discernment of spirits was regarded as an important attribute of the holy man by other writers besides Gregory. He was probably acquainted with the incident where Martin discerned that the monastery was being defiled by one of the brethren sitting naked before the fire.[43] He may also have known the stories of John of Lycopolis, who was able to distinguish which one of seven brothers was a deacon and to discern misbehaviour in the monastery; of Abba Helenus, who used to surprise his brethren by his revelations about their characters; and of the priest Eulogius, who as he stood at the altar, could discern the thoughts of the communicants.[44] There are also a number of stories of the power to discern spirits in the apophthegmatic writings, which, as we shall see in chapter six, were almost certainly known to Gregory, but these are less directly relevant for our purpose here.

Apart from section ix, *Hazäel, futur roi de Syrie*, Rousseau does not really deal with the other aspect of Benedict's gift of prophecy, *ventura praedicere*. In this section, he attempts to show that Gregory's account of Totila's visit to Benedict is based on Hazael's visit to consult Elisha.[45] P. A. Cusack has, however, successfully demonstrated that its origins, though equally literary, lie elsewhere, in the *Vita S. Martini*, in the works of Cassian and other Latin writers, and ultimately, in Plutarch's life of Solon.[46]

Mähler recognizes that there is a distinction between Benedict's two forms of prophecy, and that he possesses a power comparable to that of Elisha in 2 (4) Kings 5.25-27, when the prophet discerns the evil motives of Gehazi. It is indeed the power of which Peter is made to speak in 2.13 (2: 178-179):

---

[43] Sulpicius Severus, *Dialogue* 2(3).14, pp. 212-213.

[44] Mind-reading: e.g., *Historia monachorum* 1, PL 21: 391-393 (John of Lycopolis); discernment of spirits: e.g., ibid., 15, PL 21: 434 (John of Lycopolis); 11, PL 21: 430-431 (Helenus); 14, PL 21: 433 (Eulogius).

[45] O. Rousseau, "St. Benoît," p. 113.

[46] Cusack, pp. 87-90.

Ego sancti viri praecordiis Helisei video inesse, qui absenti discipulo praesens fuit.

However, Mähler does not sufficiently emphasize the other aspect of Benedict's prophetic gift. It is true that he devotes section xiii of his article to Benedict's prophecy of the fall of Monte Cassino (2.17, 2: 192-193), which he believes to be linked to 2 (4) Kings 8.11-12, where Elisha prophesies the harm that Hazael will do to the kingdom of Israel, but he neither indicated the significance of the gift of *ventura praedicere* in relation to Gregory's portrait of Benedict as a charismatic figure, nor attempts to find a literary source more closely related to Gregory's text than the passage in 2 (4) Kings.

There are a number of passages in earlier works which may have influenced Gregory here. Martin's powers of foreseeing the future are mentioned by both Sulpicius Severus and Gregory of Tours, but more directly relevant for our purposes are the various prophecies relating to the fall of Scete contained in the *Apophthegmata patrum latinorum*, which clearly represent different apophthegmatic traditions and which were almost certainly known to Gregory.[47] Mähler does not go into the details of Benedict's prophecy relating to the fate of Totila and the future of Rome, perhaps because it does not possess any overt biblical links. Gregory is certainly interpreting this event in the spirit of the Bible, but he may have been thinking primarily of two passages in the works of Augustine which refer to the prophecy of John of Lycopolis to the emperor Theodosius, when the latter visited him to seek advice.[48] The difference is that John of Lycopolis gave a favourable prophecy to a Christian ruler, whereas Benedict gave an unfavourable prediction to a pagan.

The following analysis shows the distinction between the two kinds of prophetic gift possessed by Benedict: *ventura praedicere*: a gift confined to Benedict by Gregory, for foreseeing large-scale events: 2.11, 2: 172-174; 15, 2: 182-183; 16, 2: 184-187; 17, 2: 192-193; 21, 2: 198-201; *praesentibus absentia nuntiare*: a gift common to Benedict and to lesser miracle-workers: Equitius: 1.4, 2: 40-41; Benedict: 2.12, 2: 174-177; 13, 2: 176-181; 14, 2: 180-185; 18-20, 2: 194-199; Sabinus: 2.5, 2: 272-277; Constantius: 3.8, 2: 284-287; Isaac of Spoleto: 14, 2: 307-311.

---

[47] E.g., *Apophthegmata patrum latinorum* 5.18, PL 73: 982; 6.1, PL 73: 993. See chapter six.

[48] *De cura pro mortuis gerenda* 17.21, p. 655; *De civitate Dei* 5.26, 1: 161; other possible sources: *Historia monachorum* 1, PL 21: 404-405; *Heraclidis paradisus* 22, PL 74: 302; Cassian, *De institutis coenobiorum* 4.23, pp. 152-155.

The gift of *ventura praedicere*, that is, the power to foresee large-scale events, appears to be confined to the type of the Old Testament prophets, particularly Elisha. The fact that Benedict is made to prophesy events which had already occurred or, as in the case of the Totila episode, had occurred to a different person and at a different time and place, is immaterial. The significance of these stories is that Gregory believed that Benedict's prophetic and charismatic gifts were so exceptional that he would have been capable of the actions and utterances of the great holy men of the past.

The one case which does not appear to fit into the scheme is that of Boniface, who foretold the death of a man with a musical instrument and a monkey, about whose personality he presumably knew nothing (1.9, 2: 82-85). This seems to be an instance of some kind of clairvoyant gift.

h. *Water and Fire*

There are two stories in the *Dialogues* relating to the supply of water: 1. the sweating rock, which supplied water to the monks of Subiaco (2.5, 2: 152-155); 2. the miraculous supply of spring water granted to Martin the hermit of Monte Marsico, as soon as he had chosen his cave (3.16, 2: 152-154). Peter has already been made to comment on the typological significance of the first of these two episodes (2.8, 2: 164-167). There is no need to confuse the issue, as Mähler has done, by citing 2 (4) Kings 3.9-15 as the type of this story.[49] The comparisons made by Mähler seem strained and far-fetched, whereas the analogy which Gregory puts into Peter's mouth is simple and straightforward. The two famous stories of Moses obtaining water for the Israelites in the wilderness (Num. 20.2-13; Exod. 17.1-6), which had often been interpreted typologically by the Fathers, would naturally occur to Gregory when recounting the search of Benedict and his community for water. The phrase *ex petra* used by Peter suggests that the story in Exodus is the more likely in this case.

The circumstances of the monks at Subiaco and of the solitary at Monte Marsico in the Campania region might well suggest to Gregory a parallel with the Israelites in the wilderness; Gregory apparently sees Benedict as a new Moses, leading the chosen into a wilderness nearer home. Water supplies might well be a problem in sixth-century Rome and its surrounding districts, because of the blocking-up of the aqueducts and of the subsequent failure to keep them in repair;[50] it seems likely that in a hot

---

[49] Mähler, "Évocations bibliques," pp. 406-407.
[50] See n. 30 above.

summer, the level of the Anio might be much reduced, and that other streams might become dried up. In such a situation, any fortunate discovery of water in the Subiaco area or in the Campania might well suggest biblical parallels.

The miracles of preservation from fire (1.6, 2: 62-65; 2.18, 2: 344-345) recall the story of the Three Holy Children in Dan. 3, to which Peter, as we have already seen is made to relate the second of these narratives (3.18). However, the earlier story (1.6) may be one of those miracle-stories like that of Constantius (1.5, 2: 58-63), which are linked to a biblical type, but for which Gregory takes an episode in some more recent work for his model. Here he appears to be thinking of a similar miracle performed by Martin (who, by placing himself against the flames, prevented a house from being destroyed) in the *Vita S. Martini*.[51] This is the closest parallel to Gregory's narrative, but there are stories of bishops extinguishing fires by their presence in the *Vita S. Caesarii arelatensis* and *De virtutibus S. Martini*.[52] This material affords yet another example of the use of the same biblical types by writers of miracles-stories belonging to different periods and different parts of the Mediterranean area.

i. *Walking on Water*

If we except the reference to the miracle of preservation, of which Benedict was the recipient rather than the agent (2.17, 2: 192-193), the story of Maurus walking on the water is the sole miracle-story based on a New Testament type to be found in *Dialogue* 2 (7, 2: 156-159) and may therefore be regarded as in a class by itself. The general aim seems clear enough. The ability to walk on the water is a Christ-like characteristic, but Peter is made by Gregory to say, *in aquae itinere Petrum ... video*, which raises certain problems of interpretation. If Maurus is regarded as following the action of Jesus in walking on the water, then Benedict ceases to be the hero. On the other hand, if Maurus is regarded as filling the role of St Peter (Matt. 14.26-31) and Benedict that of Jesus, then Placid will surely drown, and the characters of both Benedict and Maurus will be tarnished. This difficulty is experienced by Mähler, who does his best to solve it by means of a complicated piece of biblical exegesis.[53] He regards the *mise en scène* as similar to that of the Gospel, with Maurus as

---

[51] *Vita S. Martini* 14, 1: 282-283.

[52] *Vita Caesarii arelatensis* 1.22, p. 465; 2.26, p. 494; Gregory of Tours, *Vita S. Martini* 432, p. 208.

[53] Mähler, "Évocations bibliques," pp. 407-409.

analogous with Peter, and draws certain parallels; these are elucidated in the following table:

Matt. 14	*Dialogue 2.7, 2: 156-161*
28 Peter asks Jesus to cause him to walk on the water.	Maurus asks Benedict for a blessing.
29-30 Peter walks on the water and then begins to sink.	Maurus hastens over the water, while Placid sinks.
31 Jesus pulls Peter out of the water.	Maurus pulls Placid out of the water.

Matt. 3	
15 Conflict of humility between Jesus and John the Baptist on the bank of the Jordan.	Conflict of humility between Benedict and Maurus.
16 Jesus, having been baptized rises from the water and sees the Holy Spirit descending in the form of a dove.	Placid, when he is pulled out of the water, sees the *melota* of Benedict on his own head. This signifies the Second Baptism of the novice.

The suggestion that this episode is to be interpreted as the Second Baptism of Placid, because the *melota* was placed on the head of the novice, is most ingenious, but it seems unlikely that Gregory would have worked out the analogies in such detail.

An alternative possibility is that Gregory is interpreting his material not in the light of the gospel narrative but of that of some other writer. According to one text of Palladius, the sanctity of some of the monks of the Thebaid was such that they were in the habit of walking on the water without mishap. This story is not found in either of the extant ancient Latin versions of Palladius, but this is not an insuperable objection, since it may have occurred in the version of which PL 74: 343-382 is a fragment. Moreover there are similar stories in the *Apophthegmata patrum latinorum* and Rufinus's version of the *Historia monachorum*.[54]

What is clear is that Gregory is anxious to stress that there are monks in Italy whose sanctity is equal to that of the Desert Fathers. Peter the Deacon reacts to the story as any of Gregory's readers might have done, by identifying Maurus with St Peter, but what he really sees is a monk who succeeds where the Apostle failed, because his obedience to his superior is equal to that of the Desert Fathers and exceeds that of St Peter.

---

[54] *Apophthegmata patrum latinorum* 6.2, PL 73: 1000 (Bessarion); *Historia monachorum* 9, PL 21: 423 (Copres); PL 21: 425 (Patermutius).

Possibly Gregory placed a high value on the sanctity of the monks, because in the light of Matt. 22.30, he regarded them as angels.

This is not to say that Gregory's rich and fertile use of typology did not include the many biblical and other symbols here. The connection between the *melota* of Benedict, employed here to warm and comfort the half-drowned boy, and its use at the profession of a monk is certainly suggestive, but the analogy should not be pressed too far. When interpreting Gregory's miracle-stories, it is important to discover the salient points of analogy with the Bible or with the works of other writers, but not to attempt vainly to work out a complete complementary scene.

j. *Casting Out Devils*

Many of the stories in the *Dialogues* relating to the casting-out of devils are of a non-biblical character (for example, 1.4, 2: 42-45; 2.4, 2: 152-153; 8, 2: 166-171; 16, 2: 184-187; 30, 2: 220-221; 3.4, 2: 270-273; 6, 2: 276-279; 7, 2: 278-285; 14, 2: 304-305; 16, 2: 328-331; 20, 2: 350-353; 26, 2: 366-367; 33, 2: 394-401; 42, 3: 152-153); but we can distinguish a small group of stories which have as their type the story of the Gadarene swine (Matt. 8.29-34; Mark 5.1-20; Luke 8.26-40). The details of Gregory's stories do not correspond very closely with the gospel narratives about the Gadarene swine, because he was primarily interpreting non-biblical material on biblical lines, but they all involve the arrival or transfer of a devil or devils into a living creature, in two cases, a human being and in two others, a pig.

The first two stories concern bishop Fortunatus of Todi (1.10, 2: 92-99), who possessed special skill as an exorcist:

> ... qui in exfugandis spiritibus immensae virtutis gratia pollebat ita ut nonnunquam ab obsessis corporibus legiones daemonum pelleret.

The phrase *legiones daemonum* at once links him with the gospel type. Gregory had been able to learn a good deal about him from Julian the *Defensor*, who had once been a papal official and later became an episcopal colleague of Fortunatus, whose closest friend he was.

The earlier of the two stories concerns a young married woman who broke a rule by having sexual intercourse with her husband the night before she attended the dedication of a chapel. As soon as the relics of St Sebastian were brought into the service of dedication, she became possessed. The priest covered her with a veil, whereupon the devil transferred itself to him. After a good deal of trouble, including the arrival of a *legio* of devils (another recollection of the gospel story), she was cured through the devotion of bishop Fortunatus.

In the later story (1.10, 2: 98-99) Gregory makes a curious use of the text, *Si autem oculus tuus fuerit nequam, totum corpus tenebrosum erit* (Matt. 6.23), to account for the death of an innocent little boy. Fortunatus cast out a devil, which promptly roamed the streets of the city at night in the form of a man, complaining that the bishop had refused him lodging. Invited by an inhabitant to sit by the fire in his home, the devil then entered into the man's little son, who fell on the fire and died. Gregory's explanation is that the man received the visitor only in order to spite the bishop and therefore had to be punished by the death of his son. This unpleasant story is to be regarded as an example of Gregory's biblical method of interpretation, but even so, this explanation is not altogether satisfactory. It seems as though he was casting about for an explanation of a story that he had heard, of the death of an innocent child, whose father he believed, for some reason, to be worthy of punishment.

In the other two stories, Gregory is concerned with a single devil and a single pig. The first of these (3.21, 2: 353-355) forms one of the Spoleto sequence, for which his informant was the holy man Eleutherius. In this story, a consecrated virgin of Spoleto drove a devil from a countryman into a pig. The second story (3.30, 2: 378-383), like that of the young married woman, is incidentally an example of the power of the relics of the saints, when translated, to set in train unexpected and sometimes alarming events; it has already been mentioned in chapter one. As in the other story, it is the relics of St Sebastian which have this effect. During the consecration by Gregory of the church in Rome now known as Sant' Agata dei Goti, in 592, on its transfer from Arian to Catholic worship, at the moment when relics of St Sebastian and St Agatha were being brought in, members of the crowded congregation were conscious of a pig scuffling and snuffling round their feet, though they could not see it. Still invisible, it rushed through the doorway and was heard no more, which was taken as a sign that the evil spirit of Arianism had departed from the church for ever.

Gregory explicitly relates the story of the virgin of Spoleto to the Gadarene swine, but the second story is an example of his "indirect" typology. In pagan times in Rome a pig was used as one of the victims in sacrifices of purification (*suovetaurilia*). There may have been some lingering folk-memory of this among the *populum*, *sacerdotem*, and *custodes* from whom Gregory derived his information.[55]

---

[55] See *PW*, *art*. Schwein.

k. *Healing*

Among the miracles of healing described in the *Dialogues* it is possible to distinguish two groups of stories with biblical affinities. The first group consists of stories about healings, not necessarily biblical in their details, but performed by bishops as successors of the apostles. Gregory's readers would know from Acts 2.43 and 5.12-16 that in the early days of the Church in Jerusalem, the apostles were able to perform many miracles. One of the gifts of those who have within them the *vitam apostolicam* (see 1.10, 2: 108-109) is the power to enlighten the blind; in this little group of stories are two examples of cures of blindness: by Fortunatus (1.10, 2: 100-101), and by the pope John at the Golden Gate of Constantinople (3.2, 2: 268-269). Agapitus, the future pope, healed a dumb and lame man in the context of the Eucharist (3.3, 2: 268-271); Amantius, a priest with remarkable charismatic gifts, whose likeness to the apostles is particularly stressed by Gregory, healed a madman in Rome (3.35, 2: 104-107). For this last miracle Gregory's informant was Floridus, bishop of Tifernae Tiberinae, who brought Amantius to Rome at Gregory's request, but Gregory himself did not actually witness the miracle. There is also a "long-distance" healing by St Peter, through the agency of a humble *mansionarius* called Acontius, whom the saint, in a vision, instructed a paralyzed girl to approach (3.25, 2: 364-365).

The second group of healing miracles consists of those performed by Benedict in *Dialogue* 2. The fact that there is no real counterpart to the healing of Naaman by Elisha (2 [4] Kings 5.3-19) causes our two Benedictine scholars some difficulty, particularly Rousseau, who is trying to fit the miracle-stories of this *Dialogue* into the rigid framework of 2 (4) Kings 4-8; he takes the view that the healings of the servant of Aptonius's father (2.26, 2: 214-215) and of the man poisoned by an enemy (2.27, 2: 216-217) correspond to the healing of Naaman, but there is an objection to this explanation, if the *Dialogue* is to be interpreted on this kind of level: in neither case does the victim suffer from true leprosy. Mähler declares that he finds *un curieux parallélisme* between the biblical narrative and the story in 2.26. Presumably this lies in the fact that both Elisha and Benedict were approached through an intermediary for a cure; in the story of Naaman it is the master who is the sufferer, whereas in Gregory's narrative the situation is reversed.

However, Gregory was not seeking exact parallels in these accounts of healings; his object was to give examples of those who practised the *vitam apostolicam*, as described in 1.10 (2: 108-109). Among the powers of such people is *leprosos mundare*. He therefore visualizes Benedict at work in a difficult and unhealthy district and performing the kind of miracles of healing which the apostles, on the one hand, and his counterpart, Elisha, on the other, might have accomplished in the circumstances.

D. CONCLUSION

We have now seen how some of Gregory's critics have failed to understand what he was trying to do. In chapter one we observed their failure to realize that Gregory had so strong a sense of the transitory nature of this world that he regarded it as a mirror through which to see the next, and that since he possessed this kind of perspective, the historical and chronological setting of an event would be for him it least important aspect.[56] The critics whose work we have examined in chapter two, Mähler and Rousseau, while not expecting Gregory to produce an historical document, have not seen Benedict within his historical, literary, and typological background, but as a figure too rigidly enclosed within a biblical framework. The object of Gregory, as of any other author of a late antique or early medieval *Vita*, was not to create a character study based on the available evidence, but to convey to his readers a portrait of a holy man possessing the qualities expected of a holy man; prominent among these was the capacity to perform miracles. Whether or not the miracles described had actually been performed by the subject of the *Vita* was immaterial; what was important was that a holy man such as he was might have performed them. We have already seen that there is nothing surprising in finding the same miracle attributed to different holy men. Gregory describes miracles similar to those performed by Caesarius of Arles, Martin of Tours, and the monks of Egypt; Bede will not scruple to ascribe to Cuthbert[57] miracles attributed by Gregory to other holy men. More important, Gregory did not hesitate to use Antony as portrayed by Athanasius as a model for Benedict. The characters in the *Dialogues* have to be evaluated as a series of portrait types of Christian sanctity in sixth-century Italy and not primarily as a quarry for the social historian or student of folklore.

[56] Bolton, "The Supra-Historical Sense," p. 208.

[57] B. Colgrave, ed., *Two Lives of St Cuthbert* (Cambridge 1940), pp. 164-165, cf. *Dialogue* 2.35, 2: 238-241; pp. 198-199, cf. *Dialogue* 2.10, 2: 170-173; p. 200, cf. *Dialogue* 1.6, 2: 62-65.

The Bible is prominent among the various sources for these portraits, but its real importance in this connection lies in the part that it played in Gregory's mental and spiritual formation. He was not only steeped in its contents, but also practised in viewing life and literature from its standpoint. It is this biblical spirit which we need to cultivate when evaluating and interpreting Gregory's writings, rather than the habit of examining biblical minutiae and straining after scriptural parallels.

3

Gregory and the Stories
of the Italian Martyrs

A. Introduction

We have already seen that the raw material available to Gregory, when he
intended to write about the lives and deeds of holy men in Italy, was a
body of traditions which had grown up in the city of Rome and the
countryside of central Italy. This material appears to have been
transmitted to him orally, rather than in writing, by employees on the
papal estates, both clerical and lay. We need to remember that other
writers had been making use of this material in the past and would
continue to do so in future. It is important to discover how they did so and
what was Gregory's relationship to them.

This material, known collectively as the *Gesta martyrum*, can most
accessibly be studied in the Bollandists' *Acta Sanctorum*, combined with
the cautious use of the martyrologies of Ado and Usuard. The unfinished
Étude sur les Gesta martyrum romains, by Albert Dufourcq, provides
French versions of a number of the *Gesta* and some guidance through the
labyrinth, but not the least of its many shortcomings is the lack of any
kind of index. More reliable help is afforded by Lanzoni's *Le diocesi
d'Italia dalle origini al principio del secolo VII*, but the arrangement of this
book, which was written solely from the point of view of local
ecclesiastical history, often renders it difficult to use.

It is useful, at this stage, to consider once more Gregory's aim in
writing the *Dialogues*: were they solely a didactic exercise, designed to
inspire a monastic and clerical audience, as suggested at the end of chapter
one? It seems to me that Gregory had another purpose, unexpressed but
discernible. When he entered upon his pontificate, the immediate
situation in Rome was desperate. There was a serious outbreak of plague,
in which his predecessor, Pelagius II, had perished; the flooding of the

Tiber had caused severe damage to a city which had already suffered much on account of the imperial and Gothic wars and was threatened by the Lombard invasion; there was a shortage of food and other necessities.[1]

Gregory's attitude at this time of crisis was determined by two factors: his Christian faith and a combination of patriotism and a sense of *noblesse oblige* as a member of a distinguished Roman family. No doubt he realized that the only effective administration in the city at the beginning of his pontificate was provided by the papal machinery. In the long term, the Pope alone could fill the place of the vanished Emperors of the West in temporal matters, but more immediately, the situation provided an opportunity for consolidating the spiritual power of the papacy and re-creating something of the glory of Rome. Gregory saw intuitively that the significance of Rome was no longer political but religious; its position could best be restored not by recalling the great days of the Empire or even the Republic, but by stressing its links with the apostles Peter and Paul and with the long line of martyrs whose mortal remains lay near at hand. Gregory therefore set to work to collect material relating to local heroes of the faith, which would both afford examples of sanctity and help to restore the morale of his audience.

The morale of the writers of the *Gesta* was probably lowered by the situation also, but lacking Gregory's *Romanitas* and sense of public duty, they were more interested in building up their own prestige by means of stories which boosted the status of the secular clerics and stressed the continuity of their orders with those of the holy men of past ages than in enhancing the prestige of the city. Thus Gregory and the writers of the *Gesta* were using similar material for similar, but not identical, purposes.

This hypothesis would account for two facts: relatively few of Gregory's stories deal with holy men living outside Rome or the central regions of Italy; no contemporary of Gregory wrote any parallel work dealing with some other part of Italy. It may be objected that other cities had few, if any, martyrs and had forgotten about those they had, as, for example, in the case of Gervase and Protase at Milan.[2]

In reply, it may be pointed out that Rome, too, had martyrs about whom little or nothing is known, but this did not prevent the development of a corpus of material relating to them; whereas there were good reasons, in the case of Rome, for refurbishing the stories of the martyrs, the other

---

[1] E.g., *Homiliae in evangelia* 1.1, PL 76: 1078, 1080; *Dialogue* 3.19, 2: 346-347.

[2] See Paulinus, *Vita Ambrosii* 14, pp. 70-73; Augustine, *Confessiones*, ed. P. Knöll, CSEL 33 (Vienna 1900), pp. 208-209; *De civitate Dei* 22.8, 2: 816; *Ep.* 78, *Epistulae*, ed. A. Goldbacher, 4 vols, CSEL 24, 45, 57, 58 (Vienna 1895-1911), 2: 336.

cities did not require such an extensive propagandist exercise for building their reputation. It is interesting to note that Possidius's *Vita* of Augustine contains no miracle stories, whereas Paulinus of Milan felt it necessary to include an account of the miracles resulting from the finding of the bodies of Gervase and Protase; it would appear that these stories added to the lustre of Ambrose as a holy man, but that the creation of a corpus of such material was not required to enhance the status of Milan as a city and diocese in the early fifth century.

Further confirmation of this hypothesis is afforded by the case of Ravenna. According to Peter Chrysologus, this city had only one martyr, Apollinaris, though Venantius Fortunatus thought otherwise, erroneously, as Lanzoni has shown.[3] Yet in the seventh century a *Passio Apollinaris* (*BHL* 623) made its appearance, which includes the same kind of stock hagiographical characteristics and situations as the Roman and Umbrian *Passiones* of the same or earlier date, which will be discussed later. Indeed it was used by Agnellus as a source for the earliest episcopal biographies in his *Liber pontificalis Ravennatis*.[4]

What was the background to the appearance of this solitary Ravennate *Passio*? From the mid-fifth century Ravenna began to rise in ecclesiastical status through the grant of jurisdiction over various churches which had previously been subject to Milan. About a hundred years later, Justinian appears to have granted the city some special privileges, the exact nature of which is not clear.[5] Maximian, who became bishop in 546, was the first to assume the title of *archiepiscopus*, and by the 550s, this had become the normal title. Agnellus tells us that Maximian received the *pallium* at the time of his consecration.[6] This was the beginning of the famous dispute with which Gregory was called upon to deal (*Reg.* 3.54, 1: 210-214; 66-67, 1: 228-231; 5.11, 1: 291-292; 15, 1: 295-296, 61, 1: 375-380, all dated 593-595).

Gregory's relations with the exarchate had also been somewhat strained, because the exarch Romanus resented what he considered to be Gregory's interference in dealing with the Lombards (*Reg.* 5.40, 1: 329-

[3] Peter Chrysologus, *Sermones* 128, PL 52: 552-553; Venantius Fortunatus, *Vita S. Martini* 4, 680-685, MGH AA 4 (1) (Berlin 1881), p. 369; Lanzoni, 2: 724-732.

[4] Apollinaris, Aderitus, and Eleucadius: Agnellus of Ravenna, [*Liber pontificalis*] *Codex pontificalis ecclesiae Ravennatis*, fasc. 1-3, ed. A. Testi Rasponi, RIS 2.3 (Bologna 1924), pp. 21-32.

[5] See R. A. Markus, "Carthage – Prima Justiniana – Ravenna: an Aspect of Justinian's Kirchenpolitik," *Byz.* 49 (1979): 277-306.

[6] *Liber pontificalis Ravennatis* 27, ed. O. Holden Egger, MGH SRL (Hanover 1878), pp. 34-391, at p. 187.

331; 2.45, 1: 144-145). The appointment of two Romans in succession, John and Marinianus, cannot have helped to soothe wounded pride.[7]

These disputes, both religious and secular, are probably symptomatic of the feelings of the people of Ravenna who, though outwardly proud of being citizens of the city of the exarch, might, from an inner sense of inferiority, cherish a secret envy of the ancient prestige of Rome.

Against this kind of background, a mediocre writer, such as the author of the *Passio Apollinaris*, might well feel obliged to help to boost the prestige of the exarchate and, more particularly, of the archdiocese; indeed he may have wished to build up the reputation of the episcopate of Ravenna, in order to render it equal in status to the papacy. He could not succeed in this design for two reasons. First, his subject matter was inevitably inferior; Rome possessed the physical remains of SS Peter and Paul, as well as those of numerous other martyrs, whereas Ravenna, by comparison, was an upstart city, lacking a background of historical grandeur and heroic sanctity. Second, since he lacked Gregory's psychological insight, political acumen, and literary artistry, his performance in handling the meagre material at his disposal could not rise above that of the writers of the Roman *Gesta*.

B. The Nature of the *Gesta martyrum* and Their Writers and Readers

A distinction must be drawn between the narratives of the *Passiones* of the martyrs, written in the second and third centuries, and the *Gesta martyrum*, which, as we shall see, are to be assigned to the fifth, sixth, and seventh centuries. The earlier *Passiones* deal, for the most part, with Eastern Christendom or with Christians in North Africa. Probably the only narratives dealing with Italy are the *Acta Iustini* (Justin Martyr, *BHG* 973), the *Acta Apollonii* (*BHG* 149), and possibly the *Acta Euplii* (*BHL* 2728). If the last be an authentic document, then it is the only early Latin *Passio* dealing with Italy.

It is difficult, if not impossible, to devise an objective method of testing the authenticity of a passion narrative. Dufourcq's comparative method is as good as any, provided that one can be certain of the authenticity of the earlier narrative with which the comparison is made. Unfortunately Dufourcq selects a story which contains doubtful elements, the *Passio Mariani et Iacobi*; it certainly possesses that calm, grave, fervent tone, still

---

[7] John: *Reg.* 3.6, 1: 229; *Liber pontificalis Ravennatis* 98, p. 342; Marinianus: *Reg.* 5.51, 1: 351; *Liber pontificalis Ravennatis* 99, p. 343.

capable of moving the reader by its simplicity, which he contrasts with that of the stories written in the post-Constantinian era,[8] but there are certain suspicious features: for example the protagonists are both clerics, James, a deacon and Marian a *lector*, like the characters in the *Gesta*; again, like them, they happen to encounter two bishops. The prophetic visions which they see in prison recall those found in the *Acta Perpetuae et Felicitatis*[9] and the tone of the narrative is highly rhetorical. It is wiser to take as our "control" a passion narrative of which the authenticity is less doubtful. The archetypal *Passio* is that of Perpetua and Felicitas. According to its anonymous author, chapters 4-10 (the account of Perpetua) and 11-13 (the story of Saturus) were taken from the martyr's own words. It contains accounts of visions, but these are written in a straightforward, non-rhetorical manner.[10] There is a realism about Perpetua's courage and directness in dealing with the severe gaoler. The preliminary escapes of Saturus, Perpetua, and Felicitas from the animals in the arena are reported as matters of fact, not as marvels.[11] The sufferings of the young mother Perpetua and the pregnant Felicitas move us, because they are so simply described. The characters in the post-Constantinian *Gesta*, however, are stereotypes rather than real people: the persecutors are extraordinarily cruel, the persecuted, extraordinarily brave. There are no cowards, waverers, or apostates. All kinds of marvels, and prodigies occur; there are large-scale conversions of gaolers and soldiers (as against one soldier Pudens, in the *Passio Perpetuae et Felicitatis*);[12] the repetition of edifying death-scenes and executions becomes monotonous. Altogether one is reminded of the world of the apocryphal New Testament as opposed to that of the canonical New Testament.

The ecclesiastical and theological ideas put forward in the *Gesta* are anachronistic: there is a bishop in practically every city in the Roman world,[13] post-Nicene and post-Chalcedonian utterances are attributed to the martyrs,[14] and the writers assign to the first, second, and third centuries, church customs, institutions, and modes of discipline which

---

[8] A. Dufourcq, *Étude sur les Gesta martyrum romains*, vols 1-4, BÉFAR 83 in 4 parts (Paris 1900-1910, unfinished), 1: 67-75; H. A. Musurillo, ed., *The Acts of the Christian Martyrs* (Oxford 1972), pp. 194-213. The latter, pp. xxxiii-xxxiv, admits that the narrative presents problems.

[9] Musurillo, *The Acts*, pp. 202-205; 208-213; cf. pp. 110-123.

[10] Ibid., pp. 110-133.

[11] Ibid., pp. 126-131.

[12] Ibid., pp. 128-131.

[13] *AASS* Iun. 5: 413-414; 416.

[14] E.g., *BHL* 561-565.

had been common earlier or were not employed until much later.[15] For example, baptisms of entire households are common, though these must surely belong either to the apostolic or the Constantinian age.[16] Mass conversions, too, seem more appropriate to that era following the Peace of the Church.[17] The spectacle of large groups embracing celibacy is more appropriate to the fifth and sixth centuries than to the period from the first to the third.[18] We find, too, an exaggerated exaltation of virginity and a corresponding depreciation of matrimony. This is more characteristic of the period from the late fourth century onwards than of the age of the martyrs.[19]

It has been suggested in the past that these fifth and sixth-century passion narratives represent a "working over" of earlier material by later writers. There are, of course, no grounds for completely denying this possibility, but it seems more likely that they were actually composed in the later period.[20] It is unlikely, if such narratives existed in the third or fourth centuries, that they would not have been mentioned by Pope Damasus, in his quest for information about the martyrs, or by other writers, such as Augustine, Ambrose or Jerome. On the contrary, Ambrose invokes oral tradition in speaking of Agnes: *Haec* [Agnes] *duodecimorum annorum martyrium fecisse traditur.*[21] The uniformity of subject matter which marks these narratives, does not suggest that they are based on original material. It is possible to trace the literary sources from which they appear to be derived.

The many miraculous cures described in these narratives appear to be derived from *De civitate Dei* 22.8. The stories of destruction of temples may have their origin in the *Vita S. Martini* and the *Dialogues* of Sulpicius Severus.[22] The books of the Maccabees, particularly the fourth, apocryphal book, had a profound influence on Jewish and early Christian ideals of martyrdom, as W. H. C. Frend has well shown;[23] the complicated genealogical arrangements of stories such as the *Gesta*

---

[15] E.g., *BHL* 1906.

[16] E.g., *BHL* 273, 6632.

[17] E.g., *BHL* 107, 1938, 2832.

[18] E.g., *BHL* 1620, 4420.

[19] E.g., *BHL* 418, 1778, 1895.

[20] Lanzoni, *Le diocesi*, 1: 44-51.

[21] Ambrose, *De virginibus* 1.2.7, ed. O. Faller, *FlorPatr* 31 (Bonn 1933), p. 21.

[22] *De civitate Dei* 22.8, 2: 815-827; destruction of temples: e.g., *BHL* 7451-7453, 8457, 8469-8470; Sulpicius Severus, *Vita S. Martini* 14, 1: 284-285; *Dialogue* 2(3).8-9, pp. 206-207.

[23] W. H. C. Frend, *Martyrdom and Persecution in the Early Church* (Oxford 1965), pp. 44-47.

Abundii and the *Gesta XII Syrorum* (*BHL* 1620), may well exemplify the persistence of this influence in post-Constantinian times. The question of clerical celibacy was much in the air from the time of the Council of Elvira (ca. 300)[24] onwards and would achieve a new significance when the exiled Athanasius brought Eastern monastic and ascetic ideas to the West more than half a century later. These ideas were given literary form in Jerome's lives of Paul, Hilarion, and Malchus, and in his letter to Laeta it is possible to trace a connection between the *Vita Pauli* and the *Gesta Anthimii* (*BHL* 561-565) and also between the latter and the *Passio Sebastiani* (*BHL* 7453). The interest in forced marriages shown by the writers of the *Gesta* may have been aroused through Jerome's *Adversus Iovinianum* with its stress upon the superiority of virginity.[25]

What was the status and outlook of these writers? Both Dufourcq and Lanzoni suggest that the narratives may have had a monastic origin, but in this I believe they are mistaken.[26] Dufourcq suggests in his first volume that the birth and development of the stories of the martyrs were contemporary with the monastic movement of the sixth century and therefore with Cassiodorus, but as Lanzoni has shown, a number of the stories belong to the fifth century. The fact that the later stories are contemporary with Cassiodorus does not imply that they are connected with him; they show no evidence of the careful scholarship of Vivarium. The principal argument for their monastic origin is their emphasis on celibacy, but this would be equally appropriate to the secular clergy as authors. Indeed, by the time he reaches the end of his first volume, Dufourcq is obliged to admit that the tone of the narrative is more appropriate to them and to men in minor orders than to the monks.[27] Lanzoni believes that the later *Passiones* were the work of ecclesiastics or monks because the writers made wide use of words and phrases from the Bible and liturgical formulae.[28] This does not preclude monks, but on other grounds the *ecclesiastici* seem the more likely candidates for authorship. They may use biblical terminology – though its use does not

[24] Mansi 2.32, p. 11.

[25] Jerome, *Vita Pauli* 4-6, PL 23: 20-22; 17, PL 23: 28-30; *Vita Hilarionis* 2, *Vita di Ila-rione*, ed. A. A. R. Bastiaensen, VSanti 4 (Milan 1975), pp. 73-145, at pp. 74-75; *Vita Malchi* 6-10, PL 23: 58-62; *Ep.* 107, 2: 290-305 passim; *Contra Iovinianum* 1, PL 23: 221-332 passim.

[26] Dufourcq, *Étude*, 1: 30-31; Lanzoni, *Le diocesi*, 1: 41.

[27] Dufourcq, *Étude*, 1: 359-360.

[28] Lanzoni, *Le diocesi*, 1: 41; e.g., the doxologies closing the *Passiones* (see *BHL* 7558); the invocation of the so-called Jewish Trinity (see *BHL* 4420, John Penariensis); the repetition of a quasi-Nicene creed (see *BHL* 561-565).

seem to be as frequent or as striking as Lanzoni suggests – but they lack the strong biblical formation and outlook which Gregory and other monks derived from the daily *lectio divina*. Of the considerable number of fifth and sixth century passion narratives, only one bears the name of the author, the *Passio Bibianae* (*BHL* 1322-1323), which is by *Donatus subdiaconus regionarius de sede apostolica*. It is Roman and is assigned by Lanzoni to the sixth century. The contents and character of the other narratives suggest that their authors may well have been men of similar status.

The clerics who figure in the *Gesta* are generally secular priests, deacons, and subdeacons, whereas in the *Dialogues* we encounter principally monks and solitaries, though secular clerics and devout laymen are not excluded. The bishop is a figure common to both sets of material, but there are considerable differences of treatment. Both Gregory and the writers of the *Gesta* portray bishops as miracle-workers; indeed many of the stories are parallel, though a bishop is not always involved in both works. Clement, for example, like Cerbonius in the *Dialogues* (3.11, 2: 294-295), possesses the quality of remaining dry when surrounded with water. He also heals a blind man, and like Benedict (2.5, 2: 152-155) and Martin the hermit (3.16, 2: 328-329), he raises a spring in the desert. This similarity, however, is not to be used as evidence for the writers of the *Gesta* influencing Gregory or vice versa: the first story is a *topos* in Late Antiquity and the second indicates that both Gregory and the writers of the *Gesta* were working within the same framework of biblical typology. For Gregory, the miracles wrought by Fortunatus (1.10, 2: 92-111) for example, are indications of his personal holiness rather than emanations of his episcopal office, whereas the treatment of the bishop in the *Gesta* is designed for a purpose other than the display of personal holiness. The function of a bishop in the *Gesta* appears to consist of performing his episcopal duties, particularly presiding at the eucharist, and conducting confirmations and ordinations, so as to guarantee the authenticity of the orders of the lesser clergy concerned.[29] The aim of the writers was evidently to produce edifying material based on the system of church discipline prevalent in their own day and to describe a pattern of events conforming to their own ecclesiastical outlook. For example, Censurinus, a secret Christian, converts seventeen gaolers, who are baptized and confirmed by a priest – who conveniently happens to visit the prison – and later receive Holy Communion from him.[30] During

[29] See n. 32 below.
[30] Dufourcq, *Étude*, 1: 246.

another persecution, Marcellus and Marcellianus are made deacons, Tranquillinus is ordained priest, and Sebastian becomes a *defensor*. Concordius is visited in prison in Spoleto by bishop Anthemius, who ordains him at a convenient opportunity.[31] Indeed it seems as though the writers are trying to enhance their own status by making their heroes members of their own order, who, in some cases, associate with men more highly placed in the ecclesiastical hierarchy. They create two papal martyrs, Urban and Sixtus, whose fictitious fate is shared by two deacons and two priests, and two deacons respectively.[32] The heroes seem often to have been created by the writers upon so slender a basis as a name on a tombstone, a figure in local legend or a conflation of two or more holy characters.[33] Sometimes the narrative is based on wishful thinking rather than solid evidence: the populace is made to side with the martyr, though in point of fact, he or she was often lonely and sad.[34] The reason for this seems to be a desire to enable their ordinary Christian readers to identify with the Church in past ages. The writers were in fact creating in the past the situation of the Church in their own day: they were transferring to earlier times the contemporary "comprehensive" Church, whereas in fact the Church in the age of persecutions was a small, highly dedicated group. It is possible that some of them may have read Rufinus's translation of Eusebius and have thus formed the opinion that the faith must have spread as rapidly in the West as in the East. They tended to believe that the diocesan organization in Italy of their own day existed in early, perhaps Sub-Apostolic, times.

In fairness, these men must have had difficulty in their boyhood in pursuing a traditional Roman education in times of war, pestilence, and famine. This might account for some of their numerous historical errors; for example, there is a tendency to group under the reign of the same emperor persecutions which are alleged to have occurred in the same district, and a vagueness about the chronological order of the emperors.[35]

With the somewhat superficial and mechanical view of the episcopate and the sacraments of confirmation and holy orders expressed by the

[31] Ibid., pp. 186-187; *BHL* 1906; Dufourcq, *Etude*, 3: 36-37.

[32] Dufourcq, *Étude*, 1: 176-177.

[33] E.g., Calocerus and Parthenius, Dufourcq, *Étude*, 1: 185; for conflation, see Urban and Sixtus, pace n. 32 above.

[34] E.g., Aemilianus, *BHL* 107; cf. John Penariensis (*confessor*), *BHL* 4420; for a martyr without popular support, see H. A. Musurillo, ed., *The Acts of the Christian Martyrs* (Oxford 1972), pp. 244-259.

[35] E.g., *BHL* 1620, 2838, 4281; see H. Delehaye, *Les passions des martyrs et les genres littéraires*, 2nd rev. ed., SHG 13b (Brussels 1966), pp. 171-177.

writers of the *Gesta*, we need to contrast Gregory's conception of the office of the bishop and of ordination. The bishop in the *Gesta* is a kind of *deus ex machina*, who appears at convenient moments to administer the sacraments or, less frequently, to perform a miracle. He is not shown to us as a man of prayer or a pastor of souls, nor does he appear to exercise any diocesan jurisdiction. Gregory's conception, if we take all his works into consideration, is both wider and deeper. It is true that in the *Dialogues* the thaumaturgical aspect predominates; we find the figures of Boniface, who performed miracles akin to those of the prophets (1.9, 2: 78-81, 88-89); Fortunatus (1.10, 2: 92-111), Cassius (3.6, 2: 276-279), and Datius (3.4, 2: 270-273), the exorcists; Sabinus (3.5, 2: 274-277), who rendered poison harmless, to name only a few. In fact the only bishop not named as a miracle-worker or a prophet is Paulinus (3.1, 2: 256-267), who is cited as an example of humility and self-sacrifice. It is from Gregory's own correspondence and from the *Liber regulae pastoralis* that his deeper conception of the office of a bishop emerges. He sees it as the source of tensions between the desire for contemplative prayer and the call of God to an individual to be a ruler of the Church, both as an administrator and as chief pastor of his diocese.

Finally, we need to consider who were the readers of the later *Passiones*, and why they believed such reading to be important. We have to distinguish first between public and private reading. It was permitted by the Council of Carthage in 393 that the *Passiones* of the martyrs might be read in churches on the anniversaries of their deaths.[36] These were, of course, the genuine passion narratives written at the time, such as the *Passio* of Perpetua and her companions. However, as time went on, this permission was taken as a precedent for the reading of the fictitious fifth and sixth century narratives, as we learn from a letter of Pope Hadrian I to Charlemagne in 794.[37] The practice probably arose considerably earlier, as Bede, who died in 735, included a number of these *Passiones* in his martyrology, which was to serve as a pattern for those of the ninth century.[38] There are also references to them, affirming that they were read in churches, in the *De virginitate* of Aldhelm,[39] who died in 709, but we have no definite evidence as to when or where the practice of reading the

---

[36] Mansi 3.36, p. 924.

[37] *Epp. Hadriani* 1.2.18, *Epistolae selectae pontificum Romanorum Carolo Magno et Ludovico Pio regnantibus scriptae*, ed. K. Hampe, MGH *Epp.* 5 (Berlin 1899), pp. 3-57, at p. 49.

[38] PL 94: 799-1147; *AnBoll* 49 (1931): 51-101.

[39] Aldhelm, *De virginitate* 50-52, ed. R. Ewald, MGH AA 15, pp. 211-471, at pp. 305-310.

later *Passiones* publicly began; it may well have been considerably earlier than the beginning of the eighth century.

It is a mistake to assume that works such as the *Gesta* or the *Dialogues* were written only for an uneducated audience. As Vogüé points out,[40] the style of the *Dialogues* is far from "popular," and we may assume that they were read by a similar class of reader to the *Gesta*. There is evidence that the latter had a number of distinguished readers from the sixth century onwards. These included Avitus of Vienne (d. ca. 519), Ennodius of Pavia (ca. 473-521), Venantius Fortunatus (ca. 530-610), and Gregory of Tours, who was acquainted with the stories of Clement of Rome, Chrysanthus, Gervase and Protase, Nazarius and Celsus, and Felix of Nola, and perhaps also with those of Pancras, Laurence, John and Paul, and Victor of Milan.[41] Last but not least, there was Gregory himself, as we shall see in the next section.

The reading of the *Passiones* by less eminent persons was also encouraged. Cassiodorus urged his monks to engage in it.[42] Certainly the study of the *Gesta* by monks and *clerici* did much to influence subsequent generations of hagiographers, particularly in Merovingian Gaul.

C. Gregory's Relationship to the Martyr-stories

It is evident from Gregory's own writings that he was not ignorant of the *Passiones*. In a letter to Eulogius of Alexandria, dated 598 (*Reg.* 8.28, 2: 29), he states that he has never heard of the work containing the *Passiones* of all the martyrs by Eusebius of Caesarea, of which Eulogius has requested a copy, but that there are available in Rome two works which deal with the martyrs: 1. *pauca quaedam in unius codicis volumine collecta*; 2. a calendar: *paene omnium martyrum distinctis per dies singulos passionibus collecta in uno codice habemus.*[43] Probably it was from the first of these collections that he was able to read certain of the passion narratives, to which he refers in his writings: the passion of Donatus, who

---

[40] *Dialogues* introd., 1: 34-35.

[41] See Lanzoni, *Le diocesi*, 1: 72-73; Avitus of Vienne, *Carmina* 6, 503-533, *Poemata*, ed. R. Peiper, MGH AA 6 (2) (Berlin 1883), pp. 289-290; Ennodius of Pavia, e.g., 349 (*Carmina* 1.18), *Opera*, ed. F. Vogel, MGH AA 7 (Berlin 1885), p. 254; Venantius Fortunatus, e.g., *Carmina* 1.2, 13-14, ed. F. Leo, MGH AA 4 (1) (Berlin 1881), pp. 7-92, at p. 8; 4.26, 97-108, at pp. 97-98; 8.1.46, at p. 179; 4.1-36, at pp. 192-193; Gregory of Tours, *Liber in gloria martyrum* 35, p. 60; 37, pp. 61-62; 46, p. 69; 60, p. 79; 103, p. 107; possibly 38, pp. 62-63; 39, p. 163; 41, pp. 65-66.

[42] *Institutiones* 1.32.4, ed. R. A. B. Mynors (Oxford 1937), p. 80.

[43] Identified by Dufourcq, *Étude*, 1: 81-92, with Cod. Pal. Vind. Lat. 357, vol. 2, but his arguments are not fully convincing.

is mentioned in 1.7 (2: 68-69) as the prototype of Nonnosus who, like Donatus, was able to put together a glass lamp by placing the fragments upon the altar and praying; by implication, the passions of Peter and Paul and Felicitas (*Reg.* 4.30, 1: 264; *Homiliae in evangelia* 1.3.3-4, PL 76: 1086-1089).

It is not, however, possible to accept the view of Dufourcq that Gregory's spiritual formation and outlook as an adult were achieved through the influence of the *Gesta* on his early training.[44] Dufourcq cites as evidence his upbringing by a pious widowed mother, who subsequently entered a convent, his selling of his possessions in order to found seven monasteries, his own retirement into a monastery, his refusal, at first, to accept the papacy, and his continual pining for the contemplative, monastic life, which he had been obliged to leave. In his sermons, Gregory stresses the transitoriness of life in this world and frequently praised the virtue of chastity, for example in *Homiliae in evangelia* 2.37.3 (PL 76: 1213).

Let us now consider Dufourcq's arguments. In the first place they are largely based upon the lives of Gregory written by Paul the Deacon (eighth century) and John the Deacon (ninth century)[45] at a time when a regular pattern of hagiography had become established. In Late Antiquity and the early Middle Ages the pious widowed mother had become a stock figure.[46] Even if we place as high an historical value on these writings as Dufourcq does, it is by no means certain that Gregory grew up as a fatherless boy; Paul the Deacon says that Gregory came into property on the death of his parents, John, that he entered into his inheritance, *patre orbatus*. Since John has preserved the details of the story of Silvia, apparently a widow, bringing Gregory a silver dish of vegetables daily, it may well be that he had access to Roman traditions about Gregory's family which were denied to Paul.[47] The balance is therefore in his favour. Taking the two *Vitae* together, one forms the impression that Gregory was already an adult when his father died and he inherited the property.

If we consider the earlier history of female monasticism in Rome, it seems unlikely that the foundation of the two private monasteries occupied by Silvia and by Gregory's three paternal aunts, Tarsilla,

---

[44] Dufourcq, *Étude*, 1: 378-381.

[45] Paul the Deacon, *Vita S. Gregorii Magni*, ed. H. Grisar, *ZKTh* 11 (1887): 158-173; John the Deacon, PL 75: 159-192.

[46] F. Graus, *Volk, Herrscher und Heiliger im Reich der Merowinger* (Prague 1965), pp. 69, 117.

[47] Paul the Deacon, *Vita S. Gregorii Magni*, p. 163; John the Deacon, 1.5, PL 75: 65.

Aemiliana, and Gordiana (*Homiliae in evangelia* 2.38.15, PL 76: 1290-1292; *Dialogue* 4.7, 3: 68-71), was inspired by the teachings of the *Gesta*. These domestic monasteries may have been formed in accordance with the traditions established by Paula, Eustochium, and Melania in the days of Jerome,[48] which may well have continued to provide, during the fifth and sixth centuries, a framework for the lives of upper-class Roman ladies remaining in their own homes as nuns. It is perhaps no coincidence that Gregory's family lived in the same district of Rome as Paula had done; the tradition of the earlier domestic monastery may well have persisted there for a century and a half. When Gregory took over the family home for St Andrew's, it would be natural for his mother to pursue her life as a religious in a smaller abode not far away.[49]

The foundation of the seven monasteries is obviously linked with the question of Gregory's *conversio*. Gregory himself says nothing about selling his goods, and we have no information at all about five of the monasteries which he is reported to have founded in Sicily, in addition to the *monasterium meum* (*nostrum*) *Panormitanum*, which he mentions on two occasions (*Reg.* 5.4, 1: 284; 9.20, 2: 54). The sale of goods by a convert (doubtless inspired by Matt. 19.21) is a commonplace in late antique and early medieval hagiography. Gregory cites two monks of aristocratic family, Speciosus and Gregory (4.9, 3: 42-43), as having done this; an earlier example, which he may well have known, is that of Antony in the *Vita Antonii*.[50] This gesture on his part cannot therefore be attributed to the influence of the *Gesta*.

To conclude our treatment of the less complex of Dufourcq's arguments, the love of chastity and depreciation of marriage are well-known as *topoi*, quite independently of the *Gesta*. Marriage is looked upon by the hagiographers as an obstacle to real holiness, which can be achieved by a married woman only if her husband dies or if she abandons him to enter a convent. Gregory may perhaps have known the examples of both men and women cited in the works of Gregory of Tours.[51] His reading of *Vita S. Antonii*, of *Apophthegmata patrum latinorum* and of Cassian (of which more will be said in chapter six) would familiarize him with Eastern Christian ideas on this subject. The *Gesta* could only serve to

[48] *Ep.* 108, *Epitaphium sanctae Paulae, In memoria di Paola*, ed. J. W. Smit, VSanti 4 (Milan 1975), pp. 148-156 (CSEL 57, pp. 306-350).

[49] John the Deacon, 1.9, PL 75: 66.

[50] *Vita Antonii* 2, pp. 10-11; see Graus, "Volk, Herrscher und Heiliger," pp. 288-290.

[51] A. de Vogüé, "Grégoire le Grand, lecteur de Grégoire de Tours?" Gregory of Tours, *Liber historiarum* 3.7, p. 105; *Vitae patrum* 16 (1), pp. 274-275; 19 (1), pp. 286-287.

confirm him in beliefs that were held by Christians throughout the Mediterranean world during the sixth century.

When we come to consider Gregory's *conversio*, his reluctance to assume high office on account of his love of the *vita contemplativa*, and his strongly eschatological outlook, we are on more delicate ground. The first of these two are certainly *topoi*, but in the case of Gregory, the *topoi* appear to correspond to the reality.

Conversion in earlier writing was regarded in two different ways: as the conversion from paganism to Christianity, such as was the experience of Perpetua and her companions; or as the conversion of persons who had a Christian background but were notoriously of evil life, which they had been unwilling to change because of the difficulties and responsibilities involved. Of these, Augustine is the supreme example. Alongside the genuine converts, there were people who nominally became Christians when it was safe and fashionable for them to do so, from the reign of Constantine onwards, but did not undergo any real change of heart. The existence of this mass of nominal Christians was a contributory factor to the rise of monasticism. Numbers of what would today be called "committed Christians," repelled by the lukewarmness and hypocrisy of secular congregations in the towns, retired into monasteries, sometimes in towns, sometimes in remote areas, where they could practise their religion more earnestly. For such people, conversion meant neither the experience of Paul on the road to Damascus nor the turning to Christ of a Perpetua or an Augustine, but the entry into a new form of Christian living, the monastic or eremitic life. Sometimes this might be combined with a conversion in the Pauline sense, as appears to have been the case with Antony,[52] but in others it was a deliberate step. This explains Gregory's curious phrase in his letter to Leander: *diu longeque conversionis gratiam distuli*. The assumption of the monastic habit was regarded as a most important sign of conversion, and Gregory is distressed because he persisted in the wearing of lay clothes for some time after his decision to enter the monastic life (*Moralia*, ep. miss. 1). We know little of the processes by which he reached it. From this letter it appears that Leander was familiar with them as the result of their talks together in Constantinople twenty years earlier; there was therefore no need for Gregory to describe them again. Certainly his conversion was very different from that of Augustine, even though he may have experienced the same kind of preliminary tensions. Dagens suggests that there is a certain kind of

[52] *Vita Antonii* 2, pp. 9-10.

parallelism between the conversion of Benedict and the conversion of
Gregory, and that in Benedict's conversion, Gregory finds the antithesis of
his own, because Benedict did not postpone the *conversionis gratiam*.[53]
This is, to some extent, the case, but Dagens does not stress sufficiently the
difference between the conversion of Gregory and those of Antony, Benedict, or men such as Exhilaratus and Theopropus. Though these others
may have been men of good family or, at any rate, in comfortable
circumstances, they were not in the situation of Gregory, who had the
prospect of a successful career, and was, moreover, the occupant of a post
carrying great personal responsibilities. We can only imagine the agonies
of deciding between the claims of his fellow-citizens and those of the
monastic life in the circumstances of sixth-century Rome, but it seems
clear that he did not undergo that "instant conversion" so often described
in the *Gesta*.[54] Gregory's family may or may not have been in the habit of
reading the *Gesta*; what is certain is that he had a strongly Christian
background and some practical knowledge of monasticism in his own
family. The example of his living aunts might be as potent a factor as the
stories of people long dead. Moreover, there is the theological aspect of the
matter. Gregory, like his master Augustine, believed that the convert was
sought out by the grace of God; hence the frequent use of the phrase
conversionis gratia, for example, in the *Moralia* (ep. miss., 1).

"The reluctant bishop" is regarded as a *topos*, but there have always
been holy and humble men who have been unwilling to accept the
responsibility of high ecclesiastical office. Are the protests of Augustine,
Ambrose, Gregory of Nazianzus, Martin and now Gregory the Great,
merely *confessiones humilitatis*, made as a matter of form ? [55]

So far as Gregory the Great is concerned, there are passages in the *Liber
regulae pastoralis* which are reminiscent of the *De fuga* of Gregory of
Nazianzus,[56] but this work reveals his own mystical temperament, which
has such a marked preference for the *vita contemplativa*, and towards

[53] Dagens, "Structure et expérience," pp. 303-306.

[54] E.g., *BHL* 273, 1938; Dufourcq, *Étude*, 3: 129-132 (a Latin text not previously
published in its untouched form).

[55] E.g., Augustine: Possidius, *Vita S. Augustini* 8, *Vita di Agostino*, ed. A. A. R.
Bastiaensen, VSanti 3 (Milan 1975), pp. 127-141, at pp. 148-149; Ambrose: Paulinus, *Vita
Ambrosii* 8-9, pp. 63-65; Gregory of Nazianzus, *Orationes* 2, PG 35: 407-514; *Orationes* 1,
Tyrannii Rufini orationum Gregorii Nazianzieni novem interpretatio, ed. A. Engelbrecht,
CSEL 36 (Vienna 1910, repr. New York 1966), pp. 1-10; Sulpicius Severus, *Vita S. Martini*
9, 1: 270-271. See also chapter four, n. 79.

[56] Among numerous examples of *confessiones humilitatis* may be cited: Venantius
Fortunatus, *Carmina* 2.9, 1-15, pp. 37-38; Ennodius of Pavia, *Ep*. 317, p. 236; 323,
pp. 240-241; 413, p. 288.

which Dufourcq is lacking in sympathy and understanding. It is this fundamental lack of understanding which leads Dufourcq to pass such a superficial judgement.

Two factors need to be remembered in connection with Gregory's view of contemplation. In his own case, it is not a merely negative longing to return to the monastic life, because he is wearied by a burden of administration not of his own choosing, as Dufourcq seems to imply. On the contrary, he sees it as a dynamic, positive quality which enriches all aspects of the Christian life. The autobiographical fragment in *Homiliae in Ezechielem* (1.11.5-6, 171) gives us some conception of the strains and stresses of his daily life; it is not surprising that his mind was *scissa ac dilaniata* and that he feels regret for the peace of the monastery of St Andrew (*Dialogue* 1, prol. 2, 1: 12-13). He believes, however, that men may be called by God to the active life as well as to the contemplative life; both lives are good, but the contemplative life is the life of greater merit (*Homiliae in Ezechielem* 1.3.9, 37). Taking Martha as the type of active life and Mary as the contemplative, he points out that Jesus praises Mary, but does not rebuke Martha. Mary has chosen *optimam partem*, but Martha has chosen *bonam* (*Homiliae in Ezechielem* 2.2.9, 230). There may even be cases where it is better that contemplation should be eliminated altogether (*Moralia* 6.37, 327). Gregory interprets *contemplatio* as the *oculus dexter* of Matt. 5.29, which is to be plucked out if it offends. It is better to practise a good *vita activa*, without contemplation, rather than to pursue false contemplation.

Gregory recognizes that certain people, though contemplatives, are driven by the necessities of office to lead a life of activity; such people must keep a secret place in their hearts in which they can take refuge (*Moralia* 23.20, PL 76: 273-274). Contemplation cannot be separated from love of neighbour; the contemplative must be ready to perform acts of charity (*Moralia* 19.25, 991-992). They are not to be distressed if they feel spiritually diminished as the result of their charitable acts, since

> illud verbum per quod constant omnia creata, ut prodesset hominibus, assumpta humanitate, voluit paulominus angelis minorari (ibid.).

The *rector*, that is, the bishop or pastor, is to combine the active and contemplative life:

> sit rector singulis compassione proximus, prae cunctis contemplatione suspensus (*Liber regulae pastoralis* 2.5, PL 77: 32; cf. 2.1, ibid., 27).

He is to resemble St Paul, who after ascending to the Third Heaven, returned to earth to deal with the problems of fornication, or the patriarch

Jacob, who at Bethel watched the angels both ascending the ladder to God and descending again, or Moses, who emerged from contemplation in the Tabernacle to be occupied with the care of the sick (*Liber regulae pastoralis*, 2.5, PL 77: 33). Indeed it may be positively wrong for the *rector* to shun the service of his neighbours through his eagerness for contemplation (*Liber regulae pastoralis* 1.6, PL 77: 19).

Perhaps a clue to Gregory's own attitude to his acceptance of high office, which would curtail the time available for contemplation, is to be found a little later in the same chapter of the *Liber regulae pastoralis*:

> neque enim vere humilis est, qui superni nutus arbitrium ut debeat praesse intelligit, et tamen praesse contemnit. Sed divinis dispositionibus subditus, atque a vitio obstinationis alienus, cum sibi regiminis culmen imperatur, si iam donis praeventus est, quibus et aliis prosit, et ex corde debet fugere, et invitus obedire (*Liber regulae pastoralis* 1.6, PL 77: 19-20).

Secondly, Gregory's teaching is in the mainstream of Christian tradition about contemplative prayer. This is not the place for a detailed account of his links with his predecessors in the contemplative life, but there are two striking examples of his use of earlier imagery and of his adoption of earlier teaching.

Reference has already been made to one of these examples, Martha as the type of the active life and Mary of the contemplative. This is found in Augustine's sermons and in Cassian. The second is the use of Leah as the type of the active life and Rachel of the contemplative (*Homiliae in Ezechielem* 2.2.10, 231-232). This allegory is also used by Augustine in discussing the kind of contemplative life that may be lived in the world. The link between contemplation and compunction, which Gregory owes to Eastern Christian teaching, will be discussed in chapter six.

Both the positive character of Gregory's teaching on contemplation, linked with the older Christian tradition, and the profundity of his conception of the episcopal office (with which we have already dealt in this chapter) combine to indicate how unlikely it is that the *Gesta* could have made any appreciable contribution to his spiritual formation.

While not calling in question the sincerity of his conversion and his decision to change his career, it seems worthwhile at this juncture to try to see whether any more practical or worldly considerations could also have influenced his choice. It might well be the case that he had found satisfaction in his administrative work as a civil servant but at the same time saw it as a blind alley, now that the possibility of a career in the imperial civil service had disappeared. He might also have seen that entry into the service of the Church might provide wider opportunities for the exercise of his talents and for the restoration of the glory of the city of which he was so loving and loyal a son. Such a view would be compatible with his essential *Romanitas* as well as his personal sense of vocation, but we have no solid evidence for it.

D. LITERARY EVIDENCE FOR THE RELATIONSHIP
BETWEEN THE *GESTA MARTYRUM* AND THE *DIALOGUES*

The miracle-story, which formed part of the *Vita* of a holy man, was a literary *genre* scarcely known in Western Christian literature before the mid-fourth century. The rise of monasticism in the East and the knowledge of it brought to the West by the exiled Athanasius were undoubtedly contributory factors to its origin and subsequent popularity. The *Vita Antonii* showed the Christian public the lives of "the new martyrs," the monks, and the miracles wrought by their leader Antony. The ideal of monastic sacrifice and the miracle-working powers of the monks were further popularized by Jerome's three religious romances.

The notion that the monks were the contemporary equivalent of the martyrs was one solution of a problem which had beset the Church from 315 onwards. It was perhaps the destruction of Jerusalem in 70 and the subsequent dispersal of the Christian community there which caused an awakening of interest in the earlier heroes, not only in the Apostles and known martyrs, but also in the Three Holy Children and the Maccabees, who had long been regarded as martyrs by the Jews. There was even a kind of envy of the martyrs, which created a desire for voluntary martyrdom: we have only to think of Origen, as a child, and of Antony.[57] Once Christianity was established as the official religion, the Church was deprived of a most important focus of devotion and inspiration. Apart from encouraging the idea that the monks were the successors of the martyrs, the Church could adopt three other possible courses: 1. to reveal further information about existing martyrs and to stimulate interest in them by means of relics, whether already available, or newly discovered; 2. to "discover" new martyrs, an activity popular in Merovingian Gaul where there had been few martyrdoms;[58] 3. to create the portrait of a new type of Christian sanctity, the *confessor*, or *martyr occultus*. Broadly speaking, the authors of the *Gesta* concentrated on the first and second of these options and Gregory on the second (to a certain extent) and the third.

[57] Eusebius, *Historia ecclesiastica* 6.2, pp. 520-521; *Vita Antonii* 46, pp. 94-97.
[58] See Graus, "Volk, Herrscher und Heiliger," pp. 92-95.

Since it was not Gregory's intention to dwell on the past, he does not give much information about the martyrs of former ages. There are in fact only three stories of such people in the *Dialogues*. The first is that of Iuticus (3.38, 2: 428-431), which was told to Gregory by his friend Redemptus, bishop of Ferentis. Redemptus was spending the night asleep on the tomb of the martyr Iuticus in the church at Ferentis, which was dedicated to him, when the martyr appeared to him in a vision, saying three times, *Finis venit universae carni*. Iuticus may well be identified with Eutychius, a martyr in the *Gesta*, who was buried at Ferentis, but this story does not occur in the *Gesta*. A similar story is told of Faustinus the martyr (4.54, 3: 180-181), who, in a vision, told the verger of the church at Brescia (where he was buried) to warn the bishop to rid the church of the body of the unworthy Valerianus; otherwise the bishop would be dead within thirty days. The third story also relates to a vision, that of the martyrs Juvenal and Eleutherius, who came to summon Probus, bishop of Reate, to heaven (4.13, 3: 54-55). Juvenal (*BHL* 4614) figures in the *Gesta* as a saint of Narnia, but not as a martyr, which perhaps indicates that Gregory was following an alternative tradition. There may also be some significance in the fact that Gregory refers, in a letter (*Reg.* 2.4, 1: 103) written in 591 to the bishop of Narnia, to the importance of converting the local heretics (presumably Arians). We know from *Dialogue* 3.6 (2: 276-277) that there were many citizens of Narnia in Rome in 593 (presumably exiles from Lombard rule), and it may be that the combination of these two factors led to the growth of a cult of Juvenal in Gregory's day.

All these stories are examples of a type which occurs elsewhere in the West. Gregory himself provides another instance of a person receiving a vision when half-asleep (4.59, 3: 198-199) and so does Sulpicius Severus.[59] Even closer parallels are provided by Gregory of Tours, describing apparitions of saints to persons sleeping on their tombs and also the voices of saints emanating from their tombs; such pronouncements seem to be a normal feature of late antique and early medieval hagiography.[60]

Since it was Gregory's intention to show that there were holy men in Italy in comparatively recent times, it is not surprising that he was more interested in portraying modern martyrs and confessors than in delving

---

[59] *Ep.* 2.2-3, *Libri qui supersunt* [incl. *Epistolae*], ed. C. Halm, CSEL 1 (Vienna 1866), pp. 324-327.

[60] E.g., Gatianus's tomb: *Liber in gloria confessorum* 4, p. 301; Germanus's tomb: ibid., 40, pp. 322-323.

back into the past. He is evolving a definition of martyrdom appropriate to conditions of church life in the sixth century. He believes that there are two kinds of martyr, *in occulto* and *in publico* (3.26, 2: 370-371). The *martyr in occulto* is the individual who would readily accept martyrdom if there were persecutions; he is typified in Scripture by James and John, the sons of Zebedee, who expressed their willingness to drink of the cup of suffering (Matt. 20.22).[61]

Gregory extends this teaching in two subsequent chapters to cover the case of innocent people slain by their enemies. He tells the stories of two martyrdoms which occurred outside Italy (3.31, 2: 384-391; 32.2, 2: 390-393), with which we have already dealt in chapter one. The remaining stories of modern martyrdoms deal with persons murdered by the Lombards or the Goths. Of the stories of the Lombards, only one has a named informant: Valentio, who subsequently became head of Gregory's monastery in Rome, but had previously been in charge of a monastery in the province of Valeria. He related to Gregory that when the Lombards were devastating the countryside, they hanged two of his monks on the same tree. On the evening of their death, their corpses were heard singing psalms by their murderers (4.22, 3: 78-79). In the next chapters, Gregory tells how Soranus, abbot of Sura in the same province, having given all the resources of the monastery to the Lombard invaders, was asked for gold. When the Lombards found that he had none, he fled into the woods and took refuge in a hollow tree, but the Lombards found him and murdered him. As his body fell to the ground, the whole mountain shook. The Lombards also captured and beheaded a deacon in the neighbouring province of Marsia (4.23-24, 3: 78-79). In this case the source is

> quibusdam religiosis quoque viris adtestantibus,

which suggests an oral tradition.

The other three stories of the Lombards appear to cover a different part of the country, but neither the situation nor Gregory's source are explicit. The nearer he approaches his own time, the more tenuous does Gregory's link with his informants become. The informants about the deaths of forty *rustici* who refused to eat meat which had been sacrificed,

> (quid itaque isti nisi martyres fuerunt, qui ne, vetitum comedendo, conditorem suum offenderunt, elegerunt gladiis vitam finire?)

---

[61] Other examples of bloodless martyrs: *Vita Antonii* 46-47, pp. 94-98; Caesarius of Arles, *Sermones* 41.3.3, *Opera*, ed. G. Morin, 2 vols, CCSL 103, 104 (Turnholt 1953), 1: 181-182.

and the considerable proportion of the four hundred captured by the Lombards, who refused to worship a goat's head (3.28, 2: 374-377), are described as *hii testantes, qui interesse potuerunt*.[62] The authorities for the final story are

vicini eius sacerdotes, mira veritate et simplicitate praediti,

but it is one which seems to have been told under different guises all over the Mediterranean area from the late fourth century onwards. As Vogüé points out, the scriptural type appears to be Jeroboam, whose hand extended against the prophet (*virum Dei*), became withered and immobile but was later released (1 [3] Kings 13.4).[63] Gregory's description of Sanctulus, who offered his life to the Lombards in exchange for that of a deacon, and of the executioner whose arm was struck rigid is paralleled by two stories told by Gregory of Tours.[64] The details differ slightly, but the basic facts are the same. In the first of these, the attacker is a Frank, but in the second, he is a Lombard, as in Gregory's story (3.37, 2: 418-423). In each case the victim is an essentially holy person; in Gregory of Tours' stories he is a solitary and in Gregory the Great's a priest. When he is about to be beheaded, a mysterious power renders the executioner's arm immobile. He allows the victim to go free and in two of the stories he is ultimately converted to better ways. A very similar story is told by Sulpicius Severus in connection with one of the Aedui, who attacked Martin after he had destroyed a pagan temple.[65]

As the *Dialogues* did not appear until 593-594 (and there seems no good reason for rejecting the generally accepted date), the year in which Gregory of Tours died, and if the *Libri historiarum* were completed in 592, the possibility that Gregory of Tours knew the *Dialogues* is eliminated. We cannot rule out the possibility that Gregory the Great had read the *Libri historiarum*, but there scarcely seems sufficient time for the text to have arrived in Rome and for Gregory to have perused it before writing the *Dialogues*. Hospitius is mentioned in the *Liber in gloria confessorum*, which appeared ca. 588, but nothing is said of his encounter

---

[62] Little appears to be known of the pagan religion of the Lombards, but possibly it may have been a form of the worship of Dionysus or of Pan, both of which cults involved a goat. See *PW*, art. "Schweige."

[63] See *Dialogue* 3.37, 2: 420-421, at p. 421, n. 15.

[64] See *Liber historiarum* 2.37, pp. 86-87; 6.6, pp. 272-275; cf. *Dialogue* 3.37, 2: 418-423; in the second story we are told by Gregory of Tours only that the executioner promised to kill no more Christians. The convert gaoler or executioner is a *topos* of hagiography; see F. Graus, "Das Gewalt bei den Anfangen des Feudalismus....," *JWG* (1961): 94-99; "Volk, Herrscher und Heiliger," p. 102.

[65] Sulpicius Severus, *Vita S. Martini* 15, 1: 284-287.

with the Lombards.[66] We are therefore left with two possibilities, which do not appear to be mutually exclusive: the two Gregories were drawing upon a common source; or they were both making use of a story which was in general circulation. The most likely common source appears to be the *Vita S. Martini*. We know definitely that Gregory of Tours was acquainted with the works of Sulpicius Severus, and on the evidence of the miracle-stories in *Dialogue* 2 it seems highly probable that Gregory the Great was also.[67] Since the story also appears in the writing of Paulinus of Milan, Palladius, and John Moschus,[68] it may well be that Sulpicius Severus and the two Gregories were all drawing on a story which was current in the Mediterranean area from the late fourth century onwards. If this hypothesis is correct, it does not strengthen the case for Gregory the Great being a reader of Gregory of Tours; on the contrary it suggests that he was making use of traditional material which had been brought to his notice by informants, though his shaping of it may have been inspired by his reading of Sulpicius Severus, *Vita S. Martini*.

When one reflects upon Gregory the Great's treatment of Italians of a near-contemporary period who have been martyred by the Lombards, three interesting points emerge. First, these men are martyrs of a new genre; they are Christians who were put to death for their faith without any kind of legal justification. They are not accused of breaking the law nor given any kind of trial, but are hanged or beheaded by gangs of lawless invaders, without being afforded any opportunity to defend themselves or to testify to their faith. In this respect they differ both from the real martyrs of the earliest centuries and from the idealized versions of them, furnished by the writers of the *Gesta*. In fact, Gregory is probably describing the kinds of deaths which really occurred, but is adding to the accounts based on local oral tradition and supplied to him by his informants, stories of holy men, which he has derived either from other Italian or Gallic traditions or from literary sources, and which seem appropriate to the occasion. Second, there is a complete absence of stories of the *inventio* of either bodies or relics of earlier martyrs. For example, he says nothing of the finding of the tombs of the martyrs Chrysanthus and Daria, when Rome became Christian, which was reported by Gregory of Tours in the *Liber in gloria martyrum*,[69] or of the bodies of Gervase and

---

[66] *Liber in gloria confessorum* 95, p. 359.

[67] *Liber historiarum* 10.3, p. 257; e.g., *Dialogue* 2.28-29, 2: 216-219; Sulpicius Severus, *Dialogue* 2 (3), pp. 200-201.

[68] E.g., *Vita Ambrosii* 20, pp. 78-79; *Heraclidis paradisus* 38, PL 74: 326; John Moschus, *Pratum spirituale* 15, PG 87 (3): 2861.

[69] *Liber in gloria martyrum* 37, pp. 61-62.

Protase at Milan, as the result of a revelation to Ambrose in a dream.[70]
Third, his accounts of the Italian martyrs appear to owe nothing to the
Gesta; neither the scene nor the time is parallel. We have already noted
the difference between Gregory and the writers of the *Gesta* in their
attitude towards the episcopate and episcopal ordination. The *Gesta* may
tell us something about the mentality and outlook of their sixth-century
clerical authors, but their characters and *mise en scène* belong to an earlier
age, even though many anachronisms occur. In conclusion, Gregory's
stories of the Italians martyred by the Lombards show us something of his
concern for living agents. The holy man is someone who has lived and
worked in his own country, and his life is to be an inspiration to living
Christians in his, Gregory's, own day.

The case of Herculanus, who was murdered by the Goths, is somewhat
different, in that we have two accounts of the same events, one in the
Dialogues and the other in the *Gesta*, which differ in detail, but which
display certain verbal similarities. In both *Dialogue* 3.13 (2: 299-303) and
the *Gesta Abundii*, Totila has been besieging Perugia for seven years and
has finally captured the city by starving it out, but thereafter there are
differences. In the *Gesta* Totila himself orders Herculanus to be cleft from
head to heels and his head to be put on view; a strip of skin like a thong is
to be cut from the crown of his head to his heels. In the *Dialogue* 3.13 (2:
300-301) similar gruesome directions are given not by the king, but by a
comes. In both narratives, a dead baby was buried with the bishop. In the
Gesta both bodies were found a year later to be incorrupt, whereas in the
Dialogues, after an interval of only forty days, the bishop's body was
found to be incorrupt, whereas the baby's was not.

From what we have seen already of Gregory's use of his sources, it
seems unlikely that he copied the story directly from the *Gesta*. It was
clearly his practice to rely on material supplied by informants, in this case,
Floridus, bishop of Tiferniae Tiberinae. There remain two possibilities:
Gregory and the writers of the *Gesta* were using a common source; or the
writer of the *Gesta* was copying Gregory. In favour of the "common
source" theory, it may, in the first place, be urged that in both narratives
Totila is described as *perfidus rex*. This, however may have been a stock
epithet, comparable to *pius Aeneas* or *fidus Achates*. More suggestive of a
common source is the wording of the directions to the people of Perugia:

> A vertice usque ad calcaneum corrigiam tolle,

---

[70] *Vita Ambrosii* 14, pp. 70-71.

says the comes in *Dialogue* 3.13, a phrase which is rendered by the writer of the *Gesta Abundii* in *oratio obliqua*:

> tunc iussit ei corrigiam usque ad calcaneum decoriari.

This last argument, however, is really more strongly in favour of the second possibility which seems to be the solution. The narrative in the *Dialogues* is a straightforward story, probably as told by bishop Floridus to Gregory. One can imagine the local story-teller pausing, and then bringing out with relish, the words,

> A vertice usque ad calcaneum corrigiam tolle,

a phrase which Gregory, with his skill as a literary artist, would retain *verbatim* for its dramatic effect. A Gregorian touch is that the bishop was originally a monk, but was called from the monstery to become a priest:

> ex conversatione monasterii ad sacerdotalis ordinis gratiam deductus;

the writer of the *Gesta*, however, has taken over Gregory's narrative, but has raised the status of the person giving directions for the slaughter of his hero, thus emphasizing the latter's importance, which is increased further by making the end of the story even more miraculous. Lacking in literary feeling, he reduces the dramatic effect of these gruesome directions by transferring them to *oratio obliqua*. Finally he omits from his narrative the information that the bishop was originally a monk, beause he is himself a secular cleric and prefers that his hero should appear to belong to the same group as himself.

Support for the view that the writer of the *Gesta* was copying Gregory is lent by the dating of the *Gesta Abundii*. These, as we shall see shortly, contain a reference to Pope Eugenius, probably Eugenius I, 654-657. Though the possibility of a common traditional source cannot be ruled out, this reference, combined with the similar treatment of other episodes in these *Gesta*, renders this unlikely.

In the parallel stories of Equitius in *Dialogue* 1.4 (2: 38-59) and of certain incidents in the *Gesta Abundii*, we find a similar situation: a straightforward narrative in the *Dialogues*, firmly rooted in the life of the Italian countryside, is matched with a more elaborate and fantastic story in the *Gesta*, though the details of the stories and the names of the characters are quite different. In Gregory's narrative, Equitius, abbot of Valeria, was summoned to Rome by the Pope (probably John III, 561-574) through the *defensor* Julian, in order that the clergy of Rome could form a judgement on his eloquence. The sight of Equitius working in a hayfield filled Julian with trembling. The next day the Pope sent word that

Equitius was not to be brought to Rome, because he, the Pope, had been filled with fear by a vision, reproaching him for sending for him. In the parallel story in the *Gesta*, the Pope (probably Eugenius I, 654-657), sent his *cubicularii* to bring to Rome Proculus, who had become a priest in Italy and who had seen a miracle at the Eucharist. The *cubicularii*, like Julian, at first displayed pride, in their case by refusing to receive Holy Communion from the hands of Proculus. However, they were convinced of his sincerity, when on the road to Ostia he caused a doe with two fawns to give them milk. Then they espied messengers from the Pope, who had been rebuked by an angel in a vision during the night for his doubts about Proculus.

In this case, the theory of a common source is less attractive at first sight, because of the differences in names. There is, however, the strong possibility that the story of Equitius, which belongs to Valeria, was transferred, on account of local pride, to the region of Umbria, and adapted to local holy men. Once again, the monastic connection has been suppressed by the clerical author.

Lanzoni believes that the basic account of the martyrdom of Abundius belongs to the late fifth or early sixth century,[71] but there is nothing to prevent later writers from incorporating the account into stories which they had derived from Gregory's material. Dufourcq supports a seventh-century date for the whole, but believes that sixth-century texts are incorporated in it.[72] In any case, it seems highly likely that the bulk of the material in the *Gesta Abundii et Carpophori* and the allied *Passiones* of Proculus (*BHL* 6955) and Anastasius and the Twelve Syrians (*BHL* 1620) is post-Gregorian and could have derived from the *Dialogues*.

A further case of parallelism between the *Dialogues* and the *Gesta martyrum* is the story of the thieves and the spades. The story, as told by Gregory, is one of the group connected with Spoleto, for which his informants were the two Spoletan exiles, the consecrated virgin, Gregoria, and the holy man, Eleutherius, who subsequently became a monk in St Andrew's monastery in Rome. The hero is Isaac the Syrian, who possessed that characteristic of the holy man, the gift of prophecy. Foreseeing that the thieves would visit the garden of his monastery but would be converted there, he ordered his monks to prepare soup for them and to provide spades for as many men as they found in the garden early in the morning. The spirit moved the thieves to pick up the spades and to work

---

[71] Lanzoni, *Le diocesi*, 1: 39, 427-428.
[72] Dufourcq, *Étude*, 3: 76.

hard as gardeners. Isaac persuaded them to mend their ways, and they departed, laden with his gift of vegetables (3.14, 2: 306-309).

Now the same story is told in the *Passio* of Felix of Nola (*BHL* 2885), but much more briefly: Felix cultivated a garden, which was visited at night by thieves, to whom he subsequently gave spades to work in it. It could be urged that the story was borrowed by Gregory from the *Gesta* or *vice versa*, but I do not believe this to be the case.

One of the parallels is the use of the word *vanga*, meaning "spade," in both stories. This is first found in literary Latin in the works of Palladius Rutilius, a writer on agriculture, whose date and place of origin are unknown, but who may probably be assiged to the late fourth or fifth century; his works are regarded as a valuable source for the "popular" vocabulary of the period.[73] *Vanga* is used by the writer of the *Gesta* without any introduction or explanation, whereas Gregory thinks it necessary to offer one to his monastic audience:

> ... fecit iactari ferramenta, quae usitato nos nomine vangas vocamus.

It could be argued from this that the story in the *Gesta* is original, and that Gregory, in his version, supplies a gloss on the word *vanga*, because this word would not be generally known to his educated urban audience.[74] The latter is probably true; there are parallel examples in the *Dialogues* of explanations of terms not likely to be familiar to cultivated people; instances are: 2.2, 2: 136-137; 18, 2: 194-195. The use of the word *vanga* does not therefore seem sufficient in itself to link the two stories.

As Lanzoni has shown[75] the *Passio* of Felix (*BHL* 2885) appears to be an amalgam of literary borrowings. According to its author, Felix was deported from Rome to Monte Circeo, near Terracina, to cut stones, which is reminiscent of the *Passio* of Caesarius (*BHL* 1151). There he healed the daughter of the tribune Probus and punished the man who wished to arrest him. Lanzoni sees, in the episode of punishment for possible arrest, a reminiscence of the captivity of Paulinus of Nola, but surely the writer of the *Passio* is thinking of the reference to the arrest of Felix in one of the poems of Paulinus.[76] According to the writer of the *Passio*, Felix then returned to Nola, where he cultivated a small garden (an occupation mentioned in another of the poems of Paulinus[77]), in which

---

[73] See *PW*, art. "Palladius."
[74] *Dialogues*, introd., 1: 36.
[75] Lanzoni, *Le diocesi*, 1: 234-235.
[76] *Carmina* 15, 177-181, p. 59.
[77] Ibid., 16, 284-289, p. 81.

the celebrated incident of the thieves occurred. Seen against such a background of literary borrowing the story seems unlikely to have been taken from Gregory or *vice versa*. It is more probable that the writer of the *Passio* is taking his information from the poems of Paulinus.

The *motif* of this story, the generous and forgiving attitude of a holy man towards thieves who have wronged him, seems to have been common in the Mediterranean area from the fourth century onwards. It is found in two forms. In the first, the stress is on the charity of the holy man; his influence upon the thieves is a secondary consideration. There are three examples of stories with this *motif* in the *Dialogues*: 1.2, 2: 24-25, where Libertinus gives his whip to the man who has stolen his horse; 1.3, 2: 34-37, where the monk-gardener presents the would-be thief with the cabbages which he intended to steal; 3.14, 2: 310-311, where Isaac warns a servant who has stolen a basket of food that it contains a poisonous snake. This *motif* also occurs in the *Historia monachorum* (Abba Ammon).[78]

In its second form, the story concludes with the conversion of the thieves. Apart from the first of the stories of Isaac, which we have already examined, this occurs twice in the *Apophthegmata patrum* with which Gregory is likely to have been familiar.[79]

In conclusion, no connection can be proved between Gregory's story and the *Gesta*. It may well be that Paulinus of Nola, Gregory, the author of the *Passio*, and the apophthegmatic writers were all drawing on a common source.

The attractive but enigmatic figure of Isaac arrived in Spoleto from Syria, according to Gregory, *prioribus quoque temporibus Gothorum*, and survived *usque ad extrema paene Gothorum tempora*, that is, almost to Gregory's own day (3.14, 2: 302-303). We have already seen that he possessed two of the marks of the holy man: a capacity to prophesy and to discern spirits (not only did he foresee that the thieves would become gardeners, but he also perceived that some naked beggars who had hidden their clothes in a hollow tree were impostors),[80] and the power to work miracles. Gregory is, however, careful to describe only those miracles which he wrought in Italy, and to depict him as a man of prayer. Certain features of Isaac's life in the district of Spoleto, as described by Gregory (3.4, 2: 302-307, 312-315), are among the *topoi* of hagiography: crowds

---

[78] *Historia monachorum* 8, PL 21: 421.
[79] *Apophthegmata patrum latinorum* 5.16.13, PL 73: 971; 19, PL 73: 973.
[80] See *Dialogues* 3.14, 2: 309, n. 8.

collected round him, offering him presents which he refused; he made a hermitage in a desert place, where others joined him.[81]

There is a striking resemblance between Gregory's account of Isaac and the *Gesta* of John Penariensis (*BHL* 4420). We are told that John left Syria, praying to the God of Abraham, Isaac, and Jacob for protection and saying that where he gave his psalter, there he would remain until it was given back to him. He encountered a holy woman *in fundo agello*, about five miles from "the metropolis," that is, Spoleto, and remained there until the next day, when an angel led him a short distance and told him to stay under a tree. There was frost everywhere, except upon that spot. Some passing huntsmen at first thought that John was a robber, but since the tree shone like a lily, they became convinced of his real character and told the bishop of Spoleto about him. The people then built a monastery, where John remained until he died forty-four years later.

The relationship between the two accounts is, however, difficult to determine. As Dufourcq points out, there are certain parallels:

1. *The motif of unwillingness*

The unwillingness of the custodian of the church to allow Isaac to continue in prayer.	The unwillingness of the huntsmen to accept John as a genuine holy man.

2. *The need for a miracle to convince their adversaries*

Isaac drives out a demon.	John stands in an area untouched by the surrounding frost.

3. In both cases, *popular support for the holy man*

4. In both cases, *the building of a monastery*

5. *The appearance of a holy woman*

The consecrated virgin, who drove a demon from a countryman into a pig.	The woman who lived *in fundo agello*.

Dufourcq identifies John, bishop of Spoleto, who is mentioned in the *Gesta*, with an historical figure of that name, who flourished in the late fifth and early sixth centuries,[82] but this affords no clue as to the date of

---

[81] Cf. e.g., Antony: *Vita Antonii* 15, pp. 38-41; Martin, *Vita S. Martini* 10, 1: 278-279; Benedict: *Dialogue* 2.3, 2: 148-151.

[82] Dufourcq, *Étude*, 3: 59-60; *BHL* 4420, 4437.

the writing of the *Gesta*. It is not clear whether John, bishop of Spoleto, is to be identified with John Penariensis, who certainly figures in popular calendars at the beginning of the seventh century.[83] It may be that the *Gesta* dealing with John Penariensis antedate Gregory, or that the two narratives are contemporary. In this instance, as in many others, it is difficult to disentangle history and hagiography, but it seems reasonable to assume that Isaac was a near-contemporary holy man, perhaps of Oriental origin and known personally to Gregory's informants, Gregoria and Eleutherius, to whom older Umbrian stories had become attached through motives of piety, either by them or by Gregory himself. It is possible that Gregory had heard from his informants both reminiscences of Isaac and other local stories from Spoleto.

The story of the tree untouched by the surrounding frost, like the story of the thieves, contains a traditional *motif* which occurs elsewhere. There are three examples in the *Dialogues*: 3.11, 2: 294-297; 12: 296-299; 346-349. Similar stories, relating principally to relics and tombs, are to be found in the writings of Gregory of Tours.[84] The existence of two stories of parallel miracles, achieved, on the one hand, by εὐλογίαι, on the other by the prayers of the holy man himself, in the Greek *Vita Hypatii* of Callinicos shows that this *motif* is not confined to the West.[85]

Isaac also figures as a minor character under his own name in the *Gesta Abundii*, *Gesta XII Syrorum* (*BHL* 1620) and the *Gesta Laurentii* (*BHL* 4748). We have already seen that the former are post-Gregorian, because they contain a reference to a Pope Eugenius; the dates of the pontificate of the first pope of this name are 654-657. The *Gesta Abundii* indeed appear to be a shortened version of the much longer story of the twelve Syrians which contains a similar reference.

This story containing, as it does, some complicated family relationships, may well be one of those *Gesta* inspired by the books of the Maccabees. Isaac figures as one of the eleven men of the younger generation brought from Syria to Rome by Anastasius and his eleven brothers, "when Julian was pope, who afterwards became emperor and apostasized," who fled to Spoleto to escape from persecution. There can be little doubt that the figure of Isaac was derived from Gregory, though there may have been a holy man of that name living at Spoleto, who was known, at any rate by repute, to Gregory's informants.

---

[83] E.g., PL 123: 151.

[84] *Liber in gloria martyrum* 35, pp. 60-61; 43, pp. 67-68; *Liber in gloria confessorum* 1, p. 340.

[85] Callinicos, *Vita Hypatii* 38.6-9, pp. 228-233; 46, pp. 272-273.

The *Gesta Laurentii* present a further problem of dating. The story is introduced by a wealth of chronological detail, unusual in the *Gesta*, which the author has apparently taken over from the *LP*,[86] but a consular name is cited in a parenthesis:

> et a consulato suprascripto usque ad consulem Decium minorem anni CCXLV.

There are three possible candidates, whose consulates fall in 508, 529, and 534 respectively. Dufourcq favours 529 as the date of our text, as the consul for that year was Decius Minor and it is apparently confirmed by adding the 245 years to 284, the date of the first consulate of Diocletian. The text of the *Gesta* mentions the sixth consulate, but as we have seen, historical accuracy was not the concern of its writers.[87] If we accept this dating, then Isaac figures in a pre-Gregorian section of the *Gesta*, but the only information supplied about his career is that he founded a monastery at Spoleto and died there, which does not really affect the position; but since the Isaac of the *Dialogues* survived *usque ad extrema paene Gothorum tempora*, it looks as though a near-contemporary person had been woven into the *Gesta*. Thus the sequence appears to be as follows:

1. *John Penariensis*, a holy man of unknown but earlier date, perhaps of the late fourth or early fifth century, the subject of local stories upon which both Gregory and the writers of the *Gesta* were at work in the sixth century.

2. *Isaac the Syrian* or *Isaac of Spoleto*, a near-contemporary holy man who is mentioned in the *Gesta Laurentii* (probably pre-Gregorian) as having founded a monastery at Spoleto and died there, and about whom Gregory had heard from Gregoria and Eleutherius; to whom Gregory attached some of the local traditional stories about John Penariensis, which he may well have learned from the same informants.

3. *Isaac the Syrian*, a character in the *Gesta Abundii* and the *Gesta XII Syrorum*, whose existence and exploits may have been taken over by their seventh-century writers from both the *Gesta Laurentii* and from *Dialogue* 3.14 (2: 302-315).

Three other stories in the *Dialogues*, which resemble stories in the *Gesta*, are believed by Dufourcq to show that Gregory and the *Gesta* writers were at work on the same corpus of traditional material.[88] This

---

[86] *LP* 1: 161.
[87] Dufourcq, *Étude*, 3: 62-63.
[88] Ibid., 3: 8.

may well be the case, but the traditions appear to be wider than those of
the Umbrian countryside. These stories describe three returns from hell:
first, 4.19, 3: 72-75: the child who blasphemed on his deathbed, calling
out to his father that the Mauri had come to fetch him; second, 4.37, 3:
126-127: the monk of Evasa who died and saw the flames of hell, but was
given a fresh start; third, 4.37, 3: 128-133: the story of Stephen, a man
known to Gregory, who died "by mistake" and was returned to earth in
exchange for Stephen the Smith.

The first of these stories certainly has an affinity with the *Passio* of
Alexander of Baccano, and with the *Conversio* of Afra, as Dufourcq
points out,[89] but Gregory may well have derived the idea from earlier
sources. The idea of blackness as representing evil is as old as Homer.[90]
The devil disguised as a black man is mentioned in the Epistle of Barnabas
(A.D. 140)[91] and again sixty years later in the *Passio* of Perpetua and her
companions, when Perpetua in her dream sees the devil as a black
Egyptian.[92] The word "Ethiopian" is also used to describe the devil
disguised as a black man, particularly by Egyptians. Gregory probably
first met the idea in literature in the *Vita Antonii*[93] from which he
introduced it into *Dialogue* 2.4 (2: 152-153), but it was probably a
commonplace in ordinary speech. We may surmise that mothers and
nurses used the Mauri or Aethiopes to represent devilish black men who
pursued naughty children and that this was the imagery which Gregory
would naturally put into the mouth of the unfortunate little boy. The
writer of the *Gesta* of Alexander may well have had the same thought
independently of Gregory. Since the whole subject of the devil as a black
person has been dealt with fully by B. Steidle,[94] there seems no need to
pursue it further, except to conclude that both Gregory and the writer of
the *Gesta* were following a widespread tradition, probably of Eastern
origin. It may even be a Christian version of the myth of Minos and
Orpheus.

[89] Ibid., 3: 6, for Afra; Venantius Fortunatus, *Vita S. Martini* 4, 643, p. 368; *Conversio
et passio*, ed. B. Krusch, MGH SRM 3 (Hanover 1896), pp. 41-64, at p. 58, where the devil as
a black man is mentioned.

[90] E.g., μέλας θάνατος, *Iliad* 2, 834, ed. D. B. Monro, 5th rev. ed. (Oxford 1929), 1:
47; μέλαινα ἀνάγκη, Euripides, *Hippolytus*, 1388, *Opera*, ed. G. Murray, 3 vols (Oxford
n.d.), 1.

[91] *Ep.* 4.9b, *Épître de Barnabé*, ed. R. A. Kraft and P. Prigent, SC 172 (Paris 1971),
pp. 100-101.

[92] Musurillo, *The Acts*, pp. 116-119.

[93] *Vita Antonii* 6, pp. 18-19.

[94] Steidle, "Der kleine schwarze Knabe," pp. 339-350; see also Graus, "Volk,
Herrscher und Heiliger," p. 230.

The other two stories have as their background a vision of hell, regarding which it seems as if Gregory is influenced by two New Testament Apocryphal writings, the *Apocalypse of Peter* and the *Apocalypse of Paul*.[95] The former may be assigned to the second century, the latter to the fourth. It seems more likely that Gregory was familiar with the later rather than the earlier document, since a Latin version was available. It also seems to have been known to Augustine, who, however, was inclined to scorn it.[96] It includes much of the material from the *Apocalypse of Peter* including the description of the torments of hell. It purports to be a description of what Paul saw when he was caught up into the Third Heaven, but he was given the opportunity to inspect hell also. There are considerable similarities between the geographical descriptions in the *Visio Pauli* and in the fourth *Dialogue*. What is interesting is that whereas the *Apocalypse of Peter* speaks of a horrible lake, the *Apocalypse of Paul* speaks of a horrible river, just as Gregory does, which suggests that he took his inspiration from the latter document.[97] Vogüé has pointed out the close resemblance of the story of Curma, the *curialis pauper*, in Augustine's *De cura pro mortuis gerenda* to that of Stephen in *Dialogue* 4.[98] In Augustine's story, it is true, the protagonist is not completely dead; he shows a very faint breath of life while in a coma, but his spirit reaches the next world. In both stories the person who was intended to die was a blacksmith. Gregory's story of Reparatus (4.32, 3: 106-109) also has some affinities with Augustine's story. Both Curma and Reparatus return from the next world, asking that a message should be sent to another person, who subsequently dies.

What are we to make of this apparent piece of plagiarism? Gregory produces two *bona fide* informants for these stories. Stephen himself was in the habit of describing his adventures:

> nam illustris vir Stephanus, quem bene nosti, de semetipso mihi narrare consueverat....

The use of the pluperfect form suggests that Stephen may have been dead at the time when Gregory was writing. There seem to be three possibilities: either Gregory applied to Stephen the story which he had read in Augustine's works, or Gregory, Stephen himself and Augustine

[95] E. Hennecke, ed., *New Testament Apocrypha*, ed. W. Schneelmacher, trans. and ed. R. McL. Wilson, vols 1-2 (London 1963-1965), 2: 663-683, 751-798.
[96] *In Iohannis Evangelium tractatus* 124.99.8, ed. R. Willems, ccsl 36 (Turnholt 1954), p. 581; *Enchiridion*, ed. E. Evans, ccsl 46 (Turnholt 1955), pp. 112-113, 109-110.
[97] See Hennecke, *New Testament Apocrypha*, 2: 779.
[98] *Dialogue* 4.37, 3: 128-135; cf. *De cura pro mortuis gerenda* 12.15, pp. 644-647.

were making use of a traditional story or Stephen had read Augustine and had applied the story to himself, but Gregory had not. My own preference is for the second hypothesis, with the rider that the traditional story was mediated to Gregory through Augustine. At any rate it seems to have no connection with the *Gesta martyrum Romanorum*.

E. Conclusion

There is no more than a small grain of truth in Dufourcq's belief that there is a close relationship between the *Dialogues* and the *Gesta*: ... *il y a une étroite solidarité entre les Gestes et les Dialogues: ces deux séries de textes se complètent et s'éclairent l'une et l'autre*.[99] In fact, he almost appears to see Gregory as no more than a more holy and more illustrious contributor to the corpus of *Gesta*. This, however, is a simplistic view of the real situation.

First of all, let us consider the resemblance between the *Gesta* and the *Dialogues*:

1. Both Gregory and the writers of the *Gesta* appear to be working on the same kind of traditional material, principally from Umbria, but Gregory is less influenced by the *Gesta* than has sometimes been thought. We have seen that his own spiritual formation owes little or nothing to them.

2. Both Gregory and the writers of the *Gesta* take a similar attitude to history, but for different reasons. Neither they nor Gregory regarded historical accuracy as important: the writers of the *Gesta* suffered from a basic ignorance of the facts of Roman history, and in any case, probably did not know what historical accuracy was. Their object was to tell an edifying story which would redound to the credit of the secular clergy and those in minor orders. Gregory perhaps had some notion of the unity of history, but as we have already seen, to him the historical setting of an event was its least important aspect. His aim was to show how God could use unlikely people for carrying out his purposes. Because his outlook was strongly eschatological and teleological, he had a longer view and a grander design than the writers of the *Gesta*.

Secondly, we need to see in what way the *Dialogues* can be said to complete the *Gesta*. We can only hold the view that they do so, if we regard the whole corpus of material relating to Italian and Roman saints as a *gloria confessorum* as well as a *gloria martyrum*. Gregory's stories,

---

[99] Dufourcq, *Étude*, 3: 294.

with the exception of the stories dealt with in section 3 of this chapter, are accounts of the deeds of confessors, whereas the *Gesta* are stories of martyrs. Gregory himself, however, does not make the distinction quite in these terms. He defines the confessor, as we have already seen, as a *martyr occultus*. In this he shows considerable psychological acumen. Martyrdom had been held for centuries as the highest form of Christian sanctity, but obviously, with the cessation of the persecutions, opportunities of attaining this ideal became rare. If a different ideal, such as "living for Christ," were to be held up, a sense of anti-climax would result, whereas the notion of the *martyr occultus* would ensure a sense of continuity with the past and would increase the confidence of the monks in the value of their way of life, since monasticism was a form of martyrdom.

There are five ways in which the *Dialogues* differ from the *Gesta*:

1. The miracles in the *Dialogues* are generally performed by bishops, monks, solitaries, or persons of especial humility, whereas those in the *Gesta* are for the most part the work of secular clerics, though the bishop is occasionally shown as a miracle-worker.

2. The bishop in the *Gesta* is usually portrayed as the means by which ecclesiastical forms and ceremonies are correctly carried out, whereas in the *Dialogues* he is shown as a holy man and a pastor.

3. Relics are used more frequently in the *Gesta* than in the *Dialogues*, where the sole examples are: the *caligula* of Honoratus (1.2, 2: 28-31); the tunic of Euthicius (3.15, 2: 326-327); the dust from the altar (3.17, 2: 338-339); the dalmatic of Paschasius (4.42, 3: 152-153).

4. The characters in the *Gesta* are mostly stock figures of hagiography without any background, or setting, whereas Gregory creates a portrait gallery of individuals and, by means of vivid touches, enables the reader to picture the settings for himself.

5. The writers of the *Gesta* may know biblical words and phrases, but they lack Gregory's profound knowledge of the Bible and make little, if any, attempt to interpret events in the light of the Bible.

The great difference in spirit and atmosphere between the *Gesta* and the *Dialogues* is primarily due to Gregory's own combination of deep spirituality and considerable literary skill, but there were other influences at work and other sources of material, as we shall see later.

4

The Miracle-Stories in the *Dialogues*
Seen in the Context of Those
of Other Western Christian Writers

A. The Attitude of Augustine Towards Miracles

We have already noticed that Gregory's stories of holy men in the *Dialogues* owe something to the works of earlier Western Christian writers and that in the latter half of the fifth century and in the sixth century, a cultural climate had developed which was more favourable to the reception of "popular" literature, such as the *Gesta*. Actually this change of cultural climate had already begun towards the end of the fourth century. The second half of this century was a period propitious for the spread of popular literature about monasticism, an interest in which had doubtless been stimulated by the arrival in the West of the exiled Athanasius in ca. 335, and from 337-342, and by the publication of Latin versions of the *Vita Antonii*. The better known of these, by Evagrius of Antioch, appeared in 375, but a translation was available some years earlier.[1] The same kind of reader would be attracted by Jerome's *Vita Pauli*, *Vita Hilarionis*, and *Vita Malchi* (375-391); by the *Vita S. Martini* (ca. 393-397) and the *Dialogues* (404) of Sulpicius Severus; and by the *Vita Ambrosii* of Paulinus of Milan (422).

This is not the place for a detailed discussion of the reasons for this cultural change, but the political upheavals, the recurrent wars, and the

---

[1] See Athanasius, *Vita Antonii. Un témoin important du texte de la vie de S. Antoine par S. Athanase: la version latine inédite des archives du chapitre de S. Pierre à Rome*, ed. G. Garitte (Brussels and Rome 1939), pp. 4-7; H. Hoppenbrouwers, ed., *La plus ancienne version latine de la vie de saint Antoine, par S. Athanase: étude de critique*, LCP 14 (Nijmegen 1960), supplies a more satisfactory text.

generally unsettled conditions of life in Western Europe from the late fourth century onward might well lead to an interest in astrology, magic, and the supernatural. In the case of the Christian public, this interest in the supernatural took the form of a thirst for miracle-stories.[2]

The attitudes displayed by Augustine and his biographer Possidius are an interesting indication of the cultural change that was coming over educated Christians in Western Europe in the late fourth and early fifth centuries. Possidius (ca. 370-ca. 440) is the type of the conservative churchman. His brief biography of Augustine is unadorned by any miracle-story. Augustine himself, however, was a man who moved with the times: over the years we can discern a decided change in his attitude towards miracles. Augustine's baptism in 387 occurred a year after the *inventio* of the bodies of Gervase and Protase at Milan but, so far as we know, there is no connection between these events. After his return to Hippo in 391 and his subsequent ordination as *presbyter*, he could adopt the attitude of believing that the great miracles are the incarnation, the resurrection, and the ascension, the effects of which are still with us, whereas the miracles of healing, the miracles involving the increase of a substance, and the exorcisms belong to the period of the earthly life of Jesus and therefore no longer occur.[3] In the same year (391), he was to express the opinion, in *De utilitate credendi*, that miracles would cease to be marvellous if they became too frequent.[4] It was not until 397 that he referred in a passage in the *Confessions* to the *inventio* of the bodies of Gervase and Protase, which gives us the impression that he sincerely believes in what he has heard, but that he regards the incident as a sign of the defeat of the Arians.[5] This is perhaps the first indication of that change of attitude towards miracles, which was to find its full expression in *De civitate Dei* 22.8 in 427.[6]

It is at first difficult to see the reason for Augustine's *volte-face*. The explanation offered by D. P. de Vooght, that Augustine was convinced by seeing the miracles take place at Milan, is hardly adequate. After all, a number of them are commonplaces of late antique and medieval hagiography, and his own words in two of his later sermons indicate his

---

[2] P. R. L. Brown, "Society, Demons, and the Rise of Christianity from Late Antiquity into the Middle Ages," *Religion and Society in the Age of St Augustine* (London 1972), pp. 119-146.

[3] *De utilitate credendi* 15.33-16.34, ed. J. Zycha, CSEL 26 (Vienna 1891), pp. 41-44.

[4] *De vera religione* 25.47, ed. J. Martin, CCSL 32 (Turnholt 1962), pp. 216-217; cf. *Ep.* 78, 1: 335-336, CSEL 24 (2) (Vienna 1878).

[5] *Confessiones* 9.7, pp. 208-209.

[6] *De civitate Dei* 22.8, 2: 815-827.

support for the text: *beati qui non viderunt, et crediderunt* (John 20.29). No outburst of thaumaturgy would be needed to strengthen this conviction.[7]

P. Courcelle attempts to account for Augustine's more tolerant attitude in later years by suggesting that the *inventio* at Milan in 386 and its consequences are likely to have impressed him deeply enough to have brought about the change, but this does not seem to be justified by the evidence. He does, however, point out that, in several of the passages quoted by Paulinus, which describe the bodies of Gervase and Protase, Augustine uses words, such as *novi*, rather than *vidi*. This may be regarded as an indication that, even after his acceptance of the possibility of miracles similar to the gospel miracles in his own day, Augustine still maintained a certain degree of scepticism.[8]

This view is borne out by two letters written in 411, which display, on the one hand, a continuation of Augustine's acceptance of the primacy of the great miracles of the incarnation, resurrection, and ascension in relation to other biblical miracles, and on the other, a reduction in the stature of these other miracles, in that they could be performed by Moses and the prophets as well as by Jesus. The first of these letters is written by the Christian Marcellinus, the imperial commissioner, who presided over the Council of Carthage (401) and to whom Augustine dedicated *De civitate Dei*, to warn Augustine to be careful in his replies to Volusianus, the Roman proconsul, whom he, Augustine, was anxious to convert to Christianity.[9]

The second letter, addressed by Augustine to Volusianus himself, deals with the difficulties which prevent him from accepting the Christian faith. The most interesting section of the letter, for our purposes, is that in which Augustine produces arguments from miracles:

> sed nulla, inquiunt, competentibus signis tantae maiestatis indicia claruerunt, quia larvalis purgatio, debilium curae, reddita vita defunctis, si et alii considerentur, Deo parva sunt. Fatemur quidem et nos talia quaedam fecisse prophetas.

Elijah and Elisha, for example, have raised the dead. Moses and the true prophets, in prophesying the coming of Christ, proclaimed him as one

---

[7] D. P. de Vooght, "La notion philosophique du miracle chez saint Augustin dans le 'De Trinitate' et le 'De Genesi ad litteram'," *RTAM* 10 (1938): 317-343; "Les miracles dans la vie de saint Augustin," ibid. 11 (1939): 5-16, at p. 19, n. 17.

[8] P. Courcelle, *Recherches sur les Confessions de saint Augustin*, n.ed. (Paris 1968), pp. 139-153.

[9] *Ep.* 136, 2: 93-96.

who would come as Lord of all and as one made man. He would possess miraculous powers because it would be absurd for one who had performed miracles through Moses and the prophets not to be able to perform them himself. However, Jesus would preserve certain miracles as peculiar to himself alone: the Virgin birth, the resurrection, and the ascension.[10]

Probably the most satisfactory explanation of Augustine's change of attitude is offered by Brown: in Augustine's old age, "modern miracles, which had once been peripheral, now became urgently important as supports to faith"; just as he had once collected evidence regarding infant baptism with which to confront Pelagians, so he now drew together information about miraculous cures with which he could confront the pagan intelligentsia of the district.[11]

These two letters are also valuable for indicating that the change which had come over Augustine's general cultural outlook, was not confined to him or indeed to Christians. Mention is made in them of two earlier writers, Apollonius of Tyana (d. 98) and Lucius Apuleius (fl. second century), who evidently still possessed an appeal for educated pagans. In both these writers we find a blend of serious philosophical thinking and writing and a love of the miraculous. Our knowledge of Apollonius comes chiefly from the *Vita*, written by Philostratus in the third century, which consciously imitates the Gospels in its account of his miracles.

Apuleius might well be of special interest in North African cultural circles because he came from Madaura, where Augustine received part of his higher education. Apuleius studies philosophy in Athens and worked for some years as an advocate in Rome before marrying a wealthy widow and settling down in Carthage. A few of his rhetorical and philosophical works have survived, but he is now best known for his works on the occult and for his fantastic miracle stories in *The Golden Ass* (*De asino aureo*). The work which most interests Augustine is his *De deo Socratis*, which he criticizes at some length in *De civitate Dei*, particularly in bk 9.[12] The miracles to which he refers in these two letters, however, are likely to be those described in *The Golden Ass*, which are principally performed by witches and wizards and involve the transformation of human beings into animals.

The fact that cultivated men could apparently accept both the philosophical writings of Apollonius and Apuleius and the fantastic

---

[10] *Ep.* 137, 2: 96-125, at pp. 114-117.
[11] P. R. L. Brown, *Augustine of Hippo: a Biography* (London 1967), p. 415.
[12] *De civitate Dei* 9.1-7, 1: 249-256.

miracle-stories is an indication of the change of intellectual climate in North Africa – and indeed in Western Europe – in the early fifth century. This had not fully affected Augustine at the time when he was writing bk 9 (417), but its influence would become more apparent in bk 22, published in 427, when he was over seventy years old. He may well have been influenced by his own later reflections on the finding of the bodies of Gervase and Protase at Milan, though, as we have seen, he made no comment at the time. It was almost certainly the discovery of the relics of Stephen the protomartyr at Caphar Gamle in 415,[13] which contributed to his change of attitude. Some of these which had reached places in the neighbourhood of Hippo in 416, appear to have been responsible for the outburst of thaumaturgy described in *De civitate Dei*.

B. The Forms of the New Thaumaturgy

a. *Augustine*

In spite of his change of attitude, Augustine's belief in miracles is strongly coloured by his biblical and typological outlook. As we shall see later, some of the Western miracle-story writers, particularly Gregory of Tours, are intensely interested in the miracle *per se*, which they regard as the hall-mark of the holy man.[14] A man is holy *because* he can perform miracles. Gregory the Great, on the other hand, sees the miracle as the outcome of an inwardly holy life, but not as the essential mark of holiness. He points out that Peter could walk on the water whereas Paul was involved in shipwrecks, but in the sight of heaven their merits were equal (1.12, 2: 116-117). He believes in the efficacy of the presence of the bodies of the martyrs in producing miracles (2.38, 2: 246-249); indeed his attitude appears to be inherited from Augustine, who was intensely interested in the favours achieved through the intercession of the martyrs. He saw these miracles as parallel with the miracles in the Gospels, and because he believed that less was known of them than of the gospel miracles, he conceived the idea of the *libelli*, in which the beneficiaries of the miracles wrote down what had happened, in order that other church members

---

[13] Lucian the Priest, *Epistola*, PL 41: 807-818. For a useful account of the relics of St Stephen, see Prinknash Abbey, *The Findings of St Stephen's Body at Caphar Gamal in 415 A.D.* (Cheltenham, pr., 1979).

[14] See, e.g., Gregory of Tours, *Liber de virtutibus S. Iuliani* 1, ed. B. Krusch, MGH SRM 1 (2) (Hanover 1885, anastatic repr. 1969), pp. 34-111, at p. 113.

might learn about it. H. Delehaye's important work on these documents[15] has never been superseded.[16]

Some of the miracles described in *De civitate Dei* 22.8 are brought about by prayer or by the use of the sacraments, but in a number of others, the use of relics is involved. It is perhaps worth noting here that there are biblical precedents for this, with which Augustine was doubtless familiar; in the Old Testament, the Children of Israel carried the bones of Joseph with them to the Promised Land (Exod. 13.19), while in the New Testament there is mention of the practice of healing the sick by means of handkerchiefs and aprons, which had been in contact with the living body of Paul (Acts 19.12). Augustine mentions the use of flowers which had been handed by a blind woman to a bishop carrying relics of Stephen, or which had been placed on an altar containing such relics; clothing or oil placed on shrines, and the railings round a shrine containing relics.[17]

b. *Ambrose*

The discoveries of Ambrose – for the *inventio* of the bodies of Gervase and Protase was followed by those of the bodies of Vitalis and Agricola at Bologna and of Nazarius at Milan – mark a turning-point in the attitude of the Western Church towards miracles,[18] though it was some years before the changed ideas began to penetrate throughout Western Christendom.

The *Vita Ambrosii* of Paulinus of Milan, for which the date of 422 is more acceptable than 415,[19] is an indication of this change. Paulinus after having apparently been in contact with Augustine, announces that he is going to treat his subject in the same way as earlier Christian biographers, Athanasius, Jerome, and Sulpicius Severus have treated theirs.[20] Stories of dreams and visions, demons overcome, corpses brought to life, sick persons healed, sight restored to the blind, and speech to the dumb therefore follow each other in quick succession. Paulinus describes fifteen miracles which occupy one fifth of the *Vita*, and which fall into three categories: 1. miracles performed by Ambrose himself or, in two cases, by contact with his clothing or with cloth; 2. miracles performed through the

[15] *De civitate Dei* 22.8; 2: 815.

[16] H. Delehaye, "Les premiers libelli miraculorum," *AnBoll* 29 (1910): 427-434; "Les recueils antiques des miracles des saints," ibid. 43 (1925): 74-85.

[17] *De civitate Dei* 22.8: prayer, 2: 816-818; baptism, 2: 818-819; sign of the cross, 2: 818; relics, 2: 820-824.

[18] *Vita Ambrosii* 29, pp. 90-91; 32, pp. 94-95.

[19] For discussion of dates, see C. Mohrmann, Intr., VSanti 3 (Milan 1975), pp. xxix-xxci.

[20] *Vita Ambrosii* 1, pp. 54-55.

relics of Gervase and Protase; 3. miracles performed through relics of
other martyrs.[21] In addition, Paulinus describes five apparitions of
Ambrose after his death. In two cases, for which Paulinus had received
the testimony of witnesses whom he considered reliable, Ambrose
prophesied military victories. In another, the situation is more
complicated: a blind man was told to go to Milan on a certain day to meet
fratribus meis, that is, the recent martyrs, Sisinnius, Martyrius, and
Alexander. The man's sight was restored by his touching their tomb;
miracles at tombs were to become widespread particularly in sixth-
century Gaul.[22] It is also significant that in the previous chapter Paulinus
describes the creation of relics, another practice which was to become
common in the next two centuries and for which, as we have already
seen, there is a New Testament precedent. At the funeral of Ambrose,
crowds of men and women are reported by Paulinus to have flung *oraria
vel semicincta* on to his body, in order that they might possess some object
which had been in contact with him. According to Ambrose himself,
these objects, which are a species of "manufactured" relics, came to have
curative properties. The difference between these and the objects
mentioned in Acts 19.12, is that they had been in contact with the corpse
of Ambrose, whereas the handkerchiefs and aprons (*sudaria et
semicinctia*) in Acts had touched Paul's living body.[23]

c. *Jerome*

The writings of Jerome on miracle-workers possess a quality of
imagination which is lacking in Augustine and Paulinus; he was, of
course, in a rather different situation from them, in that he was writing
about holy men about whom very little was known and, indeed, whose
very existence has been questioned. His three essays are the forerunners of
a type of hagiographical literature which was to become extremely
popular in the early Middle Ages. He was certainly well-qualified to write
about ascetics in the Desert, since he had experienced their way of life at
first hand. The detailed account of the lifestyle and particularly the diet of
Hilarion, for example, must surely be the result of personal observation

---

[21] 1. Ibid. 10-12, pp. 66-69; 16-18, pp. 74-77; 20-21, pp. 78-81; 28, pp. 88-91; 34,
pp. 96-99; 37, pp. 100-101; 2. 14, pp. 70-73; Ambrose, *Ep.* 22, PL 16: 1064-1065; 3. *Vita
Ambrosii* 29, pp. 90-91; 32, pp. 94-95; 52, pp. 118-121; cf. Ambrose, *Ep.* 22, PL 16: 1062-
1066.

[22] Ibid. 48-51, pp. 114-119; cf. Prudentius, *Peristefanon* 1.97-120, pp. 255-256;
Paulinus of Nola, *Carmina* 18, 85-468, 1: 101-118; 26, 309-334, 1: 257-258.

[23] *Vita Ambrosii* 48, pp. 116-117; cf. 14, pp. 70-71.

and experience. There must too, be some personal feeling behind his testimony, in his life of Paul the Hermit, to the value of providing solitaries in the desert with food and drink.[24]

These three essays, though not all written at the same time, owe something to the sojourn of Jerome in the home of Evagrius at Antioch, probably between his period in the Desert of Chalcis and his journey to Rome, ca. 376-382.[25] Certainly his reliance upon the *Vita Antonii* is obvious, and it was during this period that Evagrius was composing his Latin version of it. Jerome may have seen his friend's work at an early stage, or he may have read it in the original Greek. The life of Hilarion, in all probability, belongs to his early days at Bethlehem, about 390-391. Jerome's debt to Athanasius is two-fold: in the first place, he borrows from him the framework of the life and, in particular, the *topos* with which it opens; both Paul and Hilarion are orphans and Hilarion, like Antony, gives away his substance; secondly, both Hilarion and Antony engage in great struggles with demons, and there is the same passing-on of hallowed objects in both lives, though these seem to be regarded as souvenirs rather than relics. We are told that Antony took Paul's tunic and always wore it at Easter and Whitsun.[26]

Both Paul and Hilarion possess characteristics which are displayed by later holy men. Paul prophesies his own death, and Hilarion, like Antony, was beset by crowds and had to retire into regions more and more remote.[27] Jerome, with his vast biblical knowledge, anticipates Gregory in treating many of his miracle stories typologically. There is a New Testament atmosphere about the miracles of Hilarion described in chapters 6-11. Three of these are miracles of healing, including the cure of a sterile woman, which is described in biblical terms: *hoc signum eius principium* (cf. John 2.11). There is also an "increase miracle" of a bunch of grapes used to feed 3000 people. In these chapters three exorcisms are mentioned and others occur in chapters 26 and 30.[28] Many of the other miracles described in these three lives are, however, frankly tales of wonder: Antony on his way to visit Paul, is met by a satyr; Hilarion

---

[24] Jerome, *Vita Pauli primi eremitae* 10, PL 23: 25; *Vita Hilarionis* 5, pp. 84-85.

[25] See P. H. Rousseau, *Ascetics, Authority and the Church in the Age of Jerome and Cassian* (Oxford 1978), p. 133; J. N. D. Kelly, *Jerome: His Life, Writings and Controversies* (London 1975), pp. 170-171.

[26] *Vita Pauli primi eremitae* 3, PL 23: 20; *Vita Hilarionis* 2-3, pp. 74-83; cf. *Vita Antonii* 1, pp. 6-11; *Vita Pauli* 12, PL 23: 26; cf. *Vita Antonii* 91, pp. 172-175.

[27] *Vita Pauli* 11, PL 23: 26; *Vita Hilarionis* 2, pp. 76-77.

[28] *Vita Hilarionis* 6-11, pp. 86-99, at p. 88; 26, pp. 128-129; 30, pp. 136-137.

summoned on to a pyre and subsequently burned a monster that was devastating the countryside.[29]

The life of Malchus was probably written a little earlier than the life of Hilarion.[30] Its hero is reported to be an old man living in Maronia (a village in the Antioch district, which, years earlier, was owned by Evagrius), whom Jerome had known when living in Antioch. It is one of the earliest examples in hagiographical literature of a story in praise of virginity and of the extreme measures that should be taken to preserve it. Malchus and his wife, living as brother and sister, are the forerunners of the many chaste couples who appear in the works of Gregory of Tours and later medieval writers.[31] Gregory the Great also furnishes the example of an aged priest and his wife, living in the province of Nursia (4.12, 3: 48-51).

The lives of Paul, Hilarion, and Malchus have one characteristic in common, which occurs frequently in later hagiographical writing. They all have a special relationship with the animal creation. As we have already seen, Antony on his way to Paul encountered a satyr; Paul's body was decently buried as a result of the convenient arrival of two lions who dug his grave with their feet because Antony lacked a spade; Hilarion's prayers caused a Christian charioteer to win a race in order to preserve the honour of the Church; Malchus and his wife were saved from their pursuers by a lioness and escaped on dromedaries.[32] Jerome was perhaps the first Western Christian writer to take note of this power over animals as a characteristic of the holy man. The Desert Fathers were familiar with it, and we shall meet it again in Sulpicius Severus's portrait of Martin, in Caesarius of Arles, and in some of the holy men described by Gregory the Great (for example Boniface: 1.9, 2: 90-93; Fortunatus: 1.10, 2: 100-101; Cerbonius: 3.11, 2: 292-293; Florentius: 3.15, 2: 316-319; Menas: 3.26, 2: 366-371). It was also commonplace in Celtic Christianity; for example, Columbanus saw himself as part of a religious universe.[33]

C. Mohrmann makes the interesting suggestion that Jerome may be working out his own experience, as it were, in the divisions into which the narrative of the life of Hilarion falls. This certainly seems true in the case of chapters 2.6-4.3, where Hilarion's experiences in the Desert would

---

[29] *Vita Pauli* 8, PL 23: 23; *Vita Hilarionis* 28, pp. 130-133.

[30] See Kelly, *Jerome*, p. 61.

[31] For parallel examples, see Graus, "Volk, Herrscher und Heiliger," p. 470.

[32] *Vita Pauli* 16, PL 23: 27-28; *Vita Hilarionis* 11, pp. 96-99; *Vita Malchi* 9-10, PL 23: 62.

[33] *Vita Hilarionis* 14, pp. 104-107; *Vita Theodori Syceotae* 30, pp. 27-28; see also J. Leclercq, *Aspects du monachisme hier et aujourd'hui* (Bourges 1968), pp. 193-212.

correspond to Jerome's in the Desert of Chalcis, and Hilarion's visit to Alexandria to Jerome's return to Rome.[34] It might also account for the representation of Dalmatia as a barren wilderness, whereas it was in fact a populous region. Jerome is combining his desire for a solitary place in which to end his days with his unfriendly sentiments towards the district in which he had grown up.

In these three essays Jerome presents a different tradition of thaumaturgy from that displayed by Augustine in *De civitate Dei* 22.8, in that they portray the miracle-worker as a living agent rather than as a relic or tomb of a dead holy man. Jerome had, however, a reverence for relics of the saints. One of his charges against Vigilantius was that the latter regarded devotion to the relics of the martyrs and other holy men as superstitious and questioned whether miracles occurred at their shrines. In reply to this, Jerome appeals to tradition and authority: the martyrs are alive in Christ, so their prayers can still be effective.[35] It is clear that he sees the relics of the martyrs and other holy men as a focus for prayer and as sources of spiritual strength rather than as the physical agents of miracles. There are no pilgrimages for healing to Paul's tomb in the Desert, nor are objects such as Paul's tunic made into relics for healing.

Why did Jerome write these three essays? Perhaps they were *ballons d'essai* for the great history of the Church, which he at one time intended to write, but which came to nothing.[36] At any rate the existence of these three essays in the corpus of Jerome's theological writings suggests that he, like Augustine, was affected by the change in the contemporary mental climate. He was eager to be a propagandist for the ascetic life, particularly the monastic life, and believed that writings of this type were the best vehicle for his ideas among the people of his day. Had there not been a public for literature of this *genre*, he would have expressed himself in some different manner.

Fontaine has suggested that "biographies" of holy men performed the function of "light literature" [37] in Late Antiquity, but this seems to reduce unduly the *Vitae* by Jerome and other authors. If they are to be compared to light literature, the nearest equivalent would be the Victorian religious novel, such as Wiseman's *Fabiola* or Newman's *Callista*; but surely it was Jerome's intention that his essays should provide edifying reading for the

---

[34] C. Mohrmann, intr. to Hieronymus, *Vita Hilarionis*, etc., VSanti 4, p. xxxi.
[35] *Contra Vigilantium* 1, PL 23: 354-355; 5, PL 23: 357-358; 8, PL 23: 361-362; 10, PL 23: 363-364.
[36] See *Vita Malchi* 1, PL 23: 55.
[37] J. Fontaine, ed., *Vita S. Martini*, 1: 76-77.

kind of Christian groups, of which he had been director in Rome and of which he would later have the oversight in Palestine. The groups would be largely monastic (though they might include some secular clerics) and well-educated.

d. *The Tradition of the Living Holy Man as Miracle-Worker: Martin, the Jura Fathers, Caesarius of Arles, Severinus*

So far we have considered the question of miracles and relics in relation to writers and holy men belonging to North Africa and Italy and have noticed the existence of two distinct traditions: Augustine and Paulinus describe miracles carried out, for the most part, by means of relics of dead holy men, though the living holy man also has his place; Jerome, on the other hand, following Athanasius, represents the miracle-worker as a living agent.

The same dual tradition is carried on in Gaul and elsewhere. Let us first consider the tradition which is slightly earlier, that of the living holy man as the agent of miracles. Sometime around 394, a lawyer of Aquitaine, Sulpicius Severus, had withdrawn himself from his professional career and entered upon a life of asceticism, probably in the neighbourhood of Narbonne. Soon he began to chronicle the works of healing and other miracles of a holy man who was still alive, Martin, bishop of Tours. The *Vita S. Martini* was in all probability written between 393 and 397, the year of Martin's death. This is not the place for a discussion of Martin's role in early Gallic monasticism.[38] What is important for our purpose is to examine the kind of miracle stories, which Sulpicius Severus recounted, in order to discover what conception of Christian sanctity was held by an educated man in fourth-century Gaul, how widely the stories themselves, whether or not by means of the writings of Sulpicius Severus, were disseminated, and how far they relate to the writings of both earlier and later authors.

The debt of Sulpicius Severus to the *Vita S. Antonii* is obvious. We find the *topoi* of the pious childhood, the desire for solitude, the conflict with the Arians, and above all, the struggles with the demons and the visions of angels.[39] As in the *Vita S. Antonii* there is an Old Testament atmosphere about this work. Just as Athanasius regards Antony, the father of the

---

[38] See F. Prinz, *Frühes Mönchtum im Frankenreich: Kultur und Gesellschaft in Gallien, den Rheinlanden und Bayern am Beispiel der monastischen Entwicklung* (Munich 1965), pp. 19-46.

[39] *Vita Antonii* 2, pp. 254-255; 24, pp. 306-309; 21, pp. 298-299.

monks, as a spiritual descendant of Elijah, so Sulpicius Severus appears to
see Martin, the overthrower of idols, as one of the long line of kings or
prophets whose earlier exploits in destroying the altars in the high places,
and the images of Baal are described in the books of Kings and Chronicles,
the successor, as it were, of Jehu, when he caused the pillar of the temple
of Baal to be broken down and burned (2 [4] Kings 10.26-27), or of Josiah,
when he caused the altars of the Baalim and the Asherim to be broken
down in his presence (2 Chron. 34.4-6).[40] This does not mean that some of
the miracle-stories do not possess New Testament overtones: in particular
the stories of the paralyzed girl at Trier, which recalls that of Jairus's
daughter (Mark 5.22-42; Luke 40-42, 56), and that of the slave of
Tetradius, which bears some resemblance to the story of the centurion's
servant (Matt. 8.5-13; Luke 7.1-10);[41] but there is not the type of
consistent New Testament background that is found in, for example,
Jerome's *Vita Hilarionis*, or in connection with some of the miracle stories
of Gregory the Great, as we have already noticed in chapter two.
Probably thinking typologically did not come naturally to Sulpicius
Severus, who, for the greater part of his life, was a layman and would not
have received in his youth the rigorous biblical formation provided in a
monastery. It seems that his cast of mind was literary rather than biblical,
and that these stories would strike him as literary parallels rather than
biblical types. We have some indication that this was so from his
treatment of Martin as destroyer of idols; in the Bible, it is usually the
prophet who inspires the destruction of the idols, and the leader who
carries it out (for example, Azariah and Obed, who encouraged Asa, 2
Chron. 15.8), whereas Sulpicius Severus assigns to Martin the role of both
prophet and physical destroyer.

As Fontaine points out,[42] the miracles performed by Martin fall into
three main groups. The first includes three miracles connected with his
conflict with the pagans, all of which also occur with variations, in the
works of Gregory of Tours and Gregory the Great.[43] The second consists
of miracles of healing, some of which are based on biblical types, but
which include the healing of a leper, through the kiss and blessing of
Martin, and of the daughter of the prefect Arborius, by means of a letter
from Martin being placed by her father on her breast. It is in connection
with this group that we find the mention of relics: besides the letter,

[40] Ibid. 14-15, pp. 282-287.
[41] Ibid. 16-17, pp. 286-289.
[42] J. Fontaine, ed., *Vita S. Martini*, 1: 93-95.
[43] *Vita S. Martini* 12-15, 1: 278-287.

threads from Martin's cloak and hairshirt are mentioned as having healing properties.[44] The third group is an account of Martin's struggles with Satan and his miraculous escapes; it is here that Martin approaches most closely to Antony.[45]

According to Sulpicius Severus, Martin believed that he was endowed with even greater miraculous powers before he became a bishop. Certainly the only miracles of this era, which Sulpicius describes, are both very remarkable: the resuscitation of a corpse on two separate occasions.[46]

The second and third *Dialogues* of Sulpicius contain a further instalment of Martinian miracles. Many of these are paralleled in other works of hagiography. The miracles of healing include the healing of the uncle of Postumianus (one of the participants in the *Dialogues*) by Martin before he arrived at the house.[47] Among the other miracles are the rendering of men and animals immobile; self-opening doors; the increase of oil; glass jars, which do not break when dropped from a height.[48] Two of the miracles are linked with the Bible: the increase of oil, already mentioned, and the healing of a woman who touched the hem of Martin's garment.[49] Only one relic is mentioned: a piece of straw on which Martin had lain was used by a virgin to heal a man who was possessed.[50]

What is new in Western hagiography is an account of Martin being visited by the saints, a theme which will recur again in the writings of Gregory of Tours and Gregory the Great. It is paralleled in numerous Eastern Christian writings.[51]

Sulpicius Severus reveals himself as a considerable literary artist, but his skill lies in his powers of description rather than in his delineation of character: Martin emerges as a kind of icon, a two-dimensional figure. We

---

[44] Ibid. 18-20, 1: 292-295; for the relics, 19, 1: 292-293.

[45] Ibid. 17-24, 1: 290-309.

[46] Sulpicius Severus, *Dialogue* 1(2).4, p. 184; *Vita S.Martini* 7-8, 1: 266-271.

[47] *Dialogue* 1(2).2, p. 182.

[48] Ibid. 1(2).9, p. 191; 3, pp. 200-201.

[49] Ibid. 2(3).3, pp. 200-201; 9, p. 207.

[50] Ibid. 1(2).8, p. 190.

[51] Ibid. 1(2).13, p. 197; cf. *Vita Ambrosii* 48-52, pp. 114-121; *Vita patrum iurensium* 153-166, pp. 402-407; Gregory of Tours, e.g., *Liber in gloria martyrum* 9, p. 44; 33, p. 59; 50, p. 63; 91, p. 99; *Vita S. Martini* 1.6, p. 142; 16, p. 148; 24, p. 151; 2.18, p. 165; 40, pp. 173-174; 4.26, pp. 205-206; *Liber in gloria confessorum* 17-18, pp. 307-308; 20, pp. 309-310; 58, pp. 331-332; Gregory the Great, *Dialogue* 3.24-25, 2: 362-365; 38, 2: 429-431; 4.12-14, 3: 48-53; 18, 3: 72-75. For Eastern narratives, see, e.g., Cyril of Scythopolis, *Vita S. Sabae* 78, p. 185; 83, p. 188; *Vita Iohannis Hesychastae* 16, p. 214; [Theodore of Sykeon], *Vita Theodori Syceotae* 63, pp. 52-53; 88, p. 73; 100, p. 80; Leontius of Naples, *Vita Iohannis Eleemosinarii* 46, ed. H. Gelzer (Freiburg i/Br. and Leipzig 1893), pp. 95-103.

are told that he loved solitude and contemplation, but what we see is a man of action, who lacks emotion, intuition, and humour.[52] His sanctity lies in his outward acts, rather than in the development of the qualities which are expressed in those acts.

It is not, however, surprising that Sulpicius Severus should draw such a portrait. It is Augustine, Athanasius, and Jerome, who furnish the exceptions to the rules of late antique and early medieval characterization of holy men – or indeed of great men in general. A possible model for Sulpicius Severus, whether direct or at several removes, might have been the lives of the Caesars by Suetonius, which were written in the first century. These portraits are distinctive, but they possess the same curiously flat quality. This tradition was to permeate later hagiographical writing. The reader would not often be shown the inward struggles of an Antony, as actualized in the conflicts with the demons, nor of a Jerome, as presented in the life story of Hilarion, let alone participate in the *Confessiones* of an Augustine.

There is evidence for the dissemination of the writings of Sulpicius Severus soon after their publication. In a letter dated 397, Paulinus of Nola thanks Sulpicius Severus for sending him a copy of the life of Martin;[53] in another, of which the date is uncertain but is probably about 403, he describes the visit of Melania the Elder to Nola on her way to Rome, after twenty-five years in the Near East; in the last paragraph he tells how he read this work aloud to her, to bishop Nicetas, and to others.[54] Finally in the first of his *Dialogues*, written in 404, Sulpicius puts into the mouth of Postumianus a rhetorical account of the dissemination of his *libellus*; beginning with the *vir studiosissimus ... Paulinus* at Rome, he describes how it is selling well in Rome and that it is being read at Carthage, Cyrene, Alexandria, Nitria, the Thebaid, and Memphis.[55] Even allowing for the rhetorical exaggeration, it nevertheless appears to have had a wide circulation.

The readers of this work would be the circles of cultivated Latin-speaking people who still existed within the Mediterranean area: groups, in fact, comparable to Augustine and his friends in Hippo, the small monastic groups, which collected round Jerome at Rome and later at Bethlehem, and round Paulinus at Nola, and indeed, the participants in the *Dialogues*. Such people would appreciate both the fine Latin and the

---

[52] *Vita S. Martini* 27, 1: 314-315.
[53] Paulinus of Nola, *Ep.* 11, 1: 70.
[54] Ibid., *Ep.* 29, 1: 247-262, at pp. 251-252, 261-262.
[55] Sulpicius Severus, *Dialogue* 1.26, pp. 178-179.

literary artistry of Sulpicius Severus as well as his miracle-stories. One would surmise that his readership would not be entirely monastic, but would include secular clergy and educated lay-people, of whom Gallus and Postumianus in the *Dialogues* of Sulpicius Severus are examples.

We shall consider in a later section of this chapter the reasons for the close resemblances between some of Sulpicius's miracle stories and those of Gregory the Great.

Ever since the completion of the publication of the *Vita patrum iurensium* in 1668 by the Bollandists, doubts have been raised from time to time as to the authenticity of this work. The most recent of these controversies occurred at the end of the nineteenth century, when B. Krusch, who at first accepted the work as genuine, later changed his mind. His objections were based on what he believed to be anachronistic linguistic usages, on the omission from the collection of lives of that of the third abbot, Minausius, on the alleged ignorance of the author, and on the discrepancies between the lives of the abbots Romanus and Lupicinus, as described by the author of the *Vita patrum iurensium* and by Gregory of Tours.[56] A spirited reply was made by Duchesne in 1898, refuting these objections, and it is Duchesne's view, with slight modifications, which prevails today.[57] Probably the solution is that which is suggested by Prinz: he believes that there is a kernel of truth in the narrative, to which later accretions have become attached.[58] A good summary of the arguments is to be found in the edition of the *Vita patrum iurensium* by F. Martine, published in 1968,[59] and an interesting footnote was provided by Riché in 1954, when he pointed out that no less than seven lives of Merovingian saints regarded by Krusch as lacking authenticity are now accepted as genuine.[60]

The datings of both the events described in the *Vita patrum iurensium* and of the work itself are not immediately obvious. It is an account of the life of a monastic colony at Condadisco or Condat in the Jura, as reflected in the lives of three of its abbots, Romanus, Lupicinus, and Eugendus or Oyend. Romanus is the founder and is joined later by his younger brother Lupicinus, who ultimately succeeds him as abbot. The third abbot was Minausius, whose omission from the narrative caused such difficulty to

[56] B. Krusch, ed., MGH SRM 3, pp. 125-130.

[57] L. Duchesne, "La vie des pères du Jura," *MÉFR* 13 (1898), pp. 1-16; see list on p. 16 for further criticisms of Krusch.

[58] Prinz, *Frühes Mönchtum*, p. 67, n. 124.

[59] F. Martine, ed., in *Vita patrum iurensium, La vie des pères du Jura*, SC 122 (Paris 1968), pp. 14-44.

[60] P. Riché, "Note d'hagiographie mérovingienne," *AnBoll* 72 (1954): 36.

Krusch. It has been suggested (by Poupardin) that he misgoverned the monastery, or (by Duchesne) that the author disliked him. Martine suggests that he was omitted, because the author was anxious to represent the portrait of the abbots in the form of a triptych.[61] This is quite possible, but may not the idea of a triptych have occurred to the author precisely because he had some personal reason for the omission? The fourth abbot, the third in our portrait gallery, is Eugendus, whom the author, *adhuc puerilis*, knew in the monastery. Thus it appears that the author, whose identity is unknown, was a member of the Condat community, an impression which is confirmed by an eye-witness account in chapter 42 and by the description of the death-bed of Eugendus.[62]

The events described appear to belong to the fifth century. There are references, direct and indirect, to fourth and fifth century writers, the most numerous being to the *Vita Antonii*, to Cassian, and to Sulpicius Severus, *Vita S. Martini*.[63] This suggests that the work was written at the end of the fifth century or early in the sixth, since no later writers are cited. The dating of the work depends on the date of the death of Eugendus, for which 516 or 517 was commonly accepted. Martine points out, however, that 512-514 is more likely. Probably the *Vita patrum iurensium* can be assigned a date ca. 520.[64]

The interesting possibility of a link between Condat, Martinian monasticism, and the Desert is suggested by Prinz, who believes that the monastery of Lugdunensis Interamnis, where Romanus, though not yet a monk, acquired his conception of the monastic life, is to be identified with the monastery of Insula Barbara, which received Maximus, one of Martin's disciples.[65] Certainly the example of Martin obviously had considerable influence at Condat. The bishop of Lyons at the time when Romanus was at the monastery, was probably Eucherius who was one of the people to whom Cassian dedicated his *Collationes* in 425-426.[66]

The identification of the monastery of Interamnis with that of Insula Barbara cannot be accepted with certainty. The word itself suggests the tongue of land between the Rhône and Saône, the present-day district of Ainay, but there is no record of any early monastery there. Be that as it

---

[61] Krusch, MGH SRM 3, p. 127; R. Poupardin, "Étude sur les vies des saints fondateurs de Condat et la critique de M. Bruno Krusch," *Le moyen-âge* 2 (1898): 31-48; Duchesne, "La vie des pères du Jura," p. 12; Martine, *Vita patrum iurensium* 33, pp. 105-112.

[62] *Vita patrum iurensium* 78, pp. 324-325; 42, pp. 285-287; 175-178, pp. 428-433.

[63] See *Vita patrum iurensium*, index 2, pp. 465-466 for details.

[64] Martine, *Vita patrum iurensium*, pp. 53-57.

[65] Prinz, *Frühes Mönchtum*, pp. 66-69.

[66] Cassian, *Collationes* 11, praef., 2: 98-99.

may, there is no reason why Romanus should not have met Maximus if they were both in Lyons at the same time.

At any rate, Romanus left the Lyons monastery equipped with some interesting spiritual literature:

> Ex quo etiam monasterio, nihil de ambitione sanctissima manifestans, librum Vitae sanctorum Patrum eximiasque Institutiones Abbatum omni elegantia ac nisu aut supplicando elicuit aut potitus est conparando.[67]

The *Institutiones* must surely be those of Cassian, which were written in ca. 425, but the identity of the lives of the Fathers is a little less obvious. The *Vita Antonii* may well have been in the collection, since its influence is most apparent in the *Vita patrum iurensium*: Romanus is described as *prisci imitator Antonii*.[68] Like earlier and later holy men he has a sister who is a nun.[69] Temptation came to him, as to Antony, from the devil in the guise of an aged monk. The goatskin scapular given by Leonianus of Vienne to Eugendus recalls the gifts of Paul the Hermit to Antony and of Antony to Athanasius.[70] The *Vita patrum iurensium* contains four reminiscences of Rufinus's translation of the *Hist. mon.* (404).[71] The parallelism between a remarkable "increase" miracle in that work and one which the author of the *Vita patrum iurensium* attributes to Lupicinus,[72] suggests that a copy was available at Condat and that it formed part of the collection brought by Romanus from Lyons. We may well conjecture that the author of the *Vita patrum iurensium* saw Condat as a kind of Thebaid, populated by holy men comparable to the hermits of Egypt. It is interesting to note that Condat, in the two earlier lives, is shown as a loosely-organized colony of hermits, but is developed by Eugendus into a *coenobium*.

Whether or not *Vita S. Martini* was included in the *Liber vitae sanctorum patrum*, the coincidences between the miracles described by Sulpicius Severus and the author of the *Vita patrum iurensium* suggest that the latter must have been acquainted with the *Vita S. Martini*. This is confirmed by the fact that the *Vita patrum iurensium* includes twenty-two

---

[67] *Vita patrum iurensium* 11, pp. 250-253.

[68] Ibid. 12, pp. 252-253.

[69] For the *topos* of the holy man's sister, see, e.g., *Vita Antonii* 17, p. 8; *Vita Pachomii* 28 (Latin; Greek 2), pp. 48-49; *Vita Ambrosii* 4, p. 54; *Vita patrum iurensium* 60, pp. 304-305; *Vita Caesarii arelatensis* 1.28, p. 467; Gregory the Great, *Dialogues* 2.33, 2: 230-235; Callinicos, *Vita Hypatii* 53, pp. 294-295.

[70] *Vita patrum iurensium* 127, pp. 374-377; cf. Jerome, *Vita Pauli* 12, PL 23: 26; Athanasius, *Vita Antonii* 91, pp. 172-173.

[71] See list, *Vita patrum iurensium*, p. 466.

[72] Ibid. 68-70, pp. 315-319; cf. *Historia monachorum* 7, PL 21: 416.

references to the *Vita S. Martini*, three of which are direct quotations. Romanus healed two lepers by embracing them, just as Martin had embraced the leper in Paris. Eugendus used holy oil in his miracles, just as Martin did, and a woman called Syagria was healed by means of a letter from him, just as the daughter of Arborius was healed by a letter from Martin. The three abbots were particularly successful in healing madmen, the possessed, paralytics, and persons bitten by snakes. Eugendus, like Martin, is reported to have had visions of saints and angels: Martin, Peter, Paul, and Andrew, and angels similar to those in the vision of Jacob's ladder.[73]

Thus this little work embodies the tradition of the living holy man as miracle-worker, but it contains two interesting new developments: Romanus inaugurates in Gaul the tradition of the dead holy man performing miracles from his tomb (Eugendus, when a child, saw criminals and others stretched over it);[74] there is an early example of a healing achieved through a sick person lying in or on a holy man's bed, a practice of which several examples are recorded by Gregory of Tours.[75]

The *Vita patrum iurensium* is an unpretentious work; its miracles are described not with a view to building up the prestige of a holy man, a shrine, or a diocese, but in order to record the examples of great holy men of the past as an ideal for the present generation. We may surmise that it was intended for a monastic audience. There is no explanation of life in a monastery as such, because its details would be familiar to readers. Nevertheless the modern reader can glean from it some information about the daily life of the community.

The early years of Caesarius of Arles are coterminous with the *Vita patrum iurensium* but the *Vita Caesarii arelatensis* was not written until after his death in 542. Its principal author was Cyprian, bishop of Toulon, whose name is mentioned in the text; he was assisted by two other bishops, Firminus and Viventius, by the presbyter Messianus, and the deacon Stephen. Since Cyprian died in 549, the work presumably appeared sometime between 542 and 549.[76]

---

[73] For list of quotations, see *Vita patrum iurensium*, p. 466; for the miracles, 45-48, pp. 288-293; 148, pp. 398-399; 145-146, pp. 394-397; cf. *Vita S. Martini* 18, 1: 292-293; 16, 1: 286-289; 19, 1: 202-203.

[74] *Vita patrum iurensium* 152-160, pp. 402-413.

[75] Ibid. 41-42, pp. 284-287; 78, pp. 324-325 (cf. *Vita Caesarii arelatensis* 1.30, p. 468); Gregory of Tours, e.g., *Vita S. Martini* 1.35, p. 155; 2.19, p. 166; *Vitae patrum* 6(6), p. 234.

[76] *Vita Caesarii arelatensis* 2.1, pp. 483-484; for evidence of date, Krusch, MGH SRM 3, pp. 451-452.

Like many late antique and early medieval *Vitae* of holy men, it contains a number of *topoi*. Caesarius as a child was so devout and unselfish that he was always giving away his clothes to the poor and was consequently *saepe seminudus*.[77] He ran away from home to enter a monastery at an early age and was privileged to receive visions of the saints. Like Jerome he received a message in a dream bidding him to forsake secular study, but in his case this took the form of a vision of a serpent.[78] Like many of his illustrious predecessors, he claimed to be reluctant to accept episcopal office.[79] In the tradition of holy men, he had a sister who was a nun.[80] His episcopate was marked by activity in ransoming captives.[81] Last but not least, he was a notable miracle-worker.

It is possible to unravel the main events of the career of Caesarius from the narrative of the *Vita Caesarii arelatensis*. He was born ca. 470 at Chalon-sur-Saône and made his monastic vows at the age of eighteen in the presence of Pope Silvester at Rome. In 490 he became a monk at Lérins, where he remained for two years. Since he ruined his health there through excessive austerities, he was sent to Arles to recuperate and found himself among a circle of cultivated people, where he took lessons in rhetoric.[82] At some point before 499, he became abbot of the monastery *in insula suburbana civitatis* (probably the modern suburb of Trinquetaille, on the right bank of the Rhône). It may have been for this community that he drew up his rule for monks.[83] In 503 he was elected bishop of Arles, to succeed Eonius, and began to build the nunnery over which his sister is reported to have presided. It was for these sisters that he drew up his celebrated rule for nuns in 534.[84] He was indeed active *de monasteriis*. We gather that after ordination, he had the status of a *clericus* but kept the rule of Lérins. After he became bishop, he seems to have lived not in a monastery, but in the *domus ecclesiae* attached to his cathedral.[85]

Yet in spite of his undoubted love of things monastic, Caesarius, as revealed by the *Vita* and by his sermons, was both an administrator and a

---

[77] Ibid. 1.3-4, pp. 458-459; cf. Boniface, *Dialogue* 1.9, 2: 90-91.

[78] *Vita Caesarii arelatensis* 1.9, p. 460; cf. Jerome, *Ep*. 22, 1: 190.

[79] *Vita Caesarii arelatensis* 1.14, p. 462; see pp. 70-71 above.

[80] *Vita Caesarii arelatensis* 1.28, p. 467; 35, p. 470; 58, p. 481; Venantius Fortunatus, *Carmina* 8, 3.39, p. 182.

[81] *Vita Caesarii arelatensis* 1.20, p. 464; 33, p. 469; 44, p. 474.

[82] Ibid. 1.5-10, pp. 459-461.

[83] Ibid. 1.12, p. 461.

[84] Ibid. 1.13, pp. 461-462; 35, p. 470; 2.47, p. 500. For the rule itself, see *AASS* Ian. 1, 730 ff.

[85] *Vita Caesarii arelatensis* 1.11, p. 461; 62, p. 483.

pastoral bishop who enjoyed going about his diocese and meeting his flock.

The two-fold vocation of Caesarius as monk and as pastoral bishop is reflected in the character of the audience to which Cyprian and his collaborators appear to be addressing the *Vita*. Ostensibly its readership consists of the nuns of the convent over which the sister of Caesarius had presided and of which a younger Caesaria was now abbess. It is addressed to

> Caesaria, cum choro sodalium monacharum tibi commisso,

but it also contains references to a number of laymen and women.[86] It may well be that it was the purpose of Cyprian to compose a work which would appeal both to the *clerici* in the household of Caesarius's successor and to the laity, as well as to the nuns. This impression is strengthened by two phrases: the first is,

> Quid diximus, fratres? Quid disseruimus, filioli?

Now *fratres* is the normal mode of address to the general congregation assembled to hear the *admonitiones* of Caesarius, and the *filioli* could well be the *clerici*, some of whom we know to have been of tender years.[87] The second phrase is,

> Misit tamen praestantissimos viros de episcopis cum presbyteris et diaco-nibus.

The *praestantissimi viri* are presumably men of the status of Peter, the doctor Helpidius (both deacons), Liberius and his wife Agretia, Eucyria, whose maid he healed, the *charterius* Desiderius, the *notarius* Messianus, and the *illustres viri*, Salvius and Martianus.[88]

The miracles performed by Caesarius in his lifetime may all be described as apostolic works. They consist of healing, exorcisms, and raising the dead. The miracles of healing are carried out sometimes directly and sometimes with the aid of relics. In two cases healing was achieved by means of the sign of the cross, once made by Caesarius himself secretly, beneath his chasuble, and once by Eucherius whom

---

[86] Ibid. prol., p. 457; lay-people: e.g., Firminus and Gregoria, 1.8, p. 460; Parthenius, 49, p. 176; Agretia, 2.13, pp. 487-489; Eucyria, 18, p. 491; Benenatus, 23, p. 493. See also n. 87 below.

[87] Ibid. 1.61, p. 482; 2.20, p. 491.

[88] Ibid. 1.60, p. 481; *praestantissimi*: e.g., Peter, 2.2, p. 484; Helpidius, 1.41, p. 473; Liberius and Agretia, 2.10-13, pp. 487-489; Eucyria, 18, p. 491; Desiderius, 39, p. 497; Salvius, 40, p. 498; Martianus, 41, p. 498.

Caesarius ordered to do it. On four other occasions, healing was achieved by contact with the clothing of Caesarius or other textiles in contact with him, or with the water in which it had been washed.[89]

The means used by Caesarius to drive out demons varied. The doctor Helpidius, who seems to have been troubled by poltergeists in his home, had his house sprinkled with holy water.[90] The maidservant of Eucyria, who was possessed by a demon called Diana, was freed by means of the laying-on-of-hands and anointing with oil.[91] In two other cases the presence and prayers of Caesarius sufficed.[92]

The two stories of raising the dead, which recall the Elijah-Elisha cycle, have already been mentioned.[93]

Like other miracle-workers, Caesarius possessed a miracle-working bed, but it could work destructive and punitive miracles. A Goth who slept in it died. Presumably he was an Arian and therefore deemed worthy of punishment.[94]

From the foregoing evidence, it seems to have been the object of Cyprian and his collaborators to create a portrait of their revered former bishop as a miracle-worker comparable in status to the prophets Elijah and Elisha, the prototypes of the monks, and to the apostles. At the same time our authors are careful to mention the names of a number of prominent laymen in the diocese.[95] They hoped, no doubt, to create the impression of a monk of surpassing holiness who followed in the footsteps of the founding fathers of monasticism, and of a bishop who was a true successor of the apostles and with whom the leading laymen of the diocese were accustomed to associate. In the first half of the sixth century, when civil government was visibly disintegrating, the picture of the Church as a seat of authority would be likely to appeal to readers of the *Vita*.

Caesarius apparently continued to perform healing miracles after his death. Patients were cured of quartan and tertian fevers by drinking water in which his corpse or portions of his clothing had been washed.[96] A Frank, who wanted a piece of clothing so that he could wash it and drink

---

[89] Ibid. 1.47, p. 475; 2.30, p. 495; 13-15, p. 489; 40-41, p. 498. See also 2.49, p. 500.
[90] Ibid. 1.41, p. 473.
[91] Ibid. 2.18, p. 491.
[92] Ibid. 2.20, p. 491; 21, p. 495.
[93] Ibid. 1.39-40, p. 472; 2.2, p. 484. See p. 34.
[94] Ibid. 1.30, p. 468.
[95] See nn. 84, 87, above.
[96] *Vita Caesarii arelatensis* 2.39-41, p. 498.

the water, had to be content with a piece of the towel with which the corpse had been dried. This proved efficacious.[97]

We do not hear of any healings, exorcism, or resuscitations at the tomb of Caesarius, but these *post mortem* healings by means of relics do point the way to later developments, which are chronicled by Gregory of Tours.

The tradition of hagiographical writing based on miracles performed by a living holy man was also carried on by Eugippius, abbot of Lucullanum, whose *Vita Severini* can be assigned with certainty to the year 511.[98] The events described in it appear to belong to the same period as those described in the *Vita patrum iurensium*, namely the latter half of the fifth century.

In recent years this little work has aroused interest and controversy out of all proportion to its length. Its importance is due to the fact that it deals with a geographical area and with characters and events for which little other literary evidence is available, and that its hero is a man of Western culture who has nevertheless had some experience of Eastern Christianity, and who, after participating in these events, has fled to the West. The *Vita Severini* is of particular interest to German and Austrian scholars, because it deals with districts which, since the First World War, have passed through a period of political changes and upheavals, just as in the fifth century.

There is no need to dwell here at length upon the recent controversy between F. Lotter and F. Prinz in the pages of *Deutsches Archiv* and the *Historische Zeitschrift*, since this is concerned primarily with the value of the *Vita Severini* as an historical source and with the possible identification of Severinus with a character of that name mentioned by Sidonius Apollinaris and Ennodius of Pavia.[99] For our purpose it is enough to observe that Lotter has seen that many of the incidents in the *Vita Severini* are *topoi*, but that, as Prinz points out, he has failed to grasp

---

[97] Ibid. 2.42, p. 498.

[98] Eugippius, *Ep. ad Pasch.* 1, in *Das Leben des heiligen Severin*, ed. R. Noll (Berlin 1963), pp. 40-41; see also pp. 14-15.

[99] See F. Lotter, "Severinus und die Endzeit der römischen Herrschaft an der oberen Donau," *DA* 24 (1968): 309-338; F. Prinz, "Zur Vita Severini," *DA* 25 (1969): 531-536; F. Lotter, "Inlustrissimus vir Severinus," ibid. 26 (1970): 200-207; "Antonius von Lérins und der Untergang Ufernorikums," *HZ* 212 (1971): 265-315; *Severinus von Norikum: Legende und historische Wirklichkeit*, MGMA 12 (Stuttgart 1976). Also of interest are B. de Gaiffier, "La vie de saint Séverin de Norique à propos d'un livre récent" [of F. Lotter], *AnBoll* 95 (1977): 13-23; and M. van Uytfanghe, "Éléments évangéliques dans la structure et composition de la vie de saint Séverin d'Eugippius," *SE* 21 (1972-1973): 147-159; "Les avatars de l'hagiologie à propos d'un ouvrage récent sur saint Séverin du Norique," *Francia* 5 (1977): 639-671 [on F. Lotter].

the significance of some of them.[100] He realizes that the prophecy of
Severinus that the Romans will win a victory at Lauriacum, at a period
when they were actually withdrawing their influence from Noricum, is a
topos which has already occurred in the pages of Sulpicius Severus, an
author actually mentioned by Eugippius[101] (indeed he goes so far as to
indicate its Eastern origins[102]), but he does not see that the freeing of the
captives after victory by Severinus, with the threat of divine punishment
by the enemy should they offend in the future, bears more resemblance to
the *topos* of the freeing of captives by holy men than to strictly historical
narrative.[103]

Nothing is known of the origins of Eugippius. H. Leclercq suggested
long ago in the *DACL* that he was an African, probably because he edited
a famous collection of *excerpta* from the works of Augustine and
numbered Fulgentius of Ruspe among his correspondents: but he may
have been of a Roman family, since he calls the non-Roman inhabitants of
Noricum and surrounding countries *barbari*.[104] He seems to have been
a monk in Severinus's community in Noricum, to have witnessed the
death of Severinus, and to have been present at the exhumation of his
body, which he and the other monks accompanied to Italy.[105] R. Noll
conjectures that he was born ca. 460, that he was twenty-two at the time
of the death of Severinus, that he became abbot of Lucullanum at the age
of fifty in 510, and died ca. 535.[106] According to his letter to Paschasius in
Rome, he gathered additional information from the older monks of the
community:

> commemoratorium nonnullis refertum indiciis ex notissima nobis et
> cottidiana maiorum relatione composui.[107]

The identification proposed by Lotter, though a possibility, is not based on
adequate evidence. Prinz points out that, in order to accept it, some
straining of the meaning of the text has to be practised.[108] In his letter to

---

[100] Prinz, "Zur Vita Severini," pp. 532-533, on Lotter, "Severinus und die Endzeit,"
p. 312.

[101] Eugippius, *Vita Severini* 36, pp. 102-103.

[102] Lotter, "Severinus und die Endzeit," p. 312.

[103] Prinz, "Zur Vita Severini," p. 533; Graus, "Die Gewalt," pp. 94-99.

[104] E.g., *Vita Severini* 1, pp. 58-59; 3, pp. 62-63; 9, pp. 70-71; 35, pp. 100-101; 40,
pp. 106-107.

[105] Ibid., pp. 43-44, pp. 108-115.

[106] Eugippius, [*Vita Severini*] *Das Leben des heiligen Severin*, ed. and German trans.
by R. Noll (Berlin 1963), pp. 13-14.

[107] *Ep. ad Paschasium* 2, pp. 40-41.

[108] Prinz, "Zur Vita Severini," pp. 531-532.

Paschasius, Eugippius tells us that Severinus laughingly refused to disclose his origins. It was, however, clear to Eugippius that he was a man of the West, who had spent some time in the East and who arrived in Noricum in 435, at the time of the death of Attila the Hun. What Eugippius tells us of his practices certainly indicates that Eastern influences persisted after his arrival in Noricum:

> Loquela tamen ipsius manifestabat hominem omnino Latinum, quem constat prius ad quandam Orientis solitudinem fervore perfectionis vitae fuisse profectum....

Severinus sometimes spoke of his travels:

> nonnullas Orientis urbes nominans, et itineris immensi pericula se mirabiliter transisse significans....[109]

The narrative of Eugippius describes the painful austerities which he practised and gives the impression that he preferred the life of a solitary, but was driven by divine revelation to found a *coenobium*; at first he departed from the other monks to a more remote place which was called *ad Vineas*. From there he was impelled to depart to found his *coenobium* at Favianis, but he later established a *secretum habitaculum* called Burgum, about a mile from the town, to which he used often to retire to escape from the crowds.[110] All this recalls the practices of Antony in his early days, and of other Desert Fathers.

Eugippius endows Severinus with gifts common to late antique holy men, but not always recognized as such by later commentators. In the first place, he possessed the gifts of prophecy (*ventura praedicere*) and discernment of spirits. We have already commented on his prophecy of the victory at Lauriacum. In addition, he prophesied that Paulinus would become bishop of Tiburnia, that the basilica at Boiotro would be destroyed, that relics of St John the Baptist would arrive, and that the town of Ioviaco would meet with a sad fate. Lastly, like many other holy men, he prophesied his own death.[111] His powers of discernment gave him a premonition that the bodies of some murdered soldiers would be found; they led him, too, to send one of the captives whom he had redeemed into enemy territory to find a man carrying relics of Gervase and Protase, to look for Maurus, who had strayed across the frontier, and to order a boat for purposes of rescue.[112] In performing acts of healing and

---

[109] *Ep. ad Paschasium* 10, pp. 44-45.
[110] *Vita Severini* 4, pp. 62-65.
[111] Ibid. 21-24, pp. 86-89; 4, pp. 106-107.
[112] Ibid. 9-10, pp. 70-73; 20, pp. 86-87.

exorcism, he did not use relics, but relied upon prayer, fasting, and the sign of the cross.[113]

Two of Severinus's miracles have literary connections. The story of the conversation between Severinus and the dead man Silvinus, who said that he did not wish to return to life, recalls Augustine's story of the *curialis* Curma in *De cura pro mortuis gerenda*, to which we have already referred.[114] The other story is of an "increase" miracle, which recalls an incident in the *Dialogues* of Sulpicius Severus, a work known to Eugippius. It describes the overflowing of a flask of oil at a time of scarcity when Severinus had collected the *pauperes* into a church for a general distribution. Eugippius here compares Severinus to Elisha.[115]

Two miracles described by Eugippius concern deliverances from disasters in the natural world. The first related to the destruction of a swarm of locusts, the second, to the holding-back of a flood by means of the sign of the cross, which has its parallel in the stories, which we have examined already, of flames held back on account of the presence of the holy man.[116]

There are, however, in this *Vita*, two kinds of miracles which anticipate developments in later writers, particularly Gregory of Tours. The first is the phenomenon of the self-lighting candle, which occurs on two occasions.[117] The second is the element of punishment which is found in certain miracle-stories. The first two illustrate punishment for disobedience: the only person whose little patch of ground was not spared by the locusts was the man who went out to look at it though Severinus had ordered all the people to remain in church to pray. The second, the removal of blight from wheat by a gentle shower of rain, after the people had repented of their sins, would not have occurred if the people had not disobeyed Severinus because there would have been no blight to be removed. In the last two cases, misdeeds were punished by demonic possession. Some monks were punished for vanity in this way; so likewise was Avitianus, for stealing a chalice from the altar on behalf of Ferde-ruchus.[118]

---

[113] E.g., ibid. 6, pp. 66-69; 14, pp. 78-79; 36, pp. 102-103; 38, pp. 104-105.

[114] Ibid. 16, pp. 80-83; see p. 87, n. 98.

[115] Ibid. 28, pp. 93-95; cf. Sulpicius Severus, *Dialogue* 2(3).3, pp. 200-201; Gregory the Great, *Dialogue* 2.28, 2: 216-219. For Eugippius's knowledge of Sulpicius Severus's *Dialogues*, see *Vita Severini* 36, pp. 102-103.

[116] *Vita Severini* 12, pp. 74-77; 15, pp. 78-81.

[117] Ibid. 11, pp. 74-75; 13, pp. 78-79.

[118] Ibid. 17-18, pp. 82-85; 36, pp. 102-103; 44, pp. 112-113.

These miracle-stories are undoubtedly *topoi*, though in some cases, the *topos* may coincide with the reality.

There are also two non-miraculous episodes in the *Vita* which may fall into the same category. The first relates to the destruction of a church and the slaying of a priest who spoke sacrilegious words. Similar stories are told by Jerome in one of his letters, and by Sidonius Apollinaris, a contemporary of Severinus.[119] The second is the instruction given upon his deathbed by Severinus to the monks to keep together and to take his bones with them, because the land would be devastated and graves would be violated. Parallel stories of Germanic origin are told of the martyr-bishop Quirinus, Pollio, and the Four Crowned Martyrs.[120]

Severinus remained buried from his death in 482 until 488, when Onoulfus, the brother of Odoacer, ordered the Romans to return to Italy. Not surprisingly in the case of a holy man, the body, when disinterred, was incorrupt and gave off a sweet smell. It was finally laid to rest at Lucullanum in the reign of Pope Gelasius, that is, between 492 and 496.[121]

Relics are mentioned in three places in the *Vita Severini*, but they are not the relics of Severinus himself, nor are they employed for the purpose of working miracles. In fact their function appears to be to consecrate and sanctify church buildings. Relics of Gervase and Protase indeed made it possible to pick out a man who was carrying them, but their real purpose was to serve as a focus of devotion in the church, and to act as the nucleus of a collection of further relics. It is probable that the relics of St John the Baptist performed a similar function at Boiotro, where great activity in collecting relics was displayed.[122]

Severinus however, continued to work miracles after his death, just as Caesarius did. When the body of Severinus first came to rest at Monte Feletro, near Rimini, various people with diseases or possessed by evil spirits, including a man who was deaf and dumb, were immediately healed. The latter crawled under the bier and prayed "in his heart." Further cures were effected by the bier when the body reached Naples, through physical contact with it or merely by being in its presence.[123] The miracles, however, appear to have ceased after the interment of the body.

---

[119] Ibid. 22, pp. 86-89; 24, pp. 90-91; Jerome, *Ep.* 60.16.3, 1: 570-571; Sidonius Apollinaris, *Ep.* 7.6.7-10, *Epistolae*, ed. C. Luetjohann, MGH AA 8 (Berlin 1887), pp. 1-72, at pp. 109-110.

[120] See R. Egger, *Der heilige Hermagoras* (Klagenfurt 1948), pp. 51 ff., for details; cited by R. Noll, "Das Leben des heiligen Severin," p. 145.

[121] *Vita Severini* 44, pp. 112-115.

[122] Ibid. 9, pp. 70-73; 22-23, pp. 86-89.

[123] Ibid. 45-46, pp. 115-117.

It is almost certain that this *Vita* was intended primarily for a monastic audience. It contains the kind of edifying stories of a holy man which were considered appropriate to such an audience and stressed the thaumaturgical aspects of his career to the exclusion of the political and economic situation in Noricum, information about which would have been of interest to posterity. The motive of Eugippius was probably to preserve the memory of the illustrious founder of his community and to provide his monks with an example of "holy living and holy dying."

C. The Origins of the Two-fold Tradition of Thaumaturgy

We have already noticed that in the period from the mid-fourth to the late sixth century two distinct traditions of thaumaturgy developed in Western Christendom. In this chapter, apart from Augustine, the writers whom we have considered belong mainly to the tradition in which the miracle-worker is the living holy man, though it is not always possible to draw up hard-and-fast dividing lines between the different classes of miracle-worker. Augustine, for example, reports healings which were achieved solely by prayer, as in the case of Innocentius who suffered from a fistula, or by holy baptism, as in the case of the doctor who suffered from gout, and the former actor who was paralyzed. Even in the works of Gregory of Tours, which we shall consider in the next chapter, we find instances of miracles performed by living holy men, though the majority of those described in his pages were brought about at the tombs of holy men or by means of relics. On the other hand, some of those who were personally active as miracle-workers sometimes employed relics: we have already noticed that objects which had been in contact with the living Martin – a letter, threads from his hairshirt, and a piece of straw – were found to be efficacious for healing, and that both objects and water which had been in contact with Caesarius, whether he was living or dead, could also work miracles. Gregory the Great himself falls into the same category: for the most part, his holy men bring about miracles by prayers, the sign of the cross, or by other physical means, but he records four cases of the use of relics, as we have already seen in chapter three.

Broadly speaking, it is the writers who have come under Eastern Christian influences, whether personally or through literature, who see the living holy man as the miracle-worker. Those whose background is more Western are more interested in the efficacy of dead holy men and their relics as miracle-workers. Augustine was led to take an interest in miracles as the result of the arrival of the relics of Stephen in North Africa. Paulinus reported the miracles achieved on the finding of the bodies of Gervase and Protase. Gregory of Tours, as we shall see, was impressed by the tombs and relics of the martyrs and confessors of Gaul, particularly of Martin and Julian, though he had Byzantine contacts, as Averil Cameron has pointed out.[124] Ambrose knew the world of Greek theology and was well-placed at Milan for receiving Byzantine news, but, like Gregory of Tours, he remained committed to Western ideas.

The remaining writers all have contacts with the East. Jerome spent some time as a solitary in the desert of Chalcis, long before he settled in Palestine, and had also lived at Antioch in the household of Evagrius of Antioch. The Jura Fathers probably had links with Lérins and thus with Eastern Christendom through the sojourn of Romanus at a monastery in Lyons. Sulpicius Severus certainly had first-hand information about monasticism in Egypt, judging by his description in his *Dialogues*. Underlying all his writings on Martin as miracle-worker, we can detect the image of Antony. P. H. Rousseau has made the interesting suggestion that Sulpicius Severus was not so much influenced by the *Vita S. Antonii* as reacting to it.[125] He was trying to show the people of Gaul that they, too, had holy men in their midst; the districts which are now known as Touraine and Poitou were as much a desert from the spiritual point of view as the sands of Egypt and formed an equally suitable habitat for hermits. There is much to be said for this view, and Rousseau's conclusion seems similarly appropriate to Gregory's *Dialogues*, particularly to the life of Benedict. Gregory is at pains to stress that he is writing of holy men in Italy and implies that the district around Subiaco forms a second Thebaid. The same kind of impression is also conveyed by the *Liber vitae patrum* of Gregory of Tours, as we shall see later.

On the other hand, the *Vita Caesarii arelatensis*, the *Vita patrum iurensium* and the *Vita Severini* seem to be straightforward accounts of the lives of holy men, even though their authors had Eastern connections. We have already seen that Lérins almost certainly forms a link between the Jura Fathers and Eastern spirituality, and that considerable emphasis is placed by Eugippius on the Eastern connection of Severinus.

What are we to make of the connections illustrated by the chart at the end of this chapter? We have definite evidence that both Eugippius and the author of the *Vita patrum iurensium* knew the work of Sulpicius Severus, but beyond that, all is conjectural only. The chart indicates that the same stories as told by Sulpicius Severus and Gregory of Tours were

---

[124] A. M. Cameron, "The Byzantine Sources of Gregory of Tours," *JTS*, n.s. 26 (1975): 421-426.

[125] P. H. Rousseau, "Ascetics, Authority and the Church," p. 144.

also known in the Eastern Mediterranean area. Greek was now little known in Western Europe. It therefore looks as though Gregory the Great was drawing upon a corpus of material which was common property throughout the Mediterranean area, and was following his usual technique of adapting literary matter which already embodied some of the traditional material for his own purposes.

From the chart on pp. 120-121 we can see that many of the stories can be traced back to biblical origins. Caesarius, like Gregory, would tend to view his material typologically because, like Gregory, he had received a monastic training; in this he was followed by his biographers. Sulpicius Severus, on the other hand, because he had been brought up as a layman, tended to look for literary parallels, as we have already seen. The resemblances between the stories do not therefore prove that Gregory was influenced by other authors of miracle-stories.

There are two other arguments in favour of his having read Sulpicius Severus, which, on first sight, appear strong, but are not completely convincing. The first is the resemblance between the stories of life after death told by Gregory and Sulpicius Severus.

The two principal points in common between the stories of life after death are 1. in both cases a dream or vision is involved; 2. in both cases a sinner is helped by the prayers of his friends in this world. This is not, however, sufficient evidence to indicate a literary borrowing. As P. Antin points out,[126] dreams and visions played an extremely important part in the Bible and in classical and late antique literature. Fontaine adds the further interesting note that this passage in *Vita S. Martini*, like the description of Jerome's dream which forms the basis of Antin's article, shows that late antique Christians envisaged the Last Judgement as being comparable to a law-court.[127] Thus Sulpicius Severus sets a scene here, which is more comparable to Jerome than to Gregory. The vision described by Gregory is more comparable to the many apparitions of holy persons described by Gregory of Tours than to the vision of the Judge in the *Vita S. Martini* or of the Tribunal which condemned Jerome as a *Ciceronianus*. Again, the efficacy of prayers for the dead is a topic which occurs as early as the beginning of the third century in the *Passio SS Perpetuae et Felicitatis*; and the practice of praying for the dead is widely commended by Tertullian and by the Latin Fathers, particularly Ambrose,

---

[126] P. Antin, "Autour du songe de saint Jérôme," *RÉL* 41 (1963): 350-377, at pp. 358-359.

[127] J. Fontaine, ed., *Vita S. Martini* 7, 1: 625-631.

Augustine, and Jerome.[128] There is therefore nothing new in the ideas expressed by both Sulpicius Severus and Gregory. They could well have thought of them independently.

Secondly, the works of Sulpicius Severus became known in Italy in his lifetime, as we have already seen, and it seems unlikely that they would have been forgotten. Indeed there is definite evidence for the extension of the Martin cult in sixth-century Italy. A church at Verona and monastic chapels in Rome itself, at Vivarium, and at Monte Cassino were dedicated to him.[129] Gregory himself tells us how Benedict, the *vir Dei*, on his arrival at Monte Cassino destroyed the image, overturned the pagan altar, cut down the sacred groves, and established a shrine to Martin on the site of a temple of Apollo (2.8, 2: 168-169). His *contrivit idolum* is not a verbal reminiscence, but there is a Martinian touch about it and about the whole description, which recalls the vivid scenes in the *Dialogues* of Sulpicius Severus where Martin destroyed the idols.[130] Indeed it is the resemblances in spirit and atmosphere in the structure of Gregory's *Dialogue* 2 as compared with the *Vita Antonii* and the *Vita S. Martini*, and above all, in the comparative portraits of Martin and Benedict that the strongest evidence for Gregory's having read Antony and Sulpicius Severus lies.

---

[128] *Acta Perpetuae et Felicitatis* 7-8, in Musurillo, *Acts of the Christian Martyrs*, pp. 114-117.

[129] Prinz, *Frühes Mönchtum*, pp. 30-31.

[130] Sulpicius Severus, *Dialogue* 2(3).8, p. 206.

TYPE OF MIRACLE-STORIES

Type of miracle	Bible	Paulinus Vita Ambrosii	Sulpicius Severus	Vita patrum iurensium
Resuscitation of corpse	1 (3) Kings 17.24 2 (4) Kings 4.29-37 Luke 7.4-6 John 11	28	Vita S. Martini 7-8	
Fire or water turned back	Dan. 3		Vita S. Martini 14	
Increase of oil	1 (3) Kings 17.12-16 2 (4) Kings 4.2-7		Dialogue 2(3).3	
Unbroken flask of oil*			Dialogue 2(3).3	
Healing of leper	2 (4) Kings 5.1-end		Vita S. Martini 1	46-47
Immobility	1 (3) Kings 13.4	20	Vita S. Martini 15	
			Vita S. Martini 12 (procession)	
			Dialogue 1(2).3 (horses)	

* Though this is not strictly based on a biblical type, it is included because it is so closely connected with the "increase miracles" in our writers.

Type of Miracle-Stories

Cyprian *Vita Caesarii*	Eugippius *Vita Severini*	Gregory I *Dialogues*	Gregory of Tours	Eastern writers
1.38-40 2.2		1.2 1.10 2.32 3.17	*Liber in gloria confessorum* 78 *De virtutibus S. Martini* 2.39	*Historia monachorum* 9.11 *Apophthegmata* 6.2 Theodoret, *Historia religiosa* 21
1.22 2.26	15	1.6		Socrates, *Historia ecclesiastica* 7.38 = Cassiodorus, *Historia tripartita* 12.10
	28	2.29	*Liber in gloria martyrum* 5 *De virtutibus S. Martini* 3, 24, 32	Theodoret, *Historia religiosa* 14
1.51	28	2.28		
	26, 34	2.26		
		3.37	*Liber historiarum* 6.6 *De virtutibus S. Martini* 1.2	*Historia monachorum* 6.30 Theodoret, *Historia religiosa* 14, 15 John Moschus, *Pratum* 15 *Historia monachorum* 8.40 (procession)
		3.22 (sheep stealer)		*Vita Spyridonis* (1) 18 (sheep stealer)
				Historia monachorum 6.2 Cyr. Scyth., *Vita Euthymii* 69 (thieves in the night)
		1.2 (horses)		

5

Gregory of Tours
and the Development of Relics

A. RELICS IN SIXTH-CENTURY GAUL

We have already noticed two distinct traditions in the writers of miracle-stories in the West, and we have dealt at some length with the slightly earlier tradition of the living holy man as agent of miracles. It is now time for us to examine the parallel tradition of the dead holy man as worker of miracles through his tomb or through his relics, of which we have already considered examples in the writings of Augustine and of Paulinus of Milan.

The cult of relics in Gaul had come into existence contemporaneously with the events described in *De civitate Dei* 22.8 and in the *Vita Ambrosii* of Paulinus. The practice of dedicating churches with relics of the saints, inaugurated by Ambrose in 386 on the finding of the bodies of Gervase and Protase,[1] spread over Western Europe within the next ten years. In 396 Ambrose gave to Victricius, bishop of Rouen, the relics of no less than thirteen saints with which to dedicate Rouen Cathedral. The sermon of Victricius on this occasion was expanded into the treatise *De laude sanctorum*, laying down the lines on which the cult of relics was to develop. Victricius told the people that in the form of relics, part of the heavenly host had visited Rouen, so that even in this life its citizens would henceforward live in its company. Since the blood as part of the body partook of heavenly fire, even the smallest relic would partake of the virtue of the whole. Thus, by means of their relics, the same saints would be able to heal the sick in many places. The relics would become, as it were, sacramental signs through which grace would be conveyed.[2]

---

[1] See *Vita Ambrosii* 14, pp. 70-73.
[2] *De laude sanctorum* 3, PL 20: 445; see E. W. Kemp, *Canonisation and Authority in the Early Church* (London 1948), pp. 4-5.

Gregory of Tours is the writer *par excellence* on miracles in late antique Gaul. He portrays a very different world from the other writers whom we have already considered, where certain aspects of thaumaturgy are stressed to the exclusion of the rest. His principal criterion of Christian sanctity is the power to work miracles. Though living holy men are not excluded, they definitely take second place; his emphasis is all on miracles worked through dead saints from their tombs or through their relics. Indeed his zeal to record miracles sometimes causes him to treat other important matters as mere side-issues. As S. Boesch Gajano has pointed out, Christ is presented as the first in the line of martyrs, and the story of the nativity is contained in an ablative absolute.[3] Gregory's interest in Helena and Radegund is due to their connection with the True Cross; Stephen the proto-martyr is seen principally as a source of relics.[4]

The one clue, which Gregory, an enigmatic personality, affords us as to the reason for his interest in miracles and indeed in church history in general, is contained in the preface to the *Liber in gloria martyrum*. He refers to the celebrated dream of Jerome, as the result of which he decides to eschew secular literature, a snare which he, Gregory, is also determined to avoid. His avowed object is to build up the Church by means of his writings:

> Ergo haec nos oportet sequi, scribere, atque loqui, quae ecclesiam aedificent et quae mentes inopes ad notitiam perfectae fidei instructione sancta faecundent. Non enim oportet fallaces commemorare fabulas....[5]

Gregory makes it quite clear that the *fallaces fabulae* are not legends or fictitious stories about the martyrs, but stories in secular literature, particularly in the *Aeneid*. It is interesting that his quotations are all taken from books 1, 2, 4, 6, and 8;[6] probably these were the books most generally read in schools in his time, as today.

Unfortunately we have no information as to the identity of the possessors of the *inopes mentes*. Boesch Gajano too readily assumes that Sulpicius Severus was writing for a cultured readership, whereas Gregory of Tours had less literate people in mind.[7] One wonders whether she has not been unconsciously influenced by the contrast between the polished

---

[3] S. Boesch Gajano, "Il santo nella visione di Gregorio di Tours," *Atti di XII convegno storico internazionale dell'Accademia Tudertina* (Todi 1971), pp. 29-91, at p. 33, commenting on *Liber in gloria martyrum* 1, pp. 37-38.

[4] Ibid., p. 34, on *Liber in gloria martyrum* 5, pp. 39-40.

[5] *Liber in gloria martyrum* prol., p. 37; cf. Jerome, *Ep.* 22.2, 1: 146.

[6] For details, see MGH SRM 1 (2), p. 37, n. 1, nn. 3-8; p. 38, nn. 1-6, 8-16.

[7] Boesch Gajano, "Il santo," pp. 46-47.

Latin of Sulpicius and the *rusticitas* of Gregory of Tours. It is more likely that Gregory's writings provide yet one more example of the cultural change which began to occur early in the fifth century; Sulpicius Severus is one of the last writers of the old world and Gregory of Tours one of the first of the new. He was probably writing for the secular clergy and the relatively few cultivated lay-people. In confirmation of this view, we find few references to the cenobitic life in the *Liber in gloria martyrum*, the *Liber in gloria confessorum* and the *Libri historiarum*.[8] We have the impression of an active diocesan bishop, much involved in the secular life of his day, though there are descriptions in the *Liber in gloria confessorum* and the *Libri historiarum* of hermits.[9] From the *Liber vitae patrum* we learn that certain hermits collected followers and founded monasteries, but the emphasis is on the holy man as miracle-worker rather than as father of a religious community.[10] In connection with the question of Gregory's potential readership, it is interesting to note that though the subject matter of his life of Martin is not dissimilar to that of Sulpicius, *Vita S. Martini*, the styles of these works are in vivid contrast, that of the latter being appropriate to the well-educated monks and laity of the fourth century; the style of the former, however, is less polished and is an indication of that cultural change which we have already noticed.

Besides his avowed intention that he would follow Jerome in providing materials,

> Deo digna et ad aedificationem ecclesiae opportuna,[11]

Gregory probably had other motives. Almost certainly he wished to win fame for his own diocese of Tours, where the tomb of Martin, the principal miracle-worker, was situated, and to support the policy of the Merovingians, whereby the Martin cult was used for political ends. He

---

[8] For *coenobia*, see, e.g., *Libri historiarum* 4.47, p. 184; 5.21, p. 228; 6.29, p. 297; 9.35, p. 455; 40, p. 464; 10.29, p. 523; *Liber in gloria martyrum* 5, p. 39; 79, pp. 346-347; *Liber in gloria confessorum* 16, p. 306; 22, pp. 311-312; 25, p. 314 (cf. *Libri historiarum* 5.7, p. 204; *Liber vitae patrum* 15 (1), p. 271); 37, p. 321; *Liber vitae patrum* 16 (1), p. 275. These references to monasteries are, for the most part, incidental, as, e.g., to Lérins, *Liber in gloria confessorum* 95, p. 359.

[9] For hermits mentioned elsewhere than in *Liber vitae patrum*, see, e.g., *Libri historiarum* 2.37, pp. 86-87; 4.37, p. 169 (cf. *Liber vitae patrum* 10 (1-3), pp. 256-259); 5.7, p. 204 (cf. *Liber vitae patrum* 15 (1-4), pp. 271-274); 6.6, p. 272; 8, p. 277; 8.34, p. 403; 9.40, p. 466; *Liber in gloria confessorum* 23-26, pp. 312-314; 80-81, pp. 348-350; 96, pp. 359-360; 101, p. 362.

[10] E.g., Romanus and Lupicinus, *Liber vitae patrum* 1 (1), p. 214; Patroclus, who remained a hermit, but founded a community of monks and nuns, 9 (1-3), pp. 252-255; Brachio, 12 (2-3), pp. 262-265; Martius, 14 (2), pp. 268-269; Sennoch, 15 (1), pp. 271-272.

[11] See n. 5 above.

may well have found the miracle-stories, "set in medallions," [12] useful as a literary device for contrasting past and present.

Gregory of Tours describes his miracles in considerably more detail than any of the earlier writers whom we have considered, apart from Augustine. It is possible to distinguish different categories, which include: 1. miracles involving animals, particularly horses; 2. miracles by which people or animals are rendered immobile; 3. apparitions of saints; 4. dreams and visions; 5. apparitions involving light, such as balls of fire, mysterious lights in churches, self-lighting lamps and candles, lights in locked churches, etc.; 6. miracles at tombs, caused by touching them, sleeping on them, or praying at them (the principal tombs for this purpose are those of Martin and Julian, but there are many others, such as those of Romanus and Illidius in the *Liber vitae patrum*); 7. changes in the nature of the elements, particularly fire and water, and of substances; 8. "increase" miracles; 9. singing by unseen choirs; 10. mysterious voices; 11. the "odour of sanctity"; 12. self-moving tombs; 13. raising the dead; 14. objects which arrive by supernatural means, or which change their weight; 15. breakages.[13]

[12] Boesch Gajano, "Il santo," p. 62.

[13] E.g., 1. *Liber de virtutibus S. Iuliani* 21, p. 123; 31, p. 127; *De virtutibus S. Martini* 1.29, p. 152; 3.18, p. 187; 33, p. 190. 2. *Libri historiarum* 6.6, p. 273; *Liber in gloria martyrum* 54, p. 76. 3. ibid. 8, p. 43; 33, p. 59; *Liber in gloria confessorum* 18, p. 308; 58, p. 331; 79, p. 347. 4. *Liber in gloria martyrum* 22, p. 51; *Liber de virtutibus S. Iuliani* 28, p. 126; *De virtutibus S. Martini* 2.31, p. 170; 38, p. 172; 56, p. 178; 4.17, p. 204; 20, p. 205; 37, p. 209; *Liber vitae patrum* 9 (2), p. 254; 16 (2), p. 275; *Liber in gloria confessorum* 17, p. 307. 5. *Libri historiarum* 2.37, p. 86; 6.25, p. 292; 33, p. 304; *Liber in gloria martyrum* 5, p. 40; 6, p. 42; 31, p. 57; 33, p. 59; 49, p. 72; *Liber de virtutibus S. Iuliani* 34, p. 128; *De virtutibus S. Martini* 2.15, p. 164; 18, p. 165; 29, p. 170; *Liber vitae patrum* 12 (3), p. 264; *Liber in gloria confessorum* 20, p. 309; 29, p. 316; 38, pp. 321-322; 69, p. 338; 102, p. 363. 6. *Liber in gloria martyrum* 29, p. 55; 32, pp. 57-58; 38, pp. 62-63; 43, p. 67; *Liber de virtutibus S. Iuliani* 10, p. 119; *De virtutibus S. Martini*, among numerous examples, 1.8, p. 143; 2.3, p. 160; 5, p. 161; 8, pp. 161-162; 3.39, p. 192; 46, p. 193; 54, p. 195; 4.21, pp. 199-200; *Liber vitae patrum* 2 (2), p. 220; 5, p. 222; 9 (3), p. 255; 14 (4), p. 270; 15 (4), p. 274; 16 (4), p. 277; 17 (6), p. 283; 18 (3), p. 285; 19 (4), pp. 289-290; *Liber in gloria confessorum*, among numerous examples, 28, p. 315; 35, pp. 320-321; 56, p. 330. 7. *Libri historiarum* 8.33, p. 402; *Liber in gloria martyrum* 9, p. 44; 10, p. 45; 35, p. 60; 36, p. 61; *Liber de virtutibus S. Iuliani* 27, pp. 125-126; *De virtutibus S. Martini* 1.2, p. 138; 9, pp. 143-144; *Liber vitae patrum* 2 (3), pp. 220-221; *Liber in gloria confessorum* 2-3, pp. 299-300; 22, p. 311; 54, pp. 329-330. 8. *Liber in gloria martyrum* 5, p. 40; 9, pp. 44-45; 14, p. 48; *Liber de virtutibus S. Iuliani* 36, p. 129; *De virtutibus S. Martini* 2.24, pp. 188-189; *Liber vitae patrum* 3 (1), p. 223; *Liber in gloria confessorum* 1, pp. 298-299; 83, pp. 351-352. 9. *Libri historiarum* 1.48, p. 32; *Liber in gloria martyrum* 33, p. 59; *Liber de virtutibus S. Iuliani* 42, p. 131; *De virtutibus S. Martini* 1.4, p. 140; *Liber vitae patrum* 7 (2), pp. 237-238; 13 (1), p. 166; *Liber in gloria confessorum* 29, p. 316; 46, p. 326; 72, p. 341. 10. *Liber in gloria martyrum* 50, pp. 72-74; 64, pp. 81-82; *De virtutibus S. Martini* 2.6, p. 161; 23, pp. 166-167; *Liber in gloria*

The miracles of healing form a class apart. The diseases from which Gregory's subjects principally suffer are paralysis, blindness, deafness and dumbness, contraction of limbs (which may be rheumatoid arthritis), various fevers (which may well include malaria), eye-diseases (which sound like ophthalmia and cataract), and demonic possession.[14]

Healing is sometimes achieved by simply being present in the basilica near the tomb and practising fasting and prayer,[15] but more often relics play their part. Sleeping in the bed of a holy man is often effective.[16] Pieces of the *fimbria* or fringe of the holy man's clothing, of the hangings round the tomb, and of the *palla* or veil of the tomb or reliquary or of the wood of the screen are also used.[17] Dust is a favourite remedy. This can be

---

confessorum 4-5, p. 301; 30, pp. 316-317; 39, p. 322; 40, p. 323; 64, p. 336; 66, p. 337; 72, p. 341. 11. *Libri historiarum* 2.16, p. 64; *Liber vitae patrum* 10 (4), p. 259; *Liber in gloria confessorum* 40, p. 323; 94, p. 359. 12. *Liber in gloria confessorum* 27, pp. 314-315; 51, p. 328; 59, p. 332. 13. *Libri historiarum* 1.39, p. 27; 2.31, p. 77 (cf. *Liber in gloria confessorum* 78, pp. 344-345); *De virtutibus S. Martini* 2.39, p. 173; 43, p. 174; *Liber in gloria confessorum* 82, pp. 350-351. 14. *Liber in gloria martyrum* 6, p. 42; 13, p. 47; 14, p. 48; 21, p. 51; *Liber de virtutibus S. Iuliani* 44, p. 131; *De virtutibus S. Martini* 1.6, p. 142; *Liber vitae patrum* 7 (3), p. 239; *Liber in gloria confessorum* 17, p. 307. 15. *Liber in gloria martyrum* 45, pp. 68-69.

[14] E.g., paralysis: *Liber de virtutibus S. Iuliani* 39, p. 130; *De virtutibus S. Martini* 1.25, p. 151; 27, p. 151; 2.3, p. 160; 5-6, p. 161; 3.58, p. 196; 4.6, p. 200; blindness: *Libri historiarum* 6.6, p. 275; *Liber de virtutibus S. Iuliani* 22, pp. 123-124; 47, p. 133; *De virtutibus S. Martini* 1.8, p. 143; 39, p. 156; 2.3, p. 160; 13, p. 163; 15, pp. 163-164; 3.16, p. 186; 19, p. 187; 15, pp. 163-164; 3.16, p. 186; 19, p. 187; 39, p. 192; 48, p. 194; 4.6, p. 200; *Liber vitae patrum* 8 (12), pp. 251-252; 9 (3), p. 255; 15 (3), p. 272; 19 (3), p. 289; deafness and dumbness: *Libri historiarum* 6.6, pp. 273-274; *De virtutibus S. Martini* 2.26, pp. 168-169; 3.17, p. 187; 37, p. 191; 49, p. 194; 54, p. 195; 4.36, pp. 208-209; *Liber vitae patrum* 19 (1), p. 287 (deafness only); (4), p. 290; contraction of limbs: *De virtutibus S. Martini* 2.42, p. 174; 49, p. 176; 56, p. 178; 3.7, pp. 183-184; 25-27, p. 189; 39, p. 192; 44, p. 193; *Liber vitae patrum* 19 (2), p. 288; various fevers: *Liber de virtutibus S. Iuliani* 24, pp. 124-125; *De virtutibus S. Martini* 2.23, p. 188; 50, p. 194; 4.3, p. 200; 10, p. 202; 37, p. 209; 43, p. 210; *Liber vitae patrum* 1 (6), pp. 217-218; 2 (2), p. 220; 6 (6), p. 234; 8 (10), p. 250; 14 (2), p. 268; 19 (4), p. 290; *Liber in gloria confessorum* 87, p. 354; eye-diseases: *Liber in gloria martyrum* 2.41, p. 174; *Liber vitae patrum* 15 (3), p. 272; 19 (3), p. 289; demonic possession: *Libri historiarum* 6.6, p. 275; *Liber in gloria martyrum* 5, p. 41; 43, p. 131; *De virtutibus S. Martini* 2.18, p. 165; 20, p. 166; 25, pp. 167-168; *Liber vitae patrum* 7 (2), p. 238; 8 (11), p. 250; 9(2), p. 254; 15 (3), p. 273; *Liber in gloria confessorum* 92, p. 357.

[15] E.g., *Liber de virtutibus S. Iuliani* 37, p. 130; *De virtutibus S. Martini* 4.14, p. 203; 44, p. 210; for vigils combined with sleep, *Liber de virtutibus S. Iuliani* 9, p. 118; 38, p. 130.

[16] *De virtutibus S. Martini* 2.21, p. 166; 45, p. 175; 3.22, p. 188; *Liber vitae patrum* 6 (6), p. 234; 8 (8), p. 248; *Liber in gloria confessorum* 84, p. 352; cf. *Vita Caesarii arelatensis* 1.29, p. 468; *Vita patrum iurensium* 78, p. 325.

[17] E.g., *fimbria*: *Liber de virtutibus S. Iuliani* 34, p. 128; *De virtutibus S. Martini* 4.43, p. 210; *Liber vitae patrum* 8 (6), p. 246; 13 (2), p. 260; *Liber in gloria confessorum* 84, p. 332; *palla, velum,* or *co-operturium*: *Liber de virtutibus S. Iuliani* 34, p. 128; 43, p. 131;

eaten, mixed with water, drunk, or carried about in a *capsa* or reliquary. Gregory of Tours invariably took a supply when going on a journey.[18] Oil from lamps and wax candles burning at the tomb of a holy man are also regarded as valuable remedies.[19] Augustine and Gregory the Great see the sacraments of Baptism and the Eucharist as a means of healing, but for Gregory of Tours, they are not so much a means of healing as an accompaniment to it.[20] The invocation of the saints, particularly Martin, plays an important part in it.[21]

The works of Gregory of Tours introduce a new element into the field of Western thaumaturgy, namely that of punishment for offences, particularly heresy, interference with tombs and blasphemy in church, and of healing as a reward when the offender has shown penitence. The usual punishment is for the offender to be struck deaf and dumb, or blind, but Gregory records the deaths of several such offenders including the priest, Leo, who moved the stone on which Martin was accustomed to sit.[22]

The Sunday workers were more fortunate. They invariably suffered some kind of paralysis of the arm or hand, but once they had repented,

---

De virtutibus S. Martini 2.10, p. 162; 36, p. 172; 43, p. 175; 54, p. 177; 3.1, p. 182; *Liber vitae patrum* 15 (4), p. 274; wood: *De virtutibus S. Martini* 1.35, p. 155; 4.2, p. 200; *Liber in gloria confessorum* 93, pp. 357-358.

[18] E.g., *Liber in gloria martyrum* 49, p. 72; *Liber de virtutibus S. Iuliani* 24, p. 125; 45, p. 131; *De virtutibus S. Martini* 1.2, p. 138; 27-28, p. 151; 37, p. 155; 2.1, p. 159; 12, pp. 162-163; 51, p. 176; 3.12, p. 185; 52, pp. 194-195; 4.9, pp. 201-202; 28, p. 206; 32-33, p. 208; 37, p. 209; 43, p. 210; 47, p. 211; *Liber vitae patrum* 8 (6), p. 246; (10), p. 250; *Liber in gloria confessorum* 35, p. 320; 52, p. 329; 63, p. 335; 73, p. 341; 103, p. 363; for Gregory of Tours carrying dust, e.g., *De virtutibus S. Martini* 3.43, p. 193; 60, p. 197.

[19] Oil: e.g., *De virtutibus S. Martini* 1.2, p. 138; 4.36, pp. 208-209; *Liber vitae patrum* 19 (4), p. 290; *Liber in gloria confessorum* 9, p. 304; wax: e.g., *Liber de virtutibus S. Iuliani* 45, p. 131; *De virtutibus S. Martini* 1.2, pp. 138-139; 28, p. 151; 34, p. 154; 2.2, pp. 159-160; 4.36, pp. 208-209; *Liber vitae patrum* 8 (6), p. 246; *Liber in gloria confessorum* 10, p. 304.

[20] Augustine, *De civitate Dei* 22.8, 2: 819-820 (Baptism); p. 820 (Eucharist); Gregory the Great, *Dialogues* 2.24, 2: 210-213; 3.3, 2: 268-271 (Eucharist); cf. Gregory of Tours, *De virtutibus S. Martini* 2.43, pp. 174-175 (Baptism); *De virtutibus S. Martini* 2.14, p. 163; 47, p. 176; *Liber in gloria confessorum* 93, pp. 357-358 (Eucharist).

[21] E.g., Julian: *Liber de virtutibus S. Iuliani* 4, p. 116; 6, p. 117; 30, pp. 126-127; Martin: *De virtutibus S. Martini* 1.2, p. 138; 9, pp. 143-144; 11, p. 145; 20-21, p. 149; 23, p. 150; 2.6, p. 161; 26, pp. 168-169; 27-28, p. 169; 47, pp. 175-176; 3.4, p. 183; 8, pp. 183-184; 26, p. 189; 28, p. 189; 35, pp. 190-191; 53, p. 195; 4.15-16, pp. 203-204; 21, p. 205; 29, p. 200; 47, p. 211; Paul: *Liber in gloria martyrum* 28, p. 54.

[22] Being struck deaf and dumb: e.g., *Liber in gloria confessorum* 17, p. 307; 28, p. 315; 66, p. 337; being struck blind: e.g., *De virtutibus S. Martini* 1.2, p. 137; *Liber in gloria confessorum* 13, pp. 305-306; being struck dead: e.g., *Liber in gloria martyrum* 13, p. 48; *De virtutibus S. Martini* 1.17, p. 148; 31, p. 153; *Liber in gloria confessorum* 6, p. 303; 47, pp. 326-327.

they were later restored after a visit to a church with the relics of a saint or to the tomb of the basilica.[23] Those who committed these offences belong to both town and country, but rural offenders appear to predominate.[24] There appear to be two main reasons for the inclusion of these stories: first, there was evidently a movement in the sixth century aiming at the stricter observance of Sunday; imperial legislation on this subject is embodied in Justinian's code, under the title *de feriis*, where all work, except agricultural labour, is forbidden.[25] Moreover, the condemnation of Sunday work is upheld by the canons of the Gallic councils: Agde (506), Orleans (538), Mâcon (585), Auxerre (561-605), and Chalon (647-653).[26] I. N. Wood has pointed out that the date of the Council of Mâcon coincides with the period when Gregory was writing his *De virtutibus S. Martini* in the third book of which he deals with the majority of the cases of Sunday work. He rightly adds that it was not the proceedings of this particular council, which first aroused Gregory's interest in the subject, since some of the Sunday miracles are anterior to 585.[27] It seems likely that an even sterner discipline prevailed in the West than in the East, and that these stories may have arisen as a result of warnings and cautionary tales propulgated on the part of the secular clergy. Second, the stories are designed, like much other material in the *Libri historiarum*, the *Liber de virtutibus S. Iuliani* and the *De virtutibus S. Martini*, to enhance the prestige of the basilica. In most cases it is the visit to the basilica rather than the visit to a living holy man, by the offender, which ultimately brings about restoration.[28]

What of the living holy man? He is not unknown in the pages of Gregory of Tours, but he seems to play a subordinate role compared with

---

[23] E.g., *Liber in gloria martyrum* 15, p. 48; *De virtutibus S. Martini* 2.24, p. 167; 57, p. 178; 3.3, p. 183; 7, pp. 183-184; 29, p. 189; 31, p. 190; 38, pp. 191-192; 45, p. 193; 55, p. 195; 4.45, pp. 210-211; *Liber vitae patrum* 7 (5), p. 240; *Liber in gloria confessorum* 80, pp. 348-349; 97, pp. 360-361.

[24] Offences committed in the country: e.g., *De virtutibus S. Martini* 2.57, p. 178; 3.3, p. 183; 7, pp. 183-184; 29, p. 189; 31, p. 190; 55, p. 195; *Liber in gloria confessorum* 80, pp. 348-349; 97, pp. 360-361. This suggests that the regulations were drawn up by urban ecclesiastics who lacked understanding of secular rural life.

[25] *Codex Theodosianus* 3.13.3, *Corpus iuris civilis* 2, ed. and rev. P. Krueger, 10th impr. (Berlin 1929), pp. 127-129.

[26] *Concilia Galliae* 47, *Concilia Galliae*, 1, A314-A506, ed. C. Munier, CCSL 168 (Turnholt 1963); p. 21; ibid. 31, p. 125; ibid. 1, 2, A511-A695, ed. C. de Clercq, CCSL 168A (Turnholt 1963), pp. 239-240; ibid. 2, p. 267; ibid. 18, p. 307.

[27] I. N. Wood, "Early Merovingian Devotion in Town and Country," *SCH(L)* 16 (1979), pp. 61-76, at p. 64.

[28] Exceptions are Gregory of Langres, *Liber vitae patrum* 7 (5), p. 240; Sennoch, ibid. 15 (3), p. 273.

the dead saint with a tomb in a great basilica. He is usually a hermit or a solitary of some kind, who seems to exist chiefly for the sake of performing miracles from the tomb when dead. The wonders carried out in his lifetime are dismissed as "many miracles," as in the case of Venantius and Ursus, fathers in the *Liber vitae patrum*.[29]

Some of the accounts in this work open with a commonplace of hagiography, the infancy narrative, wherein the future holy man, after a pious childhood, possibly with a widowed mother, flees from home and wordly life to enter a monastery at an early age.[30] There is one example of a reluctant bridgegroom, Venantius, who was betrothed by his parents, but fled to a monastery.[31] The presence of these well-known *topoi* makes us sceptical of the other information supplied in these lives. A number of miracles are achieved through the sign of the cross;[32] three of the *patres*, Gregory of Langres and Gallus (great-grandfather and uncle respectively of Gregory of Tours) and Nicetius of Lyons have miraculous beds;[33] Gallus put out a fire simply by his presence.[34] All these stories have been told of earlier holy men.[35] A particularly interesting example is the story of Friard's staff, a dry branch, which, when planted, grew into a wonderful tree. This story is probably a variant of one which originated in the Desert. The earliest version may well be that of the *Apophthegmata patrum latinorum*, the text of which probably represents an earlier Greek version than the existing Greek alphabetical version printed in PG 65. The hero of this story is John the Dwarf. Sulpicius Severus tells a similar story of an unnamed novice in an Egyptian monastery. Cassian tells it of John of Lycopolis, but in his narrative the branch never blossoms.[36] We must therefore conclude that Gregory of Tours was here employing the normal technique of hagiographical writers. He probably derived the story from Sulpicius Severus, but it is clearly of oriental origin, and the writers who

---

[29] E.g., *Libri historiarum* 6.6, pp. 272-276, at p. 276; *Liber vitae patrum* 16 (4), p. 277; 18 (3), pp. 283-285.

[30] E.g., *Liber vitae patrum* 9 (1), pp. 252-253; 10 (1), p. 156; 14 (1), p. 268; 17 (1), p. 278; 20 (1), p. 291.

[31] Ibid. 16 (1), pp. 274-275.

[32] E.g., ibid. 5 (1), p. 228; 7 (2), p. 238; 8 (1), p. 242; 9 (2), p. 254; 10 (1-2), pp. 256-257; 11 (1), p. 260; 13 (1), p. 266; 15 (3), p. 272; 16 (2-3), pp. 275-276; 17 (2), p. 279; 19 (2), p. 288.

[33] Ibid. 6 (6), p. 234; 7 (2), p. 238; 8 (8), p. 248.

[34] Ibid. 6 (6), p. 234.

[35] See chapter two, nn. 49-50; chapter four, n. 75.

[36] *Liber vitae patrum* 10 (3), pp. 257-258; *Apophthegmata patrum latinorum* 5.143, PL 73: 948; Sulpicius Severus, *Dialogue* 1.19, pp. 171-172; Cassian, *De institutis coenobiorum* 4.24, pp. 154-156.

cite it appear to be drawing upon different traditional versions. However, the miracles performed by the living *patres* are as nothing compared with those which occurred at their tombs. Gallus, Gregory of Langres, and Nicetius of Lyons were particularly active.[37]

B. A COMPARISON OF GREGORY OF TOURS AND GREGORY THE GREAT AS WRITERS OF MIRACLE-STORIES

We must now consider whether a relationship existed between Gregory of Tours and Gregory the Great, and if so, what its nature was. They were contemporaries, but so far as is known, they never met. The only evidence for their having done so is a story in the tenth-century *Vita* of Gregory of Tours, by Odo of Cluny, which sounds apocryphal.[38] We have already noticed the resemblance between stories told by Gregory the Great (3.37, 2: 418-423), Gregory of Tours, and Sulpicius Severus, which also appear in varying forms in the writings of Paulinus of Nola, Palladius, and John Moschus.[39] Vogüé makes a good case for Gregory the Great having read Gregory of Tours, by instancing two passages in *Homiliae in evangelia* (2.34.18, PL 76: 1357; 2.27.9, PL 76: 1279-1281), which may be dated 588 and 586 respectively; but he admits in his last paragraph that his case is far from proved.[40] It is quite likely that these *exempla* were in general circulation in Late Antiquity. Some support for his view is supplied by the correspondence between the stories of Sanctulus in *Dialogue* 3.37 (2: 410-427) and Hospitius in the *Libri historiarum* (which Vogüé does not mention).[41] It will be recalled that as the *Libri historiarum* did not appear until 592 and the *Dialogues* were published in 593-594, the year of the death of Gregory of Tours, there is little likelihood that Gregory the Great could have read the *Libri historiarum*. As elsewhere, it seems that the Western writers were making use of a story which was current in Western Europe at the time and which may have originated in the East, as we see from the example cited by Vogüé.[42]

Before we go on to make a detailed comparison of the types of miracles described by Gregory of Tours and by Gregory the Great, it would be as

---

[37] *Liber vitae patrum* 6 (7), pp. 235-236; 7 (4-6), pp. 239-240; 8 (8-12), pp. 248-252.
[38] Odo of Cluny, *Vita Gregorii Turonis* 24, PL 71: 126.
[39] See chapter three.
[40] A. de Vogüé, "Grégoire le Grand, lecteur de Grégoire de Tours?" pp. 225-233.
[41] *Libri historiarum* 6.6, pp. 272-273.
[42] de Vogüé, n. 40 above.

well to consider whether or not their intention was to solve the same kind of problem. It seems to me that their fundamental aims were the same, namely, to find an acceptable substitute for martyrdom as a goal for sixth-century Christians, but there are important differences of outlook and treatment. Gregory of Tours was anxious to build up the reputation of the cult-centres, particularly the basilica of St Martin at Tours, and thus to enhance the status of his own diocese. Gregory the Great, on the other hand, was primarily concerned with the spiritual needs of his own audience of monks, clerics, and devout laymen; he hoped to encourage them by means of stories of Italian holy men with whom they could identify themselves.

Gregory of Tours was in a particular difficulty over the question of martyrdom, since there was a dearth of Gallic martyrs and some of those that there were, such as the Martyrs of Lyons, originally lacked an impressive resting-place.[43] He therefore had to rely on the *inventio* of further martyr-tombs and on building up the *gloria confessorum*.[44] This he did by failing to draw a distinction between martyrs and confessors. Not only did he build up the reputation of the tomb of Julian the Martyr, to which he and his family owed so much, but he was also so successful in consolidating the shrine of the confessor Martin that it achieved equal status with the tombs of the martyrs. Gregory the Great, on the other hand, while second to none in his veneration of the martyrs, displayed considerable psychological acumen in evolving the concept of the *martyr occultus* which would both serve as an inspiration to monks, secular clergy, and laity alike, and would encourage interest in the activities of confessors, whether living or dead. We shall see that the different solutions offered by the two Gregories to the problem of finding a substitute for the martyrs, in an age when persecution had ceased, will lead to a difference of treatment and emphasis in their miracle-stories.

Both Gregory the Great and Gregory of Tours regard the ability to perform miracles as a mark of the holy man, but whereas for Gregory of Tours it is apparently a *sine qua non*, Gregory the Great accepts that a man may be holy without performing miracles; in a discussion with Peter the Deacon, he points out that the apostle Peter could walk on the water, whereas Paul suffered shipwreck:

---

[43] *Liber in gloria martyrum* 48, pp. 71-72.

[44] For *inventiones* of tombs of holy persons in Gallic territory, e.g., *Liber in gloria martyrum* 50, pp. 72-73; *Liber in gloria confessorum* 17-18, pp. 307-308; 79, pp. 346-348. For the *inventio* of a false martyr-tomb, see *Vita S. Martini* 11, 1: 276-277. For building up the reputation of a confessor, e.g., *Liber in gloria confessorum* 20, pp. 309-310; 58, pp. 331-332; 94, pp. 358-359.

> aperte igitur constat quia cum utriusque virtus fuit dispar in miraculo,
> utriusque tamen meritum dispar non est in caelo (1.12, 2: 116-117).

Again, both are convinced that miraculous powers emanate from the holy
man in his tomb, but there is a noticeable difference in the volume of such
miracles in their writings, even allowing for the greater length of the
writings of Gregory of Tours. Here again, Gregory the Great sounds a
note of caution:

> ubi sunt in suis corporibus sancti martyres iacent, dubium, Petre, non est,
> quod multa valeant signa monstrare, sicut ut faciunt, et pura mente
> quaerentibus innumera miracula ostendunt. Sed quia ab infirmis potest
> mentibus dubitari, utrumne ad exaudiendum ibi praesentes sint, ubi constat
> quia in corporibus suis non sint, ibi eos necesse est maiora signa ostendere,
> ubi de eorum praesentia potest mens infirma dubitare (2.38, 2: 246-247).

He records only three miracles connected with tombs or graves, and none
of these concerns healing. The first two (1.4, 2: 56-59) occur in a chapel
dedicated to St Laurence, where the holy man, Equitius, is buried: on one
occasion, a chest of grain placed by a peasant on the tomb was blown off
by a whirlwind which did not affect anything else in the chapel; on
another, a party of Lombards who invaded the chapel were driven off by
the invocation of Equitius by one of the monks. The third case belongs to
a class of miracles represented not only in Sulpicius Severus, Paulinus of
Milan, Gregory the Great, and Gregory of Tours, but also in works by
Eastern Christian writers, such as the *Historia monachorum*, the
Heraclidis paradisus and the *Historia religiosa*, namely animals and men
being rendered immobile.[45] In Gregory the Great's third example, a sheep-
stealer was rendered immobile and unable to let go of the sheep on the
grave of a holy man (3.22, 2: 356-359).

The picture conveyed by much of the works of Gregory of Tours is of
the great basilica – either of St Martin at Tours or of St Julian at
Brioude – peopled night and day, outside the main entrance, in the
narthex, and, above all, round the tomb of the saint, by a throng of
unfortunates: the lame, the blind, the deaf and dumb, the paralyzed who
have been carried in on stretchers and barrows by their friends, the
sufferers from fevers, eye- and skin-diseases, and, last but not least, the

---

[45] Among numerous examples, Sulpicius Severus, *Vita S. Martini* 12.5, 1: 284-287;
Dialogue 1(2).9, p. 191; Paulinus, *Vita Ambrosii* 20, pp. 78-79; Gregory of Tours, *Libri
historiarum* 6.6, p. 273; *Historia monachorum* 6, PL 21: 409-410; Cyril of Scythopolis, *Vita
Euthymii* 59, pp. 81-88; John Moschus, *Pratum spirituale* 15, PG 87 (3): 2861; [Spyridon],
Vita Spyridonis [version 1] 18, ed. P. van den Ven, Bibliothèque du Muséon 33 (Louvain
1953). See also chart on pp. 120-121 of this book for further instances and for parallels.

energumeni, gibbering, contorted, or collapsing in epileptic or cataleptic spasms. Gregory of Tours records at least one hundred and four miracles resulting from proximity to the tombs of Martin and Julian and at least one hundred and five through other wonder-working tombs. Miracles also resulted from being present in Martin's cell, a parallel to which is furnished by a lady who recovered from insanity after passing a night in Benedict's cave (2.38, 2: 246-247).

The cases of demonic possession are mostly permanent or of long-standing. There is an occasional exception, such as that of Aquilinus, who was attacked by a demon when out hunting.[46] Healing is, in most cases, achieved by the dead holy man from his tomb. Exorcisms by living holy men are only very occasional; for example, by Hospitius, the recluse, and by one of the Fathers in the *Liber vitae patrum*, Abraham the abbot, who was famous as a *fugator* of demons.[47]

In the *Dialogues*, the only example of an exorcism achieved by dead holy persons is that of a building, when the evil spirit departed from the church of St Agatha in Rome in the form of an invisible pig, as the relics of St Sebastian and St Agatha were being brought into the church (3.30, 2: 380-381). There are two other cases of buildings ceasing to be haunted, the temple of Apollo at Fundi (3.7, 2: 278-285) and the house on the way to Corinth (3.4, 2: 270-273), which will be dealt with in chapter six. As regards exorcisms of human beings, we find one example where a visit to a shrine was definitely unsuccessful: a *clericus* of Aquinum, who was troubled by a demon, was sent by his bishop *ad martyrum loca* but found no help until he visited Benedict, who expelled the demon (2.16, 2: 184-187). Two other exorcisms by Benedict are recorded: he drove off a *puerulum nigrum*, who had attached himself to the hem of a monk's garment, by striking the monk with a rod (2.4, 2: 152-153); he encountered, when on his way to St John's chapel, a devil disguised as an animal doctor, and then cured a monk, into whom this devil had entered while he was drawing water, by striking him lightly with his hand (2.30, 2: 220-221). Equitius, by his own command, expelled a devil from a nun, who had obtained him from a lettuce over which she had failed to make the sign of the cross (1.4, 2: 42-45); Cassius, bishop of Narnia, cast out a demon from one of Totila's guards by the sign of the cross (3.6, 2: 276-279); in the Spoleto area, Isaac cast out of the verger at the church a demon, who had accused him of being a hypocrite, by lying over the

[46] *De virtutibus S. Martini* 2.26, p. 152.
[47] *Libri historiarum* 6.6, pp. 274-275; *Liber vitae patrum* 3 (1), p. 122.

verger's body (3.14, 2: 304-305); a consecrated virgin drove a demon from a *rusticus* into a pig (3.21, 2: 352-35); and Eleutherius cured a little boy of an evil spirit by means of prayer and fasting (3.33, 2: 394-397). Fortunatus, bishop of Todi, finally healed a poor young woman who had broken a rule and had consequently become tormented on the entry of relics of St Sebastian at the dedication of a chapel to him (1.10, 2: 94-97).

There are eight types of miracle which are common to both our authors. The first is the apparition of Jesus or of a saint. As might be expected, those reported by Gregory of Tours are of Martin, at least ten in number.[48] He also records, among others, that Amandus, bishop of Bordeaux, saw a vision of Jesus, and a Jewish boy, of the Virgin Mary.[49] An old woman saw Stephen in the crypt of a church in Bordeaux.[50] Various lesser-known saints appeared, including Ursinus, who enabled his own tomb to be discovered.[51] Gregory the Great provides a similar but shorter catalogue: Jesus appeared to the priest who took Benedict food at Easter (2.1, 2: 134-135); to Gregory's aunt Tarsilla, at the point of death (4.17, 3: 68-69); and to the monk, Martyrius (*Homiliae in evangelia* 2.29, PL 76: 1300-1301). Besides Tarsilla, others had visions when on the point of death; an aged priest saw Peter and Paul (4.12, 3: 50-53); Probus, bishop of Reate, saw Juvenal and Eleutherius (4.13, 3: 54-55); the nun, Galla, saw Peter (4.14, 3: 56-59); the little girl, Musa, saw the Virgin Mary (4.18, 3: 70-71). Peter appeared to Theodore, the verger at St Peter's, Rome, when he was trimming the lamps, to ask him why he got up so early, and then vanished; as a result of this apparently pointless visitation, Theodore was ill for many days (3.24, 2: 362-363). A happier visit was that paid by the saint to a paralyzed girl who used to frequent St Peter's, to tell her to ask Acontius, a verger, to restore her to health (3.25, 2: 364-367).

Both Gregory of Tours and Gregory the Great record stories of mysterious voices; there are at least twelve instances in the former and seven in the latter. Among the most interesting examples are those of voices from the tomb; Gatianus asking Martin to bless him; Germanus of Auxerre giving absolution; Helius of Lyons rebuking a would-be despoiler; and Benignus (who also appeared in person) asking Gregory of

---

[48] E.g., *De virtutibus S. Martini* 1.6, p. 142; 16, pp. 147-148; 24, p. 151; 2.18, p. 165; 26, pp. 168-169; 40, pp. 173-174; 3.23, p. 188; 4.26, p. 206; *Liber in gloria confessorum* 58, p. 331; 94, pp. 358-359.

[49] Ibid. 44, p. 325; *Liber in gloria martyrum* 9, p. 44.

[50] Ibid. 33, p. 59.

[51] E.g., ibid. 50, pp. 72-75; *Liber in gloria confessorum* 18, pp. 307-308; 79 (Ursinus), pp. 346-348; 91, p. 356.

Langres (the great-grandfather of Gregory of Tours) to provide the tomb with a lid and to move it inside; on another occasion an unknown voice told the father of Gregory of Tours to read the books of Joshua and Tobit, as the result of which he was cured of gout.[52]

Four of Gregory the Great's stories are also of voices from the tomb, two of them of martyrs. The first was related to Gregory by Redemptus, bishop of Ferentis, when they were in the monastery of St Andrew together. Iuticus, or Eutychius, the martyr, appeared to him, Redemptus, when he was lying in a semi-somnolent state on the saint's tomb, and said, *Finis venit universae carni*, three times, not long after which the Lombard invasion occurred (3.38, 2: 428-431). The martyr Faustinus, who was interred in the church at Brescia, asked the verger to tell the bishop to remove the body of the unworthy Valerianus from the church. This the bishop refused to do, whereupon he died thirty days later (4.54, 3: 180-181). There follows the story of an evil *defensor*, Valentius of Milan, who, having died at Genoa, was buried in the church of St Syrus there. In the middle of the night, the guardians heard mysterious voices and saw two evil spirits binding the feet of the corpse and carrying him, screaming, from the church. The next day they found him outside, still with his feet bound, in a different coffin (4.55, 3: 180-183). This series is completed by the story of the corpse of a dyer, buried in St Januarius, Rome, who cried out, *Ardeo, ardeo* (4.56, 3: 182-185). Slightly different from these stories, but allied to them, is that of events at the monastery of Subpentoma: a voice first called Anastasius from the depths of a rock, *Anastasi, veni*. Then the voice summoned seven other brethren by name, and after a moment's interval, an eighth. Anastasius and the others soon all died in the order in which their names had been called. The eighth brother died a few days later (1.8, 2: 70-75).

It is curious that in the stories of Gregory of Tours the voice of Martin is never heard, but a plausible explanation can be offered. Gaul in the sixth century differed from Italy in the quality of its local leadership. Many of the Gallo-Roman aristocracy had survived to play some part in affairs, and some individuals had subsequently become bishops. Stories of the voice of a holy man of fairly recent date, emanating from the tomb, might serve to distract the populace from paying due respect to the aristocracy and the episcopate. Gregory, the living bishop of Tours, might well find himself in competition with his dead predecessor, Martin. On the other hand, there was little or no harm in reporting that Gatianus, the

---

[52] See n. 13.10 above.

first bishop of Tours, asked Martin to bless him, from his tomb. The other characters mentioned, like Gatianus, belong to an earlier era, but since they lack a chronicler comparable to Sulpicius Severus to proclaim their works abroad, they would be sufficiently obscure for Gregory's purposes. The fact that two of them actually spoke to his father and great-great-grandfather would give an impression of their genuineness, but would anchor them in past history.

The milieu of Gregory the Great's stories of voices from the tomb is different. In two of them bishops are involved, but bishops in Italy, apart from Gregory himself, were not political leaders to the same extent as their colleagues in Gaul. In two cases a martyr's voice is heard, but in neither is its utterance of great significance. Apart from the martyrs and the monks of Subpentoma, who, of course, heard a voice not from the tomb but from the depths of a rock, it is evil-doers who are principally involved; one of the *dramatis personae* is a workman, a dyer, not a person of noble birth.

Gregory the Great's stories are chiefly warnings to evil-doers. He tells them to bring home the enormities of sin and its consequences. Gregory of Tours, on the other hand, tells them for the sake of the miracles themselves, as indications of the holiness of former bishops.

Perhaps the two Gregories resemble each other most nearly in their stories connected with celestial choirs, sweet scents arising at or after death, light, fire, water, and the increase of various substances, though, for the most part, Gregory of Tours surpasses Gregory the Great both in the number of examples and in the detailed description of the experience. For instance, Gregory of Tours cites at least seven examples of celestial choirs,[53] whereas Gregory the Great produces only two, on the deaths of Servulus and Romula (4.15, 3: 62-63; 16, 2: 66-67). The "odour of sanctity" is a common phenomenon in hagiographical writing in both East and West. Two examples in Eastern hagiography are the scent occurring at the death of Abba Sisois and the healing scent of myrrh, which arose in the church where St John the Almsgiver was buried, some time after his death. Leontius tells us that a similar scent arose from the bodies of various holy men buried in Cyprus. It is not therefore surprising that both Gregories report a number of examples. Those reported by Gregory of Tours include the tombs of Germanus at Auxerre and of Albinus, the church at Clermont-Ferrand, which held relics of Gervase and Protase, and the cell of Friard on his death.[54] Gregory the Great's

---

[53] See n. 13.9 above.
[54] See n. 13.11 above; *Apophthegmata patrum latinorum* 6.3.5, PL 73: 1007; Leontius,

examples all occur in *Dialogue* 4, except for the church of St Agatha in Suburra, after it was consecrated for Catholic instead of Arian worship (3.30, 2: 382-383). The human examples are Servulus, Romula, and Gregory's aunt Tarsilla (4.15, 3: 62-63; 16-17, 3: 68-69), from all of whom emanated a sweet smell at death. This also occurred at the tomb of Theophanius, after he had been dead for four days (4.28, 3: 98-99), and when Peter, the abbot, came to prepare for himself a tomb next that of the holy monk, Merulus, who had died fourteen years earlier (4.49, 3: 170-171).

Phenomena connected with the splendour of light are also a common concomitant of the holy man from biblical times onwards. We have only to recall the shining glory of the face of Moses (Exod. 34.29-35), the glory of the Lord shining round about the shepherds (Luke 2.8-14), and the scene on the Mount of Transfiguration (Matt. 17.1-8; Mark 9.2-8; Luke 9.28-36). The connection between the glory of light and the beauty of holiness became well established in the minds of late antique and early medieval hagiographers. The "shining glory" or *coruscatio* seems to be primarily an Eastern concept; it is mentioned by Theodoret and twice in the *Apophthegmata patrum latinorum*.[55] The passages in the latter have certain affinities with a passage in *Dialogue* 4 (16, 3: 64-67). On one occasion a brother saw Abba Arsenius in his cell, looking as though he were on fire, but he emerged, looking quite normal. It appears that the brother was so holy that he was capable of discerning the phenomenon of holy fire in Abba Arsenius. In the other story, the former bishop of Oxyrhynchus appeared like fire before his death. Gregory the Great tells us that as Romula (whose deathbed has already come to our notice) lay dying, her cell became full of bright light, which remained during the first night after her death. Gregory of Tours reports that a brightly shining pall over the body of the holy man, Patroclus, deterred an archpriest from stealing it.[56] He also reports mysteriously bright lights over the tombs of various holy men and flashes of light due to the presence of relics: for example, on the arrival of the relics of Martin, Saturninus, Illidius, Julian, and other saints at the monastery of St Euphronius;[57] lights appeared at Poitiers above the altar in Radegund's convent, where there was the

---

Vita Iohannis Eleemosinarii 50, p. 73; cf. *Liber vitae patrum* 10 (4), p. 259; *Liber in gloria confessorum* 40, p. 323; 94, p. 359.

[55] *Historia religiosa* 3.6, 1: 256-257; *Apophthegmata patrum latinorum* 5.18.1, PL 73: 978; 6.3.12, PL 73: 1010-1011.

[56] *Liber vitae patrum* 9 (3), p. 255.

[57] *Liber in gloria confessorum* 20, p. 209.

famous relic of the True Cross, presented by Venantius Fortunatus;[58] there was great *claritas* in the crypt of the cathedral of St John at Lyons, which indicated the merits of the martyrs buried there.[59] On at least four occasions, when a healing miracle had been worked through Martin, lights appeared in the form of a *coruscatio*;[60] blazes of light in locked churches are also recorded.[61]

Gregory the Great reports that after the consecration of the church of St Agatha, the lamps lit themselves, and the verger found it impossible to extinguish them (3.30, 2: 382-383). Gregory of Tours also reports the existence of perpetually or long-burning lamps and torches as an indication of the presence of holiness.[62]

Both Gregories see as significant the phenomenon of a ball or pillar of fire in the heavens. Gregory of Tours, whose interest in astronomy is obvious (he reports seeing the Aurora Borealis),[63] records the greater number of examples, but both appear to interpret them on similar lines. On the whole, they are connected with holy men and their relics and are not visible to all and sundry.[64] The monk of Whitby writes in the same tradition: when Gregory the Great was in hiding for three days and three nights, to avoid being elected Pope, a column of light appeared nightly, which was so bright that it penetrated the forest. Apart from Gregory, it was seen by an anchorite.[65]

Sometimes a ball of fire is intimately linked with a death, as when one hovered over the church at the burial of Pelagia, mother of Arredius, the abbot.[66] Parallel but not identical phenomena are the appearance of burning lamps on the death of the martyr-king, Herminigild (3.31, 2: 386-387), or the lightning on that of Theodoric, the infant son of Chilperic,[67] but more important for our purposes is the ball of fire in which Benedict saw the soul of Germanus, bishop of Capua, ascending to heaven (2.35, 2:

---

[58] *Liber in gloria martyrum* 5, pp. 39-40.

[59] Ibid. 49, p. 72.

[60] *Liber de virtutibus S. Iuliani* 42, p. 131; *De virtutibus S. Martini* 2.15, p. 164; 18, p. 165; 29, p. 170.

[61] *Liber in gloria martyrum* 33, p. 59; *Liber in gloria confessorum* 72, p. 341.

[62] E.g., *Liber in gloria martyrum* 31, p. 57; *Liber vitae patrum* 8 (8), p. 248; *Liber in gloria confessorum* 68-69, p. 338.

[63] *Libri historiarum* 6.33, p. 304.

[64] E.g., *Liber in gloria confessorum* 20, p. 309; 38, pp. 321-322; *Liber vitae patrum* 12 (3), p. 264; cf. Sulpicius Severus, *Dialogue* 1(2).2, pp. 181-182.

[65] B. Colgrave, ed., *The Earliest Life of Gregory the Great* [by an anonymous monk of Whitby] (Lawrence, Kansas, 1968), pp. 86-87.

[66] *Liber in gloria confessorum* 102, p. 363.

[67] *Libri historiarum* 6.34, pp. 304-305.

236-243). This forms part of a general cosmic vision about which learned studies have been written by Courcelle, Steidle, and Gross.[68]

The *topos* of dryness, which we have already met in chapter three, also occurs in the works of Gregory of Tours in connection with both living people and relics.[69] Both authors describe miracles connected with storms. Gregory of Tours describes the intervention of both living and dead holy men in two separate instances. There was a beneficial storm during a siege, due to the intervention of Maximus, bishop of Lyons, who having left the monastery of Insula Barbara, had been preserved from drowning while crossing the river. On another occasion, a party of pilgrims visiting Martin's cell stilled a storm by invoking him.[70] There is one instance of the stilling of a storm by a dead holy man, that of Theophanius (4.28, 3: 96-97), in the *Dialogues*, but usually storms are mitigated in other ways. In one of these stories, the passengers received Holy Communion *in articulo mortis*, so great was the danger of shipwreck, but God preserved the lives of all who sailed on the ship with Maximianus, bishop of Syracuse and Gregory's informant (3.36, 2: 408-411). On another occasion, the sailor Varaca was saved by Mass being celebrated at a distance (4.59, 3: 196-197). Thus in one case the sacrament is, so to speak, incidental, whereas in the other it was the cause of the rescue. We have one example in the *Dialogues* of a "beneficial" storm, due to the intervention of a living agent, Scholastica (2.33, 2: 232-235).

The element of punishment is not lacking in the miracle-stories of Gregory the Great. The Franks, who charged into the chapel where Libertinus was praying, were struck blind (1.2, 2: 26-27), as was an Arian bishop (3.29, 2: 376-379); the treacherous archdeacon was struck dead (3.5, 2: 274-275); flames coming out of the grave of an evil *curialis* consumed his very bones and caused the grave-mound to sink (4.33, 2: 110-111).

A new element in some of the miracles described by Gregory of Tours, for which there is no real equivalent in the *Dialogues*, is that of trial by ordeal. Gregory of Tours tells us of a Jewish boy who was preserved from being burned; of Britius, whose body was unburned when touched by hot charcoal, thus proving it to be chaste; and of a bishop and his wife, whose

---

[68] P. Courcelle, "La vision cosmique de saint Benoît," *RÉAug* 13 (1967): 266-279; B. Steidle, "Die kosmische Vision des Gottesmannes Benedikt: Beitrag zur Gregor d. Gr., Dialog II c.35," *EuA* 47 (1971): 187-192; K. Gross, "Der Tod des heiligen Benediktus," *RBén* 85 (1975): 164-176.

[69] E.g., *De virtutibus S. Martini* 1.2, p. 137; *Liber in gloria martyrum* 43, p. 67.

[70] *Liber in gloria confessorum* 22, pp. 311-313; *De virtutibus S. Martini* 1.2, p. 138.

bodies, unharmed by fire, proved that they had not had a sexual relation-ship.[71] There are also two cases of perjurers who were struck down in the presence of the relics of the saints at Tours and Bourges respectively.[72]

Trial by ordeal is a very primitive legal process which goes back to classical times. In Greece and Rome it was usually carried out by water; the victim was set adrift in an oarless boat or a chest. It continued to be used in Late Antiquity, when it took the form of trial by fire. Abba Copres, after making the sign of the cross, passed unscathed through fire, whereas a Manichaean was badly burned; a novice in an Egyptian monastery was made to pass through a furnace, but emerged unhurt.[73] The custom was particularly common in Gaul, where under the Salic law, a Frank or a Roman, if he could not produce adequate evidence when tried under the *mallus* of the count, in the king's tribunal, or the bishop's court, could be tried by ordeal. This took varying forms: among them, plunging the hand into boiling water and – what is relevant for our pur-pose – swearing an oath on the relics of the saints.[74] It is not surprising, therefore, that Gregory of Tours should include these items and that Gregory the Great should not. Even in the story of Benedict of Campania (3.18, 2: 344-345), the element of test is absent.

Lastly, there are the "increase" miracles. These are common to both Gregory of Tours and Gregory the Great and are also found in Greek miracle stories. They are obviously the result of the different writers having before them the same biblical types, and call for little comment here.[75]

In conclusion, the differences between the miracles recorded by Gregory the Great and by Gregory of Tours are of degree rather than of kind. In Gregory of Tours, the idea of miracles by the dead holy man and his relics is uppermost, but miracles by the living holy men are not unknown; in Gregory the Great, the reverse is the case. It is too facile an explanation to say that Gregory of Tours represents the ideas of Western Christendom, whereas Gregory the Great shows more than a trace of

[71] *Liber in gloria martyrum* 9, p. 44; *Libri historiarum* 2.1, pp. 37-38; *Liber in gloria confessorum* 75, pp. 342-343.

[72] *Liber in gloria martyrum* 19, p. 50; 33, p. 58; cf. *Vita Euthymii* 58, pp. 79-81.

[73] *Historia monachorum* 9, PL 21: 426-427; Sulpicius Severus, *Dialogues* 1.18.4, pp. 170-171.

[74] *Liber in gloria martyrum* 19, p. 50.

[75] See n. 13.8 above; cf. *Historia monachorum* 7, PL 21: 416; *Vita Euthymii* 17, pp. 27-28; *Vita Hypatii* 20, pp. 134-135; Theodore, *Eulogion Theodosii* 158, in H. Usener, ed., *Der heilige Theodosios: Schriften des Theodoros und Kyrillos* (Leipzig 1890), pp. 3-101, at pp. 73-79; [Theodore of Sykeon], *Vita Theodori Syceotae* 104, p. 86; Theodoret, *Historia religiosa* 14, 2: 10-13.

Eastern spirituality. We shall see that at one time relics were commonly used for devotion and thaumaturgy in the East, and that Western ideas about the necessity for keeping corpses inviolate, on the one hand, underwent some modification, and on the other, were not unknown in the East.

C. Bodies and Relics: How Far Did the Burial Customs of East and West Influence the Cult of Relics?

We have already noticed in chapter four that there are in the West two distinctive traditions of thaumaturgy: the living holy man as the agent of miracles, and the dead holy man who performs them from his tomb or by means of relics. Broadly speaking, the writers who lay most stress on the living holy man as the agent of miracles are those most influenced by Eastern Christian traditions, but it is by no means possible to draw a hard and fast distinction.

Gregory of Tours, though the most notable writer on miracles performed by dead holy men, was nevertheless affected by Byzantine influences;[76] in the *Liber vitae patrum*, he describes the activities of living holy men. Augustine, too, though he devotes much space to the healings achieved through the relics of Stephen, mentions cases of healing achieved through prayer.[77] Ambrose, Caesarius of Arles, and certain characters in the *Dialogues* made occasional use of relics, as did certain Eastern holy men.[78] Only Hilarion, Martin, the Jura Fathers and Severinus relied principally upon personal powers, and some of these achieved miracles by means of relics soon after their deaths.

It could be argued that the attitude of Western Christians towards dead bodies was influenced by earlier, pagan burial customs and that this in its turn led to emphasis on the importance of tombs and to the creation of non-corporeal relics; also that the less rigid attitude of the Greeks towards bodies and tombs would lead to more emphasis on the qualities of the living holy man. There are, however, a number of flaws in this argument.

---

[76] A. M. Cameron, "The Byzantine Sources of Gregory of Tours," *JTS* n.s. 26 (1975): 421-426.

[77] E.g., Innocentius, healed by the prayers of Saturninus and others, *De civitate Dei* 22.8, 2: 816-818; the young man healed of demonic possession by the prayers of a bishop, whom he had never seen, ibid., 2: 821.

[78] E.g., *Vita Ambrosii* 10, pp. 66-67; *Vita Caesarii arelatensis* 2.12-15, pp. 488-490; see chapter three, for the use of relics by characters in the *Dialogues* of Gregory the Great. The examples of the living Martin healing by means of relics relate to involuntary healing, e.g., Sulpicius Severus, *Vita S. Martini* 18-19, 1: 292-293; *Dialogue* 1(2).8, p. 190.

From Republican times onwards there had been among the Romans a definite cult of the dead, probably derived from the Etruscans, in whose lavish tombs it was customary to provide the amenities of normal life, either real or counterfeit. The tomb of the Volumnii, about three miles from Perugia and dating from the first century B.C., is the first tomb known to us to be constructed in the form of a Roman house; it forms an important link between Etruscan and Roman burial customs. To the same period belongs the earliest evidence of Roman belief in personal survival, that is, the use of the word *manes* to denote the spirits of the dead. Ideas as to the whereabouts of the *manes* varied, but there was evidently an urge to keep the dead alive by means of offerings of food and drink which were inserted through special holes and pipes provided at graves. A meal known as the *cena novendialis*, in which the dead were felt to have a part, was eaten at the tomb nine days after the funeral. There were also common days for commemorating the departed: the *dies natalis* and the *parentalia* (13-21 February), of which the last day, known as the *feralia*, was the public celebration.[79] These practices were taken over by the Church when the practice of Christianity became general. The *dies natalis* became the "heavenly birthday" of the martyr, and the commemorative meal, the *refrigerium* or banquet at the tomb, so often illustrated in early Christian paintings.[80] Christian teaching about the resurrection and the communion of saints would help to promote the idea that the dead person was specially present in spirit on these occasions.

Roman and specifically Christian teaching in the West encouraged the view that a dead body must be preserved inviolate; Roman law provided severe penalties for those who interfered with tombs or bodies.[81]

There are two important literary sources which can be cited in support of this view.

The first is the well-known letter of Gregory the Great (*Reg.* 4.30, 1: 263-266) addressed to Constantina, wife of the emperor Maurice, in 594. The empress has asked Gregory to grant her the head and *sudarium* of Paul as relics for her new church to be dedicated to the Apostle. In his refusal, Gregory takes his stand on Roman custom:

---

[79] See J. M. C. Toynbee, *Death and Burial in the Roman World* (London 1971), pp. 62-63; for examples of holes and pipes, ibid., pp. 50-52.

[80] E.g., Augustine, *Sermones* 4.33, PL 38: 51, from which it appears that the *natalitia* was the day for the commemorative meal.

[81] *Codex Theodosianus* 9.17.7, *Theodosiani libri XVI cum constitutionibus sirmondianis et leges novellae ad Theodosianum pertinentes*, ed. Th. Mommsen and P. M. Meyer, 2 vols in 3 (Berlin 1954), 1 (2): 466.

Romanis consuetudo non est, quando sanctorum reliquias dant, ut quic-
quam tangere praesumant de corpore. ... in Romanis namque vel totius
Occidentis partibus omnino intolerabile est atque sacrilegium, si sanctorum
corpora tangere quisquam fortasse voluerit.

Instead he will send some iron filings from Paul's chains. In this Gregory
is following the precedent set in the time of Pope Hormisdas, when
Justinian made a request for relics of the apostles and the deacon and
martyr, Laurence, in 519. The papal *legati* at Constantinople wrote to ask
the Pope to send a non-corporeal relic, because they had explained to
Justinian that it was against Roman practice to send corporeal relics.[82]

J. H. McCulloh, analysing the use of various terms for relics in
Gregory's writings, has shown that he adhered to the custom of giving
non-corporeal relics, and that the various miracles involving the use of
relics, which are described in the *Dialogues*, are performed either at
tombs, or in a holy place, such as Benedict's cave, or by means of objects
which have been in contact with the holy person. The one translation
mentioned in the *Dialogues*, that of the body of bishop Herculanus, would
be permissible under Roman law, and other corporeal relics mentioned by
Gregory, such as the hairs of John the Baptist which he sent to King
Reccared, could have been obtained from a living person.[83]

The writings of Gregory of Tours, with certain exceptions, also testify
largely to the use of non-corporeal relics. These cover a wide range of
objects: wonder-working beds, books and documents, cords and ropes,
sacred dishes, pebbles wetted with the blood of the martyr, Symphorian,
and the staff of Gregory of Langres.[84] The objects connected with tombs,
which might serve as relics, have been mentioned earlier in this chapter.[85]
A somewhat bizarre relic consisted of little pieces of the wall of his cell
upon which Lupicinus had spat blood.[86] Martin's cell, like Benedict's

---

[82] *Ep.* 218, *Avellana collectio (367-353), Epistulae imperatorum pontificium aliorum ...
Avellana quae dicitur collectio*, ed. O. Guenther, CSEL 35 (2 pts in 1 vol.) (Vienna 1895-
1898), 2: 679-680.

[83] J. H. McCulloh, "The Cult of Relics in the Letters and *Dialogues* of Pope Gregory
the Great: a Lexicographical Study," *Traditio* 32 (1976): 145-184.

[84] E.g., beds: *De virtutibus S. Martini* 2.21, p. 166; 45, p. 175; *Liber vitae patrum*
6 (6), p. 234; 7 (2), p. 238; 8 (8), p. 248; books and documents: *De virtutibus S. Martini*
2.49, p. 176; ropes and cords: *De virtutibus S. Martini* 1.28, pp. 151-152; *Liber in gloria
confessorum* 84, p. 352; sacred dishes: *De virtutibus S. Martini* 4.10, p. 202; pebbles
wetted by a martyr's blood: *Liber in gloria martyrum* 51, p. 74; the staff of Gregory of
Langres: *Liber vitae patrum* 7 (2), p. 238.

[85] See nn. 17-19 above.

[86] *Liber vitae patrum* 13 (1), pp. 265-266.

cave, possessed healing properties.[87] There are also what may be termed foreign relics: the fragments of the True Cross, one of which had been given to Radegund by Venantius Fortunatus and was housed in her convent in Poitiers; the Instruments of the Passion; the herbs growing in contact with the statue of Christ at Paneas (erected by the Haemorrhoissa, the woman with an issue of blood in the Gospel, as a token of gratitude), which possessed healing powers.[88]

Other Western writers, insofar as they refer to relics, mention other relics in the same categories. Sulpicius Severus describes how a girl was healed through contact with a letter from Martin; sick people were healed through contact with the garments of Ambrose, Martin, and Caesarius of Arles.[89]

The real antithesis does not lies between the use of corporeal and non-corporeal relics, but between miracles wrought by a dead holy man, with or without the agency of non-corporeal relics. The reason for this antithesis appears to be political. We have already noted that the delicate balance of Church, state, and society in Merovingian Gaul might be threatened by a living holy man who could provide an alternative focus for the people's loyalty to that furnished by the surviving Roman aristocracy, which included the bishops. A dead holy man, such as Martin or Julian, was a far less dangerous cult figure.

Gregory the Great was in a somewhat different situation; the emperor was far away in Constantinople, the political situation was confused, and the machinery of civil government was uncertain, quite apart from the damage caused by the plague and the excessive floods. The Church and the Papacy were the principal sources of stability in the country. Emphasis on the existence of native holy men would achieve some kind of respect for the framework of the Church as a means of bringing order out of chaos and would provide the people, clergy and laity alike, with objects for devotion and emulation.

Let us now turn to Eastern Christendom, where, it is generally believed, a less rigid attitude towards death, burial customs, and tombs prevailed. It has been pointed out that the Mycenaeans were not troubled by scruples about moving bodies from one grave to another and that much later, in Christian times, it became quite usual to dismember bodies,

[87] *De virtutibus S. Martini* 2.19-23, pp. 165-167; 48, p. 176; 3.22-23, p. 188.
[88] *Liber in gloria martyrum* 5-6, pp. 39-42; 20, p. 50, which reproduces Rufinus, *Historia ecclesiastica* 7.14 (Eusebius, *Historia ecclesiastica* 7.18), GCS 9 (2), pp. 672-673.
[89] *Vita S. Martini* 19, 1: 290-292; cf. *Vita patrum iurensium* 145, pp. 394-397; for Ambrose and Caesarius, see n. 78 above.

in order to be able to send relics to different places. Theodore of Sykeon, for example, had acquired from the bishop of Germia (who had apparently been led by a vision to give them up) a piece of the head of St George, one of his fingers, and one of his teeth.[90] Gregory the Great, in his famous letter to Constantina, cites the case of certain Greek monks who had been caught two years earlier (in 592), attempting to exhume bodies from a Roman cemetery with the intention of taking home the bones as relics (Reg. 4.30, 1: 263-266, at p. 265). On the other hand, there is evidence of a more reverent Eastern attitude towards dead bodies. The author of the Vita prima of Pachomius tells how Pachomius instructed his disciple, Theodore, to bury his body in a secret place to avoid the attentions of relic-snatchers. Theodore and three other disciples carried out this command by night.[91] A similar story is told by Theodoret of Marcianus, who made his disciple swear to bury his body in a secret place which he would not reveal to anyone.[92] In reality, there was not as much difference between Greek and Roman burial customs as has sometimes been suggested: from the geometric period (ca. tenth to eighth century B.C.) onwards, it was customary to provide food, drink, and animal offerings; in the archaic and classical periods (eighth to fourth century B.C.), the offerings were often imitations of the real objects, and cherished possessions of the deceased were included.[93] The Greeks, like the Romans, attached great importance to the due performance of burial rites; indeed the plot of the Antigone of Sophocles turns on this very question. They held celebrations on the third and ninth days after death (τὰ τρίτα and τὰ ἔννατα), and there were also various annual celebrations, known as τὰ νομιζόμενα.[94] Thus we see definite resemblances between Greek and Roman customs.

We have now to consider whether Roman law and customary practice were as rigidly applied in fact as in theory. First of all, there is the question of the translation of bodies, which occurred in both East and West. In pagan times, such transfers could not occur without application to the college of pontiffs. Pliny, in one of his many anxious letters of consultation addressed to the emperor Trajan, enquires what he is to do in Bithynia when applications for exhumation and translation are made,

[90] [Theodore of Sykeon], Vita Theodori Syceotae 100, p. 80.
[91] [Pachomius], Vita 1.116, pp. 158-159.
[92] Historia religiosa 3.18, 1: 280-285.
[93] See F. Cumont, Recherches sur le symbolisme funéraire des Romains (Paris 1942), pp. 29-38; D. C. Kurtz and J. Boardman, Greek Burial Customs (London 1971), pp. 61-67, 355-356.
[94] See ibid., pp. 143-147, 160.

since communication with Rome is not practicable; Trajan pragmatically replies to the effect that he is to consult local custom and judge each case on its merits.[95] This exchange suggests that the laws were not applied so rigidly outside Rome. The first Christian translation of which we have a record, is that of Babylas, a bishop martyred at Antioch under Decius, which occurred when Gallus was installed at Antioch (351-354).[96] Translations in the West were made of the bodies of popes, bishops, and martyrs, who had died in exile or far from home. Among these were the popes Pontianus, Cornelius, and Eusebius, whose bodies were brought from places of exile to the Catacombs.[97] Gregory himself cites an example of the translation of an episcopal corpse: the body of bishop Herculanus, which had lain in a temporary resting-place outside the walls of Perugia, but was finally interred within the church of St Peter, when fighting had ceased (3.13, 2: 300-303). The bodies of martyrs (and indeed of other holy men too) were often translated. The most famous examples are the large-scale translations which occurred at Constantinople between the mid-fourth and mid-fifth centuries. The motive for these transfers was clearly to make the new Rome as rich in martyrs as the old. Constantine had been content with cenotaphs, but Constantius was responsible for the removal of the remains of Timothy (356), Andrew, and Luke (357) to the city, which set the precedent for many more.[98] Theodosius I (379-395) carried the head of John the Baptist into the church of the Hebdomon with his own hands; the same honour was paid by Arcadius (395-408) to the remains of the prophet Samuel.[99] The body of John Chrysostom came home from Comana in 438.[100]

Similar translations of the bodies of holy men to Antioch occurred: the remains of Ignatius were sent back from Rome and those of Symeon Stylites were brought into the city.[101]

---

[95] Plinius Cecilius Secundus, C. [Pliny the Younger], *Epp.* X, *Epistolae ad Traianum imperatorum cum eiusdem responsis*, ed. E. G. Hardy (London 1889), p. 113.

[96] See Sozomen, *Historia ecclesiastica* 5.19.4, 11-19, pp. 223-226; 20.7, p. 227; cf. 7.10, p. 313.

[97] *LP* 1: 134-135, 139, 141, 143, 145, 147-149, 153-155, 157, 159, 161-162, 164, 167-168, 187, for popes buried in the Catacombs.

[98] Jerome, *Contra Vigilantium* 1.5, PL 23: 358; Paulinus of Nola, *Carmina* 19, 349-351, 1: 129-130.

[99] Sozomen, *Historia ecclesiastica* 7.21, 1-5, pp. 333-334; Jerome, n. 98 above.

[100] Theodoret, *Historia ecclesiastica* 5.36, *Kirchengeschichte*, ed. L. Parmentier, rev. F. Schweidweiler, GCS 44 (Berlin 1954), p. 338.

[101] Jerome, *De viribus illustris liber* 16, ed. W. Herding (Leipzig 1924), p. 21; Antony, disciple of Symeon Stylites, *Vita Symeonis Stylitae* 31-32, *Das Leben des heiligen Symeon Stylites*, ed. H. Lietzmann (Leipzig 1908), pp. 72-77.

Translations were also taking place in the West. The body of Martin was brought from his cell at Candes to Tours in 395 and sixty-four years later was apparently translated in its tomb to a different place.[102] In addition to Anastasius, a number of martyrs in Illyria, as well as other Christians, appear to have been translated to Salona.[103] The body of Severinus was transferred from Noricum to a final resting-place in Italy.[104] Most famous of all were the finding and translation by Ambrose of the bodies of Gervase and Protase, Vitalis and Agricola, and Nazarius.[105]

In all this we can discern a certain pattern. In the first place, it was a question of the transfer of complete bodies, not of relics. Secondly, the provision of the Roman civil code, which permitted the removal of a body from a temporary to a permanent resting-place,[106] was being interpreted extremely generously to enable bodies which had long been buried, such as the remains of Ignatius of Antioch at Rome, to be translated, and to allow certain cities to enhance their spiritual importance by becoming receptacles for deceased holy men. Thirdly, the distinction between martyrs and confessors had become blurred; Severinus, for example, is given the status of *martyr occultus*, since martyrs were now in short supply.[107]

The cult of the dead holy man in his tomb is not unknown in Eastern Christendom. One notable example is that of Demetrius in Thessalonica. The details of his history and his date are obscure. He was certainly regarded as a local martyr and occupied a special place in the people's affections as protector of their city. The epithets applied to him, φιλόπολις, φιλόπατρις, σωσίπολις and σωσίπατρις, recall those applied to Zeus and Athene as protectors of Athens, πολιεύς and πολιάς.[108] The church

---

[102] *Libri historiarum* 1.48, pp. 32-34; *De virtutibus S. Martini* 1.6, p. 142.

[103] A. Grabar, *Martyrium*, 2 vols and album (Paris 1943-1946), 2: 96; E. Dyggve, *History of Salonitan Christianity* (Oslo 1951), pp. 84, 104-105, 125; *LP* 1: 330.

[104] *Vita Severini* 44-46, pp. 112-117.

[105] *Vita Ambrosii* 14, pp. 70-73; 29, pp. 90-91; 32, pp. 94-95.

[106] *Codex Theodosianus* 3.14.10, 2: 148.

[107] Cf. the miracles carried out through the agency of the dead: Severinus, *Vita Severini* 45-46, pp. 114-117, and those of the dead Martin. Severinus is called *beatissimus* or *sanctissimus vir*, but Martin was not classed as *martyr occultus*.

[108] E.g., φιλόπολις, *Miracula [Iohannis]* 3.41, *Les plus anciens miracles de saint Démétrius et la pénétration des Slaves dans les Balkans*, ed. P. Lemerle (Paris 1979), 1: 79; φιλόπατρις, *anonymi miracula* 1 [88], ibid., 1: 77; σωσίπολις, ibid., 1: 168; σωσίπατρις, *Miracula [Iohannis]* 13.116, ibid., 1: 133; πολιεύς, e.g., Aristotle, *De mund.* 401ª19; πολιάς, e.g., Herodotus, *Hist.* 5.82, *Historiae*, ed. C. Hude, 2 vols, 3rd ed. (Oxford 1935), 2: 5, cap. 82 (no folio numbers); Aristophanes, *Aves*, 828, ed. F. W. Hall and W. M. Geldart, 2nd ed. repr. (Oxford 1949).

dedicated to him seems to have borne a certain resemblance to the
sanctuary of Asclepius at Epidaurus. Healings by incubation seem to have
been carried out there and vast crowds thronged there in the hope of a
miraculous cure.[109] Thus the great basilica as a centre of help for the
afflicted, thanks to the presence of a dead holy man, is a phenomenon
found in the East as well as in the West. It has been suggested, as the
result of investigations made when the church was severely damaged by
fire in 1917, that the so-called tomb was in fact a cenotaph containing a
phial of blood of the saint; Grabar cites some parallel examples. In support
of this theory it is urged that it was unusual for the tomb of a martyr to be
found within town walls.[110] This, however, seems unlikely, in view of the
correspondence between the emperor Maurice (582-601) and Eusebius,
bishop of Thessalonica, who appears to be identical with Gregory the
Great's correspondent of the same name (see *Reg.* 9.10, 1: 12; 9.156, 2:
156; 196, 2: 184; 11.55, 2: 329). Maurice asked Eusebius to dispatch
λείψανα of Demetrius to Constantinople; Eusebius replied that there was
some doubt as to the actual site of the grave beneath the altar, and that the
saint would not wish a search to be made.[111] It is more likely that
Eusebius feared financial loss and a decline in the status of his diocese
than that he was troubled by theological or legal scruples about the dismemberment of the body or its parts. The use of the word λείψανα, the
Greek equivalent of *reliquiae*, certainly suggests a plurality of objects
rather than a single phial of blood.

Were corporeal relics ever in use in the West? The answer seems to be
"yes," but the evidence is difficult to assess, because of the ambiguity of
words, such as *reliquiae*.

The relics of Stephen, for example, may have been corporeal. We are
told by the priest Lucian that his coffin contained only earth and dust,[112] of
which small quantities may well have been sent as relics to North Africa
and elsewhere. On the other hand, it would have been possible to create
brandea by bringing pieces of cloth into contact with the remains. It
seems that Western Christians, while shrinking from the creation of
corporeal relics themselves, were not above accepting them from a body
which had fallen into decay, or which others had dismembered. For
example, Gregory of Tours tells us that, in accordance with a vision, the
faithful collected the ashes of the Martyrs of Lyons from the spot on

---

[109] E.g., *Miracula [Iohannis]* 3.42-44, 1: 80-81.
[110] Sotiriou, Ἀρχ. Ἐφημ. (1929), pp. 239-241, cited by Grabar, 1: 35, n. 6.
[111] *Miracula [Iohannis]* 5.51-54, 1: 89-90.
[112] Lucian the Priest, *Ep.* 8, PL 41: 815.

which they were burned,[113] and Paulinus of Nola mentions relics of the apostles as being *cineres*,[114] which suggests that they were once corporeal. Gregory of Tours also states that the limbs of Julian were buried at Brioude, whereas the head was at Vienne.[115] Presumably this was not regarded as reprehensible, because the parts had been sundered by the executioner.

The situation regarding the relics of Gervase and Protase is ambiguous, because there is doubt as to the condition of the bodies when they were found. Ambrose speaks as though they were skeletons, but complete and accompanied by a good deal of blood: *ossa omnia integra, sanguinis plurimum*; whereas Augustine says that they were incorrupt corpses.[116] At any rate, there is no suggestion of dismemberment. According to Gregory of Tours, when the bodies were being transferred to the church at Milan, a picture fell and struck their heads, from which a stream of blood then flowed. This was collected in *lenteamina, pallulae*, and *vela ecclesiae*, which were distributed throughout Gaul.[117] I believe that the account of Ambrose, the eye-witness, is to be preferred, and that the word *reliquiae*, used by Victricius, carries the same sense as when used by Gregory the Great; that is, they were probably *brandea* of some kind.[118] The practice of making these was certainly known to the people of Milan, since they touched the body of Ambrose himself with various items of clothing. The falling picture may have struck the head of some by-stander, whose blood would be collected by the people in good faith, since they probably could not see what was going on, owing to the crowd. This blood is probably what Ambrose meant by *sanguinis plurimum*.[119] Victricius also used the word *tropaea* for the relics, which suggests that they were objects rather than parts of the body, since this word can be translated as "sign" or "token." [120]

In conclusion, the differences between Eastern and Western burial customs are differences of emphasis rather than differences of kind. In the West the importance of the dead holy man and his relics seems to be

[113] *Liber in gloria martyrum* 48, pp. 71-72.

[114] *Carmina* 27, 403-405, 2: 280.

[115] *Liber de virtutibus S. Iuliani* 1, p. 114.

[116] Ambrose, *Ep.* 22.2, PL 16: 1063; Augustine, *Confessiones* 9.7.16, pp. 208-209; *Sermones* 286.5, PL 38: 1299; *Sermones* 318.1, PL 38: 1438; *De civitate Dei* 22.8, 2: 816; *Ep.* 78.3, 1: 33.

[117] *Liber in gloria martyrum* 46, p. 69.

[118] E.g., *De laude sanctorum* 3, PL 20: 445; 9-10, PL 20: 452.

[119] Ambrose, see n. 116 above.

[120] *De laude sanctorum* 1, PL 20: 443.

stressed at the expense of the living holy man. In the East, however, the living holy man assumes a greater importance, though relics play their part. In the West the relics are usually of a secondary kind, that is, objects, which have been in contact with him either in life or in death. Where necessary, they can be created, through placing objects in contact with his tomb. Respect is paid to the integrity of the human body on account of Roman law and burial customs, but Western Christians are willing to accept corporeal relics if the dismemberment of the body or the violation of the tomb has been carried out elsewhere. The Church in the Eastern Mediterranean area counted itself fortunate in possessing objects closely connected with the Virgin Mary and the apostles, as well as with local holy men, such as Symeon Stylites. Farther away from Rome the laws relating to the preservation of tombs and bodies were administered less strictly, with the result that bodies could be dismembered with impunity. Such practices did not become usual in the West until the late seventh century. Such Western writers as lay stress on the activities of the living holy man as miracle-worker have been found to be those who came under Eastern influences. In chapter six and in the Epilogue we shall consider how far and by what means Gregory the Great came under such influences.

6

The Influence of the Spirituality
of the Desert
upon Gregory the Great

A. Introduction

In the two previous chapters, we have considered the works of two groups of Western writers of miracle-stories: those in whose works we read of miracles performed by living holy men and those who describe miracles performed at the tombs of dead holy men or by means of their relics. We have seen that the line of division between the two groups is not hard and fast; both Augustine and Gregory of Tours cite examples of miracles performed by living holy men, and characters in the *Dialogues* of Gregory the Great make occasional use of relics. Broadly speaking, the writers in the first group are those whose contacts with the East, where the living holy man was an important charismatic figure, are closest. Gregory the Great, though his holy men in a few instances work miracles by means of relics, is very much in the Eastern tradition.

How did Gregory come to acquire this Eastern Christian outlook, although he was apparently ignorant of the Greek language? [1] Elsewhere I have made a detailed examination of his use of Greek words and phrases throughout the corpus of his works, which shows that his knowledge of Greek, though not non-existent as is often supposed, would probably not be sufficient to enable him to read Greek works of theology and spirituality. Here we need to consider what works were available to him in Latin to mediate Eastern Christian ideas to him. First, there was the *Vita Antonii* which gives the *portrait par excellence* of the living holy man

---

[1] J. M. Petersen, "Did Gregory the Great know Greek?," *SCH(L)* 13 (1976): 121-134; "Did Gregory the Great know Greek? A Reconsideration" (unpublished paper).

as miracle-worker;[2] the only relics mentioned in it are the *melota* and *substratorium* which Antony handed on to Athanasius and which are more in the nature of souvenirs;[3] they were not used for working miracles. He would be able to learn something of Eastern cenobite monasticism from the translation of the rule of St Basil by Rufinus and of the second *Vita* of Pachomius by Dionysius Exiguus, but since these deal with the practical organization of the monks' lives and of the monasteries themselves, they are not strictly relevant for our purpose. It is true that the *De institutis coenobiorum* of Cassian contain similar material, but as they also include what may be described as ascetic theology or spirituality, they and his *Collationes* will be considered later in this chapter. The *Dialogues* of Sulpicius Severus and Jerome's *Vitae* might help to fill in the background, together with Jerome's celebrated *Ep.* 22 and Augustine's *De moribus ecclesiae*, but the works of Cassian, together with Rufinus's version of the *Historia monachorum*, the *Heraclidis paradisus* or some other Latin version of the *Historia Lausiaca* of Palladius, and the Latin version of the subject collection of the *Apophthegmata patrum* are likely to have had a direct influence. The latter represents an older text of the original Greek than the Greek text which is extant but still unpublished.[4] It is the work of the deacon Pelagius and the subdeacon John, who as A. Mundò in his article on the authenticity of the *Reg. Ben.* has convincingly shown, are almost certainly identical with Pope Pelagius I (555-561) and John III (561-575).[5] This would mean that this work would be available to Gregory.

We have to determine how far, if at all, these writings influenced Gregory, and if they did so, was their influence mediated through other writers, or is it possible to trace in the *Dialogues* and elsewhere the independent and direct influence of any of these works?

In trying to find the answer, we need to consider: 1. the setting of the *Dialogues* in relation to Gregory's avowed aims in writing them (section B); 2. the working-out of certain theological and psychological concepts in the writings of Gregory, Cassian, and the Desert Fathers (section C); 3. a comparison between certain verbal similarities, scenes, and character-sketches found in the *Dialogues* and the Eastern Christian writings

---

[2] See chapter four, n. 1.

[3] *Vita Antonii* 91, pp. 172-175.

[4] See J.-C. Guy, *Recherches sur la tradition grecque des Apophthegmata patrum*, SHG 36 (Brussels 1962), pp. 126-171.

[5] A. Mundò, "L'authenticité de la Regula S. Benedicti," *StAns* 42 (1957): 105-158, at pp. 129-136.

(section D), culminating in 4. a detailed comparison of the descriptions of Symeon Stylites and Martin the hermit (section E).

B. Monasticism in the *Dialogues*

Gregory's underlying motives for writing the *Dialogues* have already been discussed in chapter three. In the two passages where he explicitly states his intention of writing them there is an emphasis on the Italian character of the material and an implication that there is a corpus of material about the lives and miracles of holy men living elsewhere, with which his audience of monks and devout clerics, such as Peter, are familiar (*Reg.* 3.50, 1: 206-207; *Dialogue* 1, prol., 2: 14-15). The following interchange between Gregory and Peter well conveys the impression that Gregory's audience believe that holy men who perform miracles are to be found in other countries but not in their own:

> *Gregorius*: Nonnumquam vero ad augmentum mei doloris adiungitur, quod quorumdam vita, qui praesens saeculum tota mente reliquerunt, mihi ad memoriam revocatur....
> *Petrus*: Non valde in Italia aliquorum vitam virtutibus fulsisse cognovi. Ex quorum igitur conparatione accenderis ignoro.

Since, however Gregory has evidently indicated that miracle-workers *are* to be found in Italy, the monks *fratres mei qui mecum familiariter vivunt* (*Reg.* 3.50, as above), have expressed their eagerness to learn about such people.

It could indeed be argued that such a corpus of material was provided by the works of Western writers of miracle-stories. The miracles described by Augustine, Sulpicius Severus, Gregory of Tours in his *Liber vitae patrum*, the author of the *Vita patrum iurensium*, Cyprian of Toulon and his associates, and Eugippius occurred, for the most part, outside Italy, or if performed in Italy, were the work of visitors or exiles. An Eastern flavour could be conferred upon Gregory's writings through the influence of the *Vita Antonii*, the *Dialogues* of Sulpicius Severus, and the three *Vitae* by Jerome. In particular there are several stories in Gregory's *Dialogues* which appear to owe their origins to the *Vita S. Martini* of Sulpicius Severus and which have given rise to the notion that Gregory saw Benedict as a species of Italian Martin. We have already discussed the question of the resemblances between the stories in chapter four. In the *Liber vitae patrum* of Gregory of Tours and the *Vita patrum iurensium* as in *Dialogue* 2, the background landscape is treated as a kind of Western European Desert where those with a vocation for the monastic life can establish first hermitages and then cenobitic communities. Whether or not Gregory the Great knew the other two works, his description of Benedict's call to the religious life and his subsequent foundation of monasteries follows the same lines as those found in them. This could be used in support of the view that Gregory is seeking to reproduce in an Italian setting situations which would be known to his audience as having occurred elsewhere, but it is more likely that all the individuals concerned may have undergone a similar religious experience, and that the writers may have been exposed to the same kind of Eastern influences as Gregory the Great.

The picture of Italian monasticism which emerges from the *Dialogues* strongly suggests that Gregory had in mind a corpus of material originating in Eastern Christendom. The monasticism described by Sulpicius Severus, whether in Egypt or in Gaul, is less organized and more individualistic than Gregory's. Martinian monasticism is active, missionary, and "outgoing," with emphasis upon conversion of the heathen by the monks, destruction of idols and heathen temples, and good works of all kinds. Severinus, as portrayed by Eugippius, though he had lived in the East, is also a pioneer missionary and a personage who assumes political responsibility. Jerome's writings, on the other hand, describe the circumstances of those who attempt to live the eremitical life.

Let us now see how far the *mise en scène* of monasticism in Western Europe, as reflected in Gregory's *Dialogues*, resembled the setting and organization of Egyptian monasticism, as described by Cassian, the writers of the *Apophthegmata patrum latinorum*, the author of the *Historia monachorum*, and Palladius.

Cassian's purpose is not so much to make an historical analysis of Egyptian monasticism as to rationalize what he has seen, that is, to provide a schematization of his own experience. He observes certain categories of monks: cenobites, anchorites, Sarabaïtes, and an "unattached" group. The cenobites live in community under the direction of an abbot; the anchorites, who emerge from the cenobites, live in cells as solitaries; the Sarabaïtes are persons of feeble character who make a public cult of *abrenuntiatio* but do not submit themselves to the will of the *Seniores* or Old Men; the rest live an individualistic life in private cells without submitting to discipline.[6] Cassian claims biblical precedents for these divisions: the cenobites live as the whole Church lived in apostolic times according to the celebrated description in Acts 4.32-35 and 2.44-45.

---

[6] Cassian, *Collationes* 18.4, 3: 14.

When, with increasing numbers, church discipline became lax, the more zealous spirits broke away to form *coenobia* of their own and became known as μονάζοντες or monks (μονάζειν = to live in solitude and also, to be celibate).[7] The anchorites are those who withdraw (ἀναχωροῦντες) in order to live a more perfect life. The founders of this form of monasticism were Paul the Hermit and Antony, its exponents, imitators of Elijah, Elisha, and John the Baptist.[8] According to an alternative tradition of Alexandrian origin, which Cassian cites in the *De institutis coenobiorum* and admits to having derived from Eusebius, the first monks were given a Rule by St Mark, when he was Patriarch of Alexandria, and were regarded by Eusebius as identical with the Therapeutae described by Philo. The Sarabaïtes are the spiritual descendants of Ananias and Sapphira who broke the unity of the Church by their behaviour.[9]

The Egyptian *coenobia* are familiar to us from the writings of Cassian, Palladius, and above all, from the various lives of Pachomius, who inspired the foundation of the group of monasteries centred on Tabennesis and organized on a "house" basis, foreshadowing the English public school.[10] There was another separate group of *coenobia* in the Nile delta. Cassian's definition of anchorites appears to cover two types of monk: 1. the great solitaries, Paul and Antony, and other monks who passed long periods in solitude, such as Abba Archebius and Abba Paphnutius, known from his love of solitude as The Buffalo; 2. monks who lived in individual cells, built by their own hands, sometimes in groups of two or three, but often standing in isolation miles from the nearest neighbour or from the central church where the hermits would gather on Saturdays and Sundays.[11] These are the men who are familiar to us from Cassian's own works, or from the earlier writings, the *Historia monachorum*, the *Historia Lausiaca*, and above all, the various collections of the *Apophtheg-mata patrum*. They are the *Seniores*, living in Nitria, the Cells, Scete, Diolcos, or Panephysis, who labour at simple tasks, such as the weaving of mats or baskets from palm leaves to sell in the nearest town, or the growing of a few herbs and vegetables, in order to survive. For the most part they are local peasants, but we can discern a small group of

---

[7] Ibid. 5, 1: 14-16.

[8] Ibid. 6, 1: 17-18; *De institutis coenobiorum* 1.1, pp. 36-39.

[9] Ibid. 2.5, pp. 64-69 (cf. Eusebius, *Historia ecclesiasticorum* 2.17, pp. 142-143); cf. A. de Vogüé, "Monachisme et église dans la pensée de Cassien," *Théologie de la vie monastique* (Paris 1961), pp. 213-240, at pp. 214-219; Cassian, *Collationes* 18.7, 3: 18.

[10] [Pachomius] *Vita* 1.28, pp. 34-39, at pp. 36-37.

[11] 1. Archebius: *Collationes* 2.7, 1: 269; Paphnutius: e.g., *Collationes* 18.15, 3: 28; 2. *Collationes* 18.15, 3: 30.

sophisticated intellectuals: Arsenius, Evagrius Ponticus, Macarius of
Alexandria, and, for a time, Cassian and his friend Germanus.[12]
Intellectual activity does not, however, seem to have been encouraged: we
read of monks selling codices of the Gospels, in order to help the poor, in
an atmosphere of general approval.[13] Among the *Seniores* there were even
a few women: Ammas Matrona, Sarah, Syncletica, Talis, Taor, the virgin
to whom the martyr Collythus appeared, her mother, and no doubt
others.[14]

It will be noticed that Cassian sees the cenobitic life as prior to the
eremitic life, perhaps because this accorded with the practice of his own
day. Once monasticism had become institutionalized, it would be more
usual for new recruits for the eremitic life to emerge from the *coenobia*
which they had joined earlier, rather than to attach themselves to *Seniores*
for training or to go far into the Desert straight from secular life.
Contemporary experience of the religious life supports this view.
Nowadays solitaries are almost invariably men and women who have
lived for some years as members of a religious community, generally
Benedictine or Cistercian, and who remain in some kind of relationship
with their original house. This may well have been the case in Cassian's
day also.

There is, however, an alternative tradition regarding the origins of
monasticism; this begins with individuals who, after living for some years
as hermits, become founders of religious communities.

The principal example is Antony, as described in the *Vita Antonii*,
but the same pattern is found in the *Liber vitae patrum* of Gregory of
Tours, the *Apophthegmata patrum latinorum*, the *Vita S. Martini* and the
Dialogues of Gregory the Great. The parallel between the lives of Antony
and of Benedict is particularly striking. Both are young men of good

---

[12] Arsenius: e.g., *Apophthegmata patrum latinorum* 5.2.3, PL 73: 858; 3.1, PL 73: 860;
6.2-3, PL 73: 888; 10.5-7, 9, PL 73: 913; 15.10, PL 73: 955; Evagrius Ponticus: e.g., *Historia
monachorum* 27, PL 21: 448-449; *Heraclidis Paradisus* 25, PL 74: 309-312; *Apophthegmata patrum latinorum* 5.1.4, PL 73: 855; 3.3, PL 73: 860-861; 6.5, PL 73: 889; 10.5, PL 73:
913; 19-20, PL 73: 915-916; Macarius of Alexandria: e.g., *Historia monachorum* 29, PL 21:
452-455; *Heraclidis paradisus* 6, PL 74: 270-275; Cassian, *Collationes* 14.4, 2: 186;
Germanus and Cassian: *Collationes* 1.1, 1: 78.
[13] *Apophthegmata patrum latinorum* 5.6.5-6, PL 73: 889; 12, PL 73: 890.
[14] Matrona: *Apophthegmata patrum latinorum* 5.2.14, PL 73: 860; Sarah: e.g., ibid.
5.5.10, PL 73: 876; 7.19-20, PL 73: 896-897; 10.73-74, PL 73: 925; Syncletica: ibid. 5.3.16,
PL 73: 862; 4.41-43, PL 73: 870; 6.13, PL 73: 891; 7.17-18, PL 73: 1039-1040; 8.19-20,
PL 73: 909; 10.70-74, PL 73: 924-925; 11.32-34, PL 73: 937-938; 14.9, PL 73: 949-950;
Talis, Taor, the virgin to whom Collythus appeared, and her mother: *Heraclidis
paradisus* 48, PL 74: 331-332; for women in the Desert in general, see ibid. 20, PL 74: 298-
299.

family, who are free from parental control; in Antony's case, this is due to
the death of his parents, but Benedict's situation is the result of a deliberate
act of renunciation. Both are incompletely educated: Benedict is described
as,

> scienter nescius et sapienter indoctus (2. prol., 2: 126-127)

Antony,

> cum autem crevisset et profecisset aetatem, litteras quidem noluit discere,
> volens liber esse a consuetudine puerorum.[15]

In both cases their assumption of the eremitical life entailed two stages:
Antony retired from his parental home in a centre of population into the
Desert, and then still deeper into the Desert. Gregory describes a similar
development in the vocation of Benedict: first, he departs from Rome to
the village of Effide; then he goes to the deserted district of Subiaco (2.1, 2:
129-131). Both find companions and ultimately form communities. The
same course is traced by Gregory for that enigmatic figure, Isaac of
Spoleto (3.14, 2: 304-307), who appears in Umbria as a stranger from
Syria, becomes first a solitary, and ultimately the founder of monasteries.

Thus Gregory derives his conception of the origins of monasticism not
from Cassian but from Athanasius. We have now to consider how far his
account of the Italian monastic scene accords with the writings of Cassian
and Eastern ascetic works. The principal difference is that while Gregory,
like Cassian, is describing what he has seen or heard about, he makes no
comparable attempt to schematize or rationalize it on the basis of the
internal monastic organization. There is, rather, a kind of geographical
progress from distant rural monasteries towards Rome, as Vogüé has
pointed out in the introduction to his edition of the *Dialogues*. In *Dialogue*
1 we find a group of relatively distant *coenobia*: Fundi (1.2, 2: 24-25); the
monasteries in Valeria, where Equitius was abbot (1.4, 2: 38-39); the
monastery on Soracte (1.7, 2: 66-67); and Subpentoma (ibid., also 1.8, 2:
70-71); Fortunatus, abbot of Balneum Ciceronis (1.3, 2: 36-37) is
mentioned as one of Gregory's informants. The nearest of these to Rome
is the monastery on Soracte, though a case has been made for situating
Balneum Ciceronis at Tuscolo, near Frascati. Gregory also tells an
anecdote of the monk who became a priest in the monastery of St Peter at
Praeneste (the modern Palestrina, 3.23, 2: 358-361). We enter the Holy
City only briefly, to leave it with Benedict in his quest for solitude.
Gregory's picture of the valley of the Anio bears a certain resemblance to

---

[15] *Vita Antonii* 3, pp. 10-13.

one of the Desert. Benedict arrives from the rural Effide to live as a solitary in the Subiaco district (2.1, 2: 132-133), just as Antony arrived in the deeper Desert from an area less distant from Alexandria. There Benedict is befriended by the monk Romanus, who lives in a *coenobium* under the government of Adeodatus (2.1, 2: 136-141). We find at least one other *coenobium* in the area, the monastery of which Benedict was asked to take charge because it had lost its abbot (2.3, 2: 140-141), and Benedict himself went on to found others at Monte Cassino and Terracina (2.8, 2: 26-27; 22, 2: 202-203). The twelve monasteries founded in the Subiaco area (2.3, 2: 150-151) may well have originally been anachoretic settlements, such as Cassian describes, since they appear to have been in-dependent organizations owing allegiance directly to Benedict, rather than "houses" on the Pachomian model. There is a good case for believing that the *Regula magistri* was drawn up for these little communities of a dozen monks each.[16]

Various monastic patterns can be discerned in *Dialogue* 3. Isaac of Spoleto represents the phenomenon of the solitary who collects disciples and ends with founding a *coenobium*. We also find a pair of monks, Florentius and Euthicius, who lived together, but who became separated when the latter was chosen to rule over a neighbouring monastery (3.15, 2: 315-317). There are, in addition to Florentius, four hermits: Benedict of Campania (3.18, 2: 344-345); the unknown holy man of Monte Argentaro, who restored a dead man to life (3.17, 2: 336-337); Menas (3.26, 2: 366-371); Martin of Monte Marsico (3.16, 2: 326-327). Two hermits are mentioned in *Dialogue* 4: one, living in Samnium, whose soul was seen ascending to heaven by travellers sailing from Sicily (4.10, 3: 44-45); the other, living in the Lipari islands, who, as the result of a vision, was able to give travellers news of the death of Theodoric (4.31, 2: 104-107).

Dialogue 4 brings us back to the Rome of Gregory's own day. Here he is within his own geographical and chronological framework and can speak from his own experience of monks in the monastery of St Andrew, such as Maximianus, the abbot, who subsequently became bishop of Syracuse (4.33, 3: 108-111); Theodore and his brother (4.40, 3: 140-141); Antony and Merulus (4.49, 3: 168-171); Justus (4.57, 3: 188-195). He also writes of abbot Stephanus, whom Peter will have known well (4.12, 3: 48-49). This urban monasticism is a phenomenon which is lacking in the pages of the Eastern Christian writers whom we are considering, though

---

[16] A. de Vogüé, "La Règle du Maître et les Dialogues de saint Grégoire," *RHE* 61(1966): 44-76.

we know from other sources that it existed in Constantinople and Jerusalem.

Feminine monasticism certainly existed in Italy from the late fourth century onwards. The story of the group of ladies, led by Paula and her daughter Eustochium and under the spiritual direction of Jerome, who lived a conventual life in their own homes on the Aventine Hill, is well-known, and there were doubtless other similar establishments. A hundred and fifty years later Gregory's three aunts (one of whom later defected) lived in this manner, as did his mother Silvia in a separate house near the present-day church of San Saba on the Little Aventine. Gregory refers in the *Dialogues* to a number of *sanctaemoniales*, some of whom seem to have been cenobites and others solitaries. Among the former was the bearded nun Galla, who

> abiecto saeculari habitu ad omnipotentis Dei servitium sese apud Beati Petri apostoli ecclesiam monasterio tradidit.

There is a reference to her colleague Sister Benedicta and to the mother of the whole community (4.14, 3: 58-59). Among the latter was the virgin Gregoria, who lived near the church of St Mary Major in Rome. There is also the consecrated virgin of Spoleto who drove a demon into a pig, but Gregory does not indicate her exact status. She may have been living at home. Some of the nuns in Italy may have lived rather as the groups of anchorites lived in Egypt: for example Herundo had lived in the hills above Praeneste, where she had trained a companion, Redempta, who later settled in Rome with two disciples. The evidence suggests that the monastic life for women was organized on a more informal basis than for men, and that owing to the unsettled state of the countryside resulting from the campaigns of Belisarius and later from the Lombard wars, it tended to be urban in character. Thus the individual women religious whom Gregory mentions are settled in Rome and Spoleto, and the spiritual descendants of Herundo have not remained at Praeneste, but have come down from the hills into Rome. A further indication of this movement towards the towns on the part of women religious is afforded by a letter from Gregory to Theoctista, the emperor's sister (*Reg.* 5.23, 2: 468), in which he thanks her for a gift of 30 lbs. of gold: this would be used to provide bedding for nuns, of whom there are a great number in Rome. The inference here is not that there are large cenobitic communities on the Pachomian model, but that many nuns have fled from their rural homes before the invaders and have had to leave all their belongings behind. Gregory does not furnish us with much information about the role of these women in the Christian community, but we form the impression that they were occupied principally in prayer and contemplation, though Gregoria was quite prepared to indulge in reminiscences about Isaac and Spoleto with interested visitors. There is no record that she or any other of these women performed the same kind of counselling functions as the Egyptian *amma*.

In conclusion to this section, it may be said that Gregory is reporting what he has seen or heard of Italian monasticism, without attempting to provide his knowledge with a philosophical basis or a schematic framework. Naturally, since monasticism came to Italy with the exiled Athanasius, it is not surprising that Italian monasticism should bear resemblance to Egyptian monasticism, and that Gregory's account of it should be influenced by Eastern ideas. In his conception of the origins of monasticism and of the foundation of *coenobia*, Gregory certainly follows the precedent of Antony as described by Athanasius. The type of cenobitic and anachoretic life which Gregory describes, is allied to that which is revealed in the works of Cassian, but this could be because both were writing of the same phenomenon. Nevertheless, as we shall see shortly, Gregory was almost certainly acquainted with the works of Cassian and, in spite of what has been said above, there seems to be a strong attempt to represent the valley of the Anio as a kind of Thebaid and Benedict as an Antony or even as an Elisha.

C. Some Theological and Psychological Concepts Common to Gregory and to the Eastern Christian Writers

We have now to examine the working-out of certain theological and psychological concepts found in Gregory the Great, Cassian, and the Desert Fathers. There are, of course, many such concepts, and it is possible here to examine only three of them, which seem particularly valuable: a. compunction; b. prophecy and discernment of spirits; c. chastity and sexual relations.

a. *Compunction*

One of Gregory's most valuable contributions to Western theology and spirituality is his teaching about *compunctio*.[17] Indeed, I. Hausherr has suggested that Pope Zacharias (741-752) translated the *Dialogues* into

---

[17] See *Moralia* 3.67-69, 1: 156-157; 33.68, PL 76: 716-718; 22.48, 1: 1127-1128; 33.41, PL 76: 275-278; 24.10, 2: 291-293; *Homiliae in Ezechielem* 2.10.4, p. 382; 19-22, pp. 394-399; *Dialogues* 3.34, 2: 400-405; *Reg.* 7.23, 1: 466; *Liber regulae pastoralis* 29, PL 77: 107-108.

Greek on account of their teaching about compunction, a doctrine highly esteemed by Eastern Christians.

We may distinguish three stages in compunction, the second and third of which are very closely allied: 1. a definite prick or sting of remorse or sorrow for sin; 2. the development of a permanent attitude of such sorrow and a sense that, though the sin may be forgiven, a scar has been left upon the soul; 3. an intense longing for spiritual advance. Prior to Gregory's teachings, it was the first stage which was emphasized in the West.[18] Augustine in his *Enarrationes in Psalmos* lays particular stress on the prick of compunction, as if by a thorn:

> modo delectant peccata, et quasi non compungunt ... tunc spinae illius rhamni, id est, dolores omnes et compunctiones ... spinas compunctionis paenitentiae.... Compunctus autem corde non solet dici nisi stimulis peccatorum in dolore paenitendi sicut de illis dictum est, qui cum audissent apostolos post Domini ascensionem, compuncti sunt corde, qui occiderant Dominum.[19]

He sees compunction as *initium paenitentiae*. The term is also used by Jerome in one of his letters, where he is commenting on Isaiah 6.6. He makes a distinction between *compunctio* as something which purifies – here the coal from the altar – and *compunctiones*, which are the *stimuli* of carnal passions.[20] Ambrose uses *compunctio* in the same way.[21]

A much richer teaching on compunction is found in Eastern Christendom. The idea of the prick or sting is to the fore, but Cassian enlarges upon it, discussing the means by which it can be aroused. His suggestions are: *per illuminationem Domini*; by means of verses of the psalms in public recitals of them; *exhortatio viri perfecti et conlatio spiritalis*; *fratris seu cari cuiuslibet interitu*; *recordatio quoque temporis ac neglegentiae nostrae*.[22]

At this stage it may be useful to consider the teachings of the Greek Fathers on compunction. The idea, of course, goes back to Old Testament times. We find it in those Psalms upon which Augustine commented. Its earliest use in the New Testament is in Acts 2.37; *his autem auditis compuncti sunt corde*, which is the Vulgate rendering of ἀκούσαντες δὲ

---

[18] I. Hausherr, *Penthos: la doctrine de la componction dans l'Orient chrétien*, OrChrA 132 (Rome 1944), p. 23.

[19] Augustine, *Enarr. in Ps. 57.20*, *Enarrationes in Psalmos*, ed. E. Dekkers and J. Fraipont, 3 vols., CCSL 38-40 (Turnholt 1956), 2: 725-726; ibid. 108.19, 2: 1595.

[20] Jerome, *Ep.* 18A, 1: 87-88.

[21] E.g., Ambrose, *Expositio Psalmi 118.3.8*, *Expositio Psalmorum*, ed. M. Petschenig, CSEL 62 (Vienna 1913, repr. 1962), p. 45.

[22] Cassian: e.g., *Coll.* 9.26, 2: 62; *Inst. coen.* 12.18, pp. 478-479; *Coll.* 9.26, 2: 62-63.

κατενύγησαν τὴν καρδίαν. Thereafter two distinct streams of teaching on compunction can be distinguished, each with its own vocabulary, which fortunately enables us to identify the source of Gregory's teaching. The first theologian to stress the idea of grief for sin becoming a permanent spiritual state is Origen. Even after μετάνοια, a word which is commonly translated as repentance and implies an entire change of thoughts, attitude and will, the penitent person still experiences sorrow.[23] The words which Origen uses are not ἡ κατάνυξις and κατανύσσειν, which are translated as *compunctio* and *compungere*, but τὸ πένθος and πενθεῖν, which imply a permanent state of mourning, as for example, in the Second Beatitude: μακάριοι οἱ πενθοῦντες. In this he is followed two generations later by the apophthegmatic writers who employ the words *luctus* and *lugere*. Nevertheless two stories in the *Apophthegmata patrum latinorum* illustrate that the different stages in the experience were still understood by the writers.

The first is the story of Abba Pambo who was asked by Athanasius to go from his hermitage to Alexandria where he saw a woman of the theatre. It well illustrates the idea of the sudden prick.[24] The second is a good example of the habitual state of *tristitia* resulting from *compunctio*:

> Sanctae memoriae Theophilus archiepiscopus, cum moriturus esset, dixit: Beatus es, Abba Arseni, quia semper hanc horam ad oculos habuisti.[25]

The second group of writers employs the words ἡ κατάνυξις and κατανύσσειν, which, like τὸ πένθος and πενθεῖν, have a biblical origin.[26] The earliest of these writers is Basil,[27] and the tradition is continued by Gregory of Nyssa,[28] John Chrysostom,[29] and Evagrius Ponticus, who distinguishes between different kinds of sorrow and puts into words the sense of longing for spiritual advance which should be felt by the penitent: πόθος πρὸς τὸ θεῖον ἄπειρος καὶ σπουδὴ περὶ τὸ ἔργον ἀμέτρητος.[30] For our purpose, the most important exponent of this tradition is Cassian, who

---

[23] Origen, *In Ier. hom. 16.10, Jeremiahomilien*, ed. E. Klostermann, GCS *Orig*. 3 (Leipzig 1901), pp. 141-142; ibid. 20.3, pp. 179-182; for τὸ πένθος and πενθεῖν, ibid. 6, p. 186; 15.3, p. 127; for a summary of the teaching of Eastern Christian writers on compunction, see Hausherr, "Penthos," pp. 18-24.

[24] *Apophthegmata patrum latinorum* 5.3.14, PL 73: 862.

[25] Ibid. 5.3.5, PL 73: 861.

[26] For ἡ κατάνυξις and κατανύσσειν, e.g., Acts 2.37; Rom. 11.8, citing Isa. 29.10; Ps. 108.16; Gen. 34.7; Ecclus. 12.12; 14.1; for τὸ πένθος, e.g., Jas. 4.9; Rev. 18.7; 21.4; πενθεῖν (intrans.), e.g., Matt. 5.4; 9.15; 1 Cor. 5.2; Mark 16.10; Luke 6.25.

[27] *Regulae brevius tractatae* 16, PG 31: 1092.

[28] Gregory of Nyssa, *De beatitudinibus orationes* 3, PG 44: 1224.

[29] E.g., *De statuis* 17.1, PG 49: 171; *De compunctione*, PG 47: 411.

[30] Evagrius Ponticus, *Praktikos* 57, Evagre le Pontique: *Traité pratique, ou Le moine*, ed. A. & C. Guillaumont, 2 vols, SC 170-171 (Paris 1970-1971), 2: 634-635.

was able to mediate to Gregory the spiritual treasures of Eastern Christendom, because he was a disciple of John Chrysostom and he wrote in Latin. R. Gillet has rightly stressed the debt of Gregory to Cassian for the list of deadly sins and has analyzed his teaching on compunction in the *Moralia*, but apart from Hausherr and Pegon, the author of the article on compunction in the *Dictionnaire de spiritualité*, no one appears to have tried to work out in detail what further debts Gregory owes to Cassian.[31]

Just as the authors in the first group employ πενθεῖν to cover the first two stages of compunction, although it actually describes the second, so the second group employ κατανύσσειν in a broad sense. Cassian employs *compunctio* for the first stage, but also uses *tristitia* for the second.[32] We have already seen that Cassian has given some thought to the *origines compunctionum*. He believes that the *spiritus saluberrimae compunctionis* is sometimes aroused by joy, but also comes in silence, when the soul pours out its desires to God with groaning.[33] This seems to foreshadow Gregory's teaching on the two-fold nature of the means by which compunction is aroused:

> alia quippe compunctio est quae per timorem nascitur, alia quae per amorem, quia aliud est supplicia fugere, aliud praemia desiderare (*Hom. Ez.* 2.10.20, p. 395)

and again in *Dialogue* 3.34, 2: 402-405:

> principaliter vero compunctionis genera duo sunt, quia Deum sitiens anima prius timore compungitur, post amore.

In this last sentence we also find the idea of longing for the divine, such as we have already seen in the quotation from Evagrius Ponticus. Cassian distinguishes two kinds of *tristitia*: the first is the deplorable kind of remorse felt by Cain and Judas, the second, which is *utilis*, or, as we should say, constructive, is the sensation which we feel, when we are inflamed by

> paenitudine delictorum vel desiderio perfectionis vel futurae beatitudinis contemplatione.[34]

There is an important respect in which Gregory and Cassian resemble each other in their teaching on compunction. Both see it as a state in

---

[31] R. Gillet in *Moralia*, sc 32bis (Paris 1975), pp. 89-102, 72-81; J. Pegon, *DSp.*, art. Componction.

[32] For *tristitia*, *De institutis coenobiorum* 4.8, pp. 130-131; 9 *passim*.

[33] *Collationes* 9.26-27, 2: 376-379.

[34] *De institutis coenobiorum* 4.10-12, pp. 376-379.

which the soul, stripped of superfluity, is bared and made conscious of its sin:

> De timore Domini nascitur compunctio salutaris, de compunctione cordis abrenuntiatio, id est nuditas et contemptus omnium facultatum.

As the soul acquires a more profound *puritas cordis*, so it becomes more conscious of sin.[35]

The same stress on the need for purity and purgation before contemplation is found in at least two passages in the *Moralia*. The mind needs to be trained to withdraw itself from external affairs, and after the blemish rust of sin has been burned up,

> mundatis oculis cordis illa laetitia patriae caelestis aperitur, ut prius purgemus lugendo quod fecimus... (*Mor*. 23.11, PL 76: 292; cf. 3.53, p. 148; 5.55, p. 256).

In addition to assimilating the teaching of Eastern Christian holy men through the medium of Cassian and making it his own, Gregory also goes on, so to speak, where Cassian left off. In the *Moralia* 23.37-43 (PL 76: 273-278) he lists the four modes of compunction which he says that he has learned from St Paul (1 Cor. 15.9; 9.27; 2 Cor. 5.6; Rom. 7.23; 1 Cor. 13.12; 2 Cor. 5.1; Eph. 2.18), Job (6.1), and King David (*Ps*. 38.6; 119.5; 30.23). The righteous man looks back on his sins, *considerans ubi fuit*; fearing the judgements of God, and bewailing himself, *cogitat ubi erit*; carefully looking at the sins of his present life, *moerens considerat ubi est*; when he contemplates the joys of his heavenly home, which he has not yet attained, *lugens conspicit ubi non est*.

For both Gregory and Cassian physical tears appear to be an essential part of compunction, though Germanus admits that he does not always find it easy to produce them.[36] Gregory in *Dialogue* 3.34 (2: 400-405), draws an elaborate comparison between the two kinds of compunction, the two streams of tears, and the *divisiones aquarum* which occur in the Lamentations of Jeremiah.

No more than a brief treatment can be given to the topic of compunction here, but I hope that it is sufficient to indicate how the writings of Cassian were able to stimulate Gregory to enlarge upon what he had said about *compunctio*, and to afford an example of the kind of Eastern Christian spirituality which Gregory was able to transmit to the West. The process of the Latinization of the Greek concept had already

---

[35] Ibid. 4.43, 1: 184-185; 12.15, 2: 470-471.
[36] *Collationes* 9.28, 2: 63; see also Gillet, pp. 72-81, cited in n. 31 above.

been begun by Cassian; it was Gregory who was able to disseminate these ideas to the sixth-century monastic and clerical public, whose background would be different from that of Cassian's audience, owing to the cultural change already mentioned in chapter four.

b. *Prophecy and Discernment of Spirits*

It was generally believed in Late Antiquity that the gifts of prophecy and the discernment of spirits were a special mark of the holy man. This belief was no doubt derived from the Bible; these gifts were possessed by the Old Testament prophets (for example, Elisha in 2 [4] Kings 5.25-27; 8.11-12) and are listed by Paul (1 Cor. 12.10) among the gifts of the Holy Spirit. Gregory, like Paul, distinguishes between prophecy and discernment of spirits (*prophetia, discretio spirituum* in the Vulgate; προφητεία, διαχρίσεις πνευμάτων in the Greek), but uses the term *ventura praedicere* and *praesentibus absentia nuntiare* (2.11, 2: 174-175).

We have already examined Benedict's exercise of these gifts in chapter two, where it was briefly indicated that some of Gregory's stories might be linked with Eastern prototypes. It seems appropriate to examine these prototypes in rather more detail here. We have already mentioned John of Lycopolis who, having lived thirty years as a recluse, possessed to a most remarkable degree both the power of prophecy and the power to read thoughts and to perceive an inner meaning, which Gregory describes as *praesentibus absentia nuntiare*. He was regularly consulted by the emperor Theodosius, as we learn from Augustine, Cassian, the author of the *Historia monachorum*, and Palladius. According to the author of the *Historia monachorum*, John prophesied to Theodosius that there would be a revolt that he would successfully subdue, and to a military governor that Theodosius would die a natural death.[37]

Gregory attributes similar powers to Benedict on the occasion of Totila's visit to Monte Cassino, when he uttered a combination of John's prophecies:

> multa male facis, multa fecisti. Iam aliquando ab iniquitate conpescere. Et quidem Romam ingressurus es, mare transiturus, novem annis regnas, decimo morieris (2.15, 2: 182-183; cf. ibid., 184-185).

A still more striking parallel between the Desert writings and *Dialogue* 2 is exemplified by the prophecies relating to the fall of Scete and the destruction of the monastery at Monte Cassino. In the *Apophthegmata*

---

[37] See chapter two, n. 47.

patrum latinorum there are two prophecies relating to the fall of Scete: the first of these, by Macarius the Great, is the more famous and the more apocalyptic in character:

> quando videritis cellam aedificatam iuxta paludem, scitote quia prope est desolatio Scythi; iam ante ianuam est; quando autem videritis pueros, tollite melotes vestros et discedite.[38]

It is more likely, however, that Gregory is thinking of the second passage, which occurs in the later portion translated by John, since both it and the prophecy which he causes Benedict to utter are less apocalyptic in tone and are alike in expressing regret at the destruction of buildings. The unknown old man of the *Apophthegmata* is found by his brethren weeping in his cell, though normally he rejoices: *Qui dixit eis: Desolandus est locus iste, filii.* The old man has twice seen fires put out by the brethren, but this time, ...

> et implevit totam Scythim et iam non potuit extingui. Ideo ego contristor ac maestus sum.[39]

In the parallel passage in *Dialogue* 2 (17, 2: 192-193), Theopropus, *vir quidam nobilis*, finds Benedict weeping in his cell and asks why:

> cui vir Dei ilico respondit, omne hoc monasterium quod construxi et cuncta quae fratribus praeparavi omnipotentis Dei indicio, gentibus tradita sunt.

The gift of discernment of spirits seems to have been widespread in Eastern Christendom. John of Lycopolis was able to read the minds and thought of the local Egyptians living round about and also to detect evil behaviour among his own monks. Abba Helenus was able to startle his brethren by his revelations about their characters. Abba Paul the Simple and Abba Eulogius had the power to make uncomfortable discoveries about intending communicants.[40] An unnamed bishop was able to discern that the faces of different groups among the communicants were of different colours: fornicators' faces went black, those of the blasphemers were red and bloodshot, and those of the virtuous were shining.[41] Certain holy men were able to discern when anything was slightly amiss: Basil, when visiting a convent, perceived that one of the sisters was missing;[42]

---

[38] *Apophthegmata patrum latinorum* 5.18, PL 73: 982.

[39] Ibid. 6.15, PL 73: 993.

[40] For John of Lycopolis, Helenus, and Eulogius, see chapter two, n. 43; for Paul the Simple, e.g., *Apophthegmata patrum latinorum* 5.18.20, PL 73: 985-988; *Heraclidis paradisus* 10, PL 74: 284-287.

[41] *Apophthegmata patrum latinorum* 6.1.16, PL 73: 998-1000.

[42] Ibid. 5.18.19, PL 73: 984.

John of Lycopolis could distinguish which one of seven brothers was absent;[43] Symeon Stylites discerned that a man among his visitors was really a woman in disguise.[44]

The details in Gregory's stories may not correspond to those stories by the Eastern writers, but they describe the same kind of character and incident. Benedict, like Abba John, can discern the evil thoughts and deeds of his monks. He is also able to see that certain of his monks have been thieves and liars when away from the monastery. He can detect that the man who is dressed as Totila is not Totila, but Riggo dressed up in Totila's clothes (2.14, 2: 180-183). Similar gifts are possessed by Equitius, who discerned that Basilius was not a monk but a devil (1.4, 2: 38-43); by Sabinus, the blind bishop of Canossa, who knew that it was not his servant but Totila who passed him his drink, and that his jealous archdeacon had placed poison in the cup (3.5, 2: 272-277); and by Isaac of Spoleto, who foresaw that a gang of potential thieves could be converted into honest labourers in the monastery garden (3.14, 2: 306-309).

Thus Gregory appears to have received his ideas about the power of discernment of spirits from Eastern Christian writings, but to have regarded this gift rather differently. The holy man in Eastern Christendom seems to have used them for strictly religious purposes: to discern the state of the souls of intending communicants;[45] to recognize the presence of heretics,[46] and to seek out persons of outstanding sanctity.[47] The holy man in the West, however, turned such gifts to practical account by using them to discover those who harboured evil thoughts and were failing to behave as good monks should, in short, as a means of maintaining good discipline in the monastery. However, too hard and fast a distinction cannot be drawn: for example, Hypatius used his powers in much the same way as Benedict.[48] Similarly Pachomius discerned that some carnally-inclined monks were still disobedient to him, in spite of his admonitions. After he had introduced his Rule, which appears to have been a necessary consequence of their bad behaviour, they saw that there was no future for themselves in the monastery and removed themselves.[49]

---

[43] *Historia monachorum* 1, PL 21: 394.
[44] *Liber in gloria confessorum* 26, p. 314.
[45] See nn. 40-41 above.
[46] Cyril of Scythopolis, *Vita Iohannis Hesychastae* 23, pp. 218-219.
[47] See n. 42 above.
[48] *Vita Hypatii* 14, pp. 122-123; cf. *Dialogues* 2.12, 2: 174-177; 20, 2: 196-199.
[49] [Pachomius] *Vita 1*.38, pp. 55-57; *Vita 2*.32, pp. 160-162.

c. *Chastity and Sexual Relations*

Readers of the *Dialogues* of Gregory the Great and of the writings of his contemporary Gregory of Tours are aware of the expression of a somewhat stern and puritanical philosophy regarding the relationship between men and women. Chastity, or rather, celibacy is represented as the highest good, but failing that, an unconsummated marriage is best. Late antique and early medieval hagiography abounds in stories of couples whose parents put pressure on them to marry; either they somehow escape the bonds of marriage to live celibate lives, or, if obliged to marry, they live a life of complete chastity in marriage or separate in order to become a monk or a nun. Such ideas seem to have come from Eastern Christendom: they were popular with Jerome, who expounded them in his three *Vitae*, two of which, as we have seen, were written after his sojourn in Antioch and in the deserts of Chalcis, and who put them into practice in his relationship with Paula and her family. They also seem to have come into prominence in the fourth century or even earlier. For example, Leontius regards it as a matter for congratulation rather than distress that John the Almsgiver's wife and children all died, thus leaving him free to become a monk.[50]

It is therefore not surprising to find the same ideas expressed in the *Apophthegmata patrum latinorum*, from which Gregory probably culled two of his best-known stories.

The first concerns Martin the hermit, who lived on Monte Marsico, and had decided at the very beginning of his eremitical life that he would never in future look upon a woman, not because he despised the female sex, but because he feared that by looking upon a woman he might incur the stain of temptation. A certain woman hearing this, climbed up the mountain and looked into his cave. Having caught sight of her female attire from a distance, he lay face downward on the floor in prayer. At last the woman grew so weary that she retreated from the window of the little cell. She went down the mountain and died that very day. This story will be considered further in section E of this chapter. In the meantime we may note that the literature of the Desert contains a number of comparable stories to this. Palladius tells us how Abba Pior, when he went into the Desert, vowed that he would never see any of his relatives again. After fifty years, his sister, believing that he had not long to live, asked to see him. Therefore he stood outside the door, with his eyes tight

---

[50] See nn. 50-51 below; Leontius, *Vita Iohannis Eleemosinarii* 3, p. 20.

shut, while she looked at him.[51] There is also the sad story told by Cassian of Abba Paul, who was so shocked by the sight of a woman that he turned back from an errand of charity upon which he was engaged with Abba Archebius. Consequently he was stricken with paralysis and had to live for the last four years of his life in a convent of nuns who had to do everything for him.[52]

A story concerning a chaste couple, which occurs in the *Historia monachorum* and the *Historia Lausiaca*, was probably known to Gregory. Amoun was obliged by his parents to marry, but he persuaded his bride to live secretly in virginity, like himself. Afterwards they parted, Amoun to become a monk in Nitria and his wife to establish a convent in their matrimonial home.[53] This recalls the story in 4.12 (3: 48-53) of the aged priest of Nursia, who had lived with his wife as brother and sister ever since his ordination. When on his deathbed, he drove away his wife, saying that there was a little fire still left and that she was to take away the straw. Indeed the chaste couple is a very common motif in Late Antiquity and the early Middle Ages.[54] We have already encountered Malchus and his wife in the pages of Jerome; and Gregory of Tours also affords a number of examples.[55]

Gregory the Great's informants, in both these cases, were Pope Pelagius and abbot Stephanus respectively. One may make two conjectures. Either Gregory's informants had conveyed to him stories which were common to many districts in the Mediterranean area, or he or his informants or both were acquainted with the apophthegmatic writings and moulded the material accordingly. The latter seems the more likely. Gregory, like other Western ecclesiastics, was concerned for the chastity of married clergy and any material which stressed its importance would serve as a welcome model.

D. A Comparison Between Narratives and Character Sketches in the *Dialogues* and in Eastern Christian Writings

So far we have seen that there is a strong probability that Gregory was acquainted with such Eastern Christian literature as was available in Latin or Latin translation, but can we obtain more concrete evidence?

[51] *Heraclidis paradisus* 26, PL 74: 311; cf. *Apophthegmata patrum latinorum* 5.4.33, PL 73: 869; *Historia religiosa* 3.14, 1: 274-277.

[52] *Collationes* 7.26, 1: 268-270.

[53] *Historia monachorum* 22, PL 21: 444-445.

[54] E.g., Theonas and his wife, *Collationes* 21.9, 3: 82-85; Eucharistius and Mary, *Apophthegmata patrum latinorum* 6.3.2, PL 73: 1006.

[55] E.g., *Liber in gloria confessorum* 31, p. 317; cf. *Libri historiarum* 1.47, pp. 30-31; *Liber in gloria confessorum* 41, pp. 323-324; 75, pp. 342-343; 77, p. 344.

I believe that there are two definite items which make it almost certain that he knew at any rate the *Historia monachorum* and the *Apophthegmata patrum latinorum*. The first of these is a small linguistic gloss – and one must admit that such glosses are grammatical stock-in-trade – relating to a special kind of horned serpent:

> Qui non solum coluber sed etiam cerastes vocatur. Κέρατα enim Graece cornua Latina dicuntur... (*Mor.* 31.43, PL 76 5967).

It seems likely that Gregory derived this information from the *Historia monachorum*:

> Hic [*sc.* Didymus the Blind] scorpiones et cerastas, id est bestias quas cornutas vocant, et angues ... pedibus conculcabat.[56]

Quite possibly the original source of this information was Pliny the Elder, who wrote:

> cerastis corpore eminere cornicula saepe.[57]

The second is rather more complicated. It is a story told by Gregory, by Cassian and in a long and short version by the apophthegmatic writers. Vogüé has found difficulty over this story on account of the origin which Gregory attributes to it.[58] It concerns Andrew, bishop of Fundi; according to Gregory,

> nec res est dubia, quam narro, quia paene tanti in ea testes sunt, quanti et eius loci habitatores existunt (3.7, 2: 278-279).

Yet it appears to have three literary antecedents in Cassian and the *Apophthegmata*. I myself believe that first, a reasonable solution of this dilemma can be offered; second, it is a good example of Gregory's methods of handling his material; and third, it affords strong evidence that Gregory knew the *Apophthegmata patrum latinorum*.

According to the version of the story told by Gregory, Andrew bishop of Fundi had in his household a nun. So secure did he feel in his own and her continence that he did not see any need to send her away. It so happened that a Jew travelling towards Rome, when evening was drawing on, took refuge in a temple of Apollo on the Appian Way. He feared so greatly the profane character of the place that though he had no faith in Christianity, he nevertheless took care to protect himself with the

---

[56] *Historia monachorum* 24, PL 21: 447-448.
[57] Plinius Secundus, C. [Pliny the Elder], *Naturalis historia* 8.23, ed. L. Jahn and C. Mayhoff, vols. 1-5 (Leipzig 1892-1909), 2: 106.
[58] *Dialogue*, introduction, 1: 132-134.

sign of the cross. In the middle of night he was lying awake, terrorstruck by the solitude, when he saw that a crowd of evil spirits was advancing as if in obedience to some powerful leader, and that he who was in command of the rest had sat down in the centre of the place itself. The leader then began to discuss the opportunities and actions of the spirits obedient to him, in order that he might discover how great an amount of wickedness each one of them had achieved. In the course of these discussions one of the fiends revealed how great was the carnal temptation with which he had moved the mind of bishop Andrew through the sight of the nun who was living in his house. The fiend reported that the bishop had so far yielded to temptation as to give the nun a gentle slap on the back, whereupon his leader bade him return and complete what he had begun, in order that he might hold the palm among the others for achieving ruin. The leader of the fiends perceived the Jew and asked the others to enquire who it was who presumed to lie down in the temple. They saw that he had been signed with the cross and finally disappeared, after calling him *vas vacuum ac signatum*. The Jew hastened to the bishop, whom he found in church, and asked him whether he was undergoing temptation. At first the bishop denied it, but a reminder about the gentle slap led him to confess humbly what he had previously denied. He prostrated himself in prayer and soon afterwards sent away not only the nun but also every other woman in his household. The temple became a chapel dedicated to St Andrew the Apostle, and the Jew was converted and baptized.

The protagonist in Cassian's story is a monk, *unus e fratribus nostris*,[59] who on a solitary journey takes refuge in a cave at nightfall, wishing to say his evening office there. By the time he had finished, it was past midnight. When he had been sitting down for a little while, he saw crowds of demons collecting together from all directions; some preceded their chief and others followed him. Ultimately the chief sat down on a throne, on a very high judgement seat. As in Gregory's story, there was much questioning as to the activities of the fiends and the amount of wickedness achieved. Cassian assigns the role of judge to the archfiend. He orders the weak and cowardly spirits to be driven from his presence and punished, but praises and encourages others who have been more successful. Among these is *quidam nequissimus spiritus*,[60] who announced that he had at last conquered a very well-known monk whom he had been besieging for fifteen years; the monk had now not only incurred the

---

[59] *Collationes* 8.16, 2: 23-24.
[60] Ibid., 2: 24.

charge of debauchery but had also been persuaded to retain the woman by conjugal right. For this the fiend was exalted with the highest praise and crowned with commendations. When day dawned, the crowd of demons vanished. The monk was doubtful about the assertions made by the fiend and remembered the words of the Gospel (John 8.44) that the devil is the father of lies, but he made his way to Pelusium, where he knew the other monk was staying. There he found that on the same night when the fiend had prophesied his ruin, the well-known monk had left his former monastery, had sought the village, and had lapsed into disgrace with the nun who had been named.

This story occurs in two different forms in the *Apophthegmata patrum latinorum*.[61] In the longer form, A, the narrator is a *senex* of Thebes, who is the son of a pagan priest. When he was a little boy, sitting in the temple, he had often seen his father enter and offer sacrifices to idols. On one occasion he had seen Satan seated there, with a whole host of demons around him and conducting an enquiry to discover what each fiend had been doing and how long it had taken him to do it. These fiends had all been operating on a large scale, causing bloodshed, shipwrecks, and all kinds of disasters, but all were ordered to be scourged, because they had not achieved enough in the time. Finally, a fiend approached who said that he had been in the desert and had been laying siege to a monk for forty years, but it was only on the previous night that he had been induced to commit fornication. Thereupon Satan rose and kissed him, put a crown on his head, and caused him to sit beside him on his throne. The boy was deeply impressed and said to himself, *Valde magnus est ordo monachorum*. From the Greek version of the *Apophthegmata* we learn that he was converted and become a monk himself but, of course, Gregory could infer this from the Latin, without having seen the Greek.[62]

In the shorter version, B, a monk, who had gone to draw water at a mealtime, upset the water vessel on the way back. He decided to go into the desert and to tell the *seniores* what had happened. Since night had fallen, he slept in a pagan temple by the wayside. There he heard the demons saying, "Tonight we have hastened that monk into fornication." Distressed, he returned next day to find his *senex* sad. The *senex* admitted his sin, and asked how it was that his colleague knew of it. He announced his intention of returning to the world, but the other monk persuaded him to dismiss the woman and remain where he was.

---

[61] *Apophthegmata patrum latinorum* 5.39, PL 73: 885-886 (version A); ibid., PL 73: 879-880 (version B).

[62] F. Nau, ed., "Histoire des solitaires égyptiens" 191, *ROC* 13(1908): 275-276.

As the result of this exposition, we can trace the stages through which this story has passed. What seems clear is that Gregory is thinking of the versions in the *Apophthegmata*, since the setting of his story is not a cave, as in Cassian, but a pagan temple as in both A and B.

Gregory and the writers of the *Apophthegmata* have as their intention a picture of the dangers of yielding to temptation and thus falling into sin, and of the importance of conversion, from Judaism in one instance and from paganism in the other. Cassian, while not losing sight of these important subjects, is anxious to stress the immense power of the demons and to show that a hierarchical principle permeates their organization. He appears to base his story on A, which contains an element of judgement and a hierarchy of demons. It is, as it were, the Day of Judgement in reverse, since the demons are rewarded according to the greatnesss of the sins which they induce man to commit. Since Cassian desires to impress upon his monastic audience the importance of a disciplined religious life, he places his emphasis, apart from stressing the hierarchy of demons, upon the monk searching for a suitable place in which to say his office, and of his chanting all the psalms, even though he was by himself, so that it was past midnight when he had finished. He also wishes to point the contrast between the virtuous and disciplined monk and his backsliding colleague.

The principal difficulty about Gregory's story, as I have already indicated, is his insistence on the numerous local witnesses to events which, he assures us, took place in Fundi, but which we believe to have strong affinities with stories told elsewhere. Does this mean that we cannot rely upon the testimonies of Gregory's informants? I do not believe this to be the case. My own view is that in spite of the provisions of Canon III of the Council of Nicaea,[63] bishop Andrew of Fundi had had the virtuous nun and various female domestics living in his house, but that the gossip in the town became so widespread that he felt obliged to order them all to go. This would be the story to which there were as many witnesses as there were inhabitants of Fundi. Gregory, always loyal to the episcopal order, used a collation of Cassian's story with the *Apophthegmata patrum latinorum* versions A and B, to try to resuscitate his colleague. The setting of Gregory's story is a pagan temple, as in the *Apophthegmata*, but since his object was to tell a story of conversion rather than to emphasize the hierarchic organization of the demonic host, he follows B by playing down the elements of hierarchy and of judgement.

[63] *Conciliorum oecumenicorum decreta*. 3rd ed. (Bologna 1973), p. 7.

The protagonist as a person in need of conversion is a conception linked with A; but he may perhaps also have had in mind a story told by Rufinus about Gregory Thaumaturgus, who, while on a journey, took refuge in a temple of Apollo, put to flight the demons there by his own presence, and ended by converting and baptizing the pagan priest.[64] In Gregory's finale, the visit of the Jew to the bishop and his subsequent conversion and baptism correspond to the visit of Cassian's monk to Pelusium to warn his colleague and to the conversion of the boy and his profession as a monk, described in version A.

There are two possible reasons for Gregory's writing of the conversion of a Jew. First, the conversion of a Jew would redound to the credit of Andrew of Fundi, doing much to restore his reputation in town and diocese. Second, Gregory always displays a special interest in the conversion of the Jews (Reg. 7.25, 2:27): gentleness and kindness are to be displayed in attempting it and special inducements may be offered (Reg. 13.15, 2: 383; 5.7, 1:228); there is to be no compulsion on them to be baptized (Reg. 1.45, 1:71-72). In his correspondence we find him taking their part, when their singing at their synagogue in Terracina (incidentally, not far from Fundi) is alleged to have disturbed the Christians, and when they have been required to leave their locum (Reg. 1.34, 1:47-48; cf. Reg. 3.6, 1:104-105).

Gregory's attitude to the conversion of the temple into the chapel of St Andrew is of interest in relation to the controversy over the contrary advice given regarding the destruction of pagan temples in England. Gregory's letter to Mellitus in 601 instructs the latter to destroy idols but not their temples, which are to be sprinkled with holy water and consecrated as churches (Reg. 11.56, 2:330-331). Thus he countermands the instructions to King Ethelbert given a little earlier in the same year, to destroy the pagan temples (Reg. 11.37, 2: 308-310, at p. 308). Probably this apparent volte-face was due, as Markus suggests, to further reflection by Gregory on the accounts of conditions in England brought home by Mellitus.[65] At any rate, when compared with previous precedents and later developments, it is the instructions to Ethelbert which are the exception to normal papal policy. The first example known to us of a church which had formerly been a pagan temple being converted into a Christian church, is that of SS Cosmas and Damian, which was consecrated by Pope Felix IV (526-530); later there was the Pantheon,

---

[64] Eusebius, trans. Rufinus, Historia ecclesiastica 7.28.2, pp. 954-955.
[65] R. A. Markus, "The Registrum of Gregory the Great and Bede," RBen 18(1970): 162-168.

which became *Sancta Maria ad Martyres* in 608.[66] The chapels at Fundi
and Monte Cassino (2.8, 2: 168-169) were presumably dedicated in the
second half of the sixth century. Seen against the background of these
recorded examples, it is Gregory's letter to Ethelbert which is the
aberration.

Here it will be convenient to consider another story of a haunted
building, which appears to be of Eastern origin and which also affords a
good example of Gregory's method of handling his sources.

In 3.2-4 (2:266-273) we find a group of stories about an Italian bishop
and two popes. Gregory has acquired this information, *tam religiosorum
virorum relatione*. We may conjecture that these were persons in the
episcopal or papal entourage. The scene of the first and third of these
stories is set in Corinth and of the second in Constantinople. The story
which concerns us here is the third, contained in 3.4 (2:270-273). Datius,
bishop of Milan, on his way to Constantinople, halted at Corinth and
ordered a large house which he had seen from a distance to be prepared
for his party. The local inhabitants told him that no one had lived there for
many years, because a demon dwelt in it. The bishop insisted on spending
the night there. In the silence of the dead of night (*intempestae noctis
silentio*), while the bishop was resting, the fiend began to make all kinds of
animal noises: the roaring of lions, bleating of sheep, braying of asses,
hissing of serpents and squealing of pigs and mice. The demon quoted
Isaiah 14.14, whereupon Datius told him that through his own pride he
had become like the pigs and mice. At these words the fiend became
ashamed and never again entered the house, which afterwards became the
abode of faithful Christians; because once one such person had entered it,
the lying and infidel spirit immediately departed.

The story has been told at least twice in a pagan setting. Pliny the
Younger (62-ca. 114),[67] whose version is the earlier, sets the scene in
Athens, but the house is equally large; it is described as *spatiosa et capax*.
Again, it is a house where everyone refused to live, because it was
haunted. The philosopher Athenodorus volunteered to sleep there,
although many who had previously attempted to do so had died of fright.
He settled down to write. After a time a ghost of terrifying aspect
appeared, laden with chains. Athenodorus marked the spot where it
finally disappeared. The next morning he sent for a magistrate who gave
orders for the spot to be dug. Chains and human remains were found,

---

[66] *LP* 1: 279, 363.
[67] Plinius Cecilius Secundus, C. [Pliny the Younger], *Ep.* 7.27.4-11, 1: 28-29.

which were subsequently reinterred. Thereafter there was no further trouble.

Lucian of Samosata (fl. ca. 120-post 160) [68] tells a similar story in a rather more elaborate manner. As in Gregory's story, the scene is set in Corinth; the exact location is the house of Eubatides, which is in a state of decay, with the roof falling in, because no one has had the courage to enter it. As in Pliny's story, there have been a number of deaths among the visitors. The hero is a Pythagorean philosopher, Arignotus, who is learned in Egyptian lore. Like Athenodorus in Pliny's story, he settled down quietly, but to read, not write. The ghost in this story possessed protean qualities; one moment it assumed the aspect of a dog, then of a bull or a lion. Arignotus succeeded in driving it into a dark corner by means of a fearful imprecation in the Egyptian language, whereupon it dissappeared. He observed where it went and then fell asleep. In the morning there was general surprise that he was still alive; he went to Eubatides with the news that the house was purged of terrors and that he could now live in it. Digging on the spot where the ghost disappeared revealed a mouldering body. This was reinterred, and thereafter the troubles ceased.

It seems as though Gregory is drawing upon both Pliny and Lucian. As in Lucian's story, the scene is set in Corinth, but Gregory's *larga domus* recalls the *spatiosa et capax domus* of Pliny. In all three stories the events occur in darkness. Lucian's demon assumed the appearance of various animals, whereas Gregory's only made animal noises comparable to those made by the demon who assailed Antony.[69] Pliny's demon, however, caused disturbance through the clanging of chains. In all three cases, the protagonist is a man of some standing – a bishop and two learned philosophers – and of considerable courage. In the two pagan stories, reinterment of the body is a precondition of deliverance, but Gregory's demon is unconnected with any physical remains. Again, in the pagan stories some kind of outward sanction for the reinterment is entailed: Athenodorus sends for a magistrate and Arignotus fetches witnesses who take part in the excavations. In Gregory's narrative the mere presence of a single faithful Christian effects the departure of the demon.

In connection with this story, we cannot say for certain who had read whom. There are certain resemblances between the narratives of Gregory and Lucian, but Gregory's knowledge of Greek, as I have shown

[68] Lucian of Samosata, *Philopseudes* 31, 2: 194-195.
[69] *Dialogue* 3.4, 2: 270-271; cf. *Vita Antonii* 9, pp. 28-29.

elsewhere, was not extensive.[70] A knowledge of Latin was by no means universal among educated people in the Eastern Mediterranean area; we cannot therefore be certain that Lucian could have read Pliny's version.[71] Possibly Pliny, Lucian, and Gregory were all working upon a story which was known all over the Mediterranean area. What is more likely is that either one of the *religiosi viri* who were Gregory's informants (3.1, 2:266-267) or Gregory himself was in touch with a Greek and Latin speaker who had read Lucian. This contact might also have read Pliny, but Gregory could not have done so himself. The identity of Gregory's Greek-speaking contact cannot be ascertained from the evidence at present available.

These two stories are yet another illustration of Gregory's methods of handling his material. In both cases he has apparently taken over traditional stories which have become embedded in literary works but he has selected those elements which he needed for his own purpose and created a new story from them.

Apart from his account of Benedict's early years in the religious life (2. *prol.*-3, 2:128-149), Gregory describes five hermits in *Dialogue* 3: Florentius (3.15, 2:316-327); Martin of Monte Marsico (3.16, 2:326-337); the unnamed hermit of Monte Argentario (3.17, 2:336-345); Benedict of Campania (3.18, 2:344-345); and Menas of Samnium (3.26, 2:366-371). The case of Martin will be considered in the final section of this chapter since it presents special problems of its own. In the meantime, it will be convenient to consider St Benedict and the unnamed hermit and Florentius and Menas as pairs, treating Benedict of Campania between them.

In section 2 of this chapter we considered Benedict's monastic organization in comparison with Egyptian monasticism in general. Here we shall confine ourselves to certain characteristics of his earlier life as a solitary which seem to bear a resemblance to stories in the *Apophthegmata patrum latinorum*, though not exactly parallel to them: his subjection to severe temptations, particularly sexual temptations (2.2, 2:136-139), like many of the Desert Fathers; when, figuratively speaking, he first entered the Desert he found a *senex* in Romanus; like Antony and others of the Desert Fathers, he practised for a considerable period a non-liturgical and apparently non-sacramental Christianity (for example he was not aware of

---

[70] Petersen, "Did Gregory the Great know Greek?" pp. 121-134.

[71] Ibid., at p. 132, nn. 62-66; see also I. Sevčenko, "A Late Antique Epigram and the So-Called Elder Magistrate from Aphrodisias," *Synthronon, Bibliothèque des cahiers archéologiques* 2 (Paris 1968), pp. 29-41.

the arrival of Easter, until a local priest invited him to a meal in honour of the feast [2.1, 2:134-135]); he had a love of solitude:

> tunc ad locum dilectae solitudinis rediit et, solus in superni spectatoris oculis habitavit secum (2.3, 2:142-143),[72]

which recalls the advice given by Antony:

> qui sedet in solitudine, et quiescit, a tribus bellis eripitur; id est, auditus locutionis, et visus

and by the unseen voice to Arsenius:

> Arseni, fuge, tace, quiesce: [73]

The final resemblance is one which Benedict shares with the unnamed hermit; Gregory first emphasizes the importance of the granting of the religious habit to Benedict by his *senex* Romanus, here described as *quidam monachus* (2.1, 2:132-133): the granting of the habit is paralleled by the placing of Benedict's *melota* upon Placid's head (2.7, 2:158-159). This is re-emphasized in the case of the unnamed hermit:

> vir fuit ... venerabilis vitae, qui habito monachi, quem praetendebat specie, moribus explebat (2.17, 2:336-337).

Now these examples all recall the significance which the Desert Fathers attached to the granting of the habit in marking the separation of the monk from the world.[74] The clothing of the monk was regarded as a second baptism;[75] a *senex* would interpret the monk's attire as a series of symbols and would exhort others to exercise in their lives the virtues of which their habits were the outward sign.[76]

The humility of this unnamed hermit in ceasing to visit his friend Quadragesimus, because he did not wish to receive any honour in respect of his miraculously raising a man from the dead, recalls the conduct of the great Macarius and of Abba Abraham, after a similar miracle, as described by Cassian:

> apostolicis verbis in admiratione signorum humanam gloriam refutantes.[77]

---

[72] See P. Courcelle, " 'Habitare secum' selon Perse et Grégoire le Grand," *REA* 69 (1967): 266-279.

[73] *Apophthegmata patrum latinorum* 5.2.3, PL 73: 858; cf. ibid. 5.3.2-3, PL 73: 860.

[74] E.g., [Pachomius] *Vita 1*.6, p. 10; *Vita 2*. (Lat.) 7, *La vie latine de saint Pachôme, traduite du grec par Denys le Petit*, ed. H. van Cranenburgh, SHG 46 (Brussels 1969), p. 96; *Historia monachorum* 9, PL 21: 423.

[75] *Apophthegmata patrum latinorum* 6.1.9, PL 73: 994.

[76] *De institutis coenobiorum* 1.1-11, pp. 34-55; 4.5-6, pp. 126-129.

[77] *Collationes* 13.6, 2: 216.

Thus, though the story of the unnamed hermit has no exact parallel in any of the Desert writing, some of its details are curiously reminiscent of them and tend to confirm the view that Gregory was acquainted with the *Apophthegmata patrum latinorum*.

Benedict of Campania need not detain us long. We have already met him as the man whom the Goths tried to bake in an oven. There is little to be said about him, except that he was living in an individual cell in Campania, not in the Subiaco area, and that he had a *regula*. This would probably not be a Rule in the cenobitic sense, but a collection of precepts for personal guidance.

Florentius and Menas are separated geographically, since the former lived in the province of Nursia (3.15, 2:314-315) and the latter in Samnium (3.26, 2:366-367). No dates are mentioned, but they appear to be of the same generation. Gregory had heard about Florentius from Sanctulus, who had died at the time when he was writing the *Dialogues*; Menas had died about ten years previously and there were still many witnesses to supply information about him. They are both examples of the holy man with an affinity for the animal creation. Florentius was a shepherd and Menas a bee-keeper. The contrast lies in their attitude to bears. Florentius made friends with a bear and used him as an assistant after his companion Euthicius had left him to become abbot of a neighbouring monastery. Menas, on the other hand, used to drive the bears away from his bees with a little stick. Gregory tells us that Menas was eager to possess nothing, to ask for nothing, and to inflame all who visited him for the sake of charity, with the desire for eternal life; he could administer a rebuke to the penitent sinner, but he did so, *amoris igne succensus*. The concept of the human soul set on fire by love, as Menas himself was and as he attempted to achieve in others, is common in the literature of the Desert. For example, Abba Joseph told Abba Lot that he could not become a monk, unless he became like a consuming fire. He, Abba Joseph, held his hands towards heaven; his fingers became like ten lamps of fire, and he said to Abba Lot: *si vis, efficiere totus sicut ignis*.[78]

Besides the quality of being like a flame, Menas possessed that other well-known mark of the holy man, the power to discern spirits. After Carterius, who was one of his regular visitors, had carried off a nun and married her, he became spiritually aware of what had happened and told the man to whom Carterius, in shame and fear, had confided his weekly

[78] *Apophthegmata patrum latinorum* 5.12.8, PL 73: 942.

offering in order that it be mingled with the offerings of others, to take it back to him with the message:

> ... ego tuam oblationem non accipio, qui suam abstulisti Deo.

The *oblationes* were no doubt comparable to the offerings of food brought by the shepherds to Benedict in exchange for the *alimenta vitae*, which they cherished in their hearts (2.1, 2:136-137). Such weekly offerings enabled hermits such as Menas to survive.

The hermits described by Gregory appear to live after the Egyptian pattern. Abba Lot, in consulting Abba Joseph thus describes his regime:

> secundum virtutem meam facio modicam regulam et parvum ieiunium, et orationem, et meditationem, et quietem, et secundum virtutem meam studeo purgare cogitationes meas; quid ergo debeo de caetero facere.[79]

This might well be the basis of the lives of Gregory's hermits. Benedict of Campania, as we have seen, had a *regula*, like Abba Lot. There is, however, a more positive and constructive element in the lives of these people. Benedict of Nursia and Menas were engaged in what we might call spiritual direction and counselling; Benedict indeed converted the shepherds through the character of his own life. Florentius and the unnamed hermit, however, appear to have been true solitaries. We are told that it was his colleague Euthicius who, prior to his departure to the monastery, won souls for God (2.15, 2:316-317), while Florentius lived a life dedicated to prayer. These two patterns are reflected in the spirituality of the Desert.

Gregory's Italian hermits are to be contrasted with the Syrian "hinge-men" described by Brown.[80] The political circumstances in Syria were such that the hermit provided a valuable liaison between the villagers and the local bureaucracy. The hermit in the West, however, though he may have functioned as spiritual guide to individuals like a forerunner of the Russian *staretz*, does not appear to have served as a mediator in social and political affairs. Perhaps this was because the one stabilizing force in Italy was the Church, in whose institutional machinery the hermit did not seem to have a place.

In conclusion, our examination of the literary material relating to the spirituality of the Desert has revealed a considerable volume of material covering teaching, narrative, and character study, which is common to

---

[79] Ibid.

[80] P. R. L. Brown, "The Rise and Function of the Holy Man in Late Antiquity," *JRS* 61 (1971): 80-101.

Gregory and to Eastern Christian writers. There are resemblances between Gregory and Cassian, in addition to those already noted by Gillet, which support the opinion that part of Gregory's narrative about Andrew of Fundi is derived from the apophthegmatic writers rather than from Cassian, because Gregory follows the former in setting the scene in a pagan temple rather than a cave. Thus there appear to be reasons for the belief that Gregory was familiar with both the works of Cassian and the *Apophthegmata patrum latinorum*.

E. MARTIN THE HERMIT AND SYMEON STYLITES: WAS GREGORY ACQUAINTED WITH THE *HISTORIA RELIGIOSA* OF THEODORET?

There is another work devoted to stories of Eastern holy men, which we have not so far considered in relation to Gregory, Theodoret's *Historia religiosa*. A period of over one hundred and fifty years separates this work, which appeared ca. 440, from the *Dialogues*, which appeared in 593. There are certain resemblances between the two works which might lead us to suppose that Gregory had some direct knowledge of the work of Theodoret, though *a priori* this seems unlikely. P. Canivet justly remarks that had a Latin translation been available, it would have had a circulation in the West comparable to that of the *Vita Antonii*, the *Historia monachorum* or the *Historia Lausiaca*. In his opinion, its influence was confined to the Orient, because the only language into which it was translated was Syriac. The first Latin translation was made in the sixteenth century.[81]

With the view that the *Historia religiosa* was without influence in the West I venture to disagree. Though very little critical work has been done on it until recently – a defect now remedied by Canivet himself, Festugière, and Brown – the resemblances between the *Historia religiosa* and the *Dialogues* have not gone unnoticed. As long ago as 1919, Ildefons Herwegen, then abbot of Maria Laach, wrote in the introduction to the second edition of his character study of Benedict:

> Dass Theodoret für die späteren verwandten Mönchsgeschichten in den Dialogen des hl. Gregor des Grossen als Quelle gedient habe, wage ich nicht zu behaupten.[82]

---

[81] *Historia religiosa* 1: 9.

[82] I. Herwegen, *Der heilige Benedikt: ein Characterbild*, 2nd ed. (Düsseldorf 1919), cited by C. Baur in his introd. to *Des Bischofs Theodoret von Cyrus Mönchsgeschichte*, trans. K. Gutberlet, BKV 50 (Munich 1926), p. 9, n. 2.

The examples of "increase" miracles [83] which he mentions, might well resemble each other, based as they are on the same biblical types; otherwise his choice of points of resemblance between the two works is, for the most part, far from apt. In his first comparison, he mistranslates the Greek. He grasps that Theodoret explicitly, and Gregory implicitly, are comparing their hero to Moses, but fails to realize that Theodoret is stressing the meekness of Moses, whereas Gregory is stressing his power to raise a spring (2.5, 2:152-153). The sentence selected by Herwegen, προεχεῖτο δὲ αὐτοῦ κὰι τοὺς ἔξω τὰ ἥδιστα νάματα, taken in its context, refers to springs of philosophy.[84] A more telling comparison would have been between Martin the hermit (3.16, 2:328-329) and Theodosius, both of whom obtained water from a rock like Moses.[85]

In two other cases, there is a similar failure to select the more relevant examples. The story of the unjust landlord whose chariot-wheels became locked as a punishment is better paralleled by that of the Goth's horses who were rendered immobile than by the accounts of various overbearing individuals in *Dialogue* 2.[86] Again, a more forceful comparison would have been between the resuscitation of the boy, the youngest son of his father, whose brothers have all died, and the widows' sons in the *Historia religiosa* 21 and *Dialogue* 1.2 (2:26-31). Both Theodoret and Gregory compare this story with that of Elisha and the Shunamite's child, one of many indications that their minds worked on similar typological lines. However, neither these more apt comparisons nor certain resemblances prove that Gregory had first-hand acquaintance with Theodoret's work.[87] Both were, after all, working within a common biblical background.

Gregory and Theodoret share the same traditional view of the origins of monasticism: they see Elijah and Elisha as the fathers and patrons of the ascetics and monks. There are many references to this in the Greek Fathers, from whom Theodoret may have gained his information, as well as in Jerome, and Cassian, who were presumably Gregory's sources.[88]

---

[83] *Historia religiosa* 24, 2: 148-149; cf. *Dialogue* 2.29, 2: 218-221.

[84] Herwegen, commenting on *Historia religiosa* 11 (1: 456-459); Canivet, also commenting on this passage, sees the real significance of νάματα.

[85] Cf. *Historia religiosa* 10.7, 1: 448-449. If this story is a later interpolation from the *Patrum spirituale* of John Moschus (*Pratum* 80, PG 87(3): 2937-2940), as suggested by Canivet, commenting on this passage, it only serves to show that Gregory and Moschus were thinking of the same biblical type.

[86] Herwegen, on *Historia religiosa* 14.4 (2: 14-15); cf. *Dialogue* 2.27, 2: 216-217; 31, 2: 222-227, but the closer parallel is 1.10, 2: 26-29.

[87] Ibid., *Historia religiosa* 21.14, 2: 90-91; cf. *Dialogue* 2.11, 2: 172-175; 32, 2: 226-229, but the closer parallel is 1.2, 2: 26-29.

[88] See chapter two, n. 46.

The one authority whose reference to Elijah might be known to both Gregory and Theodoret is Athanasius:

> Dicebat autem sibi Antonius: Oportebat qui studium Christi habet ex conversatione magni illius Eliae considerare, ut in speculo vitam suam.[89]

It is noticeable that in the writing of both Theodoret and Gregory the miracles linked with the Elijah-Elisha cycle are (with one possible exception in the *Dialogues*) performed by monks, as successors of the prophets.[90] Here, again, it must be stressed that the telling of stories based on a common type implies a common cultural and religious background rather than a knowledge of each other's works.

There are, however, three striking parallels between the *Historia religiosa* (and other Eastern ascetic literature) and the *Dialogues*: the stories of Martin the hermit and Symeon Stylites; [91] the stories of Benedict and Acepsimas;[92] the story of the woman visitor.[93] The first of these parallels, which Herwegen has noticed, concerns the chaining of the holy man to a rock, in order that he may travel only a certain distance from his cave, a practice which continues until a wiser holy man instructs him that it is to cease. Symeon, in the days before he mounted his pillar, chained himself to a rock on the top of a mountain until the *chorepiscopus* Melitius, thinking the chain excessive, ordered its removal on the grounds that a theoretical chain would be sufficient: ἀρκούσης τῆς γνώμης λογικὰ τῷ σώματι περιθεῖναι δεσμά. Martin, in his early days as a solitary, occupied a cave without a door and attached one end of an iron chain to his foot and the other to a rock. On hearing of this, Benedict sent word by a disciple that Martin was to remove the chain:

> si servus es Dei, non te teneat catena ferri, sed catena Christi.

Thereupon Martin removed the chain, but continued to confine himself to the area beyond which he could not travel when chained.

Theodoret's account is more factual; he tells us the length of the chain − ἄλυσίν τε ἐκ σιδήρου πήχεων εἴκοσι κατασκευάσας − and supplies the unsavoury detail that when the fetters were removed, twenty bugs were

---

[89] *Vita Antonii* 7, pp. 24-25.

[90] See chapter two, n. 11.

[91] *Dialogue* 3.16, 2: 334-335; cf. *Historia religiosa* 26.10, 2: 180-181.

[92] *Dialogue* 2.1, 2: 136-137; cf. Antony, *Vita Symeonis* 14, *Vita Symeonis Stylitae, Das Leben des heiligen Symeon Stylites*, ed. H. Lietzmann, with German trans. of the Syriac version and letters, by H. Hilgenfeld, TU 32 (Leipzig 1908), pp. 37-39; ibid., 23, pp. 57-59; *Liber in gloria confessorum* 26, p. 314.

[93] See n. 88 above.

found.[94] In both cases the writer implies that the senior holy man is suggesting that a rational Christian should not require such physical restraints as a chain.

The parallels seem too close to be coincidental, but at the same time it is difficult to see how Gregory, with his very slight knowledge of Greek, could have read the writings of Theodoret. The Greek *Vita* of Symeon Stylites, by Antony, was translated into Latin at an early date, but it does not contain this particular story. It is possible that Gregory himself provides us with a key to the mystery:

> quem [*sc.* Martinum] multi ex nostris noverunt, eiusque actibus praesentes extiterunt: de quo multa ipse, et beatae memoriae Papa Pelagio decessore meo et aliis religiosissimis viris narrantibus agnovi (3.16, 2:326-327).

Pelagius II is not known to us through the *LP* or any other source as one of the popes who were competent Greek scholars. In fact we know very little about him. The only evidence for his cultural achievements is to be found in his correspondence, which is printed as MGH *Epp.* 2 *App.* 3. The most important of the letters of Pelagius for our purpose is the third, a lengthy document addressed to the bishops of Aquileia on the subject of the Three Chapters; the difficulty is that there is some doubt about its real authorship. Gregory himself affirms that it is the work of Pelagius in a letter of 592 (*Reg.* 2.49, 1:150):

> ut igitur de tribus capitulis animis vestris ablata dubietate possit satisfactio abundanter infundi, librum, quem ex hac re sanctae memoriae decessor meus Pelagius papa scripserat, vobis utile indicavi transmittere.

By *librum*, Gregory must surely mean the letter referred to above (MGH *Epp.* 2, *App.* 3 (3), pp. 449-467), since it deals with the Three Chapters and is long enough to be regarded as a book. On the other hand Paul the Deacon, writing just over two hundred and fifty years later, affirms that Gregory was the author:

> Pelagius Heliae Aquileiensi episcopo nolenti tria capitula Calchidonensis Synodi suscipere epistulam satis utilem misit. Quam beatus Gregorius, cum esset adhuc diaconus, conscripserat.[95]

Hartmann, the editor of the second volume of Gregory's letters, not unreasonably has some doubts on the subject:

> de hac epistula [*sc. App.* 3 (3)], ut viri docti coniecerunt agi videtur. Sed an verum sit, quod Paulus tradit, affirmare non ausim ...[96]

---

[94] *Historia religiosa* 26.10, 2: 180-181.
[95] *Historia Langobardorum* 3.20, p. 103.
[96] MGH *Epp.* 2, p. 449 fn.

My own opinion is that we should accept the evidence of Gregory himself in preference to that of Paul. No doubt in the sixth century, as in our own time, public figures put their signature to letters which had been composed for them by officials, but how could Paul, writing so long after the event, be sure that this was the case?

If we accept that Pelagius was the author of the letter, we then become aware that he knew something of Eastern theological thought. It is true that a number of his references to Eastern theologians have been culled from conciliar *Proceedings* and the *Codex Encyclicus*, and that he could have read Eusebius and Origen in the translations of Jerome and Rufinus, but he mentions the commentary on the Song of Songs by Gregory of Nyssa, which had not been translated into Latin. More important from our point of view is his interest in Theodoret. He states that he does not condemn all the works of Theodoret, but only those which oppose the twelve chapters of Cyril and the orthodox faith. He also expresses approval of the opinions of Theodoret on Theodore of Mopsuestia's commentary on the Song of Songs.[97] There is naturally no mention of the *Historia religiosa* in this discussion of dogma, but since Pelagius has displayed interest in the works of Theodoret, it is not unreasonable to conjecture that he might have read it. If so, he may have become interested in the lives of the Eastern holy men and have compared them in his mind with such holy men as he knew in Italy. It would be entirely in keeping with the spirit of late antique hagiography to attach to Martin the hermit stories which had already been told about Symeon Stylites.

The second parallel between the *Historia religiosa* and the *Dialogues* involves Benedict and Acepsimas. Benedict, when he was a solitary at Subiaco, was taken by some shepherds for an animal, because he was clad in skins. Acepsimas, who had lived for sixty years in a hut in silence without having been seen by anyone, was taken by some shepherds for a wolf, because he was walking bent forward, being loaded down with chains.[98] In both cases the shepherds made the acquaintance of the hermit, but whereas the Italian shepherds were transformed as the result of their new friendship and spread Benedict's fame locally, the Syrian shepherds only came once, to beg the hermit's pardon for throwing stones at him.

Gregory may owe this story to Pelagius II or to a Greek-speaking source, or his informants may have heard it from someone who had read Theodoret. What is more likely, however, is that the story is one which

---

[97] Ibid., p. 464, 23ff.; p. 465, 38ff.
[98] *Historia religiosa* 15.2, 2: 18-21.

was common to the Mediterranean area and that there were variant local versions.

The third parallel concerns the woman visitor. This is not found in Theodoret, which is not surprising, since it bears the hall-marks of the hagiographer rather than the historian. There are four versions of this story, which it will be convenient to call A, B¹, B² and C. A is the original Greek version of the *Vita Symeonis* by Antony, a disciple of Symeon, which may be assigned to the second half of the fifth century; B¹ is the generally accepted Latin text, to be found in Lietzmann's edition, parallel with the Greek; B² is a variant version, printed in *AASS* 1, January; B¹ may have been known to Gregory of Tours; C is another Latin version, included by Gregory of Tours in *Liber in gloria confessorum*.[99] A is considerably longer than B¹, because it contains details omitted by the translator and describes the death of Symeon's mother. After twenty-seven years, having learned where he is, she ascends the column; on hearing from her son that they will see each other not now but in the hereafter, she flings herself upon the gate and expires. In B¹ she does not die, but *haec audiens lacrimas compescuit*; B² provides a further variant; she dies but is restored to life by Symeon.

Gregory of Tours stresses in C the fact that Symeon never saw women, even his own mother, but that this did not prevent them from making the attempt. He cites from a source, *in eius vitae libro*, which is presumably the *Vita* of Antony, since this includes (both in A and B¹ and B²) the story of a woman disguised as a soldier who attempted to see Symeon. It seems as though he is conflating two stories in B¹: the story of Symeon's mother and the story of the woman disguised as a soldier.[100]

The story of the bold woman who climbed Monte Marsico to try to see Martin the hermit and died on the very day of her descent is closely paralleled by Gregory of Tours. Martin's visitor, growing weary, finally departed:

> quae die eodem, mox ut de monte descendit, ut ex mortis sententia daretur intelligi, quia valde omnipotenti Deo displicuit, quod eius famulum ausu improbo contristavit (3.16, 2:330-331).

This echoes the sentiments of Gregory of Tours:

> tractans secum misera agere posse per indumentum, quod latere possit altissimum ignorans illud, quia Deus non irridetur (Gal. 6.7).[101]

---

[99] See *Vita Symeonis*, ed. Lietzmann, pp. 207-210; *Liber in gloria confessorum* 26, p. 314.

[100] See n. 89 above.

[101] *Liber in gloria confessorum* 26, p. 314.

We have already noticed that it is not intrinsically impossible that Gregory the Great may have read some of the works of Gregory of Tours, and that the latter deserves to be taken more seriously than he usually is, when he is dealing with Eastern affairs.[102]

Gregory the Great may have known the Latin *Vita* of Symeon, perhaps when he was *apocrisiarius* in Constantinople, or though the transmission of a manuscript to the West. The style of the Latin translation suggests that it was made by someone whose mother-tongue was Greek, since certain linguistic usages, such as the over-frequent employment of the present participle, are based on Greek rather than Latin constructions. Certain elements from the *Vita* of Symeon are in Gregory's story of Martin: both holy men are resolved never to see a woman; both holy men are in high places to which it is an effort for the woman to ascend, one on the top of his column, the other in his cave at the summit of a high and steep mountain. The difficulty about regarding the first Latin *Vita* of Symeon as Gregory's source is that his story ends with the death of the woman, as in the Greek version, whereas in the Latin version she restrains herself, weeping. Delehaye suggests that the text of the existing Greek is corrupt and that the Latin text represents an earlier text of the Greek, which is the true version, but this does not account for Gregory's apparently being acquainted with the later Greek version.[103]

There is, however, an alternative possibility. Both Gregory and Antony may have been linking their stories with various stories of the Desert Fathers:

1. Abba Pior, who vowed never to see any of his relatives again and stood with his eyes tight shut, when his sister visited him after fifty years;[104]

2. John of Lycopolis, who, at the age of ninety, had lived in his cave for forty years and had never seen a woman or been seen by one during that time;[105]

---

[102] See chapter three, nn. 65-67; chapter five, n. 76.

[103] H. Delehaye, *Les saints stylites*, SHG 14 (Brussels 1923), p. iv, ingeniously suggests that the Latin represents the original Greek, which he believes to have been καὶ ταῦτα ἀκούσασα μετὰ δακρύων ἐπαύσατο. The scribe, not properly understanding the meaning, paraphrased it as ἐν Κυρίῳ ἐπαύσατο. This can be neither affirmed nor denied. In any case it does not help us with the problem of Gregory's apparent knowledge of the later Greek text.

[104] *Heraclidis paradisus* 26, PL 74: 312-315.

[105] *Historia monachorum* 1, PL 21: 391.

3. Abba Poemen, who shut the door of his cell against his mother and told her that if she could bear with equanimity not to see him and his brothers now, she would do so hereafter;[106]

4. Cyril of Scythopolis, tells the story of the ψαλτρία or chantress of the church of the Holy Sepulchre in Jerusalem, who because she caused scandal, was visited by Abba John and Abba Cyriac. On their way back they found her dead.[107]

Elements from all these stories can readily be seen in the narratives of Antony and Gregory:

Antony

a. The desire not to see relatives, especially women, as in 1. and 2.

b. The rebuff to the mother, with the exhortation that they would meet in the next world, as in 3.

c. The woman who is found dead, as in 4.

Gregory the Great

a. The desire not to see a woman, as in 2.

b. The refusal to look upon a woman, as in 1.

c. The woman who is found dead, as in 4.

Gregory, if he knew Rufinus's translation of the *Historia monachorum*, the *Heraclidis paradisus* or some other Latin version of the *Historia Lausiaca* and the *Apophthegmata patrum latinorum*, as we may reasonably assume, would be able to draw on them for stories 2. and 3. of his narrative. His source for story 4. is more puzzling, since it apparently did not exist in Latin. In both cases, the woman is not altogether evil but has displayed a single fault, for which she must die. Symeon's mother and Martin's visitor were fervent in their devotion, but desired to do something which was contrary to the will of the holy man. The chantress had caused some scandal in the past and had received male visitors, giving the impression that she was a man. Here again, Gregory may either be drawing upon the recollections of Pelagius or may be giving literary form to a story common throughout the Mediterranean area.

---

[106] *Apophthegmata patrum latinorum* 5.4.33, PL 73: 869.
[107] Cyril of Scythopolis, *Vita Cyriaci* 17-19, pp. 233-234.

7

Epilogue

The assumption has been made by generations of scholars, including Homes Dudden,[1] Battifol,[2] and in more recent times, Riché,[3] that Gregory the Great was totally ignorant of Greek theological thought, because, on his own admission and in spite of six years' residence as *apocrisiarius* in Constantinople, he knew no Greek.

In the course of the present work we have observed that there are good grounds for challenging this assumption. The three previous chapters have revealed the existence of a fund of stories common to the Eastern and Western Mediterranean area which have been put into literary dress by both Greek and Latin writers. We have seen that Gregory could have become aware of stories told by Eastern writers through the medium of Latin writers who knew the Eastern Christian world, such as Sulpicius Severus, Jerome, and Cassian, or through Latin translations of Greek writers, particularly those by Jerome, Rufinus, and Pelagius and John. We have also noted that there is a small body of material which appears to have influenced Gregory but which seems to have existed only in Greek: the writings of Lucian of Samosata; the *Historia religiosa* of Theodoret; a story which is found only in the Greek version of the *Vita* of Symeon Stylites by Antony. How are we to account for Gregory's knowledge of these?

To describe in full the results of my investigations into Gregory's knowledge of the Greek Fathers and other Greek writers, and the state of his linguistic knowledge is beyond the scope of the present work, since they have been derived almost entirely from works of Gregory other than the *Dialogues*. As regards biblical exegesis, they have revealed the extent

[1] Homes Dudden, *Gregory the Great*, 1: 153-154.
[2] P. Battifol, *Grégoire le Grand* (Paris 1928), p. 34.
[3] P. Riché, *Éducation et culture dans l'occident barbare, VIe-VIIIe siècles*, 3rd ed. (Paris 1973), p. 189.

of Gregory's debt to the Greek Fathers. *Homiliae in evangelia* 2.34, based
on Luke 15.1-10, is a particularly good illustration of this. Gregory's
exegesis of the parables of the Lost Sheep and the Lost Coin owes much
to Origen, Gregory of Nazianzus, Gregory of Nyssa, and Cyril of
Alexandria.[4] He also devotes a considerable section of this sermon to the
nine orders of angels, on which his teaching appears to be influenced by
that of Ps. Denys the Areopagite, whose name is actually mentioned in the
text.[5] Here again, we are confronted with the same difficulty as in the
Dialogues: there is material which appears to be derived from works of
Gregory of Nazianzus and Gregory of Nyssa but these were not, as far as
we know, then available in Latin. Nor is it likely that a Latin translation of
the *De hierarchia caelesti* of Ps. Denys existed at that date.[6]

In 1976 I attempted to challenge the view that Gregory the Great knew
no Greek.[7] Since then my opinions have undergone some modification in
the light of further evidence, which suggests that, though Gregory was not
totally ignorant of the Greek language – his protests that he knew no
Greek may be construed as *confessiones humilitatis*[8] – his knowledge was
considerably less than I had believed earlier. My investigations since 1976
have shown how dependent Gregory was upon Augustine, Jerome,
Eucherius, and other earlier Latin writers for his etymologies and
explanations of Greek terms,[9] but I do not accept the view that he knew
no Greek at all. No doubt the dearth of suitable teachers in the troubled
Rome of his boyhood prevented him from acquiring a profound
knowledge of the language, but he knew enough to comment, for
example, on the connection between φυλάττειν and *gazophylacium*.[10] This
again is a stock instance. It is most unlikely that he knew sufficient Greek
to read patristic texts in the original. All the indications are that he relied
for his information about Greek writings upon some oral source which, in
the present state of our knowledge, it is impossible to identify. I have
discussed this question more fully elsewhere.[11]

---

  [4] J. M. Petersen, "Greek Influences on Gregory the Great's Exegesis of Luke 15.1-10,
Hom. Ev. 2.34," to appear in *Actes du colloque international CNRS "Grégoire le Grand,"*
not yet published.
  [5] Petersen, "A Reconsideration," pp. 5-16.
  [6] Petersen, "Greek Influences," pp. 5-6.
  [7] Petersen, "Did Gregory the Great know Greek?" pp. 131-134.
  [8] See p. 70, n. 56.
  [9] Petersen, "A Reconsideration," pp. 31-37.
  [10] *Homiliae in Ezechielem* 2.6.2, p. 295; see also Eucherius of Lyons, *Instructiones* 1,
Opera omnia, ed. C. Wetke, CSEL 31 (Vienna 1894), p. 161.
  [11] Petersen, "A Reconsideration," pp. 16-29.

As Peter Brown has shown,[12] the enquiry into the extent of Gregory's knowledge of Greek is inevitably only one aspect of a wider enquiry, the attempt to discover the kind of ideas that influenced sixth-century men in the Mediterranean area and to see how far they were common to both the Latin West and the Greek-speaking East. My examination of this problem has been confined to literature, theology, and spirituality rather than to the wider fields considered by Brown and Markus, but it has revealed that at this period there was a corpus of ideas, which were common to Christians in both East and West and were indeed so much part of the general Christian consciousness that they found expression in the writings of both Greek and Latin authors. This resemblance between the ideas underlying these works may be due to a common background and a common *Weltanschauung* rather than to a common literary source. Gregory was the personification of Pirenne's *Romania*[13] rather than the creator of what Ullmann describes as his "policy of bifurcation."[14] The living holy man as agent of miracles is not seen in his writings as confined to the East nor the dead holy man, who performed miracles from his tomb or by means of relics, to the West. The difference between Eastern and Western Christendom in the late sixth century lay in the relationship between Church and state and Church and society rather than in ideology.[15] Gregory's significance as a bridge-figure between Late Antiquity and the Middle Ages and between Eastern and Western Christendom lies in his ability to actualize in the *Dialogues* something of the common corpus of Eastern and Western ideas. It is not therefore surprising that the *Dialogues* were widely read in both East and West. The Greek translation by Pope Zacharias (741-752) was so popular that Gregory became known in the East as "Gregory of the *Dialogues*." They were copied so frequently in the later Middle Ages that it is impossible to trace a *stemma* among the numerous surviving manuscripts. Some modern readers may regard the *Dialogues* simply as charming and picturesque stories, but they cannot be dismissed on this score, nor, as they were by Gibbon and other older critics, as an inappropriate or frivolous work for Gregory to have produced. On the contrary they are important as evidence for the unity of Mediterranean literary culture in the sixth century and as a landmark in the history of the "thought-world" of Eastern and Western Christendom.

[12] P. R. L. Brown, "Eastern and Western Christendom in Late Antiquity: a Parting of the Ways," *SCH(L)* 13 (1976): 5-6.

[13] Pirenne, *Mahomet et Charlemagne*, pp. 1-4.

[14] W. Ullmann, *A Short History of the Papacy in the Middle Ages* (London 1972), p. 57.

[15] R. A. Markus, "Gregory the Great and a Papal Missionary Strategy," *SCH(L)* 6 (1970): 29-38.

Bibliography

1. PRIMARY SOURCES

Acta Sanctorum. Vols. 1-67. Brussels, etc.: Société des Bollandistes, 1643-1883; facs. repr., Brussels 1902-.

Aeneas Gazaeus. *Theophrastus*. PG 85: 872-1004.

Agnellus of Ravenna, abbot, 9th cent. *Liber pontificalis ecclesiae Ravennatis*. Ed. by O. Holden-Egger. MGH SRL. Hannover, 1878, pp. 34-391.

——. [*Liber Pontificalis*.] *Codex pontificalis ecclesiae Ravennatis*. Ed. by A. Testi Rasponi, fasc. 1-3. RIS 2.3. Bologna: Nicola Zanicchelli, 1924.

Aldhelm, Saint, bp of Sherborne. *De virginitate* [prose and verse]. Ed. by R. Ewald. MGH AA 15. Berlin, 1919, pp. 211-471.

Ambrosius, Saint, bp of Milan. *Epistolae*. PL 16: 913-1342.

——. *Expositio Psalmi 116, Expositio Psalmorum*. Ed. by M. Petschenig, CSEL 62. Vienna, 1913, repr. 1962.

——. *De virginibus*. Ed. O. Faller. *Florilegium patristicum* 31. Bonn: Hanstein, 1933.

Antonius, Saint, the Great [Antony], see Athanasius.

Antonius, disciple of Symeon Stylites [Antony], see Lietzmann, H.

Antonius, monk [Antony], see Ennodius.

Apophthegmata patrum: Texts – Greek

    Appendix ad Palladium: Apophthegmata patrum [alphabetical collection], PG 65: 71-412.

    [*Apophthegmata patrum*.] *Histoires des solitaires égyptiens* [anonymous collection]. Ed. by F. Nau. *ROC* 12 (1907): 1-37, 43-69; 38-62, 171-189; 63-132, 393-413; 13 (1908): 133-174, 47-66; 175-215, 266-297; 14 (1909): 216-297, 357-379; 17 (1912): 298-334, 204-211; 335-358, 294-301; 18 (1913): 359-400, 137-146.

——: Texts – Latin

    Verba seniorum 1-18 [= *Vitae patrum* 5]. Trans. by Pelagius. PL 73: 851-992; ibid. 1-43 [= *Vitae patrum* 6]. Trans. by John, PL 73: 991-1024; ibid. 1-44 [= *Vitae patrum* 7]. Trans. by Paschasius, PL 73: 1025-1066.

    Aegyptiorum patrum sententiae [= *Appendix ad Vitas patrum*]. Trans. by Martin of Dume, PL 74: 381-394.

——: Translations, English – From the Greek:

    The Sayings of the Desert Fathers: the Alphabetical Collection. [PG 65: 71-440]. Trans. by B. Ward. London: Mowbray, 1975.

The Wisdom of the Desert Fathers: the 'Apophthegmata patrum' (anony-
    mous series). Intr. by A. Bloom. Trans. [from Nau's text] by B. Ward.
    Oxford: Fairacres Press, 1975.
——: —— – From the Latin:
The Sayings of the Fathers [= *Verba seniorum* 1-17], with selections from
    18-21, PL 73: 855-1022]. Ed. and trans. by [W.] O. Chadwick. LCC 12:
    37-189. London: SCM Press, 1958.
——: —— – Selections from the Latin:
Waddell, Helen. *The Desert Fathers* [includes also material from *Historia
    monachorum in Aegypto*, Palladius, *Heraclidis paradisus*, and John
    Moschus, *Pratum spirituale*]. London: Constable, 1936.
——: Translations, French
Les sentences des pères du désert: Les apophtègmes des pères (recension de
    Pélage et Jean). Intr. by L. Régnault. Trans. by J. Bion and G. Oury.
    Solesmes, Abbaye saint Pierre de Solesmes, 1966.
*Les sentences des pères du désert, nouveau recueil: apophtègmes inédits ou
    peu connus*. Ed. L. Régnault. Trans. by the monks of Solesmes, Sable
    sur Sarthe, Abbaye saint Pierre de Solesmes, 1970.
Les sentences des pères du désert, troisième recueil et tables. Ed. and trans.
    by L. Régnault. Solesmes, Abbaye saint Pierre de Solesmes, 1976.
——: For additional material for the texts of the Desert Fathers, see Freire, J. G.;
    Wilmart, A.
Athanasius, Saint, patriarch of Alexandria, d. 373. [Vita Antonii.] *La plus
    ancienne version latine de la vie de saint Antoine*, par S. Athanase: [text
    with] *étude de critique textuelle* [by] H. Hoppenbrouwers. LCP 11. Nij-
    megen: Dekker & Van de Vegt, 1960.
——. [*Vita Antonii.*] *Un témoin important du texte de la vie de S. Antoine par S.
    Athanase: la version latine inédite des archives du chapitre de S. Pierre à
    Rome*. Brussels, Palais des Académies; Rome, Academia Belgica, 1939.
——. [*Vita Antonii.*] *Vita di Antonio*. Intr. by C. Mohrmann. Ed. by G. J. M.
    Bartelink. Italian tr. by P. Citati and S. Lilla. VSanti 1. Milan: Mondadori,
    1974.
Augustinus, Aurelius, Saint, bp. of Hippo. *Confessiones*. Ed. by P. Knöll. CSEL 33,
    Vienna, 1896.
——. *Contra academicos; De beata vita; De ordine*. Ed. by W. M. Green. CCSL 29.
    Turnholt, 1970.
——. *De civitate Dei contra paganos*. Ed. by B. Dombart and A. Kalb. CCSL 47-
    48. Turnholt, 1955.
——. *De cura pro mortuis gerenda*. Ed. by J. Zycha. CSEL 41. Vienna, 1900.
——. *De moribus ecclesiae catholicae*. PL 32: 1300-1344.
——. *De Trinitate*. Ed. by W. J. Mountain. CCSL 50. Turnholt, 1967.
——. *De utilitate credendi*. Ed. by J. Zycha. CSEL 26. Vienna, 1891.
——. *De vera religione*. Ed. by J. Martin. CCSL 32. Turnholt, 1962.
——. *Enarrationes in Psalmos*. Ed. by E. Dekkers and J. Fraipont. CCSL 37-40.
    Turnholt, 1956.

——. *Enchiridion*. Ed. by E. Evans. ccsl 46. Turnholt, 1969.

——. *Epistolae*. Ed. by A. Goldbacher. csel 34, 44, 57, 58. Vienna, 1895-1911; index, Vienna, 1923, repr. 1961.

——. *In Iohannis Evangelium tractatus 124*. Ed. by R. Willems. ccsl 36. Turnholt, 1954.

——. *Sermones de Vetere Testamento*. Ed. by C. Lambot. ccsl 41. Turnholt, 1961.

——. *Soliloquia*. pl 32: 869-1904.

Avellana collectio, see *Epistulae*.

Avitus, Alcimus Ecdicius, Saint. *Poemata: libri VI*. Ed. by R. Peiper. mgh aa 6 (2). Berlin, 1883.

Basil, Saint, the Great, abp of Caesarea, ca. 330-379. *Regula monachorum* [Latin version by Rufinus]. pl 103: 487-554.

——. *Regulae fusius et brevius tractatae*. pg 31: 889-1035.

Beda Venerabilis, 673-735. *Martyrologium*. pl 94: 799-1147.

Benedictus, Saint, abbot of Monte Cassino, see Regula Benedicti.

Bible. *Apocryphal New Testament*, see Hennecke, E.

——. *Biblia sacra iuxta vulgatam Clementinam*, n. ed. Madrid: Biblioteca de Autores Cristianos, 1965.

——. *Bibliorum sacrorum Latinae versiones antiquae, seu Vetus Italica ...* opera et studio P. Sabatier. 3 vols. Rheims, 1743-1749.

——. Ibid. Re-editio anastatica (additur Index Codicum Manuscriptorum quibus P. Sabatier usus est [by Bonifatius Fischer]). 3 vols. Turnholt: Brepols, 1976.

——. *The New English Bible, with the Apocrypha*. Oxford and Cambridge: oup and cup, 1970.

Bibliotheca Hagiographica Graeca. 3 ed. Revised and enlarged by F. Halkin. shg 8a. Brussels, 1957.

Bibliotheca Hagiographica Latina. shg 6. Brussels, 1898-1911.

Caesarius, Saint, bp of Arles, 470?-543. *Sermones*. Ed. by G. Morin. 2 vols. ccsl 103, 104. Turnholt, 1953.

Callinicos, monk of Rufinianae, fl. 447-450. [*Vita Hypatii*.] *Vie de saint Hypatios*. Ed. and trans. by W. J. M. Bartelink. sc 177. Paris, 1971.

Cassianus, Joannes, ca. 370-ca. 435. [*Collationes*.] *Conférences*. Ed. and trans. by E. Pichery. sc 42, 54, 64. Paris, 1955-1959.

——. [*De institutis coenobiorum*.] *Institutions cénobitiques*. Rev. text, intr. ed. and tr. by J.-C. Guy. sc 109. Paris, 1965.

Cassiodorus Senator, Flavius Magnus Aurelius, ca. 487-ca. 580. *Historia tripartita*. Ed. by R. Hanslik. csel 71. Vienna, 1952.

——. *Institutiones*. Ed. by R. A. B. Mynors. Oxford: Clarendon Press, 1937.

——. *Variarum libri XII*. Ed. by A. J. Fridh. ccsl 96. Turnholt, 1973.

Chrysostomus, Joannes, Saint, patriarch of Constantinople, d. 407. *De compunctione libri II*. pg 47: 393-422.

——. *Homiliae de statuis ad populum Antiochenum I*. pg 49: 15-34.

Clemens Romanus. [*Epistola ad Corinthios*.] *Épître aux Corinthiens*. Ed. by A. Jaubert. sc 167. Paris, 1971.

Codex Theodosianus. [*Theodosian Code*.] *Theodosiani libri XVI cum constitutioni-bus sirmondianis et leges novellae ad Theodosianum pertinentes* ... . Ed. Th. Mommsen and P. M. Meyer. 2 ed. Vol. 1, 1-2, 2. Berlin: Weidmanns, 1954.

Colgrave, Bertram, ed. and tr. *Two Lives of St Cuthbert* [by an anonymous monk of Lindisfarne and by Bede]. Cambridge: CUP, 1940.

——. [*Vita Gregorii Magni*.] *The Earliest Life of Gregory the Great* [by an anonymous monk of Whitby]. Ed. and trans. by B. Colgrave. Lawrence: University of Kansas Press, 1958.

Columban, Saint, 543-615. *Sancti Columbani opera*. Ed. G. S. M. Walker. SLH 2. Dublin: Dublin University Institute for Advanced Studies, 1957.

Concilia. *Concilia Galliae*. 2 vols. 1. A.314-A.506. Ed. by C. Munier; 2.A511-A695. Ed. by C. de Clercq. CCSL 168, 168A. Turnholt, 1963.

——. *Conciliorum oecumenicorum decreta*. 3 ed. Bologna: Istituto per le scienze religiose, 1973.

Conversio et passio Afrae. Ed. by B. Krusch. MGH SRM 3. Hanover, 1896, pp. 41-64.

Corippus, Flavius Crescentius. *In laudem Iustini*. Ed. by A. M. Cameron. London: Athlone Press, 1976.

Corpus iuris civilis: 3 vols. 1. *Institutes*. Ed. by P. Krueger; *Digest*. Ed. by Th. Mommsen, revised by P. Krueger, 15 impr. Berlin: 1928; 2. *Codex*. Ed. and revised by P. Krueger, 10 impr. Berlin: Weidmanns, 1929; 3. *Novellae*. Ed. by R. Schoell, completed by W. Kroll, 15 impr. Berlin: Weidmanns, 1928.

Cyprianus, bp of Toulon et al. *Vitae Caesarii episcopi Arelatensis libri II*. Ed. by B. Krusch. MGH SRM 3. Hanover, 1896, pp. 433-501.

Cyrillus, of Scythopolis, ca. 524-ca. 558. [*Opera*.] *Kyrillos von Skythopolis*. [Ed. by] E. Schwartz. TU 49. Leipzig: J. C. Hinrichs, 1939.

Davis, H., see Gregory the Great. *Pastoral care*.

Dawes, Elizabeth & Baynes, Norman Hepburn. *Three Byzantine Saints*. Oxford: Blackwell, 1948; repr. Oxford: Mowbray, 1977.

Ennodius, Magnus Felix, Saint, bp. of Pavia. *Opera*. Ed. by F. Vogel. MGH AA 7. Berlin, 1885. For *Vita Antonii*, see ibid., pp. 185-190.

Epistolae selectae Pontificum Romanorum Carolo Magna et Ludovico Pio regnantibus scriptae. Ed. by K. Hampe. MGH *Epp*. 5. Berlin, 1899. For *Epp*. of Hadrian I, see pp. 3-57.

Epistulae imperatorum pontificum aliorum [367-553] ... *Avellana quae dicitur collectio*. Ed. by O. Guenther. CSEL 35 (2 pts in 1 vol.). Vienna, 1895-1898.

Eucherius, Saint, bp of Lyons. *Opera omnia*. Ed. by C. Wetke. CSEL 31. Vienna, 1894.

Eugippius. [*Vita Severini*.] *Das Leben des heiligen Severin*. Ed. and German trans. by R. Noll. Berlin: Akademie Verlag, 1963.

Eusebius, Pamphili, bp of Caesarea. *Historia ecclesiastica*. Ed. by E. Schwartz; [with] Latin version by Rufinus. Ed. by Th. Mommsen. GCS 9 (1-2). Leipzig, 1903-1909.

Evagrius Ponticus, 345?-399. [*Praktikos*.] *Évagre le Pontique: Traité pratique, ou*

Le moine. Ed. and trans. by A. and C. Guillaumont. SC 170-171. Paris, 1970-1971.

Evagrius Scholasticus, b. 536?. [*Historia ecclesiastica*.] *The Ecclesiastical History with the Scholia*. Ed. by J. Bidez and L. Parmentier. London: Methuen, 1898; anastatic repr., Amsterdam, 1964.

Fortunatus, Venantius Honorius Clementianus, bp, ca. 540-ca. 600. *Carmina: libri XI* [and] *appendix*. Ed. by F. Leo. MGH AA 4 (1). Berlin, 1881, pp. 7-292.

——. *Vita S. Martini: libri IV*, ibid., pp. 293-370.

——. *Vita S. Medardi*, ibid., pp. 67-73.

——. *Vita S. Maurilii*, ibid., pp. 82-101.

——. *Vita S. Remedii*. Ed. by B. Krusch. MGH AA 4 (2), pp. 64-67.

Freire, José Geraldes, ed. *A versão latina por Pascasio de Dume dos Apophthegmata patrum*. 2 vols. Coimbra: Instidudo de Estudos classicos, 1971.

——. *Commonitiones sanctorum patrum*. Uma nova colecçao de apotegmas: estudo filólogico, texto critico. Coimbra: Instidudo de Estudos classicos, 1974.

Garvin, Joseph N., ed., see Paulus Diaconus, Emeritensis.

[*Gregorian Sacramentary*.] *Le sacramentaire grégorien*. Ed. by J. Deshusses. SpicFri 16. Fribourg (Suisse): Éditions Universitaires, 1971.

Gregorius I, the Great, Saint, Pope, ca. 540-604. [*Dialogues*.] *Grégoire le Grand: Dialogues*. Ed. by A. de Vogüé. Trans. by P. Antin. 3 vols. SC 251, 265, 266. Paris, 1978-1980.

——. *Expositiones in Canticum Canticorum* [et] *In librum primum Regum*. Ed. by P. Verbraken. CCSL 144. Turnholt, 1963.

——. *Gregorii Magni Dialogi: libri IV*. Ed. by U. Moricca. FSI 57. Rome: Tipografia del Senato, 1924.

——. *Homiliae in Evangelia*. PL 76: 1075-1314.

——. *Homiliae in Hiezechielem*. Ed. by M. Adriaen. CCSL 142. Turnholt, 1971.

——. *Liber regulae pastoralis*. PL 77: 9-128.

——. [*Liber regulae pastoralis*.] *Pastoral Care*. Ed. and trans. by H. Davis. ACW 11. Westminster, Md: Newman Press; London: Longmans, 1950.

——. *Moralia in Hiob*, 1-16. PL 75: 509-1162; 17-35. PL 76: 9-782.

——. Ibid. Ed. by M. Adriaen. 1-10 CCSL 143; 11-22 CCSL 143A. Turnholt, 1979.

——. Ibid. 1-2. n. rev. ed. by R. Gillet. Trans. by A. de Gaudemaris. SC 32 bis. Paris, 1975; 11-14. Ed. and trans. by A. Bocognano. SC 212. Paris, 1974; 15-16. ibid., SC 221. Paris, 1975.

——. *Registrum epistolarum*. MGH *Epp*. 1 (1). Ed. by P. Ewald; 1 (2), 2. Ed. by L. M. Hartmann. Berlin, 1887-1889.

Gregorius Nazianzenus, Saint, patriarch of Constantinople. *Orationes* 1-26. PG 35: 393-1252; 27-45. PG 36: 9-623.

——. [*Orationes*.] *Tyrannii Rufini orationum Gregorii Nazianzeni novem interpretatio* ... Ed. by A. Engelbrecht. CSEL 46. Vienna, 1910.

Gregorius, Saint, bp of Nyssa, fl. 379-394. *De beatitudinibus orationes* III. PG 44: 1193-1302.

Gregorius, Saint, bp of Tours, 538-594. *De virtutibus S. Martini episcopi [libri IV]*. Ed. by B. Krusch. MGH SRM 1 (2). Hannover, 1885; anastatic repr., 1969, pp. 134-211.

———. *Liber de virtutibus S. Iuliani*, ibid., pp. 112-134.

———. *Liber in gloria confessorum*, ibid., pp. 294-370.

———. *Liber in gloria martyrum*, ibid., pp. 34-111.

———. *Liber vitae patrum*, ibid., pp. 211-294.

———. *Libri historiarum*. Ed. by B. Krusch and W. Levison. MGH SRM 1 (1). n. ed., Hanover, 1951.

Hadrianus I, pope, d. 795 [Hadrian]., see Epistolae.

Hennecke, E., ed. [*Neutestamentliche Apocryphen*.] *New Testament Apocrypha*. Ed. by W. Schneelmacher. Trans. and ed. by R. McL. Wilson. Vols. 1-2. London: Lutterworth Press, 1963-1965.

Hieronymus, Saint [Jerome]. *Adversus Iovinianum libri II*. PL 23: 221-354.

———. *Apologia adversus libros Rufini libri III*. PL 23: 415-514.

———. *Contra Vigilantium*. PL 23: 353-367.

———. *De viris illustribus liber*. Ed. by W. Herding. Leipzig: 1924.

———. *Epistolae*. Ed. by I. Hilberg. 3 vols. CSEL 54-56. Vienna, 1910-1918.

———. [*Epitaphium sanctae Paulae*.] *In memoria di Paola [Ep. 108]*. Intr. by C. Mohrmann. Ed. by J. W. Smit. Italian trans. by L. Canali. VSanti 4. Milan: Mondadori, 1975, pp. 145-237.

———. *In Esaiam* 1-11. Ed. by M. Adriaen. CCSL 73. 12-22. CCSL 73A. Turnholt, 1963.

———. *In Hieremiam*. Ed. S. Reiter. CCSL 74. Turnholt, 1960.

———. *In Matthaeum*. Ed. by D. Hurst and M. Adriaen. CCSL 77. Turnholt, 1963.

———. [*Vita Hilarionis*.] *Vita di Ilarione*. Intr. by C. Mohrmann. Ed. by A. A. R. Bastiaensen. Italian trans. by C. Moreschini. VSanti 4. Milan: Mondadori, 1975, pp. 73-143.

———. *Vita Malchi monachi captivi*. PL 23: 55-62.

———. *Vita Pauli primi eremitae*. PL 23: 17-30.

Hilarius, Saint, bp of Poitiers, d. 367?. *Tractatus mysteriorum* 1.1. Ed. by A. Feder. CSEL 65 (4). Vienna 1916, pp. 3-38.

Hincmarus, abp of Rheims, d. 882. *Vita Remigii episcopi Remensis*. Ed. by B. Krusch. MGH SRM 3. Hanover, 1896, pp. 239-349.

Historia monachorum in Aegypto. Greek text. Ed. and trans. by A.-J. Festugière. SHG 53. Brussels, 1971.

———. Latin version by Rufinus. PL 21: 387-462.

———. *The Lives of the Desert Fathers*. Intr. by B. Ward. Trans. by N. Russell. London and Oxford: Mowbray; Kalamazoo, U.S.A.: Cistercian Publications, 1981.

Isidorus, Saint, bp of Seville. *Etymologiae*. Ed. by W. M. Lindsay. Oxford Clarendon Press, 1911.

Joannes, bp of Ephesus, 6th cent. *The Third Part of the Ecclesiastical History*. Trans. from the Syriac by R. Payne Smith. Oxford: OUP, 1860.

Joannes Diaconus, called Hymmonides, 9th cent. *Vita Gregorii Magni*. PL 75: 59-242.

Jonas of Bobbio, abbot, d. ca. 665. *Vitae Columbani abbatis discipulorumque eius libri II*. Ed. by B. Krusch. MGH SRM 4. Hanover and Leipzig, 1902, pp. 64-108.

Lemerle, Paul, ed. *Les plus anciens miracles de saint Démétrius et la pénétration des Slaves dans les Balkans*. Vol. 1. Le texte [*Premier recueil, ou recueil de l'archevêque Jean; Second recueil, ou recueil anonyme*]. Paris: Éditions CNRS, 1979.

Leontius, bp of Neapolis, fl. 615. *Vita Iohannis Eleemosinarii*. Ed. by H. Gelzer. Freiburg i/Br. and Leipzig: J. C. B. Mohr, 1903.

———. [*Vita Iohannis Eleemosinarii*.] "Une vie inédite de saint Jean l'Aumônier." Ed. by H. Delehaye. *AnBoll* 45 (1927): 5-74.

[*Liber Pontificalis*.] *Le Liber pontificalis*: texte, introduction et commentaire par L. Duchesne. Vols. 1-2. Ed. by L. Duchesne, repr. Paris: E. de Boccard, 1955. Vol. 3, corrections, etc. Ed. by C. Vogel. Paris: E. de Boccard, 1957.

Lietzmann, Hans, 1875-1942, ed. [Antonius, monk. *Vita Symeonis Stylitae*.] *Das Leben des heiligen Symeon Stylites*. Ed. by H. Lietzmann. German trans. of the Syriac version and letters by H. Hilgenfeld. TU 32. Leipzig: J. C. Hinrichs, 1908.

Lucianus Presbyter. *Epistola Luciani*. PL 41: 807-818.

Lucianus Samosatensis. *Opera*. Ed. by M. D. Macleod. Vols. 1-2. Oxford: Clarendon Press, 1972-1974.

Magister, pseud., see *Regula magistri*.

Mansi, Giovanni Domenico, abp, 1692-1769, *et al.*, edd. *Sacrorum conciliorum nova et amplissima collectio* ... 54 vols in 59 (facs. repr. of ed. Paris: Hubert Welter, 1901-1927). Graz: Akademische Druck und Verlagsanstalt, 1960-1961.

Marcellinus Comes. *Chronica minora*. Ed. by Th. Mommsen. MGH AA 11. Berlin, 1894, pp. 39-108.

Martyrologium Romanum ... C. Baronii notationibus illustratum. Novissimae ... huic editioni seorsim accedit Vetus Romanum Martyrologium ... una cum Martyrologio Adonis, ad MSS exemplaria recensito, opera et studio H. Rosweydi. Antwerp, 1613.

Martyrologium Romanum ad formam typicae scholiis historicis instructum (*AASS* vol. 69, *Propylaeum*). Brussels: Société des Bollandistes, 1940.

Methodius, Saint, bp of Olympos, d.ca. 311. [Συμπόσιον ἤ περὶ ἁγνείας.] *Le banquet*. Ed. by H. A. Musurillo. Trans. by V.-H. Debidour. SC 95. Paris, 1963.

Moschos, Ioannes, Eukratas, d. 619. *Pratum spirituale*. PG 87 (3): 2847-3116.

Musurillo, Herbert A., ed. *The Acts of the Christian Martyrs*. Intr., texts and trans. Oxford: Clarendon Press, 1972.

Noll, Rudolf, see Eugippius.

Odo, Saint, abbot of Cluny, 879-942. *Vita Gregorii Turonis*. PL 71: 115-130.

Origen. [*Homiliae in Ieronimum.*] *Jeremiahomilien*. Ed. by E. Klostermann. GCS *Orig.* 3. Leipzig, 1901.

——. *De principiis* [περὶ ἀρχῶν]. Ed. P. Koetschau. GCS *Orig.* 5. Leipzig, 1913.

Palladius, successively bp of Helenopolis and Aspona, d. ca. 430. *Heraclidis paradisus* [Latin version of part of the Historia Lausiaca]. PL 74: 243-342.

——. [*Historia Lausiaca.*] *La storia Lausiaca*. Intr. by C. Mohrmann. Ed. by G. J. M. Bartelink. Italian trans. by M. Barchesi. VSanti 2. Milan: Mondadori, 1972.

——. *The Lausiac History of Palladius*. 2 vols. Vol. 1, A critical discussion ... with notes on early Egyptian monachism, by E. C. Butler; Vol. 2, Greek text, with intr. and notes, by E. C. Butler. TaS 6 (1-2). Cambridge: CUP, 1898-1904.

Paulinus, Mediolanensis. [*Vita Ambrosii.*] *Vita di S. Ambrogio*. Ed. by M. Pellegrino. Rome: Editrice Studium, 1961.

——. [*Vita Ambrosii.*] *Vita di S. Ambrogio*. Intr. by C. Mohrmann. Ed. by A. A. R. Bastiaensen. Italian trans. by L. Canali. VSanti 3. Milan: Mondadori, 1975, pp. 51-125.

Paulinus of Nola, Saint, bp, 353-431. *Opera*. Ed. by W. von Hartel. 2 vols, CSEL 29, 30. Vienna, 1894.

Paulus, Diaconus, 720 (ca.)-797? *Historia Langobardorum: libri VI*. Ed. by L. Bethmann and G. Waitz. MGH SRL. Hanover, 1878, pp. 12-187.

——. *Vita S. Gregorii Magni*. Ed. by H. Grisar. *ZKTh* 11 (1887): 158-173.

Paulus, Diaconus, Emeritensis. *The Vitas sanctorum patrum Emeretensium*. Text and trans., with intr. and comm. by Joseph N. Garvin. Catholic University of America Studies in medieval and renaissance Latin lang. and lit. 19. Washington: Catholic University of America Press, 1946.

Petrus Chrysologus, Saint, bp of Ravenna. *Sermones*. PL 52: 183-666.

Plinius Cecilius Secundus, C. [Pliny the Younger]. *Epistularum libri IX* ... Ed. by C. F. W. Mueller. Leipzig: Teubner, 1903.

——. [*Epp.* 10] *Epistolae ad Traianum imperatorem cum eiusdem responsis*. Ed. by E. G. Hardy. London: Macmillan, 1889.

Plinius Secundus, C. [Pliny the Elder.] *Naturalis historia*. Ed. by L. Jahn and C. Mayhoff. Vols 1-5. Leipzig: Teubner, 1892-1909.

Plutarchus. *Vitae parallelae*. Rev. ed. by C. Lindskog and K. Ziegler. Vol. 1 (1). Leipzig: Teubner, 1964.

Possidius, Saint, bp of Calama, fl. 370-437. [*Vita Augustini.*] *Vita di Agostino*. Intr. by C. Mohrmann. Ed. by A. A. R. Bastiaensen. Italian trans. by C. Carena. VSanti 3. Milan: Mondadori, 1975, pp. 127-241.

Procopius, of Caesarea. *De bellis libri* 1-8. Ed. by J. Haury. Rev. ed. by G. Wirth. 2 vols. Vol. 1, *De bello Vandalico*; Vol. 2, *De bello Gothico*. Leipzig: Teubner, 1962-1963.

Procopius, of Gaza, ca. 465-ca. 528. *In Isaiam*. PL 87 (2): 1817-2718.

Prudentius Clemens, Aurelius, 348-ca. 410. *Carmina*. Ed. by M. P. Cunningham. CCSL 126. Turnholt, 1966.

Regula Benedicti. *Benedicti Regula*. Ed. by R. Hanslik. CSEL 75. 2 ed. Vienna, 1977.

——. *La Règle de saint Benoît*. Ed. by A. de Vogüé. Trans. by J. de Neufville. 6 vols. SC 181-186. Paris, 1971-1972. Vol. 7 (*hors série*). SC. Paris, 1977.

——. *The Rule of St Benedict in Latin and English*. Ed. and trans. by J. McCann. 4 impr. London: Burns & Oates, 1969.

——. *S. Benedicti Regula monachorum*. Ed. by E. C. Butler. 3 ed. Freiburg i/Br.: Herder Verlag, 1935.

——. *San Benedetto: La Regola*. Ed. and trans. by A. Lentini. 2 ed. Monte Cassino: Abbazia di Monte Casino, 1980.

Regula magistri. *La règle du maître*. Ed. and trans. by A. de Vogüé. 2 vols. SC 105-106. Paris, 1964.

Severus, Sulpicius. *Libri qui supersunt* [incl.] *Dialogi* [and] *Epistolae*. Ed. by C. Halm. CSEL 1. Vienna, 1866.

——. [*Vita et epistolae Martini*.] *Vie de saint Martin*. Ed. and trans. by J. Fontaine. 3 vols. SC 133-135. Paris, 1967-1969.

Sidonius, Apollinaris, Saint, ca. 431-ca. 487. *Epistolae*. Ed. by C. Luetjohann. MGH AA 8. Berlin, 1887, pp. 1-172.

Sigerbertus, Gemblacensis. *Chronica*. Ed. by D. L. C. Bethmann. MGH *Script*. 6. Hanover, 1844; anastatic repr., Leipzig, 1925, pp. 268-374.

Société des Bollandistes, see Acta Sanctorum; Bibliotheca Hagiographica Graeca; Bibliotheca Hagiographica Latina; Martyrologium Romanum.

Sozomenus, Hermias, 5th cent. [Sozomen. *Historia ecclesiastica*.] *Kirchengeschichte*. Ed. by G. C. Hansen. GCS 50. Berlin, 1960.

Tertullianus, Quintus Septimius Florens. *De monogamia*. Ed. by V. Bulhart. CSEL 76. Vienna, 1957.

Theodoretus, bp of Cyrrhus. *Des Bischofs Theodoret von Cyrus Mönchsgeschichte*. Trans. by K. Gutberlet, with intr. by C. Baur. BKV 50. Munich: Kosel, 1926.

——. *Historia ecclesiastica. Kirchengeschichte*. Ed. by L. Parmentier. Rev. by F. Scheidweiler. GCS 44. Berlin, 1954.

——. [*Historia religiosa*.] *Histoire des moines de Syrie*. Ed. and trans. by P. Canivet and A. Leroy-Molinghem. 2 vols. SC 234, 257. Paris, 1977-1979.

Uranius. *De obitu Paulini*. PL 53: 859-866.

Usener, Hermann Karl, 1834-1905. *Der heilige Theodosios: Schriften des Theodoros und Kyrillos* [contains Theodorus. *Panegyric on Theodosios*, pp. 3-101; *Vita Theodosii*, by Cyril of Scythopolis, pp. 105-113]. Leipzig: Teubner, 1890.

Usuard, d. ca. 895. *Le martyrologe d'Usuard*. Ed. by J. Dubois. SHG 40. Brussels, 1965.

Victor, bp of Tunnuna, 6th cent. *Chronica*. Ed. by Th. Mommsen. MGH AA 11. Berlin, 1894, pp. 165-206.

Victor, Saint, bp of Vita, fl. 484. *Historia persecutionis Wandalica: libri III; Passio beatissimorum martyrum*. Ed. by C. Halm. MGH AA 3. Berlin, 1879, pp. 1-62.

Victricius, Saint, bp of Rouen, d. ca. 407. *De laude sanctorum*. PL 20: 443-448.

Vita Arnulfi. Ed. by Soc. aperiendis fontibus rerum germanicarum medii aevi. MGH SRM 2. Hanover, 1888, pp. 426-446.

Vita Desiderii episcopi Viennensis. Ed. by B. Krusch. MGH SRM 3. Hanover, 1896, pp. 620-648.

[*Vita Pachomii*.] *S. Pachomii vitae graecae*. Ed. by F. Halkin. SHG 19. Brussels, 1932.

———. *La vie latine de saint Pachôme*, traduite du grec par Denys le Petit. Ed. by H. van Cranenburgh. SHG 46. Brussels, 1969.

———. *Les vies coptes de saint Pachôme et de ses premiers successeurs*. Trans. by L. Th. Lefort. BMus 16. Louvain, 1943.

———. *Vita* 1 [Greek and English]. Trans. by A. N. Athannasakis. SBLTT 7. Missoula, Montana: Society of Biblical Literature, 1975.

[*Vita patrum Iurensium*.] *La vie des pères du Jura*. Intr., ed. and trans. by F. Martine. SC 122. Paris, 1968.

[*Vita Spyridonis*]. *La légende de saint Spyridon, évêque de Trimithonte*. Ed. by P. van den Ven. BMus 33. Louvain, 1953.

[*Vita Theodori Syceotae*]. *Vie de saint Théodore de Sykéon*. Ed. and trans. by A.-J. Festugière. SHG 48. Brussels, 1970.

Wilmart, André. "Le recueil latin des Apotègmes," *RBen* 34 (1922): 185-198.

2. SECONDARY SOURCES

Adnès, A. & Canivet, Pierre. "Guérisons miraculeuses et exorcismes dans l' 'Histoire philothée' de Théodoret de Cyr," *RHRel* 171 (1967): 53-82, 149-179.

Antin, Paul. "Autour du songe de saint Jérôme," *REL* 41 (1963): 350-377.

Antonelli, F. "I primi monasteri di monaci orientali in Roma," *RivAc* 5 (1928): 104-121.

Auerbach, Erich. "Figura," *Archivum Romanicum* 22 (1938): 436-489.

———. *Literatursprache und Publikum in der lateinischen Spätantik und im Mittelalter*. Bern: A. Francke, 1958; Eng. trans. by R. Manheim, London: Routledge, 1965.

———. *Mimesis: dargestellte Wirklichkeit in der abendländischen Literatur*. Bern: A. Francke, 1946; Eng. trans. by R. Trask, Princeton: Princeton UP, 1953.

Bacht, Heinrich. "Antonius und Pachomius," *StAns* 38 (1956): 66-107.

———. "L'importance de l'idéal monastique chez saint Pachôme pour l'histoire du monachisme chrétien," *RAM* 126 (1950): 308-326.

———. "Pakhôme et ses disciples (IVe siècle)," *Théol. de la vie monastique*. Paris: Éditions Aubier, 1961, pp. 39-71.

Batlle, C. M. *Die "Adhortationes sanctorum Patrum" ("Verba seniorum") im lateinischen Mittelalter*. BGAM 31. Münster, 1972.

———. "De suscepta editione latinae versionis 'Verba seniorum' commune appellatae," *StMon* 1 (1959): 115-120.

——. " 'Vetera nova': vorlaüfige kritische Ausgabe bei Rosweyde fehlender Vaterspruche," *Festschrift Bernhard Bischoff*. Stuttgart: 1971, pp. 32-42.

Battifol, Pierre. *Grégoire le Grand*. Paris: J. Gabalda et fils, 1928.

Baynes, Norman Hepburn. *Byzantine Studies and Other Essays*. London: Athlone Press, 1955.

Blaise, Albert, ed. *Dictionnaire latin-français des auteurs chrétiens*. Strasbourg: Le Latin Chrétien, 1954.

Boesch Gajano, Sofia. "Dislevelli culturali e mediazioni ecclesiastiche nei Diálogi di Gregorio Magno," *QSM* 41 (1979): 398-415.

——. "La littérature hagiographique comme source de l'histoire ethnique, sociale, et économique de l'Occident européen entre l'antiquité et moyen âge," *XX Congrès international des sciences historiques*. Bucharest, 1980, pp. 177-181.

——. "Il santo nella visione di Gregorio di Tours," *Atti di XII convegno storico internazionale dell' Accademia Tudertina*. Todi, 1971, pp. 29-91.

——. , ed. *Agiografia altomedioevale* [Italian trans. of articles by var. writers, with intr.]. Bologna: Il Mulino, 1976.

Boglioni, Pierre. "Miracle et nature chez Grégoire le Grand," *Cahiers d'études médiévales* 1. Montréal: Institut d'études médiévales, 1974, pp. 11-102.

Bolton, W. F. "The Supra-Historical Sense in the *Dialogues* of Gregory the Great," *Aevum* 33 (1959): 206-213.

Bosl, Karl. "Der Adelsheilige: Idealtypus und Wirklichkeit," *Speculum historiale: Festschrift für Johannes Spörl*. Freiburg i/Br./Munich: Verlag Karl Alber, 1965, pp. 167-187.

——. "Potens und pauper. Begriffsgeschichtliche Studien zur gesellschaftlichen Differenzierung im frühen Mittelalter und zum 'Pauperismus' des Hochmittelalters," *Frühformen der Gesellschaft im mittelalterlichen Europa*. Munich and Vienna: R. Oldenbourg Verlag, 1964, pp. 106-134.

Bousset, Wilhelm. *Apophthegmata: Studien zur Geschichte des ältesten Mönchtums*. Ed. [from literary remains] by Th. Hermann and G. Krüger. Tubingen: J. C. B. Mohr, 1923.

Brovarone, Alessandro Vittorio. "La forma narrativa dei Dialoghi di Gregorio Magno: problemi storico-letterari," *AAST.M* 108 (1974): 95-103.

——. "Forma narrativa dei Dialoghi di Gregorio magno: prospettive di struttura," ibid. (1975): 117-185.

Brown, Peter Robert Lamont. "Aspects of the Christianization of the Roman Aristocracy," *JRS* 51 (1961): 1-11 (=*Religion and Society in the Age of St Augustine*. London: Faber & Faber, 1972, pp. 161-182).

——. *Augustine of Hippo: a biography*. London: Faber & Faber, 1967.

——. "Eastern and Western Christendom in Late Antiquity: a Parting of the Ways," *SCH(L)* 13 (1976): 1-24.

——. *The Making of Late Antiquity*. Carl Newell Jackson Lectures. Cambridge, Mass.: Harvard University Press, 1978.

——. *Relics and Social Status in the Age of Gregory of Tours*. Stenton Lecture (1976). Reading: University of Reading, 1977.

——. "The Rise and Function of the Holy Man in Late Antiquity," *JRS* 61 (1971): 80-101.

——. "Society, Demons and the Rise of Christianity: from Late Antiquity into the Middle Ages," *Religion and Society in the Age of St Augustine*. London: Faber & Faber, 1972, pp. 119-146.

——. *The World of Late Antiquity*. London: Thames & Hudson, 1971.

Buse, Adolf. *Paulin, Bischof von Nola, und seine Zeit*. 2 vols. Regensburg: G. J. Manz, 1856.

Butler, Edward Cuthbert. *Western Mysticism*. 3 ed. London: Constable, 1967.

Cambridge History of the Bible. Vols. 1-3. Cambridge: CUP, 1963-1970.

Cameron, Averil Millicent. *Agathias*. Oxford: Clarendon Press, 1970.

——. "The Artistic Patronage of Justin II," *Byz.* 50 (1980): 62-84.

——. "The Byzantine Sources of Gregory of Tours," *JTS* n.s. 26 (1975): 421-426.

——. "Images of Authority: Élites and Icons in Late Sixth-Century Byzantium," *Past and Present* 84 (1979): 3-35.

——. "A Nativity Poem of the Sixth Century," *CP* 79 (1979): 222-232.

——. "The Theotokos in Sixth-Century Constantinople: a City Finds Its Symbol," *JTS* n.s. 29 (1978): 79-108.

Canivet, Pierre. *Le monachisme syrien selon Théodoret de Cyr*. ThH 42. Paris: Beauchesne, 1977.

Catry, Patrice. "Épreuves du juste et mystère de Dieu. Le commentaire littéral du livre du Job par saint Grégoire le Grand," *REAug* 18 (1972): 122-144.

——. "Lire l'écriture selon saint Grégoire le Grand," *CCist* 34 (1972): 177-201.

Chadwick, Henry. "John Moschus and His Friend Sophronius the Sophist," *JTS* n.s. 35 (1974): 41-74.

Chadwick, [William] Owen. "Gregory of Tours and Gregory the Great," *JTS* 50 (1949): 38-49.

——. *John Cassian: a Study in Primitive Monasticism*. 2 ed. Cambridge: CUP, 1968.

——, ed. *Western Asceticism*. Trans. by the editor. LCC 12. London: SCM Press, 1958.

Chapman, John. *Saint Benedict and the Sixth Century*. London: Sheed & Ward, 1929.

Chitty, Derwas J. *The Desert a City*. Oxford: Blackwell, 1966; repr. London and Oxford: Mowbray, 1977.

Coleman-Norton, Paul Robinson. "The Use of Dialogue in the *Vitae Sanctorum*," *JTS* 27 (1925-1926): 388-395.

Conrat, Max. *Geschichte der Quellen und Literatur des römischen Rechts im früheren Mittelalter*. Leipzig: J. C. Hinrichs, 1891.

Conte, P. "Osservazioni sulla leggenda di S. Cerbonio, vescovo di Populonia," *Aevum* 52 (1978): 235-260.

Cooper-Marsdin, Arthur Cooper. *History of the Islands of Lérins*. Cambridge: CUP, 1913.

Corbett, John H. "The Saint as Patron in the Work of Gregory of Tours," *Journal of Medieval History* 7 (1981): 1-13.

Courcelle, Pierre. "Grégoire le Grand à l'école de Juvénal," *SMSR* 38 (1967): 170-174.

———. " 'Habitare secum' selon Perse et Grégoire le Grand," *REA* 69 (1967): 266-279.

———. *Les lettres grecques en occident de Macrobe à Cassiodore*. BÉFAR 159. Paris: E. de Boccard, 1948.

———. " 'Nosce teipsum' du Bas-Empire au haut moyen-âge: l'héritage profane et les développements chrétiens," *SSAM* 9 (1961), 1962, pp. 265-295.

———. *Recherches sur les Confessions de saint Augustin*. n.ed. Paris: E. de Boccard, 1968.

———. "Saint Benoît, le merle, et le buisson d'épines," *JS* (July-September 1967): 154-156.

———. "La vision cosmique de saint Benoît," *REAug* 13 (1967): 97-117.

Crampton, Lawrence J. "St Gregory's Homily XIX and the Institution of Septuagesima Sunday," *DR* 86 (1968): 162-166.

Cumont, Franz Marie Valéry. *Recherches sur le symbolisme funéraire des Romains*. Paris: P. Geuthner, 1942.

Curtius, Ernst Robert. *Europäische Literatur und lateinischer Mittelalter*. Bern: A. Francke, 1948; Eng. trans. by W. R. Trask. New York: Harper; London: Routledge, 1953.

Cusack, Pearse A. "St Scholastica: Myth or Real Person?" *DR* 107 (1974): 145-149.

———. "Some Literary Antecedents of the Totila Encounter in the Second Dialogue of Pope Gregory I," *StPatr* 12 (1975): 86-90.

Dagens, Claude. "La 'conversion' de saint Benoît selon Grégoire le Grand," *Rivista di storia e letteratura cristiana* 5 (1969): 384-391.

———. "La 'conversion' de saint Grégoire le Grand," *REAug* 15 (1969): 149-162.

———. "L'église universelle et le monde oriental chez saint Grégoire," *Ist.* 4 (1975): 457-475.

———. "La fin des temps et l'église selon Grégoire le Grand," *RSR* 58 (1970): 273-288.

———. "Grégoire le Grand et la culture: de la *terrena sapientia* à *la docta ignorantia*," *StPatr* 11 (1972): 20-21.

———. "Grégoire le Grand et le ministère de la Parole: les notions d'*ordo praedicatorum* et d'*officium praedicationis*," *StPatr* 12 (1975): 197-198.

———. *Saint Grégoire le Grand: structure et expérience chrétiennes*. Paris: Études Augustiniennes, 1977.

Daniélou, Jean. *Les anges et leur mission, d'après les Pères de l'Église*. Collection Irénikon n.s. 5. 2 ed. Chevetogne, 1953.

———. *Sacramentum futuri: études sur les origines de la typologie biblique*. Paris: Beauchesne, 1950.

Delehaye, Hippolyte. *Les légendes hagiographiques*. SHG 18. Brussels, 1906.

——. *Les origines du culte des martyrs*. SHG 20. 2 ed. Brussels, 1933.

——. *Les passions des martyrs et les genres littéraires*. SHG 13b. 2 rev. ed. Brussels, 1966.

——. "Les premiers libelli miraculorum," AnBoll 29 (1910): 427-434.

——. "Les recueils antiques de miracles des saints," AnBoll 43 (1925): 74-85 (as separate book, Brussels: Société des Bollandistes, 1925).

——. *Les saints stylites*. SHG 14. Brussels, 1923.

Delforge, Th. "Songe de Scipion et vision de saint Benoît," *RBen* 69 (1959): 351-354.

Dictionnaire d'archéologie chrétienne et de liturgie. Ed. by F. Cabrol and H. Leclercq. Completed by H. I. Marrou. 15 vols. Paris: Letouzy et Ane, 1907-1963.

Dictionnaire de spiritualité, ascétique et mystique. Ed. by M. Viller. Vols 1-10 (A-M). Paris: Beauchesne, 1937-1980.

Doucet, M. "La tentation de saint Benoît selon Grégoire le Grand," *CCist* 37 (1975): 63-71.

Duchesne, Louis. *L'église au VIe siècle* [unfinished]. Paris: E. de Boccard, 1925.

——. "Les évêchés d'Italie et l'invasion lombarde," *MÉFR* 23 (1903): 83-116; 25 (1905): 365-399.

——. "Le sedi episcopali nell'antica ducato di Roma," *Arch. Soc. Rom. di storia patria* 15 (1892): 475-503 (= *Scripta minora* ... Rome: École française de Rome, 1973, pp. 409-437).

——. "La vie des Pères du Jura," *MÉFR* 13 (1898): 1-16.

Dudden, Frederick Homes. *Gregory the Great: His Place in History and Thought*. 2 vols. London: Longmans, 1905.

Dufner, Georg. *Die Dialoge Gregors des Grossen im Wandel der Zeiten und Sprachen*. Padua: Antenore, 1968.

Dufourcq, Albert. *Étude sur les Gesta Martyrum romains*. Pts. 1-4. BÉFAR 83 in 4 pts. Paris: E. de Boccard, 1900-1910 [unfinished].

Dyggve, Ejnar. *History of Salonitan Christianity*. Instituttet for Sammenlignende Kulturforskning, ser. A, Forelesninger 21. Oslo: Aschenhoug; Cambridge, Mass.: Harvard University Press, 1951.

Egger, Rudolf. *Der heilige Hermagoras*. Klagenfurt: F. Kleinmayr, 1948.

Esbroeck, M. van. "Les apophthègmes dans les versions orientales," *AnBoll* 93 (1975): 38-39.

Fabre, Pierre. *Saint Paulin de Nole et l'amitié chrétienne*. BÉFAR 157. Paris: E. de Boccard, 1949.

Ferrari, Guy. *Early Roman Monasteries: Notes for the History of the Monasteries and Convents at Rome from the 5th through the 10th Century*. Studi di antichità 23. Vatican City: Pontificio Istituto di Archeologia Cristiana, 1957.

Festugière, André Marie Jean. *Antioche païenne et chrétienne: Libanius, Chrysostome, et les moines de Syrie*. BÉFAR. Paris: E. de Boccard, 1959.

———. "Lieux communs littéraires et thèmes de folklore dans l'hagiographie primitive," *WSt* 73 (1960): 133-152.

———. *Les moines d'Orient*. 4 vols. Paris: Éditions du Cerf, 1961-1965.

———. "Le problème littéraire de l'*Historia monachorum*," *Hermès* 83 (1955): 257-284.

Fischer, E. H. "Gregor der Grosse und Byzanz," *ZSRG.K* (80) 36 (1950): 15-144.

Fontaine, Jacques. "L'expérience spirituelle chez Grégoire le Grand: réflexions sur une thèse récente [of Claude Dagens]. *RHSp* 52 (1976): 141-154.

———. *Isidore de Seville et la culture classique dans l'Espagne wisigothique*. 2 vols. Paris: Études Augustiniennes, 1959.

Freire, José Geraldes. "Traductions latines des Apophthegmata Patrum," *Mélanges Christine Mohrmann*, nouveau recueil. Utrecht and Antwerp: Spectrum, 1973, pp. 164-171.

Frend, William Hugh Clifford. *Martyrdom and Persecution in the Early Church: a Study of a Conflict from the Maccabees to Donatus*. Oxford: Blackwell, 1965.

Gaiffier, Baudouin de. "Les héros des Dialogues de Grégoire le Grand inscrits au nombre des saints," *AnBoll* 83 (1965): 53-73.

———. "La vie de saint Séverin du Norique à propos d'un livre récent" [of F. Lotter] *AnBoll* 95 (1977): 13-23.

Gatch, M. McC. "The Fourth Dialogue of Gregory the Great: Some Problems of Interpretation," *StPatr* 10 (1967): 77-83.

Genestout, Augustin. "La Règle du Maître et la Règle de saint Benoît," *RAM* 21 (1940): 51-112.

Gibbon, Edward, 1737-1794. *The Decline and Fall of the Roman Empire*. Ed. by J. B. Bury. 7 vols. London: Methuen, 1911-1929.

Gillet, Robert. "Saint Grégoire le Grand," *DSp* (1967): 6, 872-910.

———. "Spiritualité et place du moine dans l'église selon saint Grégoire le Grand," *Théologie de la vie monastique*. Paris: Éditions Aubier, 1961, pp. 323-351.

Goubert, P. "Mystique et politique à Byzance," *REByz* 19 (1961): 152-156.

Grabar, André. *Martyrium*. 2 vols and album. Paris: Collège de France, 1943-1946.

Graus, František. "Die Gewalt bei den Anfangen des Feudalismus ..." *JWG* (1961): 94-99.

———. *Volk, Herrscher, und Heiliger im Reich der Merowinger*. Prague: Nakladatelství Československé Akademie ved, 1965.

Gross, K. "Der Tod des heiligen Benedictus," *RBen* 85 (1975): 164-176.

Guy, Jean-Claude. "Le centre monastique de Scété dans la littérature du ve siècle," *OrChrP* 30 (1964): 129-147.

———. *Jean Cassien: vie et doctrine spirituelle*. Paris: Lethielleux, 1961.

———. *Recherches sur la tradition grecque des Apophthegmata patrum*. SHG 36. Brussels, 1962, pp. 126-171.

———. "Remarques sur le texte des Apophthegmata patrum," *RSR* 43 (1955): 252-258.

Hadrill, John Michael Wallace. *The Long-Haired Kings*. London: Methuen, 1962.

Halkin, François. "Une courte vie inédite de saint Grégoire le Grand, retraduite du grec," *Mélanges Eugène Tisserant*. Vol. 4. Vatican City: Biblioteca Apostolica Vaticana, 1964, pp. 379-387.

———. "Le pape S. Grégoire le Grand dans l'hagiographie byzantine," *OrChrP* 21 (1955): 109-114.

Hallinger, Kassius. "Der Papst Gregor der Grosse und der heilige Benedikt," *StAns* 42 (1957): 213-319.

Hanson, Richard Patrick Crosland. *Allegory and Event*. London: SCM Press, 1959.

Hausherr, Irénée. *Penthos: la doctrine de la componction dans l'Orient chrétien*. OrChrA 132 (1944).

Heinzelmann, M. " 'Sanctitas' und 'Tugendadel': zu Konzeptionen von 'Heiligkeit' im 5. und 10. Jahrhunderte," *Francia* 5 (1977): 741-752.

Herwegen, Ildefonsus. *Der heilige Benedikt: ein Characterbild*. 2 ed. Düsseldorf: L. Schwann, 1919.

Hillgarth, Jocelyn N. "Coins and Chronicles: Propaganda in Sixth-Century Spain and the Byzantine Background," *Historia* 15 (Wiesbaden 1966): 483-508.

Hodgkin, Thomas. *Italy and Her Invaders*. Vol. 5. Oxford: Clarendon Press, 1895.

Jaspert, B. "Regula magistri - Regula Benedicti: Bibliographie ihrer Erforschung," *StMon* 13 (1971): 129-171.

Jedin, Hubert, Latourette, Kenneth S. and Martin, Jochem, edd. *Atlas zur Kirchengeschichte: die christlichen Kirchen in Geschichte und Gegenwart*. Freiburg i/Br.: Herder Verlag, 1970.

Kelly, John Norman Davidson. *Jerome: His Life, Writings, and Controversies*. London: Duckworth, 1975.

Kemp, Eric W. *Canonisation and Authority in the Early Church*. London: OUP, 1948.

Kurtz, Donna C. and Boardman, J. *Greek Burial Customs*. London: Thames & Hudson, 1971.

Laistner, Maurice L. W. *Thought and Letters in Western Europe, A.D. 500-900*. n.ed. London: Methuen, 1957.

Lambot, Cyrille. "La vie et les miracles de saint Benoît, racontés par saint Grégoire le Grand," *RLM* 19 (1934): 137-165.

Lampe, Geoffrey W. H., ed. *A Patristic Greek Lexicon*. Oxford: Clarendon Press, 1961-1968.

———. and Woollcombe, Kenneth J. *Essays on Typology*. Studies in biblical theology 22. London: SCM Press, 1956.

Lanzoni, Francesco. *Le diocesi d'Italia dalle origini al secolo VII* (604). Studi e Testi 35 [2 vols with same series no.]. Faenza: F. Lega, 1927.

Leclercq, Jean. *L'amour des lettres et le désir de Dieu: initiation aux auteurs monastiques du moyen âge*. Paris: Éditions du Cerf, 1957; Eng. trans. by C.

Misrahi. New York: Fordham University Press, 1961; n.ed., 1974; London: SPCK, 1978.

——. et al. edd. *Histoire de la spiritualité chrétienne*. Vols. 1-2. Vol. 1, La spiritualité du Nouveau Testament et des Pères [by L. Bouyer]; Vol. 2, La spiritualité du moyen âge. Paris: Éditions Aubier, 1960-1961.

Lehmann, Paul. "Der Einfluss der Bibel auf frühmittelalterliche Geschichtsschreiber," *La Bibbia nell' alto medioevo*. *SSAM* 10 (1963): 129-140.

Leroy-Molinghem, Alice. "À propos de la vie de Syméon Stylite," *Byz*. 34 (1964): 375-384.

Lieblang, Franz. *Grundfragen der mystischen Theologie nach Gregors des Grossen Moralia und Ezechielhomilien*. FThSt 37. Freiburg i/Br.: Herder Verlag, 1934.

Llewellyn, Peter A. B. *Rome in the Dark Ages*. London, Faber & Faber, 1971.

Lotter, Friedrich. "Antonius von Lérins und der Untergang Ufernorikums," *HZ* 212 (1971): 265-315.

——. "Inlustrissimus vir Severinus," *DA* 26 (1970): 200-207.

——. "Severinus und die Endzeit der römischen Herrschaft an der oberen Donau," *DA* 24 (1968): 309-338.

——. *Severinus von Norikum: Legende und historische Wirklichkeit*. MGMA 12. Stuttgart: Hiersemann, 1976.

See also Gaiffier, B. de; Prinz, F.; Uytfanghe, M. van.

Lubac, Henri de. *Exégèse médiévale: les quatre sens de l'écriture*. 4 vols. Paris: Éditions Aubier, 1959-1964.

McClure, Judith. "Gregory the Great: Exegesis and Audience" [unpublished thesis]. Oxford, 1978.

McCulloh, John H. "The Cult of Relics in the Letters and *Dialogues* of Pope Gregory the Great: a Lexicographical Study," *Traditio* 32 (1976): 145-184.

Mähler, Maximilien. "Évocations bibliques et hagiographiques dans la vie de saint Benoît par S. Grégoire," *RBen* 83 (1973): 398-429.

Malone, Edward E. "The Monk and the Martyr," *StAns* 38 (1956): 201-228.

Manselli, Raoul. "L'escatologismo di Gregorio Magno," *Atti di I° congresso di studi Longobardi*. Spoleto, 1952, pp. 383-387.

——. "Gregorio Magno e la Bibbia," *La Bibbia nell'alto medioevo*. *SSAM* 10 (1963): 67-101.

Markus, Robert Austin. "Carthage-Prima Justiniana-Ravenna: an Aspect of Justinian's Kirchenpolitik," *Byz*. 49 (1979): 277-306.

——. *Christianity in the Roman World*. London: Thames & Hudson, 1974.

——. "Country Bishops in Byzantine Africa," *SCH(L)* 16 (1979): 1-15.

——. "The Cult of Icons in Sixth-Century Gaul," *JTS* n.s. 29 (1978): 151-157.

——. "Gregory the Great and a Papal Missionary Strategy," *SCH(L)* 6 (1970): 29-38.

——. Review: *Consul of God*, by J. H. Richards, *History* 65 (1980): 459-460.

——. Review: *Saint Grégoire le Grand: culture et expérience chrétiennes*, by C. Dagens, *JEH* 29 (1978): 203-205.

Marrou, Henri Irénée. *Histoire de l'éducation dans l'antiquité*. 6 ed. Paris: Éditions du Seuil, 1965.

——. "Jean Cassien à Marseille," *Rev. du moyen âge latin* 1 (1945): 1-26.

——. "La patrie de Jean Cassien," *OrChrP* 13 (1947): 588-596.

——. *Saint Augustin et la fin de la culture antique*. Paris: Éditions du Seuil, 1938.

Marsili, S. *Giovanni Cassiano ed Evagrio Pontico: dottrina sulla carità e contemplazione*. *StAns* 5 (1936).

Masai, F. "La 'Vita Patrum Iurensium' et les débuts de monachisme à Saint-Maurice d'Agaune," *Festschrift Bernhard Bischoff*. Stuttgart: Hiersemann, 1971, pp. 43-69.

Mazzarino, S. "La democratizzazione della cultura nel 'Basso Impero'," *Actes du XIᵉ congrès des sciences historiques*. Vol. 2 Stockholm, 1960.

Meyvaert, Paul. "Bede and Gregory the Great," Jarrow Lecture 7 (1964), *Benedict, Gregory, Bede, and Others*. London: Variorum Reprints, 1977, pp. 1-26.

——. "Bede's Text of the *Libellus Responsionum* of Gregory the Great to Augustine of Canterbury," *England before the Conquest ... Studies Presented to Dorothy Whitelock*. Cambridge: CUP, 1971.

——. "Gregory the Great and the Theme of Authority," *Spode House Review* (1966): 3-12.

——. "A New Edition of Gregory the Great's Commentaries on the Canticle of Canticles and 1 Kings," *JTS* n.s. 19 (1968): 215-225.

——. "The *Registrum* of Gregory the Great and Bede," *RBen* 80 (1970): 162-166.

Mohrmann, Christine. *Études sur le latin des chrétiens*. SeL 65, 87, 103, 143. Rome: Edizioni di Storia e Letteratura, 1958-1977.

——. "Zwei frühchristliche Bischofsviten: Vita Ambrosii, Vita Augustini," *AAWW.PH* 112 (1975): 307-331.

Momigliano, Arnaldo. "Cassiodorus and Italian Culture of His Time," *PBA* 41 (1955): 207-245.

——. ed. *The Conflict Between Paganism and Christianity in the Fourth Century*. Oxford: Clarendon Press, 1963.

Moricca. *See* Gregorius I, *Dialogi*.

Morin, Germain. *L'idéal monastique et la vie chrétienne des premiers jours*. 3 ed. Paris: Lethielleux, 1921.

Mundo, Anscari. "L'authenticité de la Regula S. Benedicti," *StAns* 42 (1957): 105-158.

——. " 'Bibliotheca': Bible et lecture de carême d'après saint Benoît," *RBen* 60 (1950): 65-92.

Musurillo, Herbert Anthony, ed. *The Acts of the Christian Martyrs*: introd., texts and trans. Oxford, Clarendon Press, 1972.

Noll, Rudolf. "Neuere Literatur zur heiligen Severini [1925-1950]," *MIÖG* 69 (1951): 440-446.

——. "Die Vita sancti Severini des Eugippius im Lichte des neueren Forschung," *AAWW.PH* 112 (1975): 61-75.

Paredi, A. "Paulinus of Milan," *SE* 14 (1963): 206-230.

Paret, R. "Dometianus [*sic*] de Mélitène et la politique religieuse de l'empéreur Maurice," *REByz* 15 (1957): 67-143.

Pargoire, J. "Les débuts de monachisme à Constantinople," *RQH* n.s. 21 (1899): 67-143.

Parys, M. van. "L'accès à l'Orient monastique chez saint Benoît," *Irén.* 47 (1974): 48-58.

Patlagean, Evelyne. "À Byzance: ancienne hagiographie et histoire sociale," *Annales* 23 (1968): 106-123.

——. "Les moines grecs d'Italie et l'apologie des thèses pontificales," *Studi medievali* 5 (1964): 579-602.

Pauly-Wissowa-Kroll. *Paulys Real-Encyclopädie der classischen Altertumswissenschaft.* n.e. Stuttgart, series 1, 47 vols. 1894-1963; 2, 19 vols, 1914-1972; supplement, 15 vols, 1903-1978; register, 1980.

Peeters, P. "S. Syméon Stylite et ses premiers biographes," *AnBoll* 61 (1943): 29-71.

Pegon, Joseph. "Componction," *DSp* (1953): 2, 1312-1321.

Penco, Giorgio. "Il concetto de monaco e di vita monastica in Occidente nel secolo VI," *StMon* 1 (1959): 7-50.

——. "La dottrina dei sensi spirituali in S. Gregorio," *Ben.* 17 (1970): 161-201.

Petersen, Joan Margaret. "Did Gregory the Great Know Greek?" *SCH(L)* 13 (1976): 121-134.

——. "Did Gregory the Great Know Greek? A Reconsideration." Unpublished paper.

——. "Greek Influences on Gregory the Great's Exegesis of Luke 15.1-10, *Hom. in Evang.* 2.34, PL. 76: 1246ff." To appear in *Actes du colloque international CNRS "Saint Grégoire le Grand"* (Chantilly 1982) not yet published.

Pfeilschifter, Georg. *Die authentische Ausgabe der 40 Evangelienhomilien Gregors des Grossen: ein erster Beitrag zur Geschichte ihrer Überlieferung.* VKHSM 1 (4). Munich: J. J. Lentner, 1900.

Philippart, C. "Un petit fragment des Dialogues de saint Grégoire," *AnBoll* 88 (1970): 22.

——. " 'Vitae Patrum': trois travaux récents sur d'anciennes traductions latines," ibid. 92 (1974): 353-365.

See Batlle, C. M.; Freire, J. G.

Pirenne, Henri. *Mahomet et Charlemagne.* 7 ed. Brussels: Nouvelle Société d'Éditions; Paris: F. Alcan, 1937; Eng. trans. by B. Miall. London: Unwin, 1937 [and subsequent impr.].

Porcel, Olegario. *La doctrina monastica de San Gregorio Magno y la Regula monachorum.* Madrid: Istituto Enrique Florez, 1950.

——. "San Gregorio y el monacato: questiones controvertidas," (Scripta et documenta 12) *Monastica* 1 (Montserrat 1960): 1-95.

See Hallinger, K.; Verbraken, P.

Poupardin, R. "Étude sur les vies des saints fondateurs de Condat et la critique de M. Bruno Krusch," *Le moyen âge* 2 (1898): 31-48.

Prinknash Abbey. *The Finding of St Stephen's Body at Caphar Gamal in 415 A.D.*, Cheltenham pr., 1979.

Prinz, Friedrich. "Die Entwicklung des altgallischen und merowingischen Mönchtums," *Die erste Jahrtausend* 1 (Düsseldorf 1962): 223-255.

——. *Frühes Mönchtum im Frankenreich: Kultur und Gesellschaft in Gallien, den Rheinlanden und Bayern am Beispiel der monastischen Entwicklung.* Munich and Vienna: R. Oldenbourg Verlag, 1965.

——. , ed. *Mönchtum und Gesellschaft im Frühmittelalter* [collection of articles by var. writers]. Darmstadt: Wissenschaftliche Buchgesellschaft, 1976.

——. "Zur geistigen Kultur des Mönchtums im spätantiken Gallien und im Merowingerreich," *Zeitschrift für bayerische Landesgeschichte* 26 (1963): 29-102 (=*Mönchtum und Gesellschaft im Frühmittelalter*. Darmstadt: Wissenschaftliche Buchgesellschaft, 1976, pp. 265-353).

——. "Zur Vita Severini," *DA* 25 (1969): 531-536. See Lotter, F.; Noll, R.

Recchia, Vicenzo. "Rassegna gregoriana," *VetChr* 6 (1972): 177-199.

——. "La visione di S. Benedetto e la compositio del secondo libro dei Dialoghi di Gregorio Magno," *RBen* 82 (1972): 140-155.

Redon, O. "Les monastères italiens à la fin du viᵉ siècle, d'après la correspondance de Grégoire le Grand" [unpublished thesis]. Paris, 1958.

Richards, Jeffrey H. *Consul of God.* London: Routledge, 1980.

——. *The Popes and the Papacy in the Early Middle Ages, 476-752.* London: Routledge, 1979.

Riché, Pierre. *Éducation et culture dans l'occident barbare, VIᵉ-VIIIᵉ siècles.* rev. ed. Paris: Éditions du Seuil, 1973.

——. "Note d'hagiographie mérovingienne," *AnBoll* 72 (1954): 36.

Rousseau, Olivier. "Saint Benoît et le prophète Élisée," *RMAL* 144 (1956): 103-114.

Rousseau, Philip H. *Ascetics, Authority, and the Church in the Age of Jerome and Cassian.* Oxford: OUP, 1976.

——. "Blood Relationships Among Early Eastern Ascetics," *JTS* n.s. 23 (1972): 135-144.

——. "The Formation of Early Ascetic Communities: Some Further Reflections," *JTS* n.s. 25 (1974): 113-117.

——. "The Spiritual Authority of the 'Monk-Bishop': Eastern Elements in Some Western Hagiography in the Fourth and Fifth Centuries," *JTS* n.s. 22 (1971): 380-419.

Rudmann, Remigius. *Mönchtum und kirchlicher Dienst in den Schriften Gregors des Grossen.* Sankt-Ottilien: Eos Verlag, 1956.

Sauget, J.-M. "Saint Grégoire le Grand et les reliques de saint Pierre dans la tradition arabe chrétienne." *RivAC* 49 (1973): 301-309.

Schanz, Martinus von. *Geschichte der römischen Literatur.* 4 vols. 2 ed. Munich: C. H. Beck, 1914.

Schmitz, Philibert. *Histoire de l'ordre de saint Benoît.* 7 vols. Maredsous: Editions Maredsous, 1942-1956.

Ševčenko, Ivan, "A Late Antique Epigram and the So-Called Elder Magistrate from Aphrodisias," *Synthronon.* Bibliothèque des cahiers archéologiques 2. Paris: C. Klincksieck, 1968, pp. 29-41.

Siegmund, Albert. *Die Überlieferung der griechischen christlichen Literatur in der lateinischen Kirche bis zum zwölften Jahrhundert.* Munich: Filser Verlag, 1949.

Smalley, Beryl. *The Study of the Bible in the Middle Ages.* Oxford: Clarendon Press, 1941; 2 ed. 1952.

Spearing, Edward. *The Patrimony of the Roman Church in the Time of Gregory the Great.* Cambridge: CUP, 1918.

Stancliffe, Clare E. "From Town to Country: the Christianisation of the Touraine, 370-600," *SCH(L)* 16 (1979): 43-59

Steidle, Basilius. "Homo Dei Antonius: zum Bild des 'Mann Gottes' im alten Mönchtum," *StAns* 38 (1956): 148-200.

———. "Der kleine schwarze Knabe in der alten Möncherzählung," *BenM* 34 (1958): 339-350.

———. "Die kosmische Vision des Gottesmannes Benedikt: Beitrag zu Gregor d. Grosse, Dialog II c. 35," *EuA* 47 (1971): 187-192.

Steinacker, H. "Die römische Kirche und die griechischen Sprachkentnisse des Frühmittelalters," *MIÖG* 62 (1954): 28-66.

Stückelberg, Ernst Alfred. *Der constantinische Patriciat.* Basel: H. Georg's Verlag, 1891.

Stuhlfath, Walter. *Gregor der Grosse: sein Leben bis zu seiner Wahl zum Papst nebst einer Untersuchung des ältesten viten.* Heidelberg, C. Winter, 1913.

Tatteo, F. "La struttura dei Dialoghi di Gregorio Magno," *VetChr* 2 (1965): 101-127.

Théologie de la vie monastique [by var. writers]. Théologie 49. Paris: Éditions Aubier, 1961.

Thompson, E. A. *The Goths in Spain.* Oxford: Clarendon Press, 1969.

Thürlemann, Felix. *Die historische Diskurs bei Gregor von Tours.* Bern: Herbert Lang, 1974.

Toynbee, Jocelyn Mary Catherine. *Death and Burial in the Roman World.* London: Thames & Hudson, 1971.

Ullmann, Walter. *A Short History of the Papacy in the Middle Ages.* London: Methuen, 1972.

Uytfanghe, Marc van. "Les avatars contemporains de l'hagiologie' à propos d'un ouvrage récent sur saint Séverin du Norique," *Francia* 5 (1977): 639-671 [of F. Lotter].

——. "Éléments évangéliques dans la structure et composition de la 'Vie de saint Séverin' d'Eugippius," *SE* 21 (1972-1973): 147-159.

Verbraken, Pierre-Patrick. "Saint Grégoire sur le premier livre des Rois," *RBen* 66 (1957): 39-62, 159-217.

——. Review: (Scripta et documenta 12) *Monastica* 1 (Montserrat 1960) in *StMon* 2 (1960): 438-440 [review of Porcel's article and summing-up of arguments in the Porcel-Hallinger controversy].

Vieillard-Troïékouroff, May. *Les monuments religieux de la Gaule, d'après les œuvres de Grégoire de Tours*. Paris: Honoré Champion, 1976.

Vogüé, Adalbert de. "Un avatar du mythe de la caverne dans les *Dialogues* de Grégoire le Grand," *Homenaje a Fray Justo Perez de Urbel*. Vol. 2. Silos, 1977, pp. 19-24.

——. "Benoît, modèle de vie spirituelle d'après le deuxième livre des *Dialogues* de saint Grégoire," *CCist* 38 (1976): 147-157.

——. "Un cinquantenaire: l'édition des *Dialogues* de saint Grégoire, par Umberto Moricca," *BISI* (1976-1977): 183-216.

——. *La communauté et l'abbé dans la Règle de saint Benoît*. Paris: Desclée de Brouwer, 1961 [contains comm. on *Reg. Ben.* 1, 2, 3, 5, 7 (part), 21, 31, 60, 62-72, which have not therefore been covered in his ed. of *Reg. Ben.*, 6 vols, sc 181-186, and Vol. 7, sc *hors série*]; Eng. tr. by C. Philippi. Vol. 1. Cistercian Studies 5 (1), Kalamazoo: Cistercian Publications, 1979.

——. " 'Discretione praecipuam': à quoi Grégoire pensait-il?" *Ben* 22 (1975): 325-327.

——. "Grégoire le Grand, lecteur de Grégoire de Tours?" *AnBoll* 94 (1976): 225-233.

——. "La mention de la 'Regula monachorum' à la fin de la 'Vie de Benoît' (Grégoire, Dial. II.36): sa fonction littéraire et spirituelle," *RegBenSt* 5 (1976). Hildesheim: Gerstenberg Verlag, 1977: 289-298.

——. "Monachisme et église dans la pensée de Cassien," *Théologie de la vie monastique*. Paris: Éditions Aubier, 1961: 213-240.

——. "Le prêtre et la communauté monastique dans l'antiquité," *MD* 115 (1973): 61-69.

——. "La Règle de saint Benoît et la vie contemplative," *CCist* 27 (1965): 104-105.

——. "La Règle du Maître et les *Dialogues* de saint Grégoire," *RHE* 61 (1966): 44-76.

——. "La Règle du Maître en Italie du Sud," *RBen* 77 (1967): 155-156.

——. "La rencontre de Benoît et de Scholastique: essai d'interprétation," *RHSp* 48 (1972): 257-273.

——. "Sur le texte des *Dialogues* de saint Grégoire le Grand: l'utilisation du manuscrit de Milan par les éditeurs," *Latinität und alte Kirche: Festschrift für Rudolf Hanslik zum 70. Geburtstag*. WienerSt Beiheft 8 (1977), pp. 326-335.

———. "Les vues de Grégoire le Grand sur la vie religieuse dans son commentaire des Rois," *StMon* 20 (1978): 17-63.

Voss, Bernd Reiner. *Der Dialog in der frühchristlichen Literatur*. Munich: W. Fink, 1970.

Vooght, D. P. de. "Les miracles dans la vie de saint Augustin," *RTAM* 11 (1939): 5-16.

———. "La notion philosophique du miracle chez saint Augustin dans le 'De Trinitate' et le 'De Genesi ad litteram'," *RTAM* 10 (1938): 317-343.

———. "La théologie du miracle chez saint Augustin," *RTAM* 11 (1939): 197-222.

Wansbrough, J. H. "St Gregory's Intention in the Stories of St Scholastica and St Benedict," *RBen* 75 (1965): 145-151.

Wood, Ian N. "Early Merovingian Devotion in Town and Country," *SCH(L)* 16 (1979): 61-76.

Yerkes, David. "An Unnoticed Omission in the Modern Critical Editions of Gregory's *Dialogues*," *RBen* 87 (1977): 178-179.

Zimmerman, Odo. "An Unsolved Problem: the Rule of St Benedict and the Rule of the Master" [bibliography of 113 items]. *ABenR* 10 (1959): 86-106.

Index

Abraham, Abba 178

Abraham, abbot 133

Acepsimas: Theodoret's story paralleled by a story of Benedict 183, 185

Acontius, *custos ecclesiae* at Rome 134

Acontius, *mansionarius* at Ancona 53

Acta martyrum, see also *Gesta martyrum; Passiones martyrum*

Acta martyrum Apollonii 59

Acta martyrum Euplii 59

Acta martyrum Iustini (Justin Martyr) 59

Acta Sanctorum 56

Adeodatus, abbot 158

Adige, river 12

Aemiliana, aunt of Gregory the Great 68

Aemilianus, *notarius* 22

Aeneas of Gaza: *Theophrastus* 19

Agapitus, Pope (535-536) 53

Agapitus, subdeacon 39

Agilulf, king of the Lombards (596-616) 18

Agnellus, Andreas, of Ravenna (805-ca. 846) 58

Agnes, martyr 61

Agretia 109

Agricola, martyr, see bodies, translation of

Alaric, king of the Visigoths 17

Albinus, bp of Angers 136

Albinus, bp of Reate 12

Aldhelm, bp of Sherborne 65

Alexandria 99, 103, 158, 162

Alexandrian school 26, 30

Amandus, bp of Bordeaux 134

Amantius, priest and healer 14, 53

Ambrose, bp of Milan (374-397) 58, 61, 147: as "reluctant bishop" 70; commends practice of praying for the dead 118; healing through "manufactured relics" 96; knowledge of Greek theology 117; occasionally uses relics 141; post-mortem apparitions of 96; see also Gervase and Protase; Paulinus of Milan

Ammon, Abba, hermit of the Thebaid 82

Amoun, Abba, of Nitria 169

Anastasius, monk of Subpentoma 135

Anastasius of Illyria, martyr 147

Anastasius of Syria 84

Ancona 4, 41-42

Andrew, apostle: apparition of 107; chapel of 171, 174; translation of 146

Andrew, bp of Fundi 6, 170-171, 173-174, 181

animals, special relationship of holy man with 98, 179

Anio, river 49, 157, 160

Anthemius, bp 64

Antin, P. 118

Antioch 97-98, 117, 146, 168

Antony, disciple of Symeon Stylites, *Vita Symeonis Stylitae* 184, 186-189

Antony, monk of St Andrew's 158

Antony of Egypt 33, 103, 106, 113, 160, 178; as founder of monasteries 155-157; as model for Benedict 54, 68; as model for Hilarion and characters in Jerome's *Vitae* 97-98; as model for Martin 100-101; as potential martyr 73; conversion of 69

Apocalypse of Paul 87

Apocalypse of Peter 87

Apollinaris, martyr, of Ravenna 58

Apollonius of Tyana 93, see also Philostratus

Apophthegmata patrum latinorum 68, 129, 137, 177, 188; doctrine of compunction in 162; influence on Gregory's writings 152, 169-181 *passim*; prophecies in 165-166; setting of Eastern monasticism as described in 154-156; teaching on chastity in 168

apparitions of Jesus or of saints 107, 134; see also Ambrose; Andrew; Faustinus; Iuticus; Juvenal and Eleutherius; Martin of Tours; Paul, apostle; Peter, apostle

Aptonius 9

Apuleius, Lucius: *De asino aureo* 93; *De deo Socratis* 93

aqueducts, blocking-up of 41n30; 48-49

Aquilinus 133

Aquinum 133

Arborius, prefect 101, 107
Arcadius, emperor (395-408) 146
Archebius, Abba 155, 169
Arians and Arianism: Arian bishop struck blind 44; conversion of Herminigild 18; death of Goth in miraculous bed 110; Gregory's hatred of 45; persecutions in N. Africa by 18-19; reconsecration of church of St Agatha after use for Arian worship 15, 137-138; struggles with 100
Arignotus 176
Arles 108
Arpagius, priest 38
Arredius, abbot 138
Arsenius, Abba 137, 155, 178
Athanasius, patriarch of Alexandria 28, 54, 100, 103, 162, 183; introduces Eastern monasticism to the West 73, 90; Jerome's debt to 97; recipient of *melota* and *substratorium* 152; Gregory's conception of origins of monasticism derived from 157-160: *Vita Antonii* 27, 44, 68, 73, 86, 97, 100, 105-106, 117, 119, 151-153, 181
Athanasius, priest, of Isauria 14
Athenodorus 175
Athens 175
Auerbach, E. 29
Augustine, abp of Canterbury 22
Augustine, bp of Hippo 17, 61, 72, 88, 95-96, 116, 119, 125, 127, 141, 151, 153, 165, 190; baptism 1; Cassiciacum dialogues 24; conversion 69; correspondence with Marcellinus and Volusianus 92-93; gradual change of attitude towards miracles 91-94; Gregory's dependence upon 30, 190; *libelli* 94-95; ordination 91
     writings: *Confessiones* 91, 103; *De civitate Dei* 6, 21, 61, 91-95 *passim*, 99, 122; *De cura pro mortuis gerenda* 20-21, 87, 114; *De moribus ecclesiae catholicae* 152; *De utilitate credendi* 91; *Enarrationes in Psalmos* 161; *Epistolae* 91-92; *Excerpta*, by Eugippius 112
Avitianus 114
Avitus, bp of Vienne 66

Babylas, see bodies, translation of
Balneum Ciceronis, monastery 157
baptism 61, 63, 91, 116, 127
Basil the Great 162, 166: *Regula* 152

Basilius, devil 167
Battifol, P. 189
Bede, The Venerable 54, 65
Benedict of Campania: attempt of Goths to bake in an oven 31, 140; lives as solitary 158, 177, 179; *Regula* 179-180
Benedict of Nursia 7, 8, 23, 27-31 *passim*, 33, 63, 117, 180; compared to: Acepsimas 185; Antony 156-157, 160; Martin 119, 153; Moses 48-49; Noah 27; conversion 70; cosmic vision of 138-139; discernment of spirits 46-48, 165, 167; disciples of 38; exorcist 133; founder of monasteries 158; gift of prophecy 20-21, 45-48, 165-167; humility of 40; miracle-worker 36-41, 43-54; miraculous properties of cave 133, 143-144; *Regula* 25, 39, 46, 152; removal of Martin the hermit's chain suggested 183; *vir Dei* 27-28, 119; visit of Totila to Monte Cassino 20-21; see also Effide; Elijah; Elijah-Elisha cycle; Elisha; Monte Cassino; Subiaco
Benedicta, nun 159
Benignus 134
Bible 25-29 *passim*, 31-32, 40, 43, 55, 89, 101, 121, 165; Old Testament 26, 31, 33, 43, 48, 95, 161, 165; New Testament 34, 49, 95-96
Bithynia 145-146
bodies, translation of 143, 145-148; see also Andrew, apostle; Anastasius of Illyria; Chrysostom, John; Gervase and Protase; Herculanus; Martin of Tours; Severinus of Noricum; Symeon Stylites
Boesch Gajano, S. 123
Boiotro 113, 115
Bolton, W. F. 20
Boniface, bp of Ferentis 5, 7, 48, 65, 98
Boniface, monk of St Andrew's, 14, 44
Bordeaux, church of St Stephen 134
Brescia 4, 12, 74, 135
Brioude 132, 149
Britius 139
Brown, P. R. L. 93, 180-181, 191
Burgum 113
burial customs 141-150 *passim*
Buse, A. 16
Butilin, leader of the Franks 44

Caesaria, abbess 109
Caesarius, bp of Arles 54, 100, 144; early life and vocation 107-109; miracle-

worker 109-111; miracles post mortem 110-111, 115; raises the dead 34; *Regula* for nuns 108; relationship with animals 98; use of relics 116, 141, 144; use of typology 118; see also Cyprian of Toulon; relics
Callinicos, *Vita Hypatii* 84
Cameron, A. M. 117
Campania 48-49, 179; devastation of 15, 17; famine in 40
Cample 4, 13
Canivet, P. 181
Caphar Gamle 94
Carterius 179
Cassian, John 6, 44, 46, 68, 72, 129, 170-171, 173-174, 178, 181; *Collationes* 24, 105, 152; *De institutis coenobiorum* 20, 38, 106, 152, 155; schematization of experience of monasticism 154-157; teaching on compunction 160-165; see also compunction
Cassiodorus 62, 66; *Historia tripartita* 121
Cassius, bp of Narnia 65, 133
Castor, son of Felix 13
Cells, The 155
Censurinus 63
Cerbonius, bp of Populonium 12-13, 63, 98
Chalcis, Deserts of 97, 99, 117, 168
Charlemagne, first Holy Roman emperor 65
chastity 168-169; chaste couples 98, 168-169; "reluctant bridegroom" 129
Chrysanthus, martyr 77
Chrysologus, Peter, bp of Ravenna 58
Chrysostom, John, patriarch of Constantinople 146, 162
Claudius, monk, reporter of Gregory's sermons 22
Clement of Rome, as character in the *Gesta* 63, 66
Clermont-Ferrand 136
Codex encyclicus 185
Columbanus, abbot of Luxeuil 98
Comana 146
compunction 30, 72, 160-164
Concordius 64
Condat (Condadisco) 104-106
confessio humilitatis 70, 190
confirmation 63-64
Constantina, wife of emperor Maurice; requests relics from Gregory the Great 142, 145

Constantine, emperor (306-337) 146
Constantinople, blind man healed at 53; Datius en route to 175; emperor at 144; Gregory *apocrisiarius* at 10, 187; request for relics to be dispatched to 148; tongueless martyr bishops allegedly seen at 18-20; translations of bodies to 146; urban monasticism at 159
Constantinus, disciple of Benedict 38
Constantius, *mansionarius* 5-6, 41, 49
Constantius II, emperor (351-363) 146
contemplation 26, 71-72, 164; see also *vita contemplativa*
conversio 68-70, 72; *conversio animae* 35; see also Arians and Arianism; Augustine, bp of Hippo; Benedict of Nursia; Exhilaratus; Jews and Judaism; Paul, apostle; Theopropus
Copres, Abba 140
Corinth, haunted house at 133, 175-176
Cornelius, Pope, see bodies, translation of
coruscatio 137-138
councils: Elvira (ca. 306) 62; Nicaea (325) 173; Carthage (393) 65; Carthage (401) 92; Agde (506), Orleans (538), Auxerre (561-605), Mâcon (585), Chalon (647-653) 128
Courcelle, P. 92, 139
Crisaurius 10
Curma, *curialis* 87, 114
Cusack, P. A. 20, 46
Cuthbert 54
Cyprian, bp of Toulon 34, 153; *Vita Caesarii arelatensis* 34, 49, 107-108, 110, 117
Cyril, patriarch of Alexandria 185, 190
Cyril of Scythopolis 45, 121, 188

Dagens, C. 5, 39, 69-70
Dalmatia 2, 99
Damasus, Pope (366-384) 61
Daniélou, J. 27
Daria, martyr 77
Datius, bp of Milan 65, 175
Decius, emperor (249-251) 146
Decius Minor, consul (529) 85
Delehaye, H. 95, 187
Demetrius, martyr of Thessalonica 147-148
Denys, Ps., the Areopagite, *De hierarchia caelesti* 190
Desiderius, *charterius* 109
Deusdedit 9-10

Diocletian, consul, later emperor (285-305) 85

Diolcos 155

Dionysius Exiguus 152; see also Pachomius

Donatus, subdeacon 63

Duchesne, L. 1, 2, 105

Dudden, F. Homes 1-3, 15, 24, 189

Dufourcq, A. 8, 59, 62, 67-68, 71, 80, 83, 85-86, 88; *Étude sur les Gesta martyrum romains* 56

Effide 37, 157-158

Elba, island 12-13

Eleutherius, abbot of St Mark's, Spoleto, Gregory's informant 8-10, 14, 52, 80, 84; healer 134; weeps humble tears 35; ends days at St Andrew's, 14, 80; death 10

Eleutherius, martyr 74, 134; see also Juvenal and Eleutherius

Elijah, the prophet 35, 110, 155; as founder of monasticism, precursor of Antony 27-28, 101; as holy man who can raise the dead 34, 92; as type of obedience 31

Elijah-Elisha cycle of stories 27-28, 41, 45, 110, 183

Elisha, the prophet 34, 40, 110, 155, 160, 182; as precursor of Benedict 27-28; compared with Benedict as healer 53-54; compared with Benedict as holy man who can raise the dead 92; compared with Benedict as miracle-worker 29, 34, 36-38; compared with Benedict as prophet 46-48, 165; compared with Libertinus as miracle-worker 30; compared with Nonnosus as miracle-worker 39; compared with Severinus as miracle-worker 114

Ennodius, bp of Pavia 66, 111

Eonius, bp of Arles 108

Equitius, abbot of Valeria 4, 30, 47, 79-80, 133, 157, 167; miracles at tomb 132

Ethelbert, king of Kent 174-175

Eubatides 176

Eucharist, as means of rescue 139; communicants at 46, 166; Hannah as type of faithful communicant 30; healing in context of 53, 127, 139; miracle seen at 80; reception of sacrament by prisoner 63

Eucherius, bp of Lyons 105, 109

Eucherius, 6th cent. bishop 109

Eucyria 109-110

Eugendus (Oyend), abbot of Condat 104-107

Eugenius I, Pope (654-657) 79-80, 84

Eugippius, abbot of Lucullanum 111-114, 116-117, 153: *Ep. ad Paschasium* 112; *Excerpta* from works of Augustine 112; *Vita Severini* 111, 115, 117

Eulogius, Abba 46, 166

Eulogius, patriarch of Alexandria 66

Eusebius Pamphili, bp of Caesarea 6, 66, 155, 185; *Historia ecclesiastica* trans. by Rufinus 42-43, 64

Eusebius, Pope, see bodies, translation of

Eustochium, Julia 68, 159

Euthicius, abbot 7, 158, 179-180

Eutychius, see Iuticus

Evagrius of Antioch 27, 90, 97-98, 117

Evagrius Ponticus 156, 162-163

Evasa 86

Exhilaratus, monk of St Andrew's 8; conversion of 70

Fabre, P. 16

Faustinus, martyr, apparitions 12, 74

Favianis, monastery 113

Felix, bp of Portus 11

Felix, called Curvus 9-10

Felix, martyr, of Nola 17, 66

Felix, Minucius 23

Ferderuchus 114

Festugière, A. M. J. 181

floods 12, 24, 56-57, 144

Florentius, monk 98, 158, 177, 179-180

Florentius, priest, of Subiaco 31, 45

Floridus, bishop of Tifernae Tiberinae 11, 15, 53, 78-79

Fontaine, J. 99, 101, 118

Fortunatus, abbot of Balneum Ciceronis 157

Fortunatus, bp of Todi 4, 34, 51-53, 63, 65, 98, 134

Fortunatus, Venantius, bp of Poitiers 17, 58, 66, 138, 144; see also Poitiers; Radegund; True Cross

Franks 44, 76, 139

Frend, W. H. C. 61

Friard, recluse 136

Fulgentius, bp of Ruspe 112

Fundi 133, 173-174; see also Andrew of Fundi

Galla, bearded nun 134, 159
Gallus, emperor (251-253) 146
Gallus, participant in *Dialogues* of Sulpicius Severus 104
Gallus, uncle of Gregory of Tours 129-130
Gatianus, bp of Tours 134-136
Gelimer, king of the Vandals 19
Genoa, church of St Syrus 135
Genseric 16
Germanus, bp of Auxerre 134, 136
Germanus, bp of Capua 138
Germanus, friend of Cassian 156, 164
Gervase and Protase, martyrs 57-58, 77-78, 91-92, 117, 122, 147, 149; see also *inventio*; relics
Gesta martyrum, see also *Acta martyrum; Passiones martyrum*
Gesta martyrum Abundii 61-62, 78-80, 84
Gesta martyrum Laurentii 84
Gesta martyrum Romanorum 8, 56, 59-60, 63, 65-68, 70, 73-74, 77-79, 80, 82-84, 88-90
Gillet, R. 163, 181
Gordiana, aunt of Gregory the Great 68
Goths 12-13, 17, 31, 36-37, 40, 75, 78, 85, 110, 179, 182
Grabar, A. 148
Gregoria, nun 8, 14, 80, 84, 159
Gregory the Great: *apocrisiarius* at Constantinople 10, 187; destinations of letters 3; devotion to monasticism 27-28; early life 67-68; entry to monastic life, see *conversio*; founder of monasteries 68; known in Eastern Christendom as "Gregory of the Dialogues" 191; relationship to Eastern Christian culture 151, 157, 190; relationship to writers of the *Gesta martyrum* 88-89; reluctance to become Pope 70; replacement of secular household by monks 22; slightness of knowledge of Greek 151, 189-190; spiritual formation 67-71
—, *Dialogues*: differences between *Dialogues* and *Gesta martyrum* 89; element of hearsay in 15; geographical setting of 11-13; impossibility of tracing *stemma* among MSS 191; influence of Latin translations of Greek writers 152, 169-181 *passim*; linguistic usages 9-11; literary techniques 5-9, 170; monasticism in 153-160; need for synthesis of information 2; possible influence of Greek writers on 181-188; purpose in

writing 23-24, 56-57; significance of 191; stories of martyrs in 73-77; style 66; use of dialogue form 21-24
—, *Homiliae in evangelia* 5, 22, 41, 130, 134, 190
—, *Homiliae in Ezechielem* 5, 22, 41, 71-72, 163
—, *Liber regulae pastoralis* 65, 71-72
—, *Moralia* 5, 22, 29-30, 37, 71, 164, 170
—, *Registrum epistolarum* 2, 3, 22, 25, 41, 142, 145, 148, 153, 174, 184
—, teachings: attitude to history 15-21; attitude to physical miracles 35; audience 21-23; biblical knowledge 25-26, 89, 189-190; love of contemplation, see contemplation, *vita contemplativa*; methods of biblical interpretation 26-27, 55, see also typology; teaching on prayer 72
Gregory, bp of Langres, great-grandfather of Gregory of Tours 129-130, 134-135, 143
Gregory, bp of Nazianzus 190; *De fuga* 70
Gregory, bp of Nyssa 162, 185, 190
Gregory, bp of Tours 7, 21, 44, 47, 66, 68, 74, 76-77, 84, 98, 101-102, 107, 111, 114, 116-118, 123-130, 148-151, 168-169, 186-187; audience 123-124; Byzantine influence on 117, 141; miracles with element of punishment 127-128, 139; possible link with Gregory the Great 130-131; reasons for interest in miracles and church history 123; *rusticitas* 124; types of miracle common to Gregory the Great and Gregory of Tours 134-141; types of miracles described 125-130; see also Sunday workers, trial by ordeal
—, writings: *De virtutibus S. Martini* 121, 128; *Liber de virtutibus S. Iuliani* 128; *Liber in gloria confessorum* 121, 124, 186; *Liber in gloria martyrum* 77, 121, 123-124; *Liber vitae patrum* 117, 124-125, 129, 141, 153, 156; *Libri historiarum* 76, 121, 124, 128, 130
Gregory Thaumaturgus 174
Gross, K. 139

Hadrian I, Pope (772-795) 65
Hartmann, L. M. 184
Hausherr, I. 160, 163
Helena (ca. 225-ca. 350) 123
Helenus, Abba 46, 166

Helius of Lyons 134
Helpidius, deacon and physician 109-110
Herculanus, bp 78, 143, 146
Herminigild, Visigothic prince 18, 138
Herundo, nun 159
Herwegen, I. 181-183
Hilarion 96-99, 103, 141
Hilary, bp of Poitiers 26
"hinge-men" 180
Historia monachorum in Aegypto 44, 82, 121, 132, 154-155, 165, 169-170, 181; reminiscences of, in *Vita patrum iurensium* 106; trans. by Rufinus 29, 50, 152
Hodgkin, T. 1
Holy Communion, see Eucharist
homo Dei, see *vir Dei*
Honoratus, disciple of Benedict 38
Honoratus, miracle-worker 30
Hormisdas, Pope (514-523) 143
Hospitius, recluse 7, 76, 130, 133
Hypatius 167

Ignatius of Antioch 146-147
Illidius 125; see also relics
Ingund, wife of Herminigild 18
Instruments of the Passion, see relics
inventio 77; tombs in Gallic territory 131; tomb of Gervase and Protase 91, 95; tomb of Nazarius 95; tomb of Vitalis and Agricola 95; see also Martyrs of Lyons
Ioviaco 113
Isaac of Spoleto (the Syrian) 23, 160; arrival at Spoleto and miracles 81-84, 133-134; possible identity with character in *Gesta martyrum* 85; prophetic gifts of 47, 80-81; resemblance of stories to those in 8
Italy, political divisions in late 6th cent. 2
Iuticus, martyr, apparition of 74, 135

Jerome, priest and doctor, 61, 101, 103, 108, 115, 117-118, 123, 154, 169, 182, 185, 189; as founder of domestic monasteries 68, 159; as writer of religious romances and miracle-stories 21, 73, 96-100
—, writings: *Adv. Iovinianum* 62; *Epistola 22* 152; *Vita Hilarionis* 62, 90, 101; *Vita Malchi* 62, 90; *Vita Pauli* 62, 90; *Vitae* 152-153, 167; see also Hilarion, Paul the Hermit, Malchus

Jews and Judaism 73, 139, 170-171, 173; Gregory's interest in conversion of Jews 174
John I, Pope (523-526) 53
John III, Pope (561-575), form. John, subdeacon 79; see also Pelagius I
John, *defensor* 22
John of Lycopolis: abstention from seeing women 187; obedience of 38n26, 129; power of discernment of spirits 46, 166-167; power of prophecy 20-21, 47, 165
John of Spoleto 83-84
John Penariensis 83-85
John the Almsgiver 136, 168
John the Baptist 27, 30, 155; see also relics
John the Deacon 67
John the Dwarf 129
Joseph, Abba 179-180
Julian, *defensor* 4, 9, 30, 79-80
Julian, Gallic martyr 116, 125, 131, 133, 144; basilica at Brioude 132; limbs buried at Brioude but head at Vienne 149
Jura Fathers 100, 117, 141; see *Vita patrum iurensium*
Justinian I, emperor (527-565) 18-19, 58, 143; *Code* 128
Justus, monk of St Andrew's 158
Juvenal and Eleutherius, martyrs 74, 134

Krusch, B. 104

Langobardi, see Lombards
Lanzoni, F. 1, 16, 56, 62-63, 80-81
Laurentius, abbot of Fundi 44
Laurentius, *religiosus* 10, 33
Lauriacum 112-113
Lazarus, brother of Martha and Mary 31-32, 34-35
Leah, type of the active life 72
Leander, bp of Seville 18, 29, 69
Leclercq, H. 112
lectio divina 25-26, 63
legere et meditari 26
Leonianus of Vienne 106
Leontius, bp of Neapolis in Cyprus 136, 168
Lérins 108, 117; *Regula* 108
Liber pontificalis 15, 85, 184
Liber pontificalis Ravennatis 58
Libertinus 10, 30, 44-45, 139
Lombards 44, 135, 159; areas of Italy under control of Lombards 12-14;

Duchy of Samnium ravaged by 3; Gregory's dealings with Lombards resented 58; Lombards driven from chapel by invocation of Equitius 32; stories of persons murdered by Lombards 74-78

Lot, Abba 179-180

Lotter, F. 111-112

Lubac, H. de 29

Lucca 4, 12

Lucian, priest 148

Lucian of Samosata 6, 176-177, 189

Lucullanum 111-112, 115

Luke, see bodies, translation of

Lupicinus, abbot of Condat 104, 106

Lyons 105-107, 111; see also Martyrs of Lyons

Macarius of Alexandria 156

Macarius the Great 166, 178

Maccabees, the, as type of martyrs 61, 73, 84

McClure, J. 21

McCulloh, J. H. 143

Mähler, M. 28-29, 34, 37, 40, 43, 45-49, 53-54

Malchus 98, 169

Marcellinus, bp of Ancona 6

Marcellinus, imperial commissioner 92

Marcellinus Comes 19-20

Marcellus 32-34

Marcellus and Marcellinus, aft. deacons 64

Marcianus 145

Marinianus, abp of Ravenna 22, 59

Markus, R. A. 174, 191

Martha 35; type of the active life 71

Martianus 109

Martin, bp of Tours 38, 49, 54, 70, 76, 98, 116-117, 138, 141, 144; apparitions of 134; arrival of relics 137; cell at Candes 133, 139, 143, 147; confrontation with Maximus 20; gift of discernment of spirits 46; influence of example at Condat 105; invocation of Martin 127, 139; miracles paralleled in *Vita patrum iurensium* 106-107; portrait by Sulpicius Severus 100-103; shrine at Monte Cassino 119; tomb at Tours 124, 131-133; voice not heard from tomb 135; see also relics

Martin the hermit, of Monte Marsico 7, 23, 48, 63, 153, 158, 177; comparison with Symeon Stylites 181-188; decision never to look at a woman 168

Martine, F. 104-105

martyr occultus, in occulto 73, 75, 89, 131, 147

Martyrius, monk 134

martyrologies: Ado 56; Usuard 56; the Venerable Bede 65

martyrs, monks as 73

Martyrs of Lyons 131, 148

Mary, the Virgin 134, 150

Mary of Bethany 35; type of the contemplative life 71

Mass, see Eucharist

Matrona, Amma 156

Maurice, emperor (582-602) 142, 148

Maurilius, bp of Angers 17

Maurus, *aedituus* 113

Maurus, monk 31, 37, 43, 49-50

Maximian, abp of Ravenna 58

Maximianus, bp of Syracuse 10-11, 14, 22, 139, 158

Maximus, bp of Lyons 105, 139

Maximus, emperor (455) 20

Melania the Elder 68, 103

Melitius, *chorepiscopus* 183

Mellitus, aft. abp of Canterbury 22, 174

melota 50-51, 152, 178; see also *substratorium*

Menas, hermit 98, 158, 177, 179-180

Merulus, monk of St Andrew's 137, 158

Messianus, *notarius* 109

Milan 57-58, 91, 95-96, 117, 149

Minausius, abbot of Condat 104

miracles, categories of: casting out devils 51-52, see also *niger puer*, pig; changing one substance into another 41-43; healing 53-54; increasing a substance in short supply 38-41; raising the dead 33-35; rendering poison harmless 45; restoring lost objects 35-38; striking with blindness 43-44; walking on water 49-51; water and fire 48-49; see also Gregory of Tours; prophecy and discernment of spirits; and consult Table of Contents

Mohrmann, C. 98

monasteries, domestic 68, 159

monastic habit: importance of 69, 178; wearing of 35, 42; see also *melota; substratorium*

monasticism, Egyptian 154; compared with Italian 154-160

—, feminine 67-68, 159-160; see also nuns; virgins, consecrated

—, origins of 27-28, 153-158

—, urban 158-159

monks, categories of 154-155

Monte Argentaro, unnamed hermit of 31, 35, 158, 177-178, 180

Monte Cassino 27, 47, 119, 165; Benedict's prophecy regarding 47; foundation of monastery 158; visit of Totila to 20-21, 165

Monte Feletro 115

Monte Marsico 48; see also Martin the hermit

Moricca, U. 1, 3, 13, 15, 24, 42

Moschus, John 77, 121, 130

Moses 28, 30, 72, 92-93; power to raise a spring 48, 182; shining face of 137; title of *vir Dei* applied to 27; waters of Marah made sweet by 45

Mundò, A. 152

Musa 134

Narnia 3, 13, 74

Nazarius, see bodies, translation of; *inventio*

Nicetas, bishop 103

Nicetius of Lyons 129-130

niger puer and black men 44, 86, 133

Nitria 103, 155, 169

Noll, R. 112

Nonnosus, monk 10-11, 30, 40, 67

Noricum 112-113, 116, 147

nuns and nunneries 6, 23, 68, 108-109, 133, 159, 169, 171, 173, 179; see also Benedicta; Galla; Gregoria; Herundo; monasticism, feminine; Redempta; Romula; *Seniores*, women among; virgins, consecrated

Nursia 3, 10, 13, 169, 179; see also Benedict of Nursia; Narnia; Sanctulus

Odo of Cluny, *Vita Gregorii Turonis* 130

ordination 63-64, 91, 108; Gregory's conception of 65

Origen 27, 73, 162, 185, 190

Orosius, Paulus 17

Oyend, see Eugendus

Pachomius, organization of monasteries 155; *Regula* 167; reverence for dead bodies 145; scriptural precedents for the monastic life 27; *Vita prima* 145; *Vita secunda* 152; see also Dionysius Exiguus

Palladius, bp of Hellenopolis 50, 165; *He-*

raclidis paradisus (Latin version of *Historia Lausiaca*) 132, 152, 188; *Historia Lausiaca* 152, 155, 169, 181, 188; Latin versions of writings 50, 152; on Eastern monasticism 155-156; resemblances of stories to those of other writers 77, 130, 168

Pambo, Abba 162

Panephysis 155

Paphnutius, Abba (The Buffalo) 155

Paschasius, correspondent of Eugippius 112

Paschasius, deacon at Rome 89

Passio Afrae 86

Passio Alexandri 86

Passio Anastasii 80

Passio Apollinaris 59

Passio Bibianae 63

Passio Caesarii 81

Passio Chrysanthi 66

Passio Clementis 63, 66

Passio Donati 66-67

Passio Felicis 66, 81-82

Passio Gervasii et Protasii 66

Passio Ioannis et Pauli 66

Passio Laurentii 66

Passio Mariani et Iacobi 59

Passio Nazarii et Celsi 66

Passio Pancratis 66

Passio Perpetuae et Felicitatis 60, 65, 86, 118

Passio Proculi 80

Passio Sebastiani 62

Passio Victoris Mediolanensis 66

passiones, method of testing genuineness of narrative 59-60

Passiones martyrum 59, 62, 65-66; see also *Acta martyrum; Gesta martyrum*

Paterius, *notarius* 22

Patrimonia, situation of 2

Patrimonia of Hydruntum and Callipolis 5

Patrimonium Appiae 2

Patrimonium Samniticum 2

Patrimonium Tusciae 2

Patroclus, abbot 137

Paul, apostle 71, 94, 131; apocalyptic descriptions of his inspection of hell and heaven 87; apparitions of 107, 134; conversion experience of 69; gifts of prophecy and discernment of spirits 165; mortal remains at Rome 59; see also relics

Paul the Deacon 67, 184-185

Paul the Hermit 96-99, 106, 155
Paul the Simple, Abba 166
Paula 68, 159, 168
Paulinus, aft. bp of Tiburnia 113
Paulinus, bp of Nola, as correspondent
    103; criticism of Gregory's account of
    his life 6, 15-18; example of humility
    65; influence of writings on *Passio Feli-
    cis* 81-82; relics of apostles mentioned
    by 149; resemblances of stories to those
    of other writers 130
Paulinus of Milan 58, 77, 95-96, 100, 116,
    132; *Vita Ambrosii* 90, 95, 122
Pegon, J. 163
Pelagia, mother of Arredius 138
Pelagius I, Pope (555-561), form. deacon,
    and John III, Pope (561-575), form.
    subdeacon 152
Pelagius II, Pope (579-590); among Gre-
    gory's informants 7, 14, 169; death in
    plague 56; floods during pontificate 12;
    letters to bishops of Aquileia as evi-
    dence for possible knowledge of Greek
    184-186
Pelusium 172, 174
Peregrinus, disciple of Benedict 7, 9-10
Perpetua, martyr 69; see also *Passiones
    martyrum*
Perugia 78, 142, 146
Peter, abbot of St Andrew's 137
Peter, apostle 28; apparitions of 53, 107,
    134; mortal remains in Rome 59;
    walking on water 31, 49-51, 94, 131
Peter, deacon in diocese of Arles 109
Peter the Deacon (Gregory's interlocutor)
    22, 24, 30-31, 39, 48-50, 131-132, 153,
    158
Philo 155
Philostratus, *Vita Apollonii* 93
pig, demon driven into 8, 31, 134, 159; in
    sacrifice of purification (*suovetaurilia*)
    52; invisible, in church 15, 52, 133; see
    also virgins, consecrated
Pior, Abba 168, 187
Pirenne, H., concept of *Romania* 191
Placentia 4, 12
Placid 31, 49, 50, 178
plague 24, 56, 144
Pliny the Elder 170
Pliny the Younger 6, 145, 175-177
Po, river 12
Poemen, Abba 188
Poitiers 137, 144

Pompeianus, monk 43
Pontianus, Pope, see bodies, translation of
Populonium 12-13
Portianus 44
Possidius 91; *Vita Augustini* 58
Postumianus 102-103
Poupardin, R. 105
Praeneste 157, 159
Prinz, F. 105, 110, 112
Probus, abbot of monastery of Renatus 10
Probus, bp of Reate 74, 134
Procopius of Caesarea 19
Proculus, priest 80
Pronulfus, Count 12
prophecy and discernment of spirits 45-48,
    165-169; see also Menas
Prudentius, Aurelius Clemens 19

Quadragesimus, subdeacon 31, 35, 178

Rachel, type of the contemplative life 72
Radegund, abbess 123, 137, 144
Ravenna 2, 22, 34, 40, 58-59
Reccared, Visigothic king 143
rector, administrative official 4
rector, ruler of the Church 71-72; to
    combine active and contemplative life
    91
Redempta, nun 22-23, 159
Redemptus, bp of Ferentis 9, 10-11, 74,
    135
regula, see Basil the Great; Benedict of
    Campania; Benedict of Nursia; Caesa-
    rius of Arles; Lot, Abba; Pachomius
Regula magistri 158
relics, attitude of Vigilantius to 99; perju-
    rers in presence of 140; teaching of
    Victricius on 122; Theoctista's request
    for 142-143
—, corporeal, in West 148-150
—, foreign: herbs from Paneas 144; Instru-
    ments of the Passion 144; True Cross
    123, 138, 144
—, manufactured 96, 148-149
—, non-corporeal 126-127, 143-144
—, use of: as focus for prayer 99; in
    Dialogues and *Gesta martyrum* 89; in
    miracles of healing 95; to stimulate
    interest in saints 73
— of saints: Agatha 52, 133; Caesarius of
    Arles 109-111; George 145; Gervase
    and Protase 113, 115, 136; Illidius 137;
    John the Baptist 113, 115, 143, 146:

Julian 137; Laurence 143; Martin of Tours 102, 116, 137; Paul, apostle 142-143; Saturninus 137; Sebastian 51-52; 134; Stephen 94, 116, 141, 148

Reparatus 87

Riché, P. 104, 189

Riggo 167

Romanus, abbot of Condat 104-106, 117, 125

Romanus, exarch of Ravenna 58

Romanus, monk 158, 177-178

Rome 2-5, 10-11, 13-15, 157-159, 165; as ecclesiastical capital 57-59; capture by Totila (546) 13; monastery of St Andrew 22, 26, 68, 71, 135, 158; see also Antony, monk; Augustine of Canterbury; Boniface; Claudius; Exhilaratus; Justus; Maximianus; Mellitus; Merulus; Theodore; Valentio; Synod of (595) 22

—, churches: St Agatha 15, 52, 133, 137; SS Cosmas and Damian 174; St Januarius 135; St Martin (monastic chapels dedicated to) 119; St Mary Major 14, 159; St Peter 134; St Saba 159; Sancta Maria ad Martyres (Pantheon) 175

Romula, nun 22-23, 136-137

Rouen 122

Rousseau, O. 28-29, 37, 40-41, 43, 45-46, 53-54

Rousseau, P. H. 117

Rufinus, Tyrannius 174, 185, 188-189; see also Eusebius; *Historia monachorum in Aegypto*

Rutilius, Palladius, writer on agriculture 81

Sabinus, bp of Canossa 45, 47, 65, 167

Sabinus, bp of Placentia 12

Salona 147

Salvius 109

Samnium 3, 158, 177, 179

Samuel, the prophet, see bodies, translation of

sanctaemoniales, see nuns

Sanctulus, priest, of Nursia 7, 10, 13-14, 31, 39-40, 76, 130, 179

Sarabaïtes 154-155

Sarah, Amma 156

Scete (Scythis) 47, 155, 165-166

Scholastica, sister of Benedict 139

Scythis, see Scete

Sebastian, aft. *defensor* 64

Sebastian, martyr, see relics

secular clergy 22-23, 28n12, 63-65, 104, 128

senex, seniores 154-155, 172, 177-178; women among 156

Servulus 22, 136, 137

Severinus of Noricum, abbot 100, 112-116, 141, 147, 154; see also Eugippius

Severus, priest 28n12, 33, 35

Severus, Sulpicius 6, 20, 28, 40, 47, 74, 76, 95, 98, 101, 112, 129-130, 132, 136, 144, 154; audience 103-104, 123-124; *Dialogues* 24, 38-39, 61, 90, 102-103, 114, 117, 120-121, 152-153; dissemination of writings 103; enters upon ascetic life 100; letter addressed to Paulinus of Nola 17; reaction towards *Vita Antonii* 117; *Vita Martini* 46, 61, 77, 100, 105-106, 118-119, 120-121, 124, 153, 156

Sidonius Apollinaris 111, 115

Silvia, mother of Gregory the Great 67, 159

Silvinus 114

Simplicius, disciple of Benedict 38

Sisois, Abba 136

Socrates, *Historia ecclesiastica* 121; see also Cassiodorus

Soracte, monastery 157

Soranus, abbot of Sura 75

Spoleto 82-83, 85, 133, 159-160; exiles from, as Gregory's informants 14, 80; in Lombard hands 3, 4, 14; St Mark's monastery 10; Spoleto sequence of stories 7-8, 52; see also Eleutherius, abbot; Gregoria; Isaac of Spoleto; pig; virgins, consecrated

Steidle, B. 27, 29, 86, 139

Stephanus, abbot, d. in Rome 10, 158, 169

Stephen, *illustris* 86-88

Stephen, *protomartyr* 123, 134

Subiaco 29, 48-49, 117, 157, 179

Subpentoma, monastery 135-136, 157

substratorium 152; see also *melota*

Sunday workers, punishment of 127-128

Syagria 107

Symeon Stylites 150, 153; attitude to women 167, 186-187; resemblances in Theodoret's account to story of Martin the hermit 183-187; translation of body 146

Symphorian, martyr 143

Syncletica, Amma 156

Tabennesis 155

Talis, Amma 156

Taor, Amma 156

Tarsilla, aunt of Gregory the Great 22, 67, 134, 137

Terracina 158, 174

Thebaid 50, 103; idea of a Western Thebaid 106, 117, 153, 157-158, 160

Thebes 172

Theoctista, sister of emperor Maurice 159

Theodelinda, queen of the Lombards 18

Theodore, disciple of Pachomius 145

Theodore, *mansionarius* 134

Theodore, monk of St Andrew's 158

Theodore of Mopsuestia 185

Theodore of Sykeon 145

Theodoret, bp of Cyrrhus 137, 145, 181-184; *Historia religiosa* 23, 121, 132, 181-183, 185, 189

Theodoric, infant son of Chilperic 138

Theodoric, king of the Ostrogoths (493-526) 4, 158

Theodosius, Syrian hermit 182

Theodosius I, emperor (379-395) 20, 146, 165

Theophanius, Count 22-23, 137, 139

Theopropus 70, 166

Therapeutae 155

Thessalonica 147-148

Thrasamund, king of the Vandals (496-593) 16

Three Holy Children, The, as type of martyrs 31, 49, 73

Timothy, see bodies, translation of

Todi 3

topos, topoi 7, 8, 38, 68, 82, 97, 108, 111-112, 115; convert gaoler or executioner 76n64; dryness when all around is wet 12, 63, 139; holy man as child giving his clothes to the poor 5, 108; holy man's holy sister as nun 106n69; ransoming of captives 81, 103; "reluctant bishop" 70, 108; "reluctant bridegroom" 129

Totila, king of the Ostrogoths (541-552) 78, 133; captures Rome (546) 13; identity when disguised discovered by Benedict 167; visits Monte Cassino and hears Benedict's prophecies 20-21, 47-48, 165-166

Tours, city and diocese 130, 132, 140

Trajan, emperor (98-117) 144-145

Tranquillinus 64

Trial by ordeal 140

True Cross, see relics

typology 25-26, 28-30, 35, 51, 63; exam-ples 32-54; Gregory's use of typological interpretation 29-32; see also Caesarius of Arles; Theodoret of Cyrrhus

Ullmann, W. 191

Uranius, monk 6, 16-17

Urban and Sixtus, fictitious papal martyrs 64

Ursinus 134

Ursus 129

Valentianus, disciple of Benedict 38

Valentinian, monk 46

Valentio, aft. abbot of the monastery of St Andrew 75

Valentius of Milan, *defensor* 135

Valeria 75, 80, 157

Valerianus 12, 74, 135

Vandals 15, 16, 18

vanga 81

Varaca, sailor 139

Venantius, bp of Luna 11-12, 14

Venantius, recluse, form. reluctant bridegroom 129

Venantius Fortunatus, see Fortunatus, Venantius

Verona 4, 119

Victor, bp of Tunnuna 19

Victor, bp of Vita 19

Victricius, bp of Rouen 149; *De laude sanctorum* 122; see also relics

Vienne 149

Vigilantius 99; see also relics

vir Dei: as title of holy man 27-28, 28n12, 119

virgins, consecrated 8, 31, 80, 83, 134, 159

visions, see apparitions

vita activa 71

vita contemplativa 70

Vita patrum iurensium 104-107, 111, 117, 153

Vita Spyridonis 121

Vitae: compared to light literature 99-100; containing *topoi* 108

Vitalis, martyr, see bodies, translation of

Vivarium 62, 119

Vogüé, A. de 1, 11, 17, 66, 76, 87, 130, 157, 170

Vooght, D. P. de 91

Whitby, anonymous monk of 138

Wood, I. N. 128

Zacharias, Pope (741-752) 160, 191